EVERYONE

Nancy Conner

800 East 96th Street,
Indianapolis, Indiana 46240 USA

Zoho® 4 Everyone

ISBN-13: 978-0-789-73937-7
ISBN-10: 0-789-73937-2

Library of Congress Cataloging-in-Publication Data:

Conner, Nancy, 1961-
  Zoho 4 everyone / Nancy Conner.
    p. cm.
  ISBN-13: 978-0-7897-3937-7
  ISBN-10: 0-7897-3937-2
  1. Zoho Office. 2. Business--Computer programs. 3. Office management--Computer programs. I. Title. II. Title: Zoho for everyone.
  HF5548.4.Z64C66 2009
  005.5--dc22

Printed in the United States of America

First Printing: January 2009

Trademarks

Warning and Disclaimer

Bulk Sales

Que Publishing offers excellent discounts on this book when ordered in quantity for bulk purchases or special sales. For more information, please contact

U.S. Corporate and Government Sales
1-800-382-3419
corpsales@pearsontechgroup.com

For sales outside of the U.S., please contact

International Sales
international@pearson.com

Associate Publisher
Greg Wiegand

Acquisitions Editor
Michelle Newcomb

Development Editor
Faithe Wempen

Managing Editor
Kristy Hart

Project Editor
Betsy Harris

Copy Editor
Bart Reed

Senior Indexer
Cheryl Lenser

Proofreader
San Dee Phillips

Technical Editors
Vince Averello
Raju Vegesna

Publishing Coordinator
Cindy Teeters

Book Designer
Anne Jones

Page Layout
Eric S. Miller

Contents at a Glance

Table of Contents

II SPREADSHEETS AND DATABASES

III COMMUNICATION AND SCHEDULING TOOLS

V   APPS FOR BUSINESS

About the Author

Nancy Conner writes and edits tech books from her home in central New York state, on topics ranging from eBay to WAN optimization to Google Apps. She's also worked as a medievalist, an English teacher, and a corporate trainer. Nancy holds a PhD from Brown University.

Dedication

To Steve, with masses of love

Acknowledgments

A book is the result of many people's hard work. I'd like to thank Michelle Newcomb for discussing the initial idea for this book and offering guidance throughout its writing. Thanks to Raju Vegesna at Zoho for all his help—your enthusiasm is contagious, Raju! Thanks also to Faithe Wempen for her excellent suggestions, Vince Averello for his conscientious and thorough technical review, and copy editor Bart Reed for making sure all those i's are dotted and t's are crossed. Project editor Betsy Harris kept the book on schedule with patience and a sense of humor.

Thanks to Steve Holzner, as always, for his loving support and patience. You make everything possible.

We Want to Hear from You!

As the reader of this book, *you* are our most important critic and commentator. We value your opinion and want to know what we're doing right, what we could do better, what areas you'd like to see us publish in, and any other words of wisdom you're willing to pass our way.

As an associate publisher for Que Publishing, I welcome your comments. You can email or write me directly to let me know what you did or didn't like about this book—as well as what we can do to make our books better.

Please note that I cannot help you with technical problems related to the topic of this book. We do have a User Services group, however, where I will forward specific technical questions related to the book.

When you write, please be sure to include this book's title and author as well as your name, email address, and phone number. I will carefully review your comments and share them with the author and editors who worked on the book.

Email: feedback@quepublishing.com

Mail: Greg Wiegand
Associate Publisher
Que Publishing
800 East 96th Street
Indianapolis, IN 46240 USA

Reader Services

Visit our website and register this book at informit.com/register for convenient access to any updates, downloads, or errata that might be available for this book.

Introduction

Zo-*who?* Getting to Know Zoho

Never heard of Zoho? You will. Zoho has been around only since 2005, but in that time it's launched a complete suite of business- and productivity-related applications—from Writer, its word processor and first program, to CRM, a sophisticated tool for managing customer relationships.

Zoho's name comes from a play on SOHO, which stands for *small office home office,* and the SOHO market was one of the company's first targets. As word spread, and as Zoho released more applications, small-to-medium businesses showed interest. And large enterprises weren't far behind. In summer of 2008, Zoho's millionth customer signed up.

What's the buzz about? In a nutshell: sharing, collaboration, and affordability. Because Zoho offers software as a service over the Internet, you can access your applications (and their documents, data, and records) from anywhere you can connect to the Internet and use a web browser to sign in. Storing documents and data online also makes it easy for you to share, publish, and collaborate with others. So, for example, when your team members are putting together a report or a PowerPoint-style presentation, they can work on it anytime, from anywhere—several people can work on the document at once, updating a single copy in real time.

As for affordability, all Zoho services are free, or have a free version you can try. Business applications have different pricing structures for different subscription levels, so you're never paying for more than your business actually needs.

 A note about security: Zoho knows how important it is to keep your data safe and private. Zoho locates its servers in super-secure datacenters behind sophisticated, state-of-the-art firewalls. Servers are regularly checked to prevent vulnerabilities and are constantly scanned to protect from viruses and other suspicious traffic. In addition, your data is backed up daily on multiple servers at multiple locations. How does that compare to your desktop?

A Quick Overview of This Book

Zoho 4 Everyone is designed to be what its name implies: a book for anyone and everyone who's interested in learning how to use Zoho's online programs. Whether you're looking for a free, easy-to-use online word processor to write your memoirs or a suite of productivity tools for your business, this book has something for you. Even if you're new to web-based applications or you're still learning your way around keyboard, *Zoho 4 Everyone* will get you up to speed in using Zoho's most popular programs.

This book is organized into parts, and each part groups programs by what they do: create and organize documents and slideshow-style presentations, track data, communicate and keep track of your to-dos, meet and collaborate online, and streamline your business processes. This section describes how the book is put together.

Part I: Documents and Presentations

Part I is all about information: writing documents and reports, adding content to a virtual notebook, and communicating your ideas in a slideshow format. In Part I, you'll find these chapters:

- **Chapter 1: "Have Your Say with Zoho Writer"**—Writer is Zoho's word-processing program. Because your documents are stored online, you have access to those documents wherever you have a web browser and Internet access. But you can also work on your documents when you're not connected to the Internet and then sync them with Writer when you're back online. If you've never tried a web-based word processor, you'll be surprised at the way Writer steps up to the job, letting you format documents, use templates, and insert images, links, and tables—pretty much everything you expect and need in a word-processing program.

- **Chapter 2: "Zoho Notebook: Clip, Snip, and Organize"**—Notebook is an online program that lets you gather and organize different kinds of content—text, images, audio, and video—and then easily share that content with others.

- **Chapter 3: "Presenting...Zoho Show"**—A presentation is a slideshow, similar to those made with Microsoft's PowerPoint. Presentations are meant to be shared, and Show makes it easy for you to do just that. With Show, there's no need for your audience to be in the same room, because you can run your presentation over the Web.

Part II: Spreadsheets and Databases

Everybody needs to keep track of something. Whether you're keeping the family to a monthly budget, cataloging your stamp collection, or updating your business's inventory, spreadsheets and databases have become indispensable tools for life in the twenty-first century. This part of the book has chapters that cover these data-management tools:

- **Chapter 4: "Track Data with Zoho Sheet"**—Zoho's spreadsheet program lets you organize, analyze, and store your data in a single, secure, easy-to-access location. For power users, Sheet also offers advanced features such as recording macros and creating pivot tables.

- **Chapter 5: "Zoho Reports: Online Databases and Reports"**—Use this online database to enter data and use it to create reports in the form of charts, pivot tables, and summaries (and that's just for starters) by simply dragging and dropping. Because the data is stored on the Web, your whole team can access that information from anywhere: on the road, at home, or at a far-flung branch office.

- **Chapter 6: "Do-It-Yourself Applications: Zoho Creator"**—Who said you need to know how to program to design a database? With Zoho Creator, if you know how to use a computer mouse, you can create a database of your very own. Design one or more forms, and then use those forms to capture data and view it in different ways.

Part III: Communication and Scheduling Tools

A big part of the attraction of web-based applications is the ease of communication and sharing that the Web allows. This part of the book focuses on applications that let you communicate with others and share your schedule:

- **Chapter 7: "Zoho Mail: Web Mail Redux"**—If you've tried just one web-based application, chances are you've tried a web-based email program, such as Hotmail or Gmail. After you give Zoho Mail a try, you're likely to make it your email program of choice. Zoho Mail lets you organize your email messages in a way that makes sense to you: folders, labels, or both. It also integrates seamlessly with other Zoho applications.

- **Chapter 8: "Instant Communication with Zoho Chat"**—Chat is Zoho's instant-messaging (IM) program, which you can use to send and receive messages with any of your contacts who are online: friends, family, coworkers, business contacts, and more. Unlike some other IM programs, there's no software to download, so you can chat from any computer with a web browser and an Internet connection. Chat one on one or in groups, and save a transcript of the conversation to read later.

- **Chapter 9: "Zoho Planner: Your Online To-Do List"**—Keep yourself organized with this simple, streamlined program that lists your upcoming events, tasks, and appointments as to-dos and lets you share them with others. If you tend to be forgetful or are always running late, you'll appreciate Planner's automatic email reminders.

Part IV: Meeting and Collaboration Tools

The whole point of online applications is how easy they make it to collaborate. This part of the book covers Zoho's state-of-the-art collaboration tools:

- **Chapter 10: "Zoho Meeting: Web Conferencing Made Simple"**—Online meetings are all the rage—not because they're fashionable, but because they're convenient. Zoho Meeting lets you schedule and run online meetings through your web browser. Participants can join immediately—there's no special software for them to download and install. Zoho Meeting works with Skype, a service that lets you make free voice calls over the Internet, to add voice conversations to the meeting.

■ **Chapter 11: "Build Collaborative Sites with Zoho Wiki"**—A *wiki* is a collaborative website; when you create a wiki, you can make it your own personal website, or you can invite people to work on it with you. So a class can work together to create a group website on, say, saving the whales; a family can share photos, memories, and news; and a business team can create a site dedicated to its current project. Zoho Wiki works with other Zoho services, such as Writer and Show, making it easy for you to fill up its pages.

Part V: Apps for Business

You can use any of Zoho's applications for your business, but this part of the book focuses on those designed to meet specific business needs:

■ **Chapter 12: "Manage Customers with Zoho Invoice and Zoho CRM"**—Whether you're a self-employed consultant or work for a large company, business is all about keeping your customers happy—and getting paid. And that's what these two programs are designed to help you do. Invoice is a good choice for small-to-medium businesses looking for a way to streamline and track their invoicing procedure. CRM is for companies looking for an all-in-one customer-relationship management solution—from launching a marketing campaign, to following up on leads, to closing the sale, to processing payments.

■ **Chapter 13: "Keep the Team on Task with Zoho Projects"**—Managing a project is a complex set of overlapping objectives, tasks, and deadlines. Whatever the project, if you're managing it, you have to assemble a team, assign roles and tasks, create a document library, set up meetings, and keep an eye on approaching deadlines. That's a lot of juggling, and Zoho Projects helps you keep all the balls in the air by managing all these activities with a single application.

■ **Chapter 14: "Zoho People: Your Online HR Office"**—Zoho People provides a common-sense workflow for managing your organization's hiring process—from posting a new job opening, to identifying qualified candidates through making an offer and bringing the new employee on board. But that's not all—People also has tools for managing current employees, including a self-service page where employees can update their information, request time off, sign up for training, and so on. People is customizable, so you can be sure it fits your organization's needs.

 Zoho is responsive to user feedback and feature requests, which means Zoho frequently updates its applications. Because of these frequent updates, you may find that some of the pages and steps on the live applications differ from what you see in this book.

What Are You Waiting For? Signing Up and Signing In

When you sign up for a Zoho account, you get access to most of Zoho's applications with just one user ID and password. It's called *single sign-on*, and it saves you both time and the effort of remembering multiple passwords. (Some of the business apps, such as CRM, still require you to set up an account, although you can use the same username and password for that account as you use for all your other Zoho apps.)

To sign up for a Zoho account, a good place to start is Zoho's home page: www.zoho.com. (You can also create an account from the home page of any individual Zoho service, such as wiki.zoho.com or writer.zoho.com or mail.zoho.com.) On the right side of the page, click the Sign Up link to open the page shown in Figure I.1. It takes just a little information to create your account:

- **Username**—The ID you want to use with your Zoho apps.
- **Email address**—Where Zoho can send the confirmation email.
- **Password/Confirm Password**—Type in a hard-to-guess password (it's best to use a combination of letters and numbers) to gain access to your account.
- **Image text**—To prove you're a person and not some kind of web bot, type the sequence of letters and numbers into the text box.
- **Agreement**—Click the links to read Zoho's Terms of Service and Privacy Policy. If you agree, check this box.
- **Newsletter**—If you want Zoho's newsletter delivered to your email inbox, check the box that subscribes you.

Look good? Then click Sign Up. Zoho emails you a confirmation notice; click the link in the email, and you've got a Zoho account of your very own.

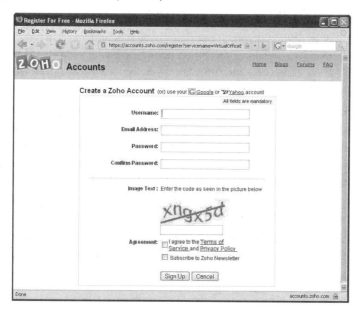

Figure I.1
Fill out this short form to create a Zoho account.

Signing In to Zoho Through a Google or Yahoo! Account

If you have a Yahoo! or a Google account, you can use that account to sign in to Zoho. This is helpful if you want to take a look at a few Zoho services before you decide whether to sign up, but you also get full access to Zoho services when you sign in this way. So if someone shares a Zoho Writer document with you, for example, you don't have to create a whole new Zoho account to access it—you can sign in through your existing Google or Yahoo! account.

When you sign in to Zoho through your Google or Yahoo! account, you give Zoho temporary, limited access to your account. Zoho doesn't store your password or poke around in your personal documents.

To sign in using your Yahoo! or Google account, go to Zoho's home page at www.zoho.com (or go to the home page of any Zoho service). In the Sign In box on the right side of the page, look for where it says Sign In Using Google or Yahoo. Click Google or Yahoo!, depending on which service you use.

If you're not currently signed in to the service you clicked, a page opens asking for your user ID and password. Type these in and click the Sign In button. When you're signed in, another page opens, asking for your permission to grant Zoho limited access to your account to log you in. Click I Agree (in Yahoo!) or Grant Access (in Google) to sign in to Zoho.

Getting Help with Zoho Applications

In the Zoho suite of services, different applications have different levels of help. Some have an FAQ (a list of frequently asked questions), others have a Help wiki, still others have a phone number you can call for live assistance, and some leave you more or less on your own (so it was smart of you to pick up this book).

If you can't find a Help link in a Zoho program, or if the FAQ for that program doesn't answer your question, the best place to try is one of the Zoho forums. Each Zoho app has forums for feedback, feature requests, bug reports, and announcements. Most apps have a Forums link at the top of their pages. If you don't see a link, you can get directly to the Forum page for that app by pointing your web browser to forums.zoho.com. Zoho services are listed along the right side of the page; click the one you want, and then use the upper-right Quick Search box to look for keywords related to your issue.

To ask a question, choose a particular forum from the Forums Categories list on the right. On the page that opens, click New Topic to open a form where you can ask your question and add it to the ongoing discussion.

Have Your Say with Zoho Writer

If you're like most people, when you hear the term *word processor*, you think of a program residing on your computer—such as Word, WordPerfect, or OpenOffice.org Writer—that lets you create, edit, and save documents. When you want to use a different computer, you have to make sure the other computer has the same word-processing program installed, and you have to transfer your document somehow—perhaps by emailing to yourself or saving it on a flash drive or external hard drive.

Zoho, along with a handful of other companies, is changing all that. Writer, Zoho's *online* word processor, lets you access your documents from any computer that's connected to the Internet. All you have to do is point your web browser to http://writer.zoho.com, sign in, and get to work. The most recent version of your document is right there, waiting for you. (And if you need to work on a document when you're offline, you can do that, too.)

But that's not all. Perhaps the biggest reason to use Zoho Writer is that it lets you share documents and collaborate on them in real time. You don't have to wait for someone to edit a document and then email it back to you. And there's no more wondering which version is the current one. With Writer, all collaborators work together on a single document, so the version in your documents list is *always* the current one. (But don't worry about someone messing up the document—Zoho keeps track of previous versions, and you can view a document's history and, if necessary, revert to an earlier version.)

This chapter gives you the ins and outs of working with Zoho Writer—from creating your first document to sharing, collaborating, and working offline.

A Quick Spin Around the Workspace

To start using Zoho Writer, go to http://writer.zoho.com and sign in to your Zoho account. (If you don't yet have a Zoho account, the Introduction to this book tells you how to get one.) The first time you open Writer, you see a screen that looks like the one in Figure 1.1, complete with Welcome message. The Welcome message is itself a document—and a helpful one, with lots of tips for getting started—that Zoho adds to your list of documents. The first time you create a new document (see the upcoming section, "Creating a Document"), the new document-in-progress takes over, appearing in the main part of the screen. If you want the Welcome message back, simply click it in the left side My Docs list.

This is the Writer workspace, where you'll create, edit, save, and share documents. Let's take a quick look around to get oriented.

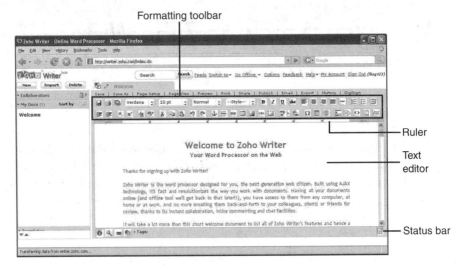

Figure 1.1
The Zoho Writer workspace has a menu on the left, listing your collaborators, documents (docs), templates, and so on, and a text editor on the right.

On the left side of the screen, a menu gives you an overview of your Writer stuff:

- **Collaborators**—Shows who else (if anyone) is currently viewing or editing your document. When a collaborator is online, you can chat with him or her, right here.
- **My Docs**—This is your documents list, with the most recent document at the top.
- **Templates**—Lists any templates you've got in Writer. (See "Working with Templates" later in this chapter to learn more about templates.)
- **Shared to Me**—Shows documents that others have invited you to view or edit.
- **Public Docs**—Lists any of your documents that you have published on the Web.
- **Trash**—This is the place where all your deleted documents end up (until you empty it).

Moving to the right, the main part of the screen is devoted to Writer's text editor, where you get a generous amount of space for typing your document's text. Above the text area are a row of links for working with the document, such as Save, Save As, Page Setup, and so on, and the Formatting toolbar (two rows of buttons, explained later in this chapter). Below the text area is Writer's status bar, which holds these buttons:

- **Document Information**—When you click this button (a blue circle holding a white italic *i*), Zoho shows you the current document's version number, author, last-modified date, and creation date.

- **Search**—To search within the current document, click this button. A search box appears, where you can type your search term and then click Find.

- **Tags**—As Zoho likes to say, tags are the new folders: Tags provide a newer, more flexible way for organizing your documents than the folders you might have used in other word processors. Tags label a document; you can add several tags to a single document, or you can label several documents with the same tag. The section "Working with Text," later in this chapter, tells you all about how to use tags. Click this button to add a tag to the current document or view its existing ones.

- **Shared Info**—Clicking this button shows whether the current document is publicly or privately shared. This is also the button to click if you want to share the document. The "Sharing and Collaborating on Documents" section of this chapter explains how to share.

- **Comments**—All by itself on the right, this button opens a pane that shows all comments in a document. From that pane, you can edit or delete existing comments. You'll find more about working with comments later in this chapter.

Above the text editor, at the top of the screen, are a series of links:

- **Feeds**—Click this link to view sharing and collaboration information for documents that others have shared with you. For example, when someone has shared a document with you or changed the permission level of a shared document, you can see that sharing history here.

- **Switch to**—Click this link; then make a selection to open a different Zoho application in a new window.

- **Go Offline**—As the section "Working Offline" explains later in this chapter, this link lets you take up to 25 of your documents and 25 of your shared documents offline, so you can work on them even when you're not connected to the Internet.

- **Options**—This link opens a box that lets you customize Writer (more on that later in this chapter).

- **Feedback**—Got a suggestion or a complaint for the folks at Zoho? Click this link to send them an email.

- **Help**—Click here to open a menu that lets you choose one of these options: FAQ (help for using Writer), Zoho API (for developers), Template Library, Zoho Writer Forums, Zoho Blogs, or Keyboard Shortcuts (which offer an alternative to clicking buttons).

- **My Account**—This link opens your Zoho Dashboard in a new window. From there, you can adjust your account settings or open another Zoho program.

- **Sign Out**—Done with Zoho for the moment? This link logs you off. Click it and say bye-bye.

Info 4U — If your web browser is set to block pop-up windows, you might have to tell it to allow pop-ups from Zoho. This ensures that Zoho can open a new window when necessary. Check your web browser's Help section to learn how to allow pop-ups from a particular site.

Getting Started with Zoho Writer

As you can see from looking around the workspace, there's a lot you can do with Writer. Even with all the features Writer offers, getting started is as simple as placing your hands on the keyboard and typing.

This section gets you up to speed with using Writer, walking you through some of the most common tasks—from creating a new document to saving, exporting, or deleting it.

Creating a Document

Creating a document couldn't be easier. Just click the New button in the upper-left part of the screen, shown in Figure 1.2. When you click New, Writer opens a new document, giving it the not-so-imaginative name *Untitled*.

To rename your document with something more descriptive, simply save the document. (Alternatively, you can click the tab where you see the current title and type the new title there.) You can save the document on which you're working in two ways. Both are located in the upper-left part of the Formatting toolbar:

- Click the Save link.
- Click the Save Document button, which looks like an old-style floppy disk.

When you click either of these items in a brand-new document, Writer pops up the Save dialog box. Type in your document's name and click OK to save it with that name.

 When you create a new document or open an existing one, Writer places it in a new tab. This makes it easy to have several documents open at once and switch between them.

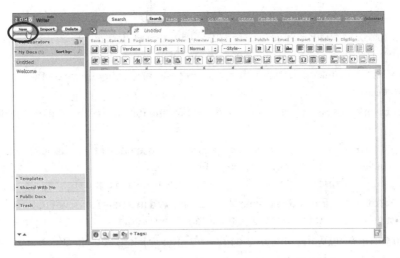

Figure 1.2
Click the New button (circled) to open a new, untitled document in a new tab.

Page Setup

If you like Writer's standard settings—10-point, single-spaced Verdana font—you can just click inside the text area and start typing. If, however, you want to customize the setup of the pages in your document, first save the document (click Save, give the document a name, and then click OK), and then click the Page Setup link above the Formatting toolbar. (Or you can click the Page Setup button, third from the left in the Formatting toolbar's top row of buttons.) This opens the dialog box shown in Figure 1.3. From here, you can tweak general page settings and create or edit headers and footers.

As you choose your settings, the Page Preview on the right side of the dialog box shows you how they'll look. When you've got the page set up the way you want, click Save and then Close.

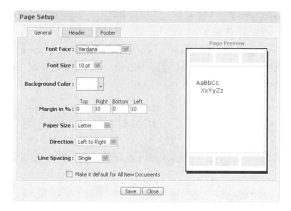

Figure 1.3
The Page Setup dialog box lets you fine-tune your document's page settings and work with headers and footers.

The General Tab

Click the General tab to adjust the following aspects of your document's pages:

- **Font Face**—Choose from more than a dozen fonts.
- **Font Size**—For normal text (as opposed to headings), sizes range from 8 to 36 points.
- **Background Color**—If you want your document's background to be a color other than white, click here and choose from a palette of colors.
- **Margin in %**—Set the top, bottom, left, and right margins here. Choose a number between 0 and 40 to indicate what percentage of the page a margin should take up. For a typical 8.5" x 11" piece of paper, one-inch margins translate to about 11.5 percent for the left and right margins and 9 percent for the top and bottom margins.
- **Paper Size**—Your choices here are A4 (a standard size based on the metric system and used outside the U.S.), Letter (8.5" x 11"), Legal (8.5" x 14"), and Executive (7.5" x 10.5").
- **Direction**—This option sets the way your cursor moves across the screen as you type: left to right (for Western languages) or right to left (for languages such as Hebrew and Arabic).

- **Line Spacing**—Choose Single, 1.5, or Double spacing.
- **Make It Default for All New Documents**—Check this box if you want the page setup you've specified to become the standard for all new documents you create.

The Header and Footer Tabs

These tabs look the same, except one deals with the space at the top of the page and the other with the space at the bottom. Headers and footers are split up into three sections: Left, Center, and Right. For any of these parts, click the drop-down list to select from these options:

- **None**—This is the standard choice for all header and footer sections. It leaves the section blank.
- **Date**—If you select Date, you can then choose from a variety of formats, such as 12/31/09, 31/12/2009, 2009-Dec-31, and so on.
- **Page Number**—This option also offers a number of formats. If, for example, you've written a 10-page document, the first page could be numbered 1, 1/10, 1 of 10, Page 1, or Page 1 of 10, among other options.

Info 4U At this time, there's no way to tell Writer to skip showing the number on a document's first page.

- **Custom**—Choose this option to type in your own text, such as your name or the document's title.
- **Image**—If you want to display a company logo, for example, choose Image and then upload the image file from your computer.

If you want a border between the main text and the header and/or footer, turn on the Apply Border check box. (Its exact name varies depending on whether it is on the Header or Footer tab.)

Whatever aspect of Page Setup you're working with, click Save when you're done to apply your changes. Then click Close to close the dialog box.

Importing Documents

Uploading a copy of an existing document into Writer is called *importing*. You can import documents from your computer, from Google Docs (another web-based word-processing program) or from elsewhere on the Web. Wherever you're importing from, the first step is to click Writer's upper-left Import button. This opens the Import Document dialog box shown in Figure 1.4.

From Your Computer

If a document currently lives on your computer and you want to get a copy of it into Writer, click the Import Document radio button and then click Browse. In the window that opens, find and select the document you want to import. Click Open, and the filename appears in the Import Document box. Click Import to open the file in Writer.

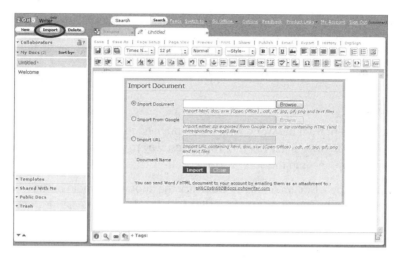

Figure 1.4
Click the Import button (circled) to open this dialog box and get existing documents into Writer.

 You can import files that end with any of these extensions (the part of the filename that comes after the dot): doc, docx, rtf, txt, text, odt, html, sxw, jpg, gif, and png.

From Google Docs

The label for this radio button is a little misleading, because you're not importing directly from Google Docs into Writer. (To do that, you need to email your Google Docs file as an attachment; see the following tip.) Instead, this option allows you to upload a zip file that contains an HTML file from your computer into Zoho Writer.

 A *zip file* contains another file that has been compressed to make it smaller. When you're importing files into Writer, the zip file must hold an HTML file—a file for display on the Web. You can also import HTML files that aren't zipped by using the Import Document option described in the previous section. The main reason to import a zipped HTML file is that Google Docs zips HTML files before exporting them.

Importing a Google Docs zip file into Writer requires two steps:

1. Export the file from Google Docs to your computer. To do this, open Google Docs and check the box next to the document you're exporting in your Docs list. From the menu bar, select More Actions, Save as HTML (zipped). A dialog box opens, asking whether you want to open or save the file. Select Save to Disk and then click OK. In the window that opens, select where you want to store the file on your computer and then click Save to export it.

2. Import the file from your computer into Zoho Writer. This is just like importing any other kind of file that's stored on your computer (see previous section). Turn on Import from Google and click Browse. Then find and select the zipped HTML file you want to import. Click Open and then click Import.

Want a faster, simpler way to get a Google Docs document into Writer? Just email it! In Google Docs, open the document you want and then click Share, Email as Attachment. This opens the Email Document dialog box. Use your unique Zoho Writer email address (see the upcoming section "Via Email") to send Writer the file.

From the Web

To import a document from the World Wide Web, you need to have the document's web address (called a URL, for *uniform resource locator*). The easiest way to get the URL is to open the document and then copy what's in the address bar.

Then, in Writer's Import Document dialog box, click the Import URL radio button and type or paste the URL of the document you're importing. Give the document a name and then click Import.

Using this method, you can import HTML, DOC, SXW, ODT, RTF, JPG, GIF, PNG, and text files.

Via Email

A quick-and-easy way to get an existing document into Writer is to email it there. The bottom of the Import Document dialog box has an email address that's assigned to your Writer account, and yours only. Click that email address to open a new message, with your unique Zoho Writer address already in place, in your email program. Attach a DOC or HTML file to the email and send it. When Zoho receives the email, your document is automatically added to My Docs in Writer's left menu. Click the document's name to open it.

 You can also find your unique email address for importing documents into Writer by clicking Email, Email In. This address is not the same as the username with which you log in to Zoho; it is a long string of letters and numbers followed by @docs.zohowriter.com.

Saving a Document

After you've created or imported a document and made some changes, you'll want to save it. You've got several options for doing so.

As a Document

To do a straightforward save, click the upper-left Save link or Save button. If the document is a new one that you haven't yet named, Writer asks you to name it. Otherwise, it simply saves the document.

 When you save a document, a pop-up box appears briefly in the lower-right part of the screen, giving you a word count and a character count for the document. So if you're writing away and you want to know how many words you've written, click Save to see the current word count.

As a Different Document

To create a copy of your document, click the upper-left Save As link. From the menu that pops up, select New Document. A box opens so you can name the new version. Type in the name you want and then click OK. After you save a document as a new document, both the original copy and the new copy remain open onscreen, on separate tabs.

As a Template

If you want to save a document's setup as a starting point for creating new documents, make it a template. To do that, click Save As, Template. Give your template a name (such as *resume* or *invitation*) and click OK. (Keep reading to learn more about working with templates, in the section "Working with Templates" later in this chapter.) After you save a document as a template, the original document remains open onscreen; the template does not open.

Autosaving

They say three things in life are inevitable: death, taxes, and data loss. Zoho can't do much about the first two, but it can help you avoid the third. To make sure you don't lose your work if your web browser freezes up or you lose your Internet connection, Writer periodically (and automatically) saves your documents. You can tell if a document has been autosaved (as opposed to being saved when you clicked the Save button) by looking at your My Docs list. If there's an asterisk (*) at the end of a document's name, that document was most recently saved automatically. When you do a manual save, the asterisk disappears.

 To compare two saved versions of a document, click History and choose the versions you want from the drop-down lists (more on that later in this chapter). Then click Revert to switch to the earlier version or click Edit to return to editing the latest version.

Exporting a Document

Just as you can import documents from other programs into Zoho Writer, you can also export documents from Writer to other programs. When you do, Writer converts the file into the format that's compatible with the program you're exporting to.

If you want to export a document, simply open the document and click the Export link in the upper-right part of the Formatting toolbar. A menu appears, as Figure 1.5 shows. From that menu, choose the kind of document you want to export:

- **Word Document**—This kind of file, with the extension .doc, can be read by most versions of Microsoft Word.
- **DOCX**—This is the file format for Word 2007.
- **ODF (ODT)**—ODF stands for *OpenDocument Format*, which is an open format that anyone can use to create programs that can read and write files using this format. ODT is the OpenDocument format for word-processed documents; it's the format for OpenOffice Writer documents.

- **PDF**—*Portable Document Format* preserves a document's formatting, layout, graphics, and so on, so that the document can be viewed in Adobe Reader or edited in Adobe Acrobat.

- **Latex**—This is a typesetting system widely used to produce scientific and technical documentation.

- **SXW**—This is a file format used by StarOffice and OpenOffice (version 1) text documents.

- **Rich Text Format**—This format, which has the extension .rtf, preserves a document's formatting. These files can be read in Microsoft and Microsoft-compatible word processors (Word, Works, OpenOffice.org Writer) and in text editors such as Microsoft Notepad and WordPad.

- **Text File**—Text files don't preserve any formatting you may have added to your document.

- **HTML**—*Hypertext Markup Language* creates documents that can be displayed in a web browser.

Choose the file format you want. A dialog box appears, asking what you'd like to do with the file you're exporting. For example, if you choose Word Document, the box asks whether you want to open the file in Microsoft Word or save it to your computer. Make your choice and then click OK. You've just exported a file.

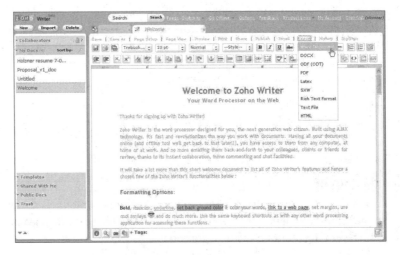

Figure 1.5
You can export Zoho Writer documents in a variety of formats.

Emailing a Document

A simple way to export a document from Writer is to email it, either to yourself or to someone else. To send a copy of your document, open the document you want to send and click Email, Email Out. This opens the Email Out dialog box shown in Figure 1.6.

Zoho needs the following info to email your document:

- **Email ID**—Type in the recipient's email address here.

- **Format**—This tells Zoho what kind of file to make the document you're exporting. These formats are currently available: HTML, PDF, DOC, SXW, ODT, RTF, and TXT.

- **Send As**—Click the appropriate radio button to send the document inside your email (inline) or as an attachment.

- **Email Language**—The language you choose here is the language Zoho uses for the email that holds your document.

Make your choices, click Send, and off whizzes your document through cyberspace to your recipient's Inbox.

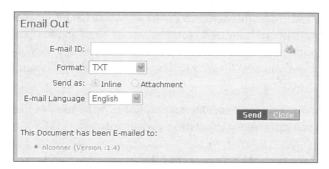

Figure 1.6
Use Email Out to send documents via email. (If you've already emailed this document to someone, this info appears at the bottom of the box.)

Deleting a Document

"Parting is such sweet sorrow," said Juliet to Romeo. That may be true, but at least Zoho makes it a snap to part with documents you no longer want. If the document you're deleting isn't currently open, click its name in the My Docs list to open it. When you see the document in the text editor, click the upper-left Delete button. In a flash, Writer dumps the document into the Trash.

If you deleted a document by mistake, it's just as easy to get it back. Click Trash in the menu on the left to see the list of trashed documents. Find the document you want to restore, and click its name. When the document opens in the text area, you don't see the Formatting toolbar. Instead, there's just one link, Restore, above the document and on the left. Click Restore to recover the document and put it back on your My Docs list.

You can get an item out of Writer entirely by deleting it from the Trash. Find the document in the Trash list and click its name; then click the Delete button. Writer asks whether you're sure you want to get rid of the document; click OK to confirm.

If you're *really* in the mood to clean house, you can make a clean sweep of all the documents you've trashed by opening Trash and then clicking Empty. Zoho asks whether you're sure. Click OK to permanently get rid of all deleted files.

Working with Templates

A *template* is like a cookie-cutter: Just as a cookie-cutter produces lots of different cookies with the same basic shape, a template lets you produce a lot of different documents with the same formatting. Templates are a super-helpful way to make sure you've got a document's format the way you want it—which means you can focus on its content.

Of course, a template can also contain boilerplate text. That's text that you use over and over again for lots of different documents. For example, an invoice has information about your company—name, address, phone number, a customer service email address, perhaps a thank-you note—that appears on every invoice you send, even though the specifics of each order are different. With a template, you can create a new document with all that boilerplate info already in place, saving you a lot of typing.

Zoho provides a library of more than 50 templates, just to make your life that much easier. However, if you prefer, you can create a template of your very own.

Selecting a Template from the Template Library

To see what's offered in Zoho's Template Library, click Product Links at the top of the screen and then select Template Library. This opens the window shown in Figure 1.7.

Figure 1.7
Writer's Template Library helps you find and select a format that meets your document's needs.

In the Template Library, use the Search Templates box to find a template using a keyword or phrase, such as *resume, invitation, purchase order, report*—something that describes the kind of document format you're looking for.

If you're the window-shopping type and would rather browse through the templates to see what's available, just click the numbers above the top template to page through the current list.

When you see a template you like, click its Preview link to open a full-size view of the template in a new window. If the template looks useful, click Add to My Templates. (Look in the upper-left part of the preview window or find it next to the template you want in the Template Library.) This saves a copy of the template in Writer. You'll find it listed in the left menu's Templates section. (You may have to refresh Writer to see it there.) When you are finished working with the Template Library, close its window.

Creating Your Own Template

To create a template, start by setting up the document the way you want it, including formatting and any boilerplate text. For example, you might create an invoice that has your company's name and address (boilerplate), a section for the customer's name and address, a table where you type in order information, and more boilerplate text such as *Thanks for your purchase!* at the bottom. When you have the document all set up, click Save As, Template. When prompted, enter a name for the template and click OK. Writer saves the document as a template.

 When you've created a document, save one copy as a document and—if you'll need to create similar documents in the future—save another as a template. Give them different names to avoid confusion.

Using a Template

After you've added a template to your Templates list, whether you found it in the Templates Library or created your own, you can use it to create a new document. To open a template, click Templates in the left menu. The section expands, showing your templates. Click the name of any template to open it.

The template opens in the main part of the screen, looking very much like any open document. But, as Figure 1.8 shows, instead of the text editor with its Formatting toolbar across the top, you see the template with these three links above it:

- **Create Document**—Click this link to create a new document based on this template.
- **Edit Template**—If you want to tweak your template—change a font or the line spacing, for example—click this link.
- **Export to Template Library**—Love your template and think others will, too? Click this link to add it to Writer's Template Library.

Creating a Document from a Template

When you open a template and click Create Document, the document opens in a new tab in the text editor, where you can work with it as you would any other document.

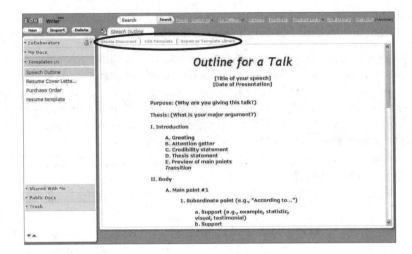

Figure 1.8
Opening a template gives you the options to create a document, edit the template, and add it to the Zoho Writer Template Library.

Editing a Template

Editing a template lets you change its formatting and setup. The template is shown in the text editor, complete with the Formatting toolbar. Editing a template is a lot like editing a document, except you have different options at the top of the Formatting toolbar:

- **Create Document**—After you've adjusted the template, you can use it as the basis for a new document.

- **Save Template**—Save the edited template with its current name.

- **Preview Template**—Click this link to see how the template will look as a document when it's displayed outside of Zoho's text editor.

- **Export to Template Library**—Add this template to Zoho's Template Library for others to use.

Exporting a Template to the Template Library

It can be helpful to build on the work of somebody else who has already created a template. (You already know this if you've added a few templates to your Writer account from the Template Library.) So if you've created a template that you think other people will appreciate and use, click the Export to Template Library link.

This opens the Template Library Details dialog box. Type in your template's name and give it a type. (What category does it fit into?) Then write a description of the template. Click Export to add your template to the library.

Working with Text

So far, we've been talking about how to work with Writer at the document level. But as everyone knows, text is the "meat and potatoes" of any letter, report, memo, itinerary, or other document you create. Writer offers a lot of options for working with text, as this section explains.

 If Writer's text editor—the part where you type in your text—feels a bit crowded to you, you can expand it. Next to the tab that shows the name of your document (the left tab if you have several documents open), click the Maximize Editor icon: two stacked squares, the top square with a diagonal arrow pointing upward. Clicking Maximize Editor makes the left pane disappear and increases the space you have for working on your document. To make the left pane reappear, click Minimize Editor.

The Formatting Toolbar

With Writer, you can apply whatever formatting you want as you write, thanks to the Formatting toolbar. This toolbar has two rows of buttons that take care of just about any text formatting you might want, as well as other functions related to word processing.

In the top row of the Formatting toolbar's buttons, moving from left to right, here's what you'll find:

- **Save**—Click this button to save the current document.
- **Print**—Later, this chapter explains all about printing from Writer. (It's a bit different from what you may be used to in a desktop program such as Word.) This button gets you started.
- **Page Setup**—An earlier section of this chapter covers how to set up the general formatting of your document. Click this button to set up that formatting or to add or edit a document's header and footer.
- **Font Style**—In Writer, the standard font is Verdana, but you have a range of options, including popular choices such as Times New Roman, Courier, Arial, and Garamond. Click this button to see and choose from a menu of fonts.

 To change the font for an entire document, use Page Setup. To change the font for some text you've selected within a document, use the Font Style drop-down.

- **Font Size**—Your choices here range from 8 to 36 points.
- **Text Styles**—This menu offers six levels of headings, from Heading 1 (huge) to Heading 6 (tiny), as well as options for regular text.
- **Styles**—The options on this drop-down apply various styles to the text you've selected: Highlight gives the text a light yellow background; Title Heading and Sub Heading make the letters light blue or gray, respectively, and insert a space between the selected text and the next line; Quote boxes the selected text and gives it an orange background; and Insert Style Sheet lets you apply a CSS style sheet to the document.

Info 4U CSS stands for *Cascading Style Sheets,* which let developers control the style and layout of multiple web pages.

- **Bold**—Click the familiar dark *B* to boldface some text.
- **Italic**—This button italicizes the text you've selected.
- **Underline**—Need to underline something? Click this button.

Tip 4U Because hyperlinks are underlined, use underlining sparingly in your document. Otherwise, readers might get confused.

- **Strikethrough**—This formatting button can be helpful when you're editing someone else's text. If you want to suggest deleting something, apply strikethrough to the text you think should go.
- **Alignment buttons**—When you *justify* text, the text lines up evenly along the margin. Most word-processing documents, for example, are left-justified, meaning the text is straight along the left margin but not along the right. These buttons let you align your text in any of the following ways: Justify Left, Justify Center (each line is centered on the page), Justify Right, and Justify Full (text lines up straight along both margins).

Tip 4U For ease of reading, Justify Left is probably your best choice.

- **Line Spacing**—Click this button to adjust the spacing for the text you've selected. When you do, the Line Spacing dialog box opens, where you can choose Single, 1.5 Lines, or Double. Make your selection and then click Done to apply it.
- **List buttons**—Click Ordered List to create a numbered list. If you prefer bullets, click Bulleted List. For more on working with lists, skip ahead to the next section.
- **Format**—If you want to put a box or border around some text, click this button. Doing so opens the Quick Format dialog box shown in Figure 1.9. Here, you can position a border and set its style and thickness. If you like, you can give the boxed text a background color and set a padding amount (that is, the distance, in pixels, between your text and its border).

Tip 4U If you've applied a lot of formatting and have decided you don't like it, you can get rid of it all in just two clicks. Right-click the document and then select Remove All Text Styles from the context menu.

The bottom row of the Formatting toolbar has these buttons, going from left to right:

- **Decrease Indent**—Click this button to move selected text closer to the left margin.
- **Increase Indent**—This button puts a little more distance between the text and the left margin. It's helpful when you want, for example, to create sub-bullets in a bulleted list.
- **Subscript and Superscript**—If you're writing a formula, such as $E=mc^2$, the Superscript button lets you put that little 2 up where it belongs. Similarly, the Subscript button reduces the font size of the selected text and places it slightly below the line of text, as in H_2O.

Format

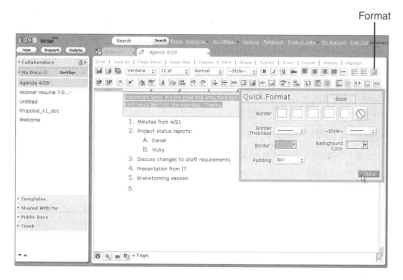

Figure 1.9
To put a border around some text, click the Format button (on the far right) to open the Quick Format dialog box.

- **Font Color**—If you want to make some text stand out from the rest (making a deadline, for example, stand out in red), select the text and then click this button. A box opens that lets you choose your color (red or anything you want) from a palette of dozens of options.
- **Background Color**—If you filled up page after page of your college textbooks with yellow highlighting, you'll love this button. Select the text you want to highlight, click the Background Color button, and then choose a highlighting color.

 To remove highlighting, click Background Color and then choose white. (If you speak hexadecimal—that's the combination of six letters and/or numbers at the top of the color selection box—white is #FFFFFF.)

- **Clipboard buttons**—The next three buttons let you move text around. Click one of the first two buttons (Cut Selection and Copy Selection) in this set to cut or copy text, putting it on the Clipboard. To paste that text somewhere else, position the cursor where you want the text to appear and then click the group's third button (Paste from Clipboard).
- **Undo/Redo**—These buttons are self-explanatory: Undo your most recent action or Redo whatever it was you just undid.
- **Anchor**—An anchor works like a bookmark, so you can find a particular section of your document by creating a named anchor and linking to it. Anchors are useful when you're creating a table of contents; a later section in this chapter ("Creating a Table of Contents") explains how to do that.
- **Horizontal Rule**—Insert a horizontal line between sections with just one click. This is a nice way to break up your text, making it easier on readers' eyes.

- **Insert Web Link**—As you'll see later in this chapter, this button opens a dialog box that lets you link text to a web page or a section of your document.

- **Insert Table**—This button lets you create a table. (More details on working with tables can be found later in this chapter.)

- **Insert/Modify Image**—This button is your starting point for adding an image to your document (or editing one that's already there). Read on for details.

- **Insert HTML**—Use this button to directly insert Hypertext Markup Language (HTML) code.

- **Insert Layer**—A *layer* is like a transparent sheet that you can overlay on your document. It can contain text, images, or whatever you want. After you've inserted a layer using this button, you can position that layer wherever you want it in the document.

- **Spell Check**—Click this button to find possible spelling errors in a document. Unlike other spell checkers you may have used, Writer checks the entire document at once, marking all potential errors when it's done. Questionable words are colored red and have a dotted underline. Click any flagged word to get spelling suggestions and the option to Ignore This One Instance or Ignore All.

 Writer's spellchecker can automatically detect the language you're using. If you want to force it to use a particular language, click the button's down arrow and choose from the list that appears.

- **Find and Replace**—When you click this button, a dialog box opens that lets you find any word or phrase in your document and (if you want) replace it with something else. You can tell Writer to match the case of your search term and to search up or down in the document.

 Grasping for just the right word? Use Writer's built-in thesaurus. Select the word that's close (but not quite it), right-click, and then select Thesaurus from the menu that appears. This opens the Thesaurus dialog box, which offers synonyms and related words.

- **Special Character**—Clicking this button brings up a dialog box with special characters— Greek letters, accented vowels, dashes, mathematical signs, and so on. Click any symbol to insert it where the cursor is.

- **Table of Contents**—This button makes it fast and easy to create a table of contents based on the heading levels in your documents. (Detailed instructions appear later in this chapter.)

- **Emotions**—Express your feelings with a variety of smiling, frowning, surprised, embarrassed, and other faces. Click this button to see the options and insert one in the text.

- **Insert Page Break**—This is a helpful option for long documents made up of numerous chapters. If you want a new chapter to begin on a new page, click this button, and Writer starts the new page just before your cursor.

- **Add Comment**—Writer's comments feature is useful when you've got several people collaborating on a document. You can comment on someone else's text without actually changing it. The "Commenting" section dishes up all the how-to details you'll need.

- **Toggle HTML Source**—Because they live on the Web, Writer documents are HTML documents. If you want to see (or tinker with) the HTML for a document, click this button to open a new window, where you'll see the document's HTML displayed in all its complex glory.

- **Insert Endnote/Footnote**—Scholarly types will find this button indispensable. Click it to open a dialog box, where you can choose where to position your note (at the bottom of the page or the end of the document), pick the numbering system for the in-text reference (1, 2, 3; a, b, c; I, II, III; and so on), and type your note. Writer automatically inserts the in-text reference number, which links to the note.

Info 4U If you're inserting an endnote, you have the option of starting the reference numbers over again from 1 on each new page.

- **Equation Editor**—If you're writing a mathematical or scientific document that requires a lot of equations, you'll appreciate this button. Click it to open the LaTeX Equation Editor, shown in Figure 1.10, where you can create your equation; click Insert to put the equation into your document.

Tip 4U To learn more about using LaTeX to write and edit equations, visit www.latex-project.org.

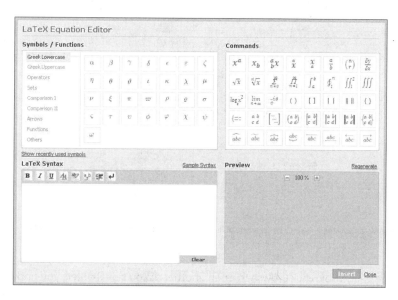

Figure 1.10
Use the LaTeX Equation Editor to create a mathematical or scientific equation and insert it in your document.

Tip 4U For a shortcut that gives you quick access to some of the most popular formatting options, right-click in the document. The context menu that pops up lets you cut, copy, paste, consult a thesaurus, insert an endnote or footnote, add a comment, create a link, realign the text, select the whole document, or remove all formatting.

Using Images in a Document

Sometimes words alone won't get your point across. If you're writing a letter about your recent vacation, for example, you can write paragraphs describing the palm trees, sand, and surf, but it won't have the same impact as a photo of your favorite beach. Read this section to learn how to insert images into a document and edit them when they're there.

Inserting an Image

To get a photo or other image into your document, position the insertion point where you want the image to appear and then click the Insert/Modify Image button in the bottom row of the Formatting toolbar. (It looks like the sun over some mountains.) This opens the Insert Image box shown in Figure 1.11.

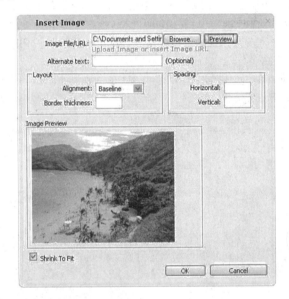

Figure 1.11
To insert an image into your document, first tell Writer where to find the image; click Preview to make sure you've got the right one.

In the Insert Image box, click Browse to open another dialog box that lets you find the picture you want on your computer's hard drive. Or if the image you want is on the Web (in an online photo album, for example), you can type or paste its web address into the Image File/URL text box. Click Preview to get an advance look at the image before you insert it into the document.

Next, you can specify or adjust these settings:

- **Alternate Text**—If you want to label your image, do so here. Alternate text appears if for some reason the browser cannot display the image, or if the page is being read by a reading program for the blind.

- **Layout**—Specify the image's alignment (bottom, left, right, and so on) and the thickness of its border, if any.

- **Spacing**—If you want to adjust the horizontal or vertical spacing of the image on the page, use this section.
- **Shrink to Fit**—Check this box to let Writer adjust the size of your image to fit the page.

When everything looks good, click OK, and Writer inserts the image into your document.

Editing an Image

If you want to adjust an image you've inserted—for example, change its alignment or add or remove a border—click the image to select it. Then click the Insert/Modify Image button (the same one you clicked to insert the image) to open the Insert Image dialog box. Make the adjustments you want; then click OK to apply them.

Resizing an Image

If the image you've inserted is bigger or smaller than you want, you can resize it. Click the image, and a border appears; at the four corners and the halfway points between them, eight small white boxes appear. These are called *handles*. When you place your cursor on a handle, the cursor changes to a double-headed arrow. Click the handle and drag it to resize the image.

Here are some points to keep in mind when resizing:

- When you make a small image bigger (especially if the image is relatively low resolution), the image may become pixelated—that is, it looks as though the image is made up of a lot of small squares.
- To keep the image in proportion, click a corner handle and drag it diagonally. This adjusts the image's size and width at the same time.

Deleting an Image

To remove an image from your document, click the image to select it and then hit your keyboard's Delete or Backspace key. Poof! The image is gone.

Working with Tables

Tables offer an at-a-glance way to categorize and compare information. You might be used to typing your data first, then using that data to create a table. In Writer, however, you create the table first—from there, you can fill in your info and adjust the table itself in various ways.

Creating a Table

To insert a table, put the cursor where you want the table to appear. Click the Insert Table button (it's in the bottom row of buttons on the Formatting toolbar), and you'll see a table-creation box that looks like the one in Figure 1.12. Move your cursor across and down the box to select the number of cells you want your table to have (you can add or delete rows and columns later) and then click to insert the table. Now you can start filling your data into individual cells. Click in a cell and start typing; hit the Tab key to move from one cell to the next. Shift+Tab takes you back to the previous cell.

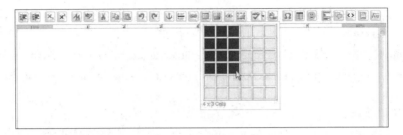

Figure 1.12
When you're creating a table, start by choosing the number of rows and columns you want.

Adding or Deleting Rows or Columns

If your table is bigger (or smaller) than you need it to be, just delete (or add) some rows or columns so it fits your data. Writer offers two ways to do this.

Add or Delete Using the Context Menu

Click inside a cell, or click-and-drag to select a range of cells, and then right-click. A context menu appears. From here, you can select a command to insert or delete a row or column, as shown in Figure 1.13.

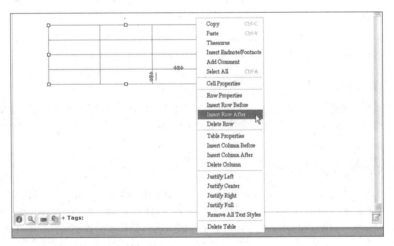

Figure 1.13
Right-clicking a table gives you many options for working with the table.

The choices on the context menu include the following:

- Insert Row Before
- Insert Row After

- Delete Row
- Insert Column Before
- Insert Column After
- Delete Column

Of course, these menu options apply to the cell or cell range you've selected. So if you want to insert a new column on the right side of the table, select a cell in the column that's currently farthest to the right, right-click, and then choose Insert Column After.

 Tip To insert more than one row or column at a time, select the number of rows or columns you want to insert. Then, when you choose your insertion option (Insert Row/Column Before/After), Zoho inserts the same number of columns you selected.

Quick Add or Delete

When you click a table to select it, an icon (two arrows and a circle with an *x* in it) appears on both a vertical and a horizontal line, as Figure 1.14 shows. To quickly add a row or column, click the arrow pointing in the direction where you want the new row or column to appear. To delete a row or column, click the circled *x* on the horizontal line (to delete a column) or on the vertical line (to delete a row).

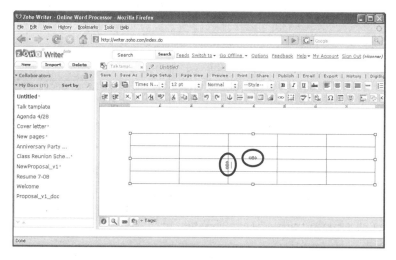

Figure 1.14
Use the circled icons to add or delete rows or columns with a single-click.

Resizing a Table

The quickest way to resize a table is to click it, which makes eight small, square handles appear (see Figure 1.13). Click any handle and then drag to resize the table. Let up on the mouse button to make the new size permanent.

Alternatively, you can adjust the table's properties to resize it. To take this route, right-click the table and then choose Table Properties from the context menu. This opens the Table Properties box shown in Figure 1.15.

To adjust the table's size, look in the Table Properties box's Layout section. Here, you can adjust the table's height, width, or both, in terms of percentage (as this relates to the table's current size) or pixels. If you want, you can also adjust the horizontal and vertical alignment of the text within the cells. Click OK to apply your changes.

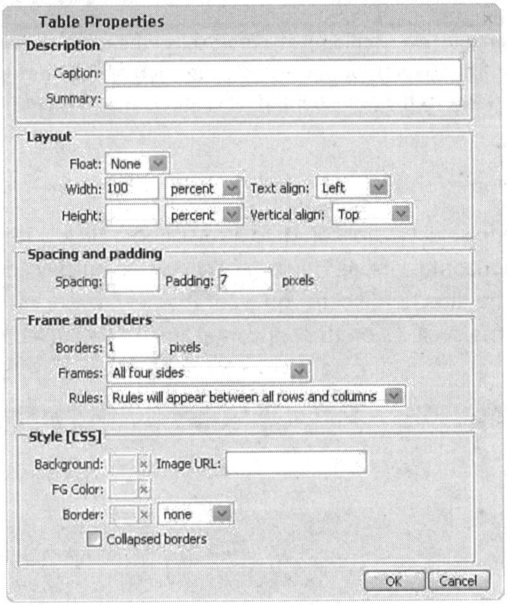

Table Properties

Description

Caption: [   ]
Summary: [   ]

Layout

Float: [None ▾]
Width: [100] [percent ▾] Text align: [Left ▾]
Height: [   ] [percent ▾] Vertical align: [Top ▾]

Spacing and padding

Spacing: [   ] Padding: [7] pixels

Frame and borders

Borders: [1] pixels
Frames: [All four sides ▾]
Rules: [Rules will appear between all rows and columns ▾]

Style [CSS]

Background: [ ][x] Image URL: [   ]
FG Color: [ ][x]
Border: [ ][x] [none ▾]
☐ Collapsed borders

[OK] [Cancel]

Figure 1.15
Use the Table Properties box to adjust various aspects of a table, including size, cell padding, and gridlines.

 You can resize an individual row or cell in the same way. When you right-click the table, choose Row Properties or Cell Properties; then choose the dimensions you want. At this writing, Writer doesn't offer a Column Properties option.

Showing or Hiding Gridlines

Writer's standard table has a border on all four sides and lines separating all cells. You can change the appearance of a table by adjusting its settings to hide all these lines or show just some of them (lines between rows but not columns, for example). To change a table's gridlines, right-click the table and select Table Properties to bring up the Table Properties box (see Figure 1.15). In Table Properties, go to the Frame and Borders section, where you can make these adjustments:

- **Borders**—If the table has a border, you can adjust its thickness with this setting. (If you don't want a border around the whole table, set this to 0).
- **Frames**—This refers to the border around the whole table. You can have a frame appear on all four sides, on just the top and/or bottom, on just the left and/or right, and so on.
- **Rules**—This refers to the horizontal and vertical lines that separate cells within the table. You can hide all rules, show all rules, show just vertical rules (between columns), or show just horizontal rules (between rows).

Wrapping Text Around a Table

Often you want a table to appear on its own, standing apart from the text, to emphasize it. Sometimes, though, you may want text to wrap around the table; this is called *floating* the table, and it allows text to appear beside a table. To float a table, right-click the table, select Table Properties, and in the Table Properties box find the Layout section. Here, use the Float drop-down menu to select one of these options:

- **None**—No text wraps around the table.
- **Left**—The table appears to the left of any text you add.
- **Right**—The table appears to the right of any text you add.

Adjusting Cell Padding

Padding describes the space between a cell's content and its border. If your table's looking a bit cramped, increase the padding to give the cells' contents some room. On the other hand, if the contents of its cells seem overwhelmed by too much whitespace, decrease the padding.

To increase or decrease padding, right-click the table and select Table Properties to open the Table Properties box. In the Spacing and Padding section, adjust the number of pixels that pad each cell. (Writer's standard is 7 pixels.)

Deleting a Table

If you've inserted a table and then change your mind, you can get rid of it with just a couple of clicks. Right-click the table you want to delete; from the context menu, select Delete Table.

 Writer doesn't ask you to confirm before it deletes a table, so make sure you really want the table gone before you click Delete Table. Clicking Undo will bring back an empty table—that is, the table minus the data it held. Be careful!

Creating a Table of Contents

In a long document, your readers will appreciate a table of contents that lets them jump ahead to a particular chapter or section. This saves a lot of scrolling when they're reading online.

To create a table of contents, first make sure your document makes consistent use of headers throughout. For example, you might use Heading 1 for chapter titles, Heading 2 for section titles, and Heading 3 for subsection titles throughout the document. (To assign a heading level to a title, use the Text Style menu in the top row of Formatting toolbar buttons.)

After you've checked through the document to make sure your headings are consistent, you're ready to create the table of contents. All you have to do is click the Table of Contents button (it's in the bottom row of the Formatting toolbar), and Writer does all the work for you: It creates a table of contents and places it at the beginning of the document; each entry in the table of contents is a link that, when clicked, jumps right to the section it references.

If you make changes to the document that affect the table of contents, just click the Table of Contents button again, and Writer updates the table of contents for you.

 If you decide you don't need a table of contents, here's how to delete it: Right-click the table of contents. From the context menu that appears, select Delete TOC.

Working Offline

Storing your documents online is smart. You always have access to all your files from anywhere you can connect to the Internet. That means no more worrying about whether you remembered to transfer the latest version from your desktop at work to the laptop you're taking along on your business trip. Whenever you open a document, you know it's the most recent version.

Sometimes, though, you need to be able to work when you don't have an Internet connection. Maybe your hotel's Wi-Fi is down or you can't get a good signal. In those situations, you don't want to waste time just because you don't have access to a hotspot or other way of connecting to the Internet.

No worries. With Zoho Writer, you can work on your documents offline. Later, when you connect to the Internet again, Writer automatically synchronizes your documents with the work you did offline. Working offline takes a little setting up, but the freedom it offers is worth the effort.

Step 1: Install Google Gears

Google Gears is an open-source extension for your web browser that lets you work with Zoho Writer documents even when your computer isn't connected to the Internet. The documents get stored on your computer, where you can open, read, edit, and save them. The next time you connect that computer to the Internet, fire up your web browser, and sign in to Zoho Writer, your online and offline documents get synched, automatically.

So before you can use Zoho Writer offline, you need to install Google Gears on your computer. (If you work offline using more than one computer, you need to install Google Gears on each of them.) To work with Google Gears, your computer's operating system and browser have to be one of the following combinations:

- Windows XP or Vista with Internet Explorer 6 or higher
- Windows XP or Vista with Firefox 1.5 or higher

- Windows XP or Vista with Google Chrome (which offers built-in support for Google Gears— and that means you can skip the rest of this section)
- Mac OS X 10.2 or higher with Firefox 1.5 or higher
- Linux with Firefox 1.5 or higher
- Windows Mobile 5 or higher with Internet Explorer 4.01 or higher

 If you need to install or upgrade to one of these browsers, you can download Firefox at www.firefox.com, Internet Explorer at www.microsoft.com/windows/downloads/ie, and Google Chrome at www.google.com/chrome. All of these browsers are free.

If your computer meets these requirements, go to http://gears.google.com to download Google Gears. Click the big blue Install Gears button. This opens a page that presents Google's Terms of Service and Privacy Policy as these relate to Gears. If you want, you can check the box that authorizes Google to collect information about how you use Gears. Any info Google collects is anonymous. If you don't feel like sharing that info with Google, though, leave the box unchecked. Click Agree and Download.

A window opens, requesting your okay to download the Gears installation file, called GoogleGearsSetup.exe, to your computer. (If you are using Internet Explorer, the information bar might tell you that IE has blocked the site from downloading the file; if so, click the information bar and click Download File.)

Click Save File (Firefox) or Save (Internet Explorer). If using Internet Explorer, you are prompted for a location in which to save; with Firefox, the file is saved to the default download location.

After downloading the GearsSetup.exe file, run it to install the program.

After the setup program installs Gears on your computer, you need to close your web browser and then restart it. (Save your work in Writer first if needed.) After you've done that, the installation is complete, and you're ready to get back to Zoho Writer.

Step 2: Set Up Zoho Writer to Work with Google Gears

After you've restarted your web browser, point it to http://writer.zoho.com and sign back in. At the top of the screen, click the Go Offline link. This opens the boxes shown in Figure 1.16.

You need to tell Google Gears that Zoho Writer can be trusted to transfer files to your computer. (That's the whole point of working offline, after all.) Check the box labeled "I trust this site. Allow it to use Gears." Next, click Allow.

Google Gears connects to Zoho and downloads your documents. Now you can disconnect from the Internet and still have access to your documents.

 You only need to green-light Zoho Writer to work with Google Gears once. After that, when you click the Go Offline link, Writer and Gears work together to download your documents.

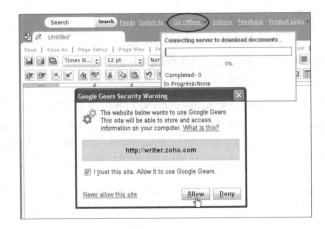

Figure 1.16
Let Google Gears know that you trust Zoho Writer to download files to your computer.

After you've let Gears know that you trust Writer, all you have to do to transfer documents from Writer to your computer is click the Go Offline link. This transfers up to 25 of the most recently worked-on documents from Writer to your computer.

 If you expect to work offline a lot, get in the habit of clicking the Go Offline link before you sign out of Writer.

Step 3: Work Offline

When Gears transfers your documents, they're stored in your computer's web browser. To work offline, open your web browser (even though you're not connected to the Internet). In the address bar, type `http://writer.zoho.com/offline` and hit Enter.

The familiar Writer workspace opens, showing the documents you downloaded. Open any document and work on it just as you normally would. Don't forget to save your document. When you're done, you don't have to sign out. (You're offline, so you're not signed in.) Just close your browser.

Step 4: Synch Your Online and Offline Documents

The next time you're online, sign in to Writer at this address: writer.zoho.com/offline.

Zoho notices that there's a difference between your online and offline documents and opens the Synchronization Summary box shown in Figure 1.17. This lists any documents that have changed due to your offline editing. Click Synchronize, and Writer uploads your offline edits as a new version.

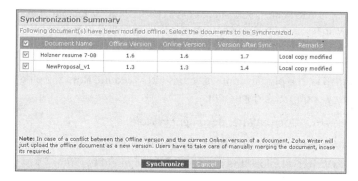

Figure 1.17
When you sign back in to Writer, Zoho notifies you of which documents have changed so you can sync them with the online versions.

Plugging into Microsoft Office

Zoho has a plug-in that you can install to add Zoho functionality to Microsoft Word and Excel. That means you can create and edit a document in Word and then save it right inside Zoho Writer. Or you can create a document in Zoho, open it in Word to do some editing, and then save it in Writer. The plug-in integrates Microsoft Word and Zoho Writer, giving Word users tons of flexibility in how they work.

 The Zoho plug-in works with Microsoft Office 2000 and higher. Currently the plug-in works only with the English version of Office, although Zoho plans to support other languages in the future.

Installing the Plug-In

First, if you've got Word or Excel open on your computer, close it. Then point your web browser to www.zoho.com. Below the list of apps, click the Zoho Plugin for Microsoft Office link. This opens a page explaining about the plug-in, complete with slideshows about how to download, install, and use it.

To download the plug-in, look in the "Installation and Use" section for this sentence: *Users can download the Zoho plug-in here.* The word *here* is a hyperlink; click it to start the download. Tell your computer where you want to save the file. After the download has finished, run the file to start the installation. The program walks you through the installation. When it's done, you get the choice of whether you want to open Microsoft Word or Excel, complete with its shiny new Zoho plug-ins.

Using the Plug-In

After you've installed the Zoho plug-in, open Word. If you use Word 2007, the new Zoho buttons are on the Add-Ins tab. (In earlier versions of Word, look for the buttons by selecting View, Toolbars.) To use the plug-in, you need to be signed in to your Zoho account, but you can do so right from Word. On the Add-Ins tab, click Zoho Writer and then click Login.

When you sign in to Zoho, the sign-in box has a check box at the bottom labeled Keep a Local Copy. To save a copy of your document in Word as well as Zoho, make sure this box is checked.

After you've signed in, the plug-in contacts your Writer account. Now, the plug-in gives you these options for working with documents:

- **Open Document**—Open a Writer document in Word.
- **Save in Zoho Writer**—Save an existing document in Writer.
- **Add to Zoho Writer**—Upload the current Word document to Writer.

Organizing Your Documents

As you work with Writer, your documents will start piling up. And just as you don't want to dig through towering stacks of paper to find a particular memo or report, you don't want to spend a lot of time hunting for a document in Writer.

Writer gives you a lot of flexibility in how you organize and find your documents. Use tags to label your documents, making them easy to find. (You can even convert a tag into a folder.) Or do a lightning-fast search to find a particular document or set of documents. This section helps you find the file you want—fast.

Tagging

When you *tag* a document, it's like slapping a label on it. This label helps you find the document (or groups of related documents) later. For example, if you're planning a trip to Paris for an industry conference, you might label related documents *2010 conference* or *Paris* (or both). One of the great things about labels is that you can attach several labels to the same document. This is an advantage over traditional folders, where it can be all too easy to squirrel away a document in some folder somewhere—and then drive yourself crazy trying to remember which folder it's in.

 When you're working offline, you can't use the status bar buttons at the bottom of the screen—this includes tagging it.

Tagging a Document

To tag a document with a label, open the document you want. In the status bar at the bottom of the screen, click +Tags. The status bar changes to show a text box. In this box, type in the tag you want and then click Add. Your new tag appears to the right of the text box and its buttons. If you want to add another tag, repeat the process. When you're done, click Close.

 To see what tags you've already created, double-click inside the Tags text box. A list of existing tags appears; click any one to apply it to the current document.

Finding Tagged Documents

After you've given your documents a few tags, you can find all the documents that have the same tag. Open a tagged document; its tags (if any) appear at the bottom of the screen. Click the tag you want, and a menu appears, as shown in Figure 1.18. At the top of the menu is a list of documents that have this tag; click any document to open it.

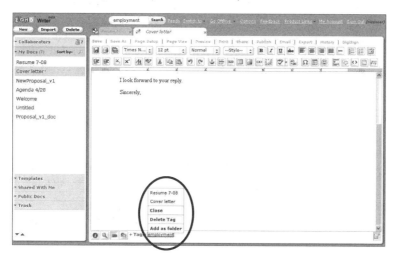

Figure 1.18
Click a document's tag to see a list of documents with that tag.

Turning a Tag into a Folder

If you're used to working with folders, using tags can take some getting used to—after all, it's a whole new way of thinking about organizing your documents. You may find you love tags, or you may miss your folders. Lucky you—you can have it both ways.

Writer lets you turn a tag into a folder. To do this, start by adding a tag to a document or opening a document that has the tag you want to become a folder. At the bottom of the screen, click the tag. From the menu that appears, choose Add as Folder.

Now, the tag appears in the left list, where documents, collaborators, templates, and so on show up. (Look for it at the bottom of the list; you may have to collapse items above it to make it visible.) For example, if you've turned a tag called *Collins Project* into a folder, you'll now see *Collins Project* in the left list. Click the Collins Project folder to see all documents tagged *Collins Project*. Click any document to open it.

Info 4U
After you've turned a tag into a folder, any subsequent documents that you label with that tag get added to the folder.

If you're done with a folder and want to delete it, just click the X to the right of its name. Deleting a folder *doesn't* delete the documents in that folder, it just removes the folder from the left list. And you can always re-create the folder in the same way you created it in the first place. (Open a tagged document, click its tag, and then select Add as Folder.)

Removing a Tag

If you want to take the tag off a document, open the document you want to untag. Click the tag and then click Delete Tag. Writer removes the tag from that document only.

 If you want to delete a tag completely, so that no documents have it, first turn the tag into a folder. In the left menu, open the folder and then open all its documents. Remove the tags from each document and then delete the folder from the list.

Searching

Trying to find a particular document among hundreds of files can make the proverbial hunt for a needle in a haystack seem easy in comparison. But with full-text search capability, Writer can help you find just the document you're looking for.

Searching for a Document

To search for a document, use the Search box above Writer's document tabs. Just type in your search term and click Search. Writer returns the list of results on a new tab. Click the name of any document on the list to open it on a new tab.

For example, if you're looking for a particular document—say, a memo you wrote about employee benefits—type **benefits** into the search box and then click Search. Writer rummages through the contents of all your documents and returns a list of those that have the word *benefits* in them. From there, you can find the exact document you're looking for.

 Searching for a phrase, such as Mary Smith, returns all documents that have either the word *Mary* or the word *Smith*. To tell Writer to look for an exact match, put quotation marks around your search phrase, like this: "`Mary Smith`".

Searching Within a Document

Looking for a certain word or phrase inside the active document? When you've got the document open, Writer gives you two ways to search for it.

Quick Search

To do a quick search, click the little picture of a magnifying glass at the bottom of the screen. To its right, a Find text box appears; type in your search term and click Find. Writer jumps to and highlights the first instance of the word in the document. If that's not the instance you're looking for, click Find again to jump to the next (and so on until you've found the right spot).

Find and Replace

To find and replace a word or phrase, click the Find and Replace button in the bottom row of the Formatting toolbar. This opens the Find and Replace box shown in Figure 1.19.

Type your search term in the Find What box. Optionally, you can tell Writer to match the case of what you typed and to search up or down in the document. Click Find Next to start searching.

If you want to replace your search term with something else—for example, Mary Smith has married Fred Jones and changed her last name—type the new term in the Replace With box. Click Replace All if you want to change all instances of *Smith* to *Jones* in one fell swoop; if you'd rather replace terms one at a time, click Find Next and Replace Next to work your way through the document.

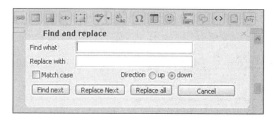

Figure 1.19
Find and Replace lets you fine-tune your in-document searches.

Sharing and Collaborating on Documents

Your kindergarten teacher was right: It's nice to share. And when it comes to your documents, not only is sharing nice, it can also end a lot of headaches. No more emailing documents around and losing track of which version is which. No more drumming your fingers on your desk, waiting for someone to check a report back into SharePoint so you can have your turn to work on it. When you share a document in Writer, you give others access to that document so that they can view it or, if you prefer, work on it with you. And all in real time—so when someone makes a change, the document gets updated for everyone.

Personal Sharing

You've got a document you want to share with a just a few people—maybe you want your siblings' reaction to the toast you wrote for your parents' upcoming anniversary party or a quick proofread of your resume from a grammar-savvy friend. You don't want to share these documents with the whole world, just with a couple of people. By sharing a document privately, you can invite others to read or edit a document.

Sharing with Individuals

To share a document with one or more individuals, open the document you want to share. In the status bar at the bottom of the page, click the Shared Info button. The status bar changes to give information about the document's current sharing status. Because you haven't yet shared this document, Writer tells you that it's not currently shared, either publicly or privately. Click the Click to Share Privately link to open the dialog box shown in Figure 1.20.

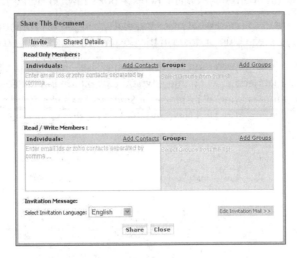

Figure 1.20
Use the Invite tab of the Share This Document box to share a document with others.

On the Invite tab, you can invite people to become Read Only Members (able to view the document but not edit it) or Read/Write Members (able to both view and edit the document). Type or paste the email addresses of the people you're inviting into the appropriate text box. If you're adding multiple addresses, use commas to separate them.

 To speed add members, click Add Contacts in the section you want (Read Only Members or Read/Write Members). Another box opens, listing your Zoho contacts. Simply click a contact to add that person to the list of people you're inviting. To add multiple contacts all at once, check the box next to those you want to add (or check Select All); then click Add.

Next, you can choose a language for the invitation message that Zoho sends. English is the standard, but you can also send the email in Chinese or Japanese.

If you want, you can also customize the invitation email to tell recipients about your document. Click Edit Invitation Mail, and the dialog box expands to let you edit the email's subject line and content. This step is optional; if you don't customize the email, Zoho sends a brief message informing recipients that you've shared a document and including a link to access that document.

When you've got your collaborators, their permissions, and your invitation email all set up, click Share to send the invitations. Zoho shoots off the invitation emails and shows you the "shared details" for this document. (Keep reading to find out more about working with shared details.) Also, the status bar updates to show how many people are now sharing this document.

Accessing a Shared Document

You've invited a few people to your Zoho party—now how do they join the fun?

The invitation email that Writer sends out has a link to your document. When the recipient clicks that link, a new window opens. Across the top is the document's name, the author's name (your Zoho username), and a Sign Up Now link. Collaborators can use the Sign Up Now link to create or sign in to their Zoho Writer accounts.

After signing in, collaborators can find shared documents in the left menu, under Shared to Me. That section lists two kinds of shared documents:

- **Personally Shared**—Here you'll find documents that someone shared with you as an individual.
- **Personal Groups**—This lists documents that were shared with you as part of a group.

 If you're not sure how the author of a document shared it with you, check both kinds of sharing.

Sharing in Groups

When there's a group of people with whom you regularly share documents—your project team at work, for example, or classmates for the upcoming class reunion—you don't want to type in everyone's email address each time you've got a new document to share. Fortunately, you don't have to. Just collect your collaborators into a group and then share with the group.

Creating a Group

Before you can share with a group, you have to create the group. Open a document you want to share. In the status bar, click the Privately Shared link. (This may say the document is not privately shared or it may list the current number of sharers, depending on whether you've already shared the document.) In the dialog box that opens, click Add Groups, which opens another box listing any groups you've created. Click Create New Group, and the box changes to look like the one shown in Figure 1.21.

To create a group, fill in these fields:

- **Group Name**—Give your group a descriptive name to make it easy, later on, to find the group you want.
- **Description (Optional)**—If you want to add a few lines about the group or its purpose, type that in here.

 If you write a description, it appears in the email invitation Zoho sends to potential group members, so *don't* write a description such as "All my loser friends."

- **Members Mail IDs**—Type or paste in the email addresses of everyone in the group. Put a comma between addresses to separate them.

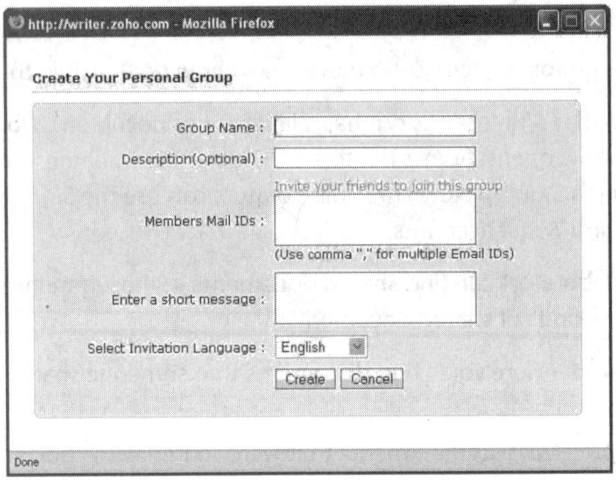

Figure 1.21
Create a group to make sharing even easier.

■ **Enter a short message**—When you create a group, Zoho lets members know they're part of it. If you want, you can include a message telling members the purpose of the group, such as "This group is to keep the Class of '99 up to date on reunion information."

■ **Select Invitation Language**—This determines the language Zoho uses for its standard invitation email (not for any optional message you include). The choices are English, Chinese, and Japanese.

When you're done, click Create. Zoho mails out invitations to each person in the group.

 When you add someone to a group, that person has to accept your invitation to become part of the group. Zoho sends an invitation email; any recipient who doesn't yet have a Zoho account is invited to sign up.

Sharing with a Group

After you've created a group, you can share a document with all its members in just a couple of clicks. Start by opening the document you want to share. In the status bar, click Shared Info and then click the private sharing link. (It may tell you that you're not yet sharing this document privately or that you're privately sharing it with *x* number of people.) In the dialog box that opens, click the Add Groups link for the kind of sharing you want (Read Only or Read/Write).

A new dialog box pops up, showing a list of the groups you've created. Click any group's name to add it to the Share This Document box. Or check the box next to the group (or groups) you want and click Add. When you're done adding groups, click the Groups List box's upper-right x to close it.

Back in the Share This Document box, you can tweak the invitation email if you want (the "Sharing with Individuals" section tells you how.) When you're ready to send out the invitations to the group, click Share. Writer grants access to everyone in the group and adds your document to their Shared to Me list.

Managing Groups

After you've created a group, you may have to make changes to it. After all, people switch projects and change email addresses. To edit an existing group, click Shared Info in the status bar and then click the private sharing link on the right. This brings up the Share This Document dialog box (Figure 1.20); click either Add Groups link, to open a list of your groups. Beneath the list of groups, click the My Groups link to open a window that looks something like the one in Figure 1.22.

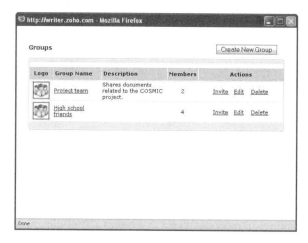

Figure 1.22
The Groups window lists existing groups you've created—to see who's in a group, click its name.

The Groups window lists all the groups you've created for Writer. For each group, you see the name of the group, its description (if you wrote one), and how many members it has. There are also links that let you manage the group: You can invite new members, edit the group's information, or delete the group entirely.

Inviting New Members

To add one or more new members to an existing group, open the Groups window, find the group you want, and then click its Invite link (shown in Figure 1.22). The box changes to let you type in the new members' email addresses (use commas to separate multiple addresses), add an optional message, and choose a language. Click Invite to send out emails asking the new members to join your group.

Reinviting a Group Member

Until an invitee responds to your invitation to join a group, that person is listed under Pending Invitations. To give invitees a nudge to hurry up and RSVP already, you can reinvite them. In the

Groups window, click the name of the group and then click Pending Invitations. Find the name of the person you want and then click Reinvite. Zoho fires off another email asking them to join the group.

Deleting a Group Member

When someone leaves a project or moves away from the neighborhood book club, you don't want that person to have continued access to the group's shared documents. Deleting someone from a group takes just a couple seconds. Open the Groups window, find the soon-to-be-former member, and then click Delete.

 Writer doesn't ask you to confirm the deletion, so make sure you're deleting the right group member.

You can also delete members you've invited who haven't yet confirmed. In the Groups window, click Pending Invitations. To the right of the name of the person you want to delete, click Delete. Deleting pending members means you're not stuck in limbo, waiting for potential group members who never bother to respond to your invitation.

Adding a Group Logo

As Figure 1.22 shows, each group you create has a picture associated with it. You don't have to stick with the standard image Zoho assigns; you can personalize a group by uploading your own image, such as a company logo.

To add your own logo or image, open the Groups window, find the group you want, and then click Edit. The box changes to show details for that group. Click Upload Logo. A new window opens, letting you browse to the image file you want on your computer. Find and select the image and then click Open. Zoho uploads the image and displays it with your group.

Here are a few tips for uploading an image to use as a group's logo:

- You can upload a file that ends in any of these extensions: .jpg, .gif, .png, or .jpeg.
- The file you upload should be 300KB or smaller. (Otherwise, it may not display correctly.)
- Any image you upload must be your own property; don't violate someone else's copyright.
- No nudity or obscene images, please.

Changing a Group's Name or Description

You get one of those top-down memos saying that the COSMIC project has been renamed Project Galaxy. If you want your project team's group to reflect the change, you can rename the group. Open the Groups window; then, for the group whose name you want to change, click Edit. When you see the details for that group, click Edit Group Details. Now, you can change the name's group or description by typing in the relevant text box. When you're done, click Save to apply the changes.

Deleting a Group

The project has been completed, the class reunion was a great success—whatever the reason, the time may come when you no longer need a particular group to share your documents with.

To delete a group, simply open the Groups window, find the obsolete group, and click the Delete link to its right. Zoho asks you to confirm that you really want to get rid of the group. Click OK, and that group is history.

Changing Sharing Privileges

As you share a document with individuals or groups, Zoho adds them to the Share This Document dialog box's Shared Details tab, shown in Figure 1.23. From this tab, you can change the sharing privilege level for any person or group. You can also delete a person or group, taking away their access to your document.

To change sharing privileges, open the Share This Document dialog box (Shared Info, Privately Shared to xx Users); then click the Shared Details tab. Find the person or group whose access level you want to change:

- Click Change to change the sharing level from View Only to View/Edit (or vice versa).
- Click Remove to stop giving that person or group access to your document.

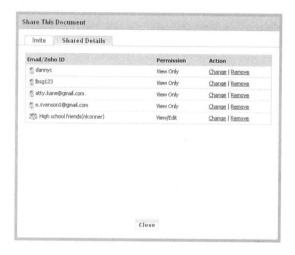

Figure 1.23
The Shared Details tab lists current sharers and their permission levels.

Collaborating with Others

The whole point of inviting others to share your documents is so that you can work together—in real time. So if Ben's on the road, Michelle is telecommuting from home, and you're in the office, all three of you can work on and discuss the document, at the same time.

 Tip To collaborate with others on a document you created, give those people Read/Write permission when you share the document with them.

What happens when two or more people work on a document at the same time? When you're working on a document and a collaborator opens it, Zoho pops up a message box in the lower-right part of the screen to let you know.

As you and your collaborators work, changes that people make to the document appear in real time. That means you don't have to refresh your screen to see the work that others have done.

But what if two people are working on the same section of the document at the same time? Won't that get confusing? Not at all. When you put your cursor in a section of the document, such as a paragraph, and start working on it, Zoho locks that part of the document so only you can work on it. Your collaborators see that section as highlighted. They can view the section, but not work on it until you've moved on to another section. (And this works both ways; if you see part of your document highlighted, it means someone else is working on it right now.)

Locking a Document

If you want a shared document all to yourself, you can lock it. In the list on the left, there's a little picture of a padlock next to the Collaborators heading. When the document is unlocked, the padlock is open. Click the padlock to lock the document. The picture changes to show that the padlock is locked, and now no one else can edit the document until you've unlocked it.

 You can't lock a document if a collaborator is also working on it.

When someone else has locked a document, you can view it but not edit it. To see who locked it, click the padlock icon. The Collaborators section expands to tell you who has put a lock on this document. If you need access, open a chat with that person (see next section).

 You can't keep a document locked up forever. When you sign out of Zoho, the document gets unlocked automatically.

Discussing Shared Documents

If you're editing a document at the same time as someone else, you may have a question about a change the other person made, or you may want to discuss who's doing what. You might even want to keep a running conversation going, just to be sociable as you work. Collaborators can chat as they work together on a document.

When you're editing a document simultaneously with others, your collaborators' usernames appear in the Collaborators list. At the same time, the Users Online icon (a picture of a person to the right of the Collaborators heading) starts flashing. To launch a chat, click either the Collaborators heading or the flashing icon.

The Collaborators section expands, showing you who else is working on the document. Below the names is a chat area. If more than one collaborator is online, select the name of the person you want to chat with. In the text box at the bottom of the chat area, type a message and then hit the Enter key.

Your message appears in the chat window just above the text box, on both your screen and the screen of the person you're chatting with. When the other person answers, the message appears below yours, pushing yours up the screen.

Commenting on a Document

Another way to communicate with collaborators is to comment on a shared document. Comments don't become part of the text in a document. Instead, they annotate the text. When you insert a comment, Writer indicates the comment with a speech-bubble icon, as shown in Figure 1.24. The speech bubble shows that someone has inserted a comment, so others can read and respond to it.

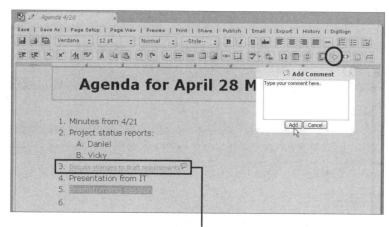

There's a comment on this text.

Figure 1.24
To add a comment, click the Add Comment button (circled). After you've added a comment, a speech bubble appears in the text at the site of the comment.

Inserting a Comment

To insert a comment, select the text you want to comment on and then click the Add Comment button, which looks like a comic strip's speech bubble. (It's in the bottom row of buttons in the Formatting toolbar, on the right side.) This opens the Add Comment box shown in Figure 1.24.

Type your comment into the text box and then click Add to insert your comment into the document.

Writer inserts the speech-bubble icon, makes the selected text pink, and underlines it, to show others a comment is there.

Viewing a Comment

When you want to read a comment in a document, click the speech bubble. This opens the Comments dialog box, where you can read the comment. The Comments box also shows who made the comment and when. When you're done reading the comment, click the upper-right X to close the Comments box.

If you want to respond to the comment, click the Add Comment link at the bottom of the box. This expands the Comments box to include a text box where you can type in your response. Click Add when you're done.

 To view all the comments in a document, click the status bar's lower-right Comments button, which looks like a pencil writing on a piece of paper. This opens the Contextual Comments pane, which shows all the document's comments, along with any responses.

Editing a Comment

You can edit any comment in a document (whether you wrote the original). To edit a comment, click the lower-right Comments button to open the Contextual Comments pane. Scroll through to find the comment you want to change and click its Edit link.

The comment changes to appear inside an editable text box. Make your changes to the comment and then click OK.

 Opening the Contextual Comments page pushes the left menu off the screen; to get it back, close the Contextual Comments pane or click the left-pointing arrow on the left side of the screen.

Deleting a Comment

You don't want tons of comments cluttering up your document. So when an issue has been dealt with, you can get rid of the comment that raised that issue. Click the lower-right Comments button; the Contextual Comments pane opens. Find the comment you want to delete, and click its Delete link. Writer asks you to confirm that you want to delete the comment. Click OK, and the comment's gone.

 Deleting a comment doesn't delete responses to that comment. To delete a comment *and* its responses, click the Trash Can icon to the right of the comment's name.

Publishing Documents

Sharing with a handful of friends or colleagues is all well and good, but sometimes you've got a document that you want to share with the whole world. So Zoho lets you publish any Writer document on the Web, either as its own web page or on your blog. Read on to learn more.

Putting a Document on the Web

When you publish a document on the Web, the document gets its very own web address, so anyone can view it. To put a document on the Web, open the document you want to publish and click Shared Info in the status bar at the bottom of the screen.

The status bar changes to show this document's sharing status. Click the Click to Make Public link to open the Public Share dialog box. This dialog box explains that you're about to publish your document on the Internet. Click Publish. The box changes to look like the one in Figure 1.25.

 For a shortcut to the Public Share dialog box, select Publish, Make Public from the menu options at the top of the text editor.

Click the published document's title to see how it'll look in its new home.

Embedding a Document in a Web Page

You can also *embed* the document in a different web page, which means that the document appears as a part of that web page. To embed your published document, copy the HTML code in the text box in the Public Share dialog box (see Figure 1.25) and then paste that code in a page you upload to your website.

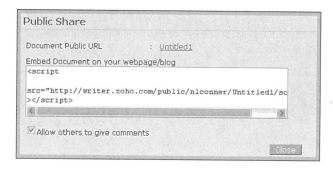

Figure 1.25
When you publish a document on the Web, Zoho gives you the HTML code you need to embed the document on a different web page.

Working with Readers' Comments

When you publish a document as a web page, readers who see the page can comment on it. They do this by clicking the lower-left comments link and then filling out a form with their email address (which is required) and their comment.

You can see comments by looking at the published document and clicking its comments link. You can also see comments on the document right in Writer. Open the document and click Shared Info; then click the Comments link. A box opens to display any comments the document has received, along with the email address of the person who left the comment. If someone has posted an unhelpful or inappropriate comment, you can delete it by clicking the red X to its right.

Disabling Comments on a Published Document

As Figure 1.25 shows, when you publish a document, you have a choice of whether to allow comments on that document. The standard is to allow comments. If you'd rather not be getting comments on your document, uncheck the Allow Others to Give Comments check box and then click Close.

If you share all your documents strictly on a read-only basis, you can turn off comments on all your public documents. In Writer, click Options, Settings. Uncheck the Allow Comments for Public Documents box and then click Save. Now, any document you make public will have comments disabled.

Removing a Published Document from the Web

You can remove a document you've published at any time. Simply open the document and select Publish, Cancel Public Sharing. That's all there is to it.

Publishing a Document in a Blog

If you keep an online journal, commonly known as a *blog* (which is short for *web log*), you can use Writer to create and polish up a new entry and then post it straight to your blog.

After you've written the document you want to post, click Publish, Post to Blog. This opens the Blog Settings box shown in Figure 1.26.

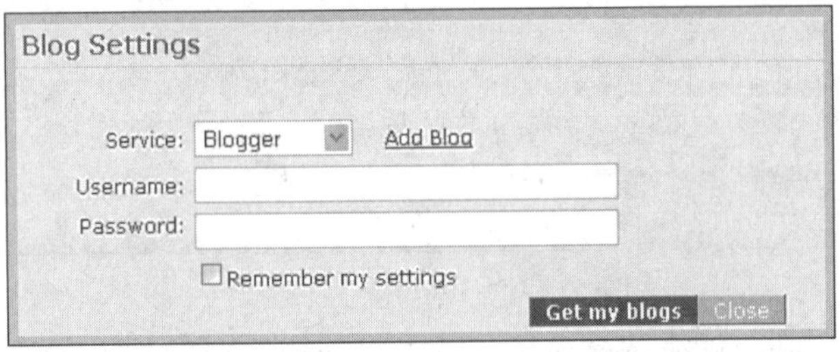

Blog Settings

Service: Blogger   Add Blog
Username:
Password:
☐ Remember my settings
Get my blogs   Close

Figure 1.26
Writer can post a document straight to your blog.

To allow Writer to post the document to your blog, you need to tell Zoho which blogging service you use, as well as your username and password. This lets Zoho log in on your behalf. Zoho currently supports these blogging services:

- Blogger
- LiveJournal
- WordPress
- TypePad

Select the service and type in your username and password. (If you're going to be using Writer frequently for blogging, check Remember My Settings.) Then click the button labeled Get My Blogs.

Zoho logs in to your blog site and fetches your blog. If you have more than one blog hosted on the same site, you'll see a drop-down list that lets you choose the blog you want. If you've created categories for your blog, you can choose the category you want for this post.

Checking the With Tags check box means that any tags you've added to your Writer document will become Technorati tags (which label posts to help people who use Technorati, a blog search engine, find what you've written) when posted to your blog. If this post is a draft not yet ready for public consumption, check the Post as Draft check box.

When everything's all set, click Publish to put the post on your blog.

Viewing and Comparing Document Versions

Ever wish you could go back to an earlier version of a document, before tangential ideas or other people's changes messed everything up? With Writer, you can.

Zoho is kind of like a pack rat, saving *everything*. When you save a document, Writer saves not just your recent changes, but also versions that existed before you made and saved those changes. At any time, you can view a document's history, seeing those previous versions and, if you want, reverting to an earlier draft. It's like having a secretary who files everything, just in case you'll need it later.

Viewing a Document's History

To see earlier versions of a document, open the document and click its History link (on the right above the Formatting toolbar). This opens the History page, shown in Figure 1.27. The History page shows the document's most recent version; use the Show Version drop-down list to choose the version you want to see.

You can't edit a document while viewing its history; that's because you're looking at a snapshot of the document as it existed at a certain moment in time. If you want to go back to an earlier version, making that version the current one, click the Revert button. Writer reverts to the version you chose and takes you back to the text editor.

If you don't want to revert to a previous version, but you do want to get back to work on the current one, click the Edit link to return to Writer's text editor.

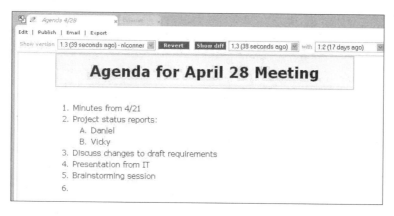

Figure 1.27
Click History to view or compare earlier versions of a document.

Comparing Versions

Not sure whether the version you want was saved yesterday or the day before? Writer lets you compare two versions of a document, so you can see specific changes and (if you want) revert to one.

To compare two versions, open the document and click its History link. On the page that opens, use the two right drop-down lists (you can see them in Figure 1.27) to choose the two versions you want to compare. Click the Show Diff button.

Writer doesn't show two different versions; what it does is highlight differences between the two versions. To revert to one of these compared versions, select the version you want from the left drop-down to display that version and then click Revert.

Who Said One Size Fits All? Customizing Writer

Zoho knows that you like to set things up your own way. So you can customize Writer (along with other apps) in a number of ways, as this section describes.

Changing Writer's Appearance

Maybe purple is your lucky color, or maybe Writer's color scheme clashes with your office decor. You can change Writer's basic appearance, called its *skin*, by clicking the Options link at the top of the page. The box that opens, shown in Figure 1.28, has the Skins tab already selected.

Click the drop-down menu to see a list of color schemes you can apply to Writer. Not sure how a color will look? Watch the preview below the list, which changes as you select a color. When you find a look you like, click Save to apply it to Writer.

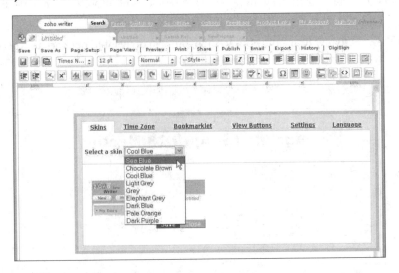

Figure 1.28
Zoho offers a variety of color schemes for Writer.

Setting a Time Zone

Writer timestamps your documents when you create or save them, so it can be helpful to make sure those times are accurate. To match up Writer with your time zone, click Options. Then in the box that opens, click Time Zone. Click the drop-down list, choose your current time zone, and then click Save.

Showing or Hiding Buttons

As you work with Writer, you may find that some buttons on the Formatting toolbar you hardly ever use. If you don't want those buttons taking up space in the text editor, you can hide them. Click Options and then View Buttons to see the box shown in Figure 1.29.

As the figure shows, this box groups buttons of related functions together. You can show or hide groups of buttons but cannot pick and choose which buttons within a group you want to display. By default, all button groups are displayed. To hide a group, uncheck its box, click Save, and then click Close.

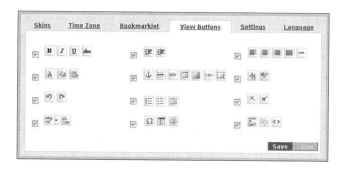

Figure 1.29
You can choose whether to show or hide groups of buttons on the Formatting toolbar.

To show a group of buttons that has been hidden, click Options, View Buttons. Then check the group's box, click Save, and then click Close. The previously hidden buttons reappear on the Formatting toolbar.

Choosing an Interface Language

Writer's language setting determines the language with which Writer communicates with you. If the language is set to English, then Writer's interface—its links, buttons, dialog boxes, and so on—are all in English. If you change the language to Russian or Japanese or Swedish, then the interface appears in the language you chose.

To change the language of Writer's interface, click Options, Language. From the drop-down list, pick the language you want (currently, Writer offers about a dozen). Click Save and then Close.

Setting a Language for the Spellchecker

Normally, Writer checks spelling using the same language your web browser uses. But if you're writing a letter or essay in another language, you can change the spellchecker to work with that language. (This can be a great help for the kids' Spanish homework.)

To set a language for Writer's spellchecker, click Options, Language. Click the Spellcheck Language drop-down and then select the language you want from the list. (You can even specify regional variations in a common language, such as British, Australian, Canadian, and U.S. English.) Click Save and then click Close to shut the box.

Customizing Other Settings

Writer lets you customize several other settings. When you select Options, Settings, you get these options:

- **Show Toolbar**—To hide the Formatting toolbar at the top of the text editor, uncheck this check box. (Hiding this toolbar makes it a little hard to work, but you can do it if you want.)

- **Show Ruler**—Writer's ruler is a thin bar across the top of the screen that helps you line up your text. It doesn't take up much room, but if you find it distracting, you can hide it.

- **Show Statusbar**—The status bar, at the bottom of the screen, has several buttons: Document Information, Search, Tags, Shared Info, and Comments. If you don't want the status bar visible, uncheck this box.

- **Allow Comments for Public Documents**—As this chapter's section on sharing documents explains, when you make a document public, people have the option of commenting on it. Don't want just anyone chiming in about your public documents? Uncheck this box.

- **Open Each Document as a New Tab**—When you create or open a new document, Writer opens it on a new tab in the text editor. If you'd prefer to have just one document open at a time, uncheck this box.

After you've customized these settings to meet your preferences, click Save and then Close.

Zoho Notebook: Clip, Snip, and Organize

If you've ever kept a journal, you know the joys of writing in a spiral-bound notebook. You can jot down thoughts, doodle, sketch, and paste in newspaper clippings and photographs—a notebook is a catchall for your thoughts and musings, a place to collect and organize information, a sketchpad that fosters your creativity.

Zoho Notebook takes this concept of the spiral-bound notebook and puts it online. You can write journal entries or notes to yourself, add shapes and other doodles, and collect interesting tidbits that you find as you surf the Web—from blogs to photos to videos. Because your notebook is online, you can access it from anywhere you have an Internet connection. Even better, you can share your notebook (or just part of it) with others. This chapter gets you up to speed with creating, editing, and sharing Zoho notebooks.

Creating a Notebook

To sign in to Zoho Notebook, point your web browser to http://notebook.zoho.com. If you're not signed in to your Zoho account, do that now. The first time you use Notebook, you'll see a screen that looks like the one in Figure 2.1. Zoho has already created your first notebook for you—it's just waiting for you to fill it in.

The Notebook workspace is easy to use. Use the menu on the left to choose the kind of content you want to add. When you do, a box appears on the current page so you can get to work filling up your notebook. (The sections "Adding Content" and "Editing Content," later in this chapter, tell you everything you need to know about working with your notebook's content.) Toolbar buttons across the top of the notebook let you save, edit, and share your notebook or a page from it. Tabs along the right side let you move between the notebook's pages. Also on the right side of the screen is a drawing toolbar, for working with lines and shapes. Side and bottom scroll bars let you move around in a particular page.

Figure 2.1
Before you add content, your notebook looks like this.

To create a new notebook (you might want several for different purposes), click New Book in the upper-left part of the page. You can give it a name by clicking the arrow on the tab, choosing Rename, and then typing in the notebook's name.

Now you're ready to fill your notebook up with all kinds of good stuff.

 As in a physical notebook, each notebook you create is made up of multiple pages—and it's helpful to think in terms of a physical notebook as you create Zoho notebooks and fill them up with pages. A notebook consists of a group of related pages. For example, you might create a notebook for planning your wedding. Within that notebook, you'd create individual pages to hold wedding-related articles, pictures of wedding dresses, honeymoon ideas, your guest list, possible caterers and reception venues, and so on.

Working with Pages

A one-page notebook wouldn't do you much good, so one of the first things you'll want to do with Zoho Notebook is stock it up with a few pages. You can add a blank notebook page, but you're not limited to just that. You can also add and work with Zoho Docs pages—word-processing documents from Writer and spreadsheet pages from Sheet—as well as interesting web pages you find while cruising around the Internet.

Adding Pages

You can add several kinds of pages, such as a blank notebook page, a page that holds a document from Writer or spreadsheet from Sheet, and a web page that becomes part of your notebook. Whichever kind of page you want to add, this section tells you how.

Notebook Page

A blank notebook page can hold images, notes, blog posts—whatever you want. To add a blank notebook page (like the blank page in Figure 2.1), click the upper-left Add Blank Page link. Zoho adds a new page and opens the notebook to that page.

 To move from one page to another, click the tab of the page number you want.

Writer or Sheet Page

If you want to add to your notebook a document you've created in Zoho Writer (discussed in Chapter 1, "Have Your Say with Zoho Writer") or Zoho Sheet (discussed in Chapter 4, "Track Data with Zoho Sheet"), find the More link (below the upper-left Add Blank Page link) and click it. Then click the kind of page you want to add: either Add Writer Page or Add Sheet Page. A dialog box opens, letting you choose whether you want to create a new page right in Notebook or import an existing page into Notebook:

- To create a new page, click the New tab. Give your about-to-be-created document a name and then click Insert. Notebook inserts a new page with that name into the notebook.

- To import an existing page, click the Existing tab, which shows you a list of all your Writer or Sheet documents. Find and select the one you want and then click Insert.

Whether you create a new page or add an existing one to your notebook, the page changes to look just like the editor you use in Writer or Sheet. Therefore, you can work with documents and spreadsheets inside Notebook in exactly the same way you would in Writer or Sheet.

 When you change a document or spreadsheet in Notebook, that document also changes in Writer or Sheet—and vice versa. In other words, change the document in Writer or Sheet, and it also changes in Notebook.

Web Page

As you're zipping around the Web, you'll probably find lots of pages you'd like to add to a note-book. For example, if you're keeping a notebook to organize a job search, you'll want to save job ads, company websites, articles about your industry and prospective employers—anything you can find online that makes you a more competitive candidate—along with documents such as your resume and cover letter. If you're planning a vacation, you can save the websites of hotels, restaurants, attractions, tour companies, and more, all in a single notebook.

To add a web page to your notebook, you need the web page's address (also called its URL, which stands for *uniform resource locator*). When you find a web page you want to save in your notebook, copy its URL from your browser's address bar.

In Notebook, click the upper-left More link and then click Add Web Page. This opens the Add Web Page dialog box. In that box, paste (or type) the URL for the web page you want to add; then click Create.

Zoho creates a new page that displays the web page in your notebook. There, you can interact with the page as you normally would—click links, fill out forms, and so on.

 The number of tabs you see to the right of the current page depends on the size of your computer's screen. If don't see the tab you want, hover your cursor over the up or down arrow (above or below the tabs, respectively) to move through the tabs before or after the currently displayed set.

Renaming Pages

After your notebook has accumulated some pages, it can be easy to forget what's on which page: For example, is that yummy cheesecake recipe on page 14 or page 15 of your Favorite Desserts notebook?

You don't need to stick with the numbers Notebook assigns as the names for pages. To give a notebook page a new name, double-click the right-side tab of the page you want to rename. This opens the Rename Page dialog box. Type in the name you want to give the page and then click Rename. Now it'll be easy to find the page you want when you want it.

 If a page's name is too long to appear in the tab, hover your cursor over the tab. A tooltip appears, giving the page's full name.

Moving Pages Around

Here's a big advantage that Zoho Notebook has over its spiral-bound cousin: You can rearrange its pages to keep your thoughts and clippings organized. So instead of being stuck with having your thoughts appear in the order in which they occurred to you, you can move them around in whatever way makes the most sense.

To move a page in your notebook, simply click the right-side tab of the page you want to move. Holding down the mouse button, drag that page to its new position. When the page is where you want it, let up on the mouse button. Presto—the page moves to its new location.

Exporting a Page or a Notebook

If you want to store a copy of your notebook or some of its pages on your computer, simply export what you want to save. Zoho Notebook exports files in MHTML format. MHTML stands for *MIME HTML*, a format that holds together objects such as video and sound files with the HTML that describes web pages. Your exported file will end with the extension .mht.

To export a notebook, open it. In the menu bar, click Export and then choose what you want to export: book or page. A dialog box opens, asking how to deal with the file. You can choose to open it with Internet Explorer or save it to your computer. If you open the file with Internet Explorer, be sure to save it when you're done.

Deleting a Page

In the physical world, when you don't want a page in your notebook any more, you tear it out, crumple it up, and toss it into the nearest recycling bin. Getting rid of a page from Zoho Notebook is even easier (no crumpling or recycling bin needed).

Open the notebook that has the page you want to delete and then find the page you want to get rid of. In the toolbar at the top of the page, click Delete, Page. Zoho opens a confirmation box asking whether you *really* want to tear this page out of your notebook. Click OK, and Zoho removes that page from your notebook.

 When you've deleted a page, clicking the Undo button won't bring it back. So be extra sure you want to get rid of the page before you confirm deletion.

Deleting a Whole Notebook

The work project is finished, the vacation taken, the wedding a big success—and now you no longer need the notebook you used while doing the work or setting things up. If you want to delete a notebook, open the notebook you plan to delete and then go to the toolbar and click Delete, Book. Zoho asks you to confirm; click OK to delete the whole notebook.

Filling Up Your Notebook with Content

A blank notebook may be full of potential—but it needs information to be useful. In Zoho Notebook, you can add and edit all kinds of information—from your own jottings and doodlings, to audio, image, and video files, and more. This section tells you all about how to work with your notebook's content.

Adding Content

To add content, use the left-side menu to select the kind of content you want to add. Instructions for specific kinds of content follow.

Text

To add text to a notebook page, click Add Text in the left menu. This opens a text box inside the current notebook page, as shown in Figure 2.2. Simply click inside the text area and start typing.

As Figure 2.2 shows, the box for adding text has some formatting buttons across the top. These are for the basics—bolding or italicizing text, choosing a font and color, creating or breaking links, highlighting, and so on. If you want more extensive formatting, insert a Writer page (covered earlier in this chapter).

 If the text box feels a bit cramped, you can resize it by clicking and dragging its lower-right corner.

After you've typed in your text, click outside the text box (or click its upper-right X) to insert your words into your notebook page. You can also edit or reposition text, as explained later in this chapter.

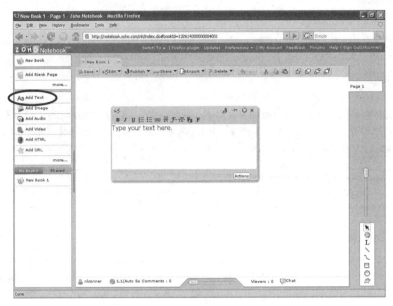

Figure 2.2
When you click Add Text (circled), Notebook gives you a mini text editor to type in.

Images and Audio Files

Whether you want to add an image (such as a photograph) or an audio file (such as an MP3 of your favorite song) to a notebook page, you follow the same steps. From the left menu, click Add Image or Add Audio, as appropriate. This opens a dialog box that looks like the one shown in Figure 2.3.

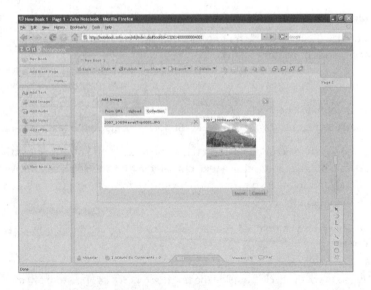

Figure 2.3
You can insert images and audio files from a Web location, by uploading the file from your computer, or by selecting a file you've already uploaded.

To insert an image or audio file, choose one of these three tabs:

- **From URL**—This tab lets you grab an image or audio file from the Web and insert it in your page. Just type or paste the file's web address into the text box here. For example, if you use an online photo service (such as Flickr, Snapfish, Photobucket, or Picasa Web Albums), use this option to let Zoho find your photo.

- **Upload**—To transfer a file from your computer's hard drive, select this tab. Click the Browse button and locate the file on your computer for Zoho to upload.

- **Collection**—After you've uploaded some files to Zoho, those files are listed here. Just select the file you want to insert into the current page.

Whichever method you choose, click the Insert button to put the file in your notebook.

 You can insert any kind of computer file into a Zoho Notebook page—not just images and sounds. To insert another kind of file, go to the left menu, click the More link, and select Add File. Then select your insertion option. (They're the same as those shown in Figure 2.3.) Click Insert, and Zoho puts the file in your page as an icon. Click the icon to open the file using the appropriate program.

Video

You can embed a video into a notebook page. The video appears in a mini player and plays when someone clicks its Play button.

To make this work, you need to know the code that embeds it in a web page. Fortunately, you don't need to be a programmer to find this code; most video sites, such as YouTube and AOL Video, make it easy to find a video's embedding code.

So the first step in embedding a video in a notebook page is to find the embedding code of the video you want. In YouTube (www.youtube.com), for example, it's to the right of the video, in a text box labeled Embed. In AOL Video (http://video.aol.com), there's an Embed button beneath the video player that opens a box containing the embedding code. When you've found the code, copy it.

Now, go to your Zoho notebook and select the page where you want to embed the video. Click the Add Video link (on the left). This opens the Add Video dialog box, which has a roomy text box for the embedding code. Paste in the code and then click Insert. Zoho puts the video into your notebook.

 Sometimes, the owner of a video may not want others to put a copy of the video into their own web page. Although this can be disappointing, it's a legitimate copyright issue. If a video's owner doesn't want the video popping up all over the Internet, you'll see a notice that tells you embedding has been disabled for this video.

HTML

If you're a whiz at creating and working with web pages, you can use your knowledge of HTML to insert content on your notebook page. Select Add HTML from the left menu. In the dialog box that opens, type or paste your HTML code into the text box and then click Insert.

URL

You can add a web page as a whole new page in your notebook (as discussed earlier), or you can insert a web page into any notebook page. The method you choose depends on whether you want the web page to appear on its own page or as part of a page that has other content. To insert a web page, click Add URL in the left menu to open the Add URL dialog box. In that box, type or paste the web address of the page you want and then click Insert. The web page appears as part of your notebook page.

RSS

Depending on whom you ask, RSS stands for *really simple syndication* or *rich site summary*—take your pick. Either way, it's a format that lets you get news headlines, blog posts, and other online content as it's updated. You can subscribe to an RSS feed in your notebook, so you're always up to date about changes to your favorite new sites and blogs. For example, if you're planning a vacation, you can subscribe to the local newspaper's RSS feed and automatically receive local news headlines.

To add an RSS feed to your notebook, you need to know the web address that lets you subscribe to your target site's newsfeed. This is a different URL from the site's main web page. Open the news site or blog you want to subscribe to and find its Subscribe to RSS button or link. Right-click the button or link and, using the context menu that appears, copy the link. (In Firefox, select Copy Link Location; in Internet Explorer, choose Copy Shortcut.)

In Zoho Notebook, open the page where you want the newsfeed to appear. From the left menu, click the More link and select Add RSS. The Add RSS dialog box opens, looking like the one in Figure 2.4. Click inside the Enter RSS text box and paste in the newsfeed address. Click Insert, and you have a newsfeed on that page.

Depending on how the newsfeed is set up, you can click a headline to see the story's preview. Click the icon to a headline's right to open that story in a new window.

Sheet and Writer

Earlier in this chapter, "Writer or Sheet Page" explains how to create a new notebook page by inserting a Zoho Sheet spreadsheet or a Zoho Writer document. If you'd rather insert the spreadsheet or document into an existing notebook page, you can do that, too. Click the left menu's More link and then select either Add Sheet or Add Writer. In the dialog box that opens, you can name and create a new document, or choose from a list of existing documents. When you've named or selected your document, click Insert.

Show

Chapter 3, "Presenting…Zoho Show," tells you all about creating, editing, and showing slideshow-style presentations with Zoho Show. If you've created a presentation that you want to include in your notebook, click More in the left menu and then choose Add Show.

The Add Show dialog box lists all your Zoho Show presentations. Select the one you want and then click Insert.

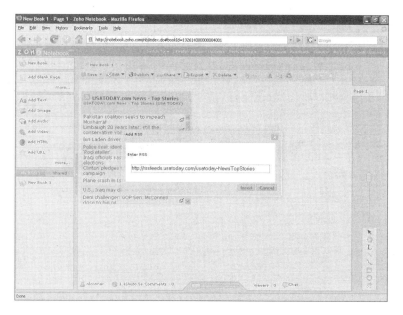

Figure 2.4
The RSS feed address in the Add RSS box inserts the newsfeed shown in the background.

Zoho displays the presentation on your notebook page. People viewing your notebook can page through the presentation slide by slide, at their own pace. Use the left and right arrows in the slideshow viewer to move between slides.

 You can't edit a Zoho Show presentation in Notebook (as you can spreadsheets and documents).

Editing Content

Adding content to a notebook is only half the fun. Once it's there, you can work with it in various ways. Whichever kind of content you're editing, click the content itself. This puts a frame around the content, offering editing and other options, as shown in Figure 2.5.

Moving Content

When you add new content, Zoho places it more or less in the middle of the current page. Obviously, you don't want all your images, text, and videos piling up on top of each other. To move a piece of content, click the content to bring up its frame. Move your cursor to the top of the frame; it'll turn into a four-way arrow. Then just click-and-drag the content to where you want it. Let go of the mouse button to drop the content into its new location.

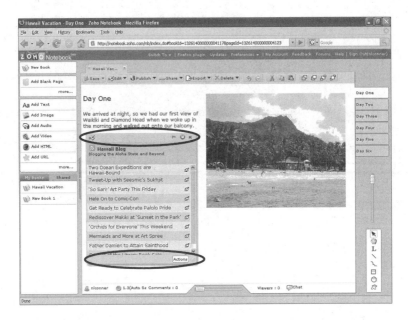

Figure 2.5
When you click a page's content, a frame appears that lets you work with that content.

Making Content Stay Put

When you have a page's content arranged the way you want it, you can pin individual pieces of content into place to make sure they stay put. When you click a piece of content to reveal its frame, you'll notice a Pushpin icon in the upper-right part of the frame. When the content is unpinned (that is, when you can click-and-drag it around), the pushpin is horizontal. Click the pushpin, and it becomes diagonal, like a pin pushed into a bulletin board. The diagonal pushpin means that your content is now kept in place; before you can move it, you have to unpin it (by clicking the pushpin again).

 If you prefer, you can also pin and unpin a piece of content using the Menu icon (a white arrow in a green circle in the upper-right part of the frame). Click the Menu icon; from the menu that appears, choose Pin or Unpin.

Resizing Content

If text is running over onto an image or a photo you uploaded or takes up too much room on the page, it's easy to resize the content. Click the content and move your cursor to the lower-right corner of the frame. When the cursor becomes a double-headed arrow, you can click-and-drag the frame to resize it. When the piece of content is the size you want, let up on the mouse button to keep the new size.

 When you resize content, different kinds of content respond differently. For example, when you resize a text box, the size of the text inside the box doesn't change. When you resize a picture or a shape, on the other hand, the entire image or shape changes as you adjust the size.

Moving Content Forward or Backward

Sometimes you want to layer one piece of content over another. For example, you might want to overlay labels on an image. When you have two or more pieces of content stacked up, you can move any of those pieces forward (on top of another piece of content) or backward (behind another piece of content). To do this, click the Menu icon in the upper-right part of any content frame. As Figure 2.6 shows, this opens a list of options for working with this piece of content:

- Send Backward moves the piece of content back one layer.
- Bring Forward moves the piece of content forward one layer.
- Send to Back moves the piece of content behind all other content on the page.
- Bring to Front moves the piece of content in front of all other content on the page.

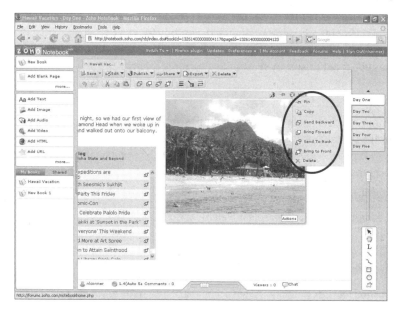

Figure 2.6
The Menu icon offers several options for working with a selected piece of content.

Copying Content

Here's an easy way to move a piece of content from one page to another. Select the piece of content you want and then click the Menu icon in the upper-right part of its frame. Select Copy or press Ctrl+C (Cmd-C on a Mac).

Go to the page where you want to paste the content and press Ctrl+V or, if your using a Mac, Cmd-V. (These are shortcuts for Paste.) The content appears on the new page.

 When you use copy content in Zoho Notebook, you can only paste it within Notebook. You can't paste it, say, into a Word or Writer document.

Editing Text

No need to let a little thing like a typo ruin your day. When you need to make changes to text you've added to a notebook page, click the text to make its frame appear. Then, click the Edit icon in the upper-left corner of the frame. (As Figure 2.5 shows, it looks like a pencil writing on a piece of paper.) This turns the frame back into the mini–text editor you used to create the text. When you're done editing, click outside the frame.

 Here's a shortcut for opening the mini-text editor: Just double-click the text you want to edit.

Editing URLs and HTML

As with text, URLs (whether for a web page or an RSS feed) and HTML also have the upper-left Edit icon in their frames. Click Edit to open a dialog box that looks just like the one you used to insert the original content, except it already has the URL or other content filled in. Make whatever changes you need to and then click Save to apply them.

Deleting Content

When you want to remove content from a physical notebook, you have to tear out a page or scribble out the unwanted content. In Zoho Notebook, all you have to do to delete some content is click the content you want to delete so that you can see its frame and then take one of these two actions:

- Click the upper-right X.
- Click the Menu icon and then select Delete.

Either way, the content is history.

 Oops! If you clicked that upper-right X by mistake, you can get your content back—if you act fast. Go to the Toolbar and click the Undo button. (It's a curved arrow that points left.) This button reverses your most recent action—so if the last thing you did was accidentally delete some content, clicking Undo brings it right back.

Working with Shapes

What would a notebook be without doodles? Whether you want to unleash your inner artist, annotate content, or separate sections of a page, you'll find Notebook's Drawing toolbar helpful in snazzing up your pages. It's on the right side of the screen, as Figure 2.7 shows.

Moving from top to bottom, the Drawing toolbar has these buttons for you to use:

- **Select Tool**—This button looks like a cursor, and for good reason—after you've used a drawing tool, click this button to get your cursor back. And if you want to select a shape for editing (see upcoming section), make sure this button is clicked.

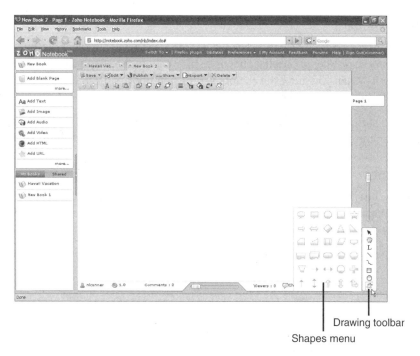

Drawing toolbar

Shapes menu

Figure 2.7
Use the Drawing toolbar to add shapes, lines, and symbols to your page.

- **Hand Tool**—You can scroll through a notebook page using the sliders at the right side and bottom of the screen. Alternatively, you can click this button. When the cursor changes to a hand, click-and-drag to scroll up, down, left, or right.

- **Text Tool**—Less elaborate than the Add Text box, this button lets you add a quick label to a page. Click this button and then click the notebook page. A text box appears. There are no formatting buttons in the text box, but this is an easy way to insert a quick, basic label.

- **Line Tool**—Need to get from point A to point B? Use this tool to draw a super-straight line. The Line Tool is helpful for putting a vertical rule between columns or a horizontal separator between sections of a page.

- **Free Hand**—Perfect for doodling. Click this button for drawing wavy lines or curves or writing in cursive.

- **Rectangle**—To draw a perfectly proportioned square or rectangle, use this tool.

- **Circle**—Ever try drawing a perfect circle freehand? You'll never have to worry about lopsided circles again, thanks to this tool.

- **Shapes**—Click this button to open a menu of more than two dozen shapes (as shown in Figure 2.7). You'll learn more about shapes in the next section.

Inserting a Shape

To put a shape on a notebook page, click the appropriate Drawing toolbar button—line, rectangle, circle, and so on. (If you click the Shapes button, choose the shape you want from the Shapes menu.) When you move the cursor over the notebook page, the cursor changes shape to represent the kind of tool you chose.

Position the cursor where you want the shape to appear; then click-and-drag to create the shape. When the shape is about the size you want it, let go of the mouse button to insert it.

Editing Shapes

After you've inserted a shape, line, or label using the Drawing toolbar, you can edit it—change its size, flip its orientation, or pick a new color. When you select the shape, a row of formatting buttons appears on the toolbar, as shown in Figure 2.8.

The formatting buttons vary according to the object you've selected, as the following sections explain.

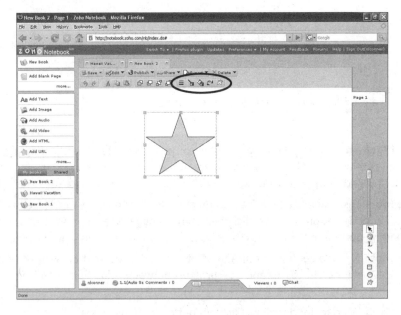

Figure 2.8
When you select a shape, formatting buttons (circled) appear.

Formatting Rectangles, Circles, and Shapes

These objects share the following formatting buttons:

- **Stroke Width**—This changes the width of the lines that outline a shape. You can choose from 0 pixels (no outline) all the way up to 10 pixels (wide outline).

- **Stroke Color**—To change the color of a shape's outline, click this button and then choose the color you want from the palette that appears. To make it easier to create a consistent color scheme, Zoho shows you the most recent colors you've worked with; click one to choose it. Whichever way you choose the color, click OK to apply it to the shape.

- **Fill Color**—This works just like the Stroke Color button, except it fills in the interior of the shape you've selected. Choose from the palette or from recently used colors.

In addition to these buttons, rectangles have a formatting button called Rectangle Type. Click it to create a rounded rectangle, or to sharpen a rounded rectangle's corners.

Shapes also have a couple special buttons of their own:

- **Flip Type**—Click the button to change the orientation of the shape. You can flip a shape along its horizontal axis, its vertical axis, or both.

- **Shapes**—This isn't a formatting button, but a shortcut to opening the Shapes menu so that you can change the selected shape into a different one. For example, if you want to change a single-headed arrow to a double-headed one, just click this button and select the new shape.

 Notebook's Shapes menu contains the most commonly used symbols in process diagrams—such as decision points, actions, predefined processes, and terminators—making it easy to sketch out this kind of diagram on a notebook page.

Formatting Lines

As explained earlier in this section, you can use Notebook to draw straight lines or free-hand lines. For either type, you can change the line's width and color by using the Stroke Width and Stroke Color buttons described in the previous section.

For straight lines, there's also a Line Style button in the formatting toolbar. Use this button to add an arrowhead (left, right, or double) or to change an arrow to a plain ol' straight line.

 The arrowhead that Zoho adds from the Line Style button is tiny. You can make it bigger by increasing the line width. Alternatively, you can insert an arrow using the Drawing toolbar's Shapes button, which offers several arrow styles.

Formatting Labels

When you insert a label using the Drawing toolbar's Text Tool, you don't have as many formatting options as you would selecting Add Text from the left menu, but you do have some, as Figure 2.9 shows.

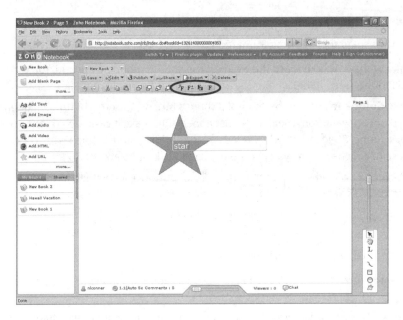

Figure 2.9
Text inserted using the Drawing toolbar's Text Tool can be formatted using the circled buttons.

Here are the formatting buttons for labels:

■ **Font**—Zoho offers eight fonts for labels inserted with the Text Tool: Arial, Courier, Georgia, Serif, Tahoma, Times, Trebuchet, and Verdana.

■ **Text Size**—Choose from sizes ranging from 9 to 18 points. The font size you choose when creating the label resizes the text box, making it hard to change from a smaller font to a larger one. (The larger size gets cut off.)

■ **Text Color**—Click this button to choose a color for your label. (Choose from a palette or from recently used colors.) Click OK to change the letters' color.

■ **Highlight Text**—This changes the color of the label's background (as opposed to the text itself). Applying a highlight changes the color of the entire length of the text box.

Resizing Shapes and Lines

To change the size of a shape or a line, make sure that the Select Tool is active in the Drawing toolbar. Then, click the object you want. If it's a shape, a dotted line surrounds the shape to show it has been selected (as shown earlier in Figure 2.8). If it's a line, a circle appears at either end.

To resize a shape, click one of the square handles and drag. As you do, the shape changes its size and dimensions. When you like the new size, let go of the mouse button.

To resize a line, click one of the circles at either end of the line and then drag to make the line longer or shorter. You can also change the direction of the line by clicking and dragging. When the line looks good, let up on the mouse button.

You can't resize label boxes or lines drawn using the Free Hand tool.

Deleting Shapes

There are two ways to delete a shape, line, or label that you've inserted into a notebook page. The easiest is to select the object (make sure the Select Tool is active in the Drawing toolbar) and then hit your keyboard's Delete key.

If you like to keep your hand on the mouse as you draw, you can take this route: Select the object and click Delete, Object in the menu bar. A confirmation box appears asking whether you're sure you want to delete the object; click OK to make the object disappear.

Web Clipping (for Firefox Users)

If you use Firefox to browse the Web, Notebook has a plugin that you can install to clip web pages (or sections of them) and add those clippings to your notebook. It's called Zoho Notebook Helper, and this section tells you how to get it and how to use it.

Clipping web pages and putting them into your notebook is like clipping articles from a newspaper or magazine and pasting them into a scrapbook. When you clip an image, article, or page from the Web and insert it into your Zoho Notebook, you're creating an image of that page. In effect, you're taking a snapshot of it. This means that, in your notebook, the links on the page won't work. If you want a full, working version of the web page in your notebook, use Add URL from the left menu (explained earlier in this chapter).

Installing the Plugin

Before you can start web clipping, you need to install the plugin. Open Notebook, and at the top of the page click the Firefox Plugin link. This opens the Firefox Add-ons page for the plugin. Click Add to Firefox. A dialog box opens asking you to confirm that you want to add this plugin to Firefox. Click Install Now.

It takes only a second or two to install the plugin, but you have to start Firefox up again to get it working. After Firefox has added the plugin, a new Add-Ons window tells you to restart Firefox to complete the installation. Save any work you've been doing in Firefox and then click Restart Firefox. (If you prefer, you can close the Add-Ons window by clicking its upper-right X and waiting until the next time you start Firefox to finish installing the Notebook plugin.)

If you click Restart Firefox, Firefox shuts down and then restarts (restoring your previous session). Now you're ready to start clipping—or, as Zoho calls it, *snapping* (as in taking a snapshot).

 You need to be signed in to your Zoho account and have Notebook open on another tab or window to capture web clippings.

Snapping a Web Page

To take a snapshot of a web page and add it to your Notebook, follow these quick steps:

1. Make sure you're signed in to your Zoho account and Notebook is open. If you know the page where you want your snapshot to appear, have that page open. (You can always copy and paste the snapshot to move it later.)

2. When you find a web page you want to clip, right-click anywhere on that web page. The menu shown in Figure 2.10 pops up.

3. Select the menu item Snap Page to Zoho Notebook.

4. Zoho asks you to name your clip. Type in a name and click OK.

The plugin takes a snapshot of the page and inserts it into your notebook.

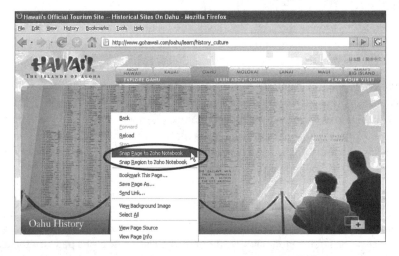

Figure 2.10
If you use Firefox as your web browser, the Zoho Notebook Helper plugin lets you capture a web page or a section of a page by right-clicking it.

Snapping a Section of a Web Page

If you want to clip just a portion of a web page, rather than take a snapshot of the whole page, you can. Start off with steps 1 and 2 for snapping an entire web page. When the context menu appears, select Snap Region to Zoho Notebook.

A capture area, which looks like a transparent gray square, appears on the web page, as shown in Figure 2.11. When you put your cursor on the square, it changes to a four-way arrow. Click-and-drag the capture area to the region of the page you want to clip. If the selection area doesn't quite fit that region, click-and-drag the lower-right corner to resize it.

When the capture area matches the region you want to clip, click the capture area's upper-right Camera icon. A dialog box opens, asking you to name the clipping. Do that and then click OK. Within seconds, a snapshot of the region you selected appears in your notebook.

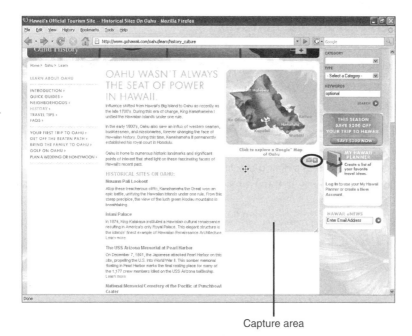

Capture area

Figure 2.11
By dragging the capture area, you can capture just a section of a web page, using the upper-right Camera icon (circled).

Working with Web Clippings in Your Notebook

Web clippings are snapshots, so Notebook treats them as images. After you've inserted a clipping, you can work with it in exactly the same way you'd work with any other image (see "Editing Content" earlier in this chapter).

 When you insert a web clipping, Zoho adds the name you give it to the Collection list in your Add Image box. This lets you add the clipping to another notebook or page in the same way you'd add any other existing image.

Sharing Your Notebooks

When you've created a great notebook, you want to let people know about it—share your thoughts, doodles, web clippings, or anything else you've collected in your notebook's pages. You can share an object, a page, or an entire notebook. Sharing all or part of your notebook is as easy as sending an invitation by email.

Inviting Others to Share Your Notebook

To share your notebook, open the notebook you want to share. If you're sharing a single page or object, select it. Then, in the toolbar at the top of the page, click Share. This opens a menu with three options:

- Book
- Page
- Object

Make your selection to open a dialog box like the one in Figure 2.12. If you've already shared your selection with someone, that person's email address appears in the bottom half of the box.

Figure 2.12
Use this dialog box to share your notebook with other people.

Next, fill in these sections of the Share dialog box:

- **Username/E-Mail**—In this section, type or paste in the email addresses of everyone you want to share with. If you're sharing with more than one person, separate email addresses with commas.
- **Permissions**—You can invite others to simply look at your notebook contents (Read Only), or you can invite them to collaborate on it with you (Read/Write). Click the permission level you want these sharers to have.
- **Add Custom Message**—If you want to add a personalized message to Zoho's standard one, check this box. The section expands, giving you a text box where you can type your message.

Click Save to share your notebook. If you're finished inviting people to share, click Done to close the Share box.

Here's a shortcut for sharing an object: Select the object and click its lower-right Actions button and then choose Share from the menu that appears. This opens the Share Object dialog box.

When the person you've shared with signs in to Zoho and opens Notebook, the notebook you shared appears in the left menu's Shared list of that person's browser.

Managing Sharers

After you've shared a notebook (or part of it) with others, you may want to adjust or take away sharing privileges. To do either, click Share and then choose Book, Page, or Object to open the appropriate Share dialog box.

Current sharers are listed in the lower part of the Share box. Find the person you're looking for and then take one of these actions:

- Click either Read Only or Read/Write to reset that person's privilege level.
- Click the red X at the right to remove that person's ability to share.

When you're finished, click Done.

Publishing on the Web

Sharing with a few close friends or colleagues is one thing, but what if you want to share your notebook more widely—like with anyone who has Internet access? As with other Zoho documents, you can publish a notebook on the Web. (If you don't want to share the whole notebook, you can publish just a page or an object.)

When you want to take your notebook public, open the notebook you want. If you're publishing just a page or an object, select the part of the notebook that you want to publish. In the toolbar above the notebook, click Public and then select Book, Page, or Object.

A dialog box opens, giving you two choices:

- **General**—Use this tab if you want to publish your selection on the Web, complete with its own URL that you can send to friends, family, and colleagues.
- **Embed**—Use this tab if you want to make your selection part of an existing web page or blog.

The sections that follow describe each option.

Publishing Your Notebook on the Web

The General tab creates a website for your notebook (or the page or object you've selected from it). When this tab is selected, you see a notification from Zoho that publishing a notebook means that anyone with Internet access can see it. Because that's what you want, click Publish.

Zoho puts your notebook on the Web and gives you the notebook's URL, which looks something like this:

http://notebook.zoho.com/nb/public/nlconner/book/132617000000003206

Use the URL to link to your notebook from other websites, or email it to those you want to share your notebook with.

 When you publish all or part of a notebook to the Web, Zoho creates a cover page for what you've published. This cover page is like the title page of a book; it shows the title of the notebook and your Zoho ID as its author. If you don't want a cover page (maybe you've already created your own), click Publish, Book. In the Publish Book dialog box, check the Remove Cover Page box. This changes the notebook's URL, adding this to the end:

?nocover=true

When you click the new URL (or paste it into your browser's address bar), the Zoho-created cover disappears.

Taking a Published Notebook off the Web

They say all good things come to an end. If that's the case, there may come a time when you want to take your published notebook off the Internet. To do this, open the notebook in Zoho Notebook. Click Publish and then select what you want to stop publishing: Book, Page, or Object. The Publish dialog box opens, showing the URL of the notebook (or page or object). Click the Revoke Publish button, and Zoho removes the item from the Web. Click Cancel to close the dialog box.

Now, if someone tries to go to the URL for that published notebook, a message appears saying that the item is no longer public.

Embedding Your Notebook in an Existing Web Page

Another option for publishing your notebook on the Web is to insert it into an existing web page or blog; this is called *embedding* the notebook in your web page. To embed a notebook (or some part of it), you need some HTML code—and Zoho makes things easy by generating that code for you.

To get it, you first have to publish the notebook, page, or object, as described in the previous section. After that's done, follow these steps to embed what you've published in a web page or blog:

1. Open the notebook you're embedding. If you're embedding just a page or an object, select it.
2. Click Publish and then choose Book, Page, or Object.
3. The Publish Book dialog box opens; click the Embed tab. This dialog box changes to look like the one shown in Figure 2.13. In the center of the dialog box is some HTML code. Select and copy that code.
4. Paste the code you copied into an HTML document and upload that document to your blog or website.

Now, your web page or blog will show whatever you embedded—an object, a page, or the entire notebook—as an element of that page.

Figure 2.13
Copy the Zoho-supplied HTML code to embed a notebook (or part of it) in a web page or blog.

Collaborating with Others

Why do all the work yourself when you can invite others to share the load? Whether it's a team project for work or school, a group notebook for a club or for family, or something else, you can give other people permission to help you create and develop your notebook.

Before you can collaborate on a notebook, you have to share it with your collaborators. If you haven't done that yet, flip back a few pages and read the section on sharing, "Sharing Your Notebooks." When you set up sharing, be sure to give Read/Write privileges to anyone who'll work on the notebook with you.

When you're working on a notebook and one of your collaborators opens it, too, you get a message box in the lower-right part of your screen to let you know who else is there. In addition, as Figure 2.14 shows, Zoho tells you how many other people are viewing the notebook by putting a number next to Viewers in the status bar. Click Viewers to get a list of who else is looking at the notebook with you.

Chatting with Collaborators

Zoho integrates its Chat program with Notebook, so when you're collaborating with someone and have a question or comment, you can open a chat window and discuss whatever it is you need to discuss. Chapter 8, "Instant Communication with Zoho Chat," tells you all about using Zoho Chat. Here, we'll just take a quick look at the basics for launching Chat from Notebook.

As Figure 2.14 shows, when your collaborators are online, Zoho tells you how many and, when you click Viewers, who they are. Double-click any collaborator's name to start a chat. Or you can click Chat and then the person's name to get the same result. When you click Chat, the list of names shows who's online:

- A smiling yellow face means that the person is online.
- A frowning gray face means that the person is offline.

Click the name of anyone who's online to launch a chat with that person.

Figure 2.14
To see who else is looking at a notebook, click Viewers to get a list.

Zoho opens a chat box. Just type your message in the lower part of the box and then press Enter to start the conversation. When you do, a chat box opens on the other person's screen, containing your message.

Talking with Collaborators via Skype

Skype is a service that uses VoIP (Voice over Internet Protocol) to let you make free voice calls, using your computer, to any other Skype user, anywhere in the world. If you and your collaborator each have a Skype ID, you can use it to chat over the computer as you work together.

First, if you don't already have one, get a Skype ID. You can do this by going to www.skype.com and clicking Download Skype. Follow the instructions to install Skype on your computer and get your ID.

Next, tell Zoho your Skype ID. Sign in to your Zoho account. From any Zoho application, click the My Account link at the top of the screen. Zoho opens your account in a new window. In the menu on the left, click Personal Information.

Zoho opens the Personal Information page, shown in Figure 2.15. Type your Skype ID in the appropriate text box and then click Save.

After you've entered your Skype ID in your Zoho account's personal information, collaborators with whom you share a notebook can use Skype to talk to you while you're both working on a notebook.

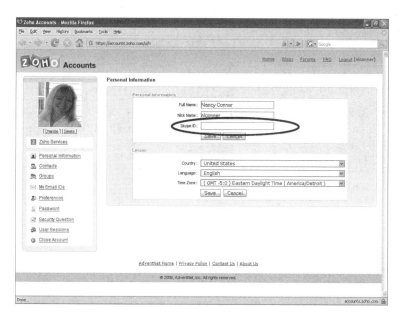

Figure 2.15
If you have a Skype ID, type it in this text box on your Personal Information page.

 A collaborator who wants to call you using Skype must have Skype installed on his or her computer and a Skype ID to make the call.

When you're collaborating on a notebook, you see some Skype icons on the status bar, in the lower-right portion of the screen, as shown in Figure 2.16:

- **Online Status**—The first icon shows whether the notebook's owner is currently online and available. If this icon shows a check mark on a green cloud, you're good to go.
- **Call**—Click this icon to place a call.
- **Chat**—Click this icon to launch Skype's Chat program. (Alternatively, use Zoho Chat, as described in the previous section.)
- **User Info**—Opens a Skype profile for the person you're calling.

Click the one that looks like a telephone to call the notebook's owner using Skype.

 The first time you click a Skype icon, you may see a dialog box asking your permission to launch Skype to handle the action you requested. If you don't want to see that dialog box every time you make a Skype call from Zoho, check the box that tells your computer to remember your choice for all Skype links. Then click Launch Application to continue with your Skype call.

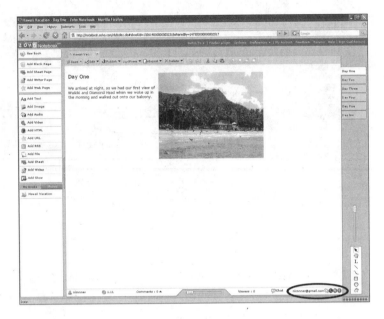

Figure 2.16
Skype icons (circled) appear at the right side of the status bar.

Comparing Versions

Whether you're collaborating on a notebook with someone else or working on it alone, the notebook will change and evolve with time. And even though change can be good, there will probably be times when you wish you could roll back your notebook to an earlier version.

Zoho keeps track of the versions of your notebook, allowing you to compare them and, if you want, revert back to an earlier version.

In the status bar at the bottom of the page on the left side is a version number. (You can see an example in Figure 2.16, where the version number is 1.11.) Click the version number to open a page like the one in Figure 2.17. By default, this page shows the current version (on the left) and most recent previous version (on the right), but you can compare any two versions you choose.

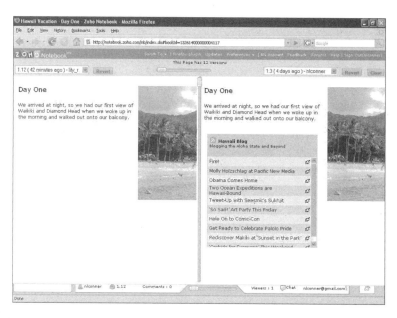

Figure 2.17
Compare versions of your notebook and, if you want, revert to an earlier one.

Info 4U You can't edit a notebook while you're viewing its past versions. You need either to revert to a specific version or to close the Versions window to edit the notebook.

Use the drop-down lists near the top of each half of the page to choose the versions you want to compare. The scrollers at the top and in the middle of the page let you see in full what you're comparing. If you want to switch from the current version to an older one, click the Revert button. When you do, Zoho switches back to the previous version while giving it a new version number. If you don't want to revert to a different version, click the Close button (in the top-right corner) to go back to your notebook.

When you revert to an earlier version, you don't lose the later version—it becomes a version in your revision history.

Presenting...Zoho Show

Slideshows are a powerful way to make your points during a meeting. Used to be, you'd have to get everyone into the same room at the same time to show your presentation. And with busy schedules and people on the road, that could be hard to do.

Zoho Show solves that problem. Create your slideshow and store it on the Web. When it's time for that meeting, you can give the presentation over the Internet—so if Tom is on the road, Betty's in a branch office, and Michelle is working from home, they can all watch your presentation in real time. You can even publish the presentation so that others can go through it on their own time, at their own pace.

Creating a Presentation

To get started with Show, point your web browser to show.zoho.com (and log in if you're not already signed in to your Zoho account). When you first open Show, you see a home page that looks like the one in Figure 3.1. This is the place for creating presentations, whether you start a brand-new presentation using Show or import an existing presentation.

Starting from Scratch

To create a brand-new presentation in Show, start on the Show home page (see Figure 3.1). Click the Create a New Presentation link. (If you've already added a presentation or two, click the Create New button in the upper-left part of the page.) This opens the Create New Presentation page shown in Figure 3.2. Here's where you tell Show the basics so it can get started on your presentation:

- **Presentation Name**—After you've created a bunch of presentations, you want it to be easy to find the one your looking for, so give your presentation a descriptive name.

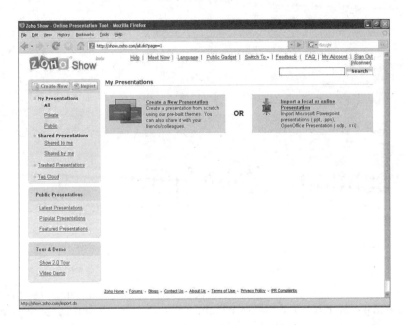

Figure 3.1
Start creating presentations on the Zoho Show home page.

- **Description**—This section gives you the option of writing a lengthier description of your presentation, who it's for, its purpose—whatever might be helpful.
- **Tags**—In Show, tags work just as they do in Zoho Writer (see Chapter 1, "Have Your Say with Zoho Writer"). They help you organize your presentations by labeling them. Tagging a presentation is optional, and you can always add tags later.

Info 4U As you type in your presentation's name, Show fills the same text into the Tags text box. You can keep, edit, or delete the Tags text, as you prefer.

Tip 4U Use tags to find related presentations. On the Zoho Show home page, click the Tag Cloud link (on the left). This shows all the tags you've added to your presentations. The more presentations that are associated with a tag, the bigger the tag appears in the cloud. Click any tag to see a list of the presentations tagged with that word.

- **Choose Theme**—In Show, a *theme* is a design template for your presentation. Zoho offers dozens of predefined themes, from plain to jazzy, so you can give your presentation the feel you want it to have.

After you've set up the presentation, click Start to create your presentation.

Figure 3.2
When you create a presentation from scratch, Show collects some basic information to get you started.

Importing an Existing Presentation

You don't have to start from square one to get a presentation into Show; you can import existing presentations and work on them in Show. Presentations you import must be either on the Web or stored on your computer. Either way, the import process is fast and easy.

Info 4U To import successfully into Show, a presentation file must be 10MB or smaller.

Importing a Presentation from Your Computer

Show can handle presentations that you created using Microsoft PowerPoint (files that end with the extension .ppt or .pps) or OpenOffice.org Impress (files that end with the extension .odp or .sxi).

To import a file, go to the Show home page at show.zoho.com. (Make sure you're signed in to your Zoho account.) If you don't currently have any saved presentations, click the Import a Local or Online Presentation link; if you've already got one or more presentations in Show, click the upper-left Import button. Either way, Show opens the Import Presentation page, shown in Figure 3.3.

Tip 4U If you're already working on a presentation, you can import a new presentation by clicking the Import link at the top of the page.

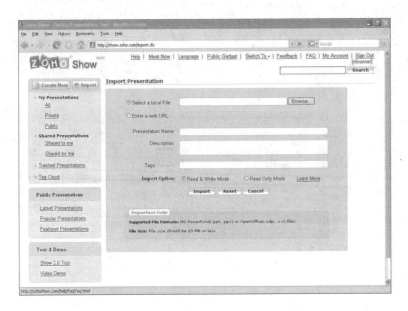

Figure 3.3
Whether a presentation is displayed on the Web or stored on your computer, you can import it into Show.

To import a PowerPoint or Impress presentation, make sure the Select a Local File radio button is turned on. (Zoho preselects it for you.) Click the Browse button; a new window opens, where you can find the file you want on your computer. Select that file and click Open to make the filename appear in Show's Import Presentation page.

Show automatically fills in the file's name and uses that name to tag the presentation, but if you want, you can change the presentation's name, its tag, or both. Just click inside the Presentation Name or Tags box and edit as you like. You can also write an optional description of the presentation.

You've got one more decision to make before you import the presentation, and that's in the Import Option section: In Show, do you want the presentation to be Read Only or Read/Write? If a presentation is done and you only want a copy of it in Show, select Read Only mode. If you know you're going to be doing more work on the presentation, select Read/Write mode.

When you've made your choices, click Import to upload a copy of the presentation into Show. Zoho imports the presentation and sends you an email to confirm that the import has taken place.

Importing a Presentation from the Web

To import a presentation that has been published somewhere on the Web, you need to know the URL (that is, the web address) of the presentation. The easiest way to get this is to go to the presentation and then copy what's in your web browser's address bar.

Next, go to the Show home page and click Import. The process of importing a presentation from the Web is almost identical to importing a presentation from your computer (see the previous section). The main difference is that, when you're importing from the Web, you turn on the Enter a Web URL option on the Import Presentation page (see Figure 3.3) and paste or type the presentation's URL into that text box.

When you've set up the presentation the way you want it, click Import. Show imports the presentation, adds it to the list on its home page, and emails you to let you know that the import succeeded.

Presentation Views

Sometimes you want to work on a presentation one slide at a time; other times, you want to get an overview of the presentation as a whole. And eventually, of course, you're going to want to give the presentation a trial run. As you're working on a presentation, you have the following options for viewing it:

- **Normal View**—This view displays your presentation in the optimal way for working on individual slides: The slide sorter pane on the left, the slide editor in the middle, and a right-side pane for activities such as adding shapes or tags, changing the theme, and viewing the presentation's history. This is the default view when you create or open a presentation. If you're in a different view, get back to Normal View by selecting Slide View, Normal View.

- **Master View**—If you want to change the look, size, or style of the standard fonts in a presentation, switch to Master View (Slide View, Master View). This view shows two master slides: Title Master and Slide Master (see Figure 3.4). Any changes you make to these master slides automatically apply to all the slides in the presentation.

- **Sorter View**—Shown in Figure 3.5, Sorter View gives you an overview of your presentation as a whole. From here, you can easily move slides around. To switch to Sorter View, select Slide View, Sorter View.

 To make a fast switch from Sorter View back to Normal View, double-click the slide you want to work on, and it opens in Normal View's slide editor.

- **Slideshow**—Before you share your presentation, you'll want to give it a couple of run-throughs to make sure everything looks okay. To view your presentation as a slideshow, click Slideshow in the top row of toolbar buttons. This previews the slideshow in a new window. And, of course, if you're giving an onsite slideshow (as opposed to one that brings together remote users from different locations), this is the button to click to start your show.

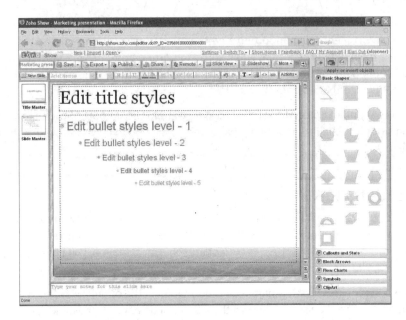

Figure 3.4
Tweak the formatting of all slides in a presentation using the master slide.

Figure 3.5
Sorter View shows thumbnails of all the slides in your presentation.

Editing a Presentation

Whether you're adding content to a shiny new presentation or editing an existing one, you work in the presentation editor, as shown in Figure 3.6. The presentation editor has three main areas: a pane on the left that shows thumbnails of your presentation's slides, a center area where you can edit individual slides, and a pane on the right that lets you do the following things:

- Add shapes or clip art to a slide.
- Change a presentation's theme.
- View the presentation's history (that is, the different versions you've saved).

- View or work with a presentation's tags. (See the upcoming section on working with tags.)
- Get information about your presentation.

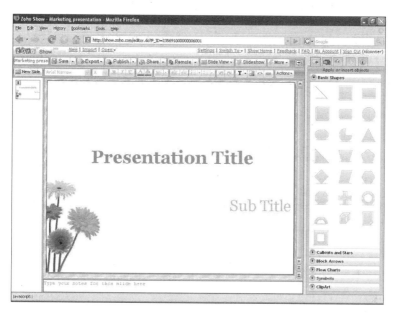

Figure 3.6
Show's presentation editor is where you add slides and content to your presentations.

Adding Slides

When you first create a new presentation, Zoho helps you out by inserting a blank title slide at the start. (As Figure 3.6 shows, this slide has placeholders for a title and subtitle.) But a presentation consisting of just one slide is not very useful. To add a new slide, click the New Slide button on the left end of the Formatting toolbar. Show opens the dialog box shown in Figure 3.7.

 When you click the New Slide button, Show inserts the new slide right after the one that's currently selected.

The Create New Slide – Select Slide Type dialog box offers these formats for blank slides:

- **Blank Slide**—No predetermined formatting here, so you can go to town adding content wherever you want.
- **Title Slide**—This format has text boxes already inserted and formatted for a title and subtitle.
- **Title with Text**—There's a slot for a title at the top of the slide and a text box for normal-sized text below it.

- **Title with Points**—This is just like the Title with Text format, except that the lower text box is preformatted as a bulleted list.
- **Two Text Blocks**—Below the titles are two text boxes, side by side. Use this kind of slide when you want the slide's text to appear in columns.

Click a slide type to select it; then click Create Slide to insert a blank slide with that format into your presentation.

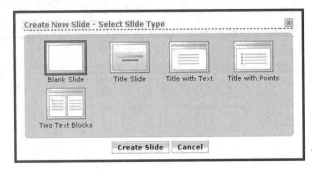

Figure 3.7
Choose a format for each new slide you add to a presentation.

Working with Text

When you create a new slide, such as the title slide shown in Figure 3.6, that slide already has preformatted text boxes placed on it. (The exception, of course, is when you create a blank slide, which has no text boxes already inserted.) These text boxes help you put content on the slide without having to worry about font, color, size, or placement. However, you can change any of these as you like, as this section explains.

Adding Text to a Slide

When you've added a slide that has some text boxes (you'll know because the slide has place-holders such as Title or [Insert your text here]), click the placeholder text. The placeholder changes to a text box like the one in Figure 3.8, so you can start typing. At the same time, Show activates the formatting buttons above the slide editor.

You're not limited to Show's placeholders for putting text on a slide. If you want to add text to a blank slide, or if you want to add a new text box to a preformatted slide, click the downward-point arrow on the Text Box button (see Figure 3.8) or right-click the slide and select Add Text. This brings up a menu of choices for the kind of text box to add: Title Box 1, Sub Title Box, Title Box 2, Text Box, or Bullet Box (for creating a bulleted list).

Whichever kind of text box you choose, Show inserts it into the current slide. Click the place-holder to turn it into a text box and then start typing. Show pays no attention to existing content when inserting the new text box, so the new text box might overlap other text boxes or graphics. You can move or resize the text boxes to eliminate this problem, as the next section explains.

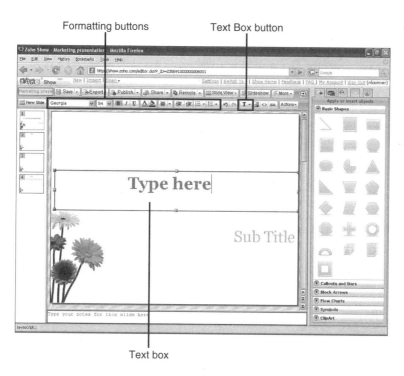

Formatting buttons   Text Box button

Text box

Figure 3.8
To replace a placeholder with your own text, click the placeholder to turn it into a text box and then start typing.

Resizing or Moving a Text Box

You're not stuck with Show's standard positioning of text; you can move text around on the slide. You can also make a text box larger or smaller to get your text looking just the way you want—maybe you want it to stretch all the way across the screen or be limited to a narrow column.

To move a text box, click the text it holds to make the text box visible, as in Figure 3.8. Position your cursor on the border of the text box so the cursor becomes a four-way arrow. When the cursor changes, click and drag the text box to its new location. Let up on the mouse button when you've got the text where you want it.

To resize a text box, click the text you want so the borders of the text box appear. The border has eight small squares, called *handles*, at its corners and its lines' halfway points. Click any handle and drag it to make the text box smaller or larger. As you drag, the text inside the box repositions itself, so you can see how it looks on the slide. When the text looks good, let up on the mouse button to apply the new text box size.

Formatting Text

To format text, click the text to reveal the text box and activate the formatting buttons above the slide editor. Then select the text you want to format. (Press Ctrl+A or Cmd-A to select all the text in the box.)

If you've worked in Writer, the text buttons will be familiar. (Chapter 1 has a list of formatting buttons and what they do.) You can change the font style, size, or color; add a background color to the text box; align text; change the indent; create lists; and more.

 Want your list to have a different bullet or numbering style from the standard? Click the arrow next to the Bullets or Numbering button to select from a variety of styles.

Creating Hyperlinks

When you give a slideshow, you can insert a link that opens a web page when you click it. First, make sure you know the correct URL (web address) of the web page you want to link to—the easiest way to do this is to open the web page and copy what's in your browser's address bar.

Back in Show, select the text that will hold the link and then click the Insert Hyperlink button on the right side of the toolbar. (Or press Ctrl+K for a keyboard shortcut.) The Insert Link dialog box opens. Paste or type in the URL of the page you're linking to and then click Insert. The text is now linked to the web page.

 If you haven't yet written the text for the hyperlink, you can do that at the same time you insert the link. When you click the Insert Hyperlink button with no text selected, just type the text into the Text to Display box, above where you paste in the URL, and then click Insert. Zoho inserts the text *and* the link, all at once.

Working with Shapes

A slideshow with nothing but text might make your points, but visually it's kinda boring. To add a little pizzazz to your slides, try adding some shapes. You can create a flow chart, emphasize important points with stars or lightning bolts, add a speech or thought bubble, and more. Show even comes preloaded with ready-to-use clip art in more than a dozen different categories.

Inserting a Shape

At the top of Show's right pane are five tabs; the leftmost one, called Shapes, is where you choose and insert a shape into your slide. Show offers six categories of shapes; click a category to see its options:

- **Basic Shapes**—Includes squares, circles, diamonds, rectangles, trapezoids, and just about everything else you may remember from geometry class.
- **Callouts and Stars**—This is where you'll find a variety of star shapes and bubbles to indicate speech or thoughts.
- **Block Arrows**—Offers quite a few styles beyond the run-of-the-mill single- or double-headed arrows.

- **Flow Charts**—Includes all the common symbols you need to create this kind of diagram: terminators, actions, processes, decision points, and more.

- **Symbols**—This is Show's "miscellaneous" category, including smiley faces, hearts, flowers, scrolls, and more.

- **Clip Art**—This is where you can browse categories ranging from animals and people, to computers and technology, to entertainment and sports (and that's just for starters) to find cartoon-like illustrations for your slides.

Whatever kind of shape or illustration you want, click the shape to select it. Then move your cursor to the approximate place on the slide where you want the shape to appear. (Don't worry if your placement isn't exact; you can move the shape later.) From there you have two options:

- Click to make a standard-sized shape appear.

- Click and drag to size the shape you're inserting.

Voilà! You've inserted a shape, and your slide looks something like the one in Figure 3.9.

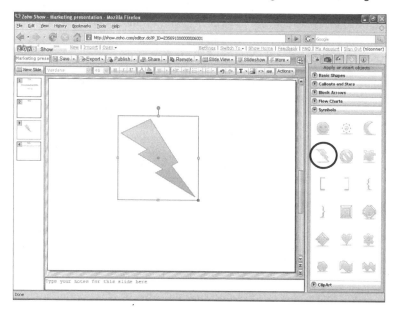

Figure 3.9
Use the right pane to insert a shape. When you select a shape, Show puts a box around it.

 Here's a quick 'n' easy way to get a shape onto your slide: Click the shape you want, drag it onto the slide, and then let go of the mouse button to drop the shape into place.

Resizing Shapes

Often, you'll want to adjust a shape's size after you've inserted it. Piece of cake. Click the shape to select it, revealing a frame around the shape (as shown in Figure 3.9). The shape's frame has five square handles; place your cursor on any of these handles so that the cursor becomes a double-headed arrow; then click and drag to change the shape's size.

 To keep a shape in proportion, click and drag the handle in the lower-right corner of the shape's frame. This adjusts the shape's horizontal and vertical dimensions simultaneously.

 Here's a keyboard shortcut for resizing objects: First, select the shape (or other object) you want to resize. Then, while holding down the Shift key, use the arrow keys to adjust the size.

Rotating a Shape

If you want a right-pointing arrow to switch around and point left, up, down, or at an angle, you can rotate that arrow to make it point exactly where you're aiming it. In fact, you can rotate any shape you insert into a slide.

When you select a shape, you see a circle connected to the top of its frame (take a look back at Figure 3.9 to see it). Put your cursor on this circle, and the cursor becomes a four-way arrow. When it does, click the mouse button and drag to make the shape rotate around its center point (which is a gray circle in the middle of the shape's frame).

Alternatively, if you'd prefer a keyboard shortcut for rotating a shape, just hold down Alt while pressing an arrow key to rotate the image.

 To flip an image (that is, show its mirror image), select the image and right-click. From the context menu that appears, choose Properties. This opens the Properties dialog box. In this box, select Flip & Rotation and then choose Flip Horizontal or Flip Vertical, as you prefer.

Moving a Shape

If a shape isn't quite where you want it on the slide, you can move it to a new location. Doing so is as easy as selecting the shape (so you can see its frame) and then clicking the shape and dragging it to its new location.

 Here's a keyboard trick: Select the shape you want to move and then use the arrow keys to reposition it.

Adding Images

If a picture is worth a thousand words, it's got to be worth at least a few hundred bullet points. You can insert an image from your computer or an online photo album into any slide. To do so, click the Insert Image button in the toolbar above the slide editor. This opens the Insert Image dialog box shown in Figure 3.10.

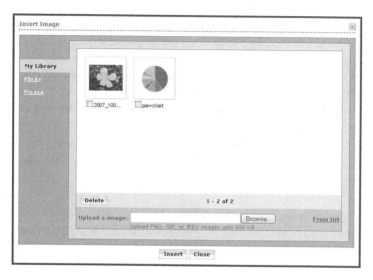

Figure 3.10
Use the Insert Image box to upload an image from your computer, insert an image you've already uploaded, or link to an online image.

The Insert Image box gives you several choices for getting pictures onto your slide.

- To transfer a copy of an image from your computer to Show, click the Browse button, find and select the image on your computer, and click Open to put the file's name and location in the Upload an Image box. Images you upload in this way must be in one of four formats— .png, .gif, .jpg, or .jpeg—and 600KB or smaller in size.

 Show may give you an error message telling you that the image is 0 bytes and couldn't be uploaded. If you see that, close the Insert Image box and then open it again. Despite the error message, your image should be there.

- To insert an image you've already uploaded, find the image you want in the Insert Image box. Check the box below the image.

- To insert an image from your Flickr or Picasa Web Albums account, look in the left part of the dialog box and click the name of your service. The first time you use one of these services to transfer images to Show, you need to configure that service to work with Show. Click the Click Here to Configure Account link and log in to your Google account (for Picasa Web Albums) or your Yahoo! account (for Flickr). You have to give permission for Zoho to access these applications, just as you do when you sign in to a Zoho app through Google or Yahoo! (see this book's Introduction for more info about that). Zoho transfers your files to Show; just check the box of the one you want to insert.

 After you've configured Picasa Web Albums or Flickr to work with Show, any new photos you've added to those sites automatically get transferred to Show when you click Insert Image and then select the service in the left side of the Insert Image dialog box.

■ To transfer an image from a web location other than Picasa Web Albums or Flickr, start by finding the image and copying its URL. Most online photo services, such as Photobucket and Snapfish, have a direct link you can copy (it begins with *http*). After you've copied that link, open Show's Insert Image dialog box and select My Library from its left side; then click the From URL link. The text box changes its label to "Insert Image from URL." Paste the URL you copied into the text box. (This does *not* add the image to your Show image library; instead, it creates a link to the image.)

Whichever method you choose, click Insert to put the image on your slide. Show inserts the image, and you can work with it as you would any other object (see the previous section on working with shapes).

 You can also embed videos in a slideshow. Chapter 2, "Zoho Notebook: Clip, Snip, and Organize," tells how to embed videos in a Zoho Notebook page; in Show the process is similar. Copy the code that embeds the video from its source site (such as YouTube). In Show, select the slide you want, click the Insert HTML Code Snippet button, and then paste in the code and click Insert.

Sometimes, you may insert an image and then find that it's too big for the slide; the top and bottom resizing handles, for example, may not appear when you select the image. When that happens, you can resize the image using its properties. Right-click the image and choose Properties from the context menu to open the Properties dialog box. There, select Size & Position and then adjust the image's height and width manually. For example, you might make both height and width 75 percent of the original image to shrink the image while keeping it in proportion.

Copying and Pasting an Object

Sometimes you've got a great picture or chart on one slide that you want to revisit on a later slide. And that's when copying and pasting comes in handy. Copying and pasting is a piece of cake for any kind of object: text, a shape, an image—whatever. Just right-click the object. As Figure 3.11 shows, this brings up a context menu. Select Copy Object or Cut Object (as you prefer). Then move to the slide where you want to paste the object (just click it in the left pane), right-click there, and select Paste Object. Presto! The copied object magically appears.

Deleting an Object

There are two ways to delete an object from a slide (an object can be a text box, shape, image, and so on):

■ Click the object to select it. From the toolbar above the editing pane, select Actions, Delete Object.

■ Right-click the object and select Delete Object from the context menu (see Figure 3.11).

However you delete an object, Show doesn't ask for confirmation before it removes the object from the slide. If you delete an object by mistake, click the toolbar's Undo button to bring it back.

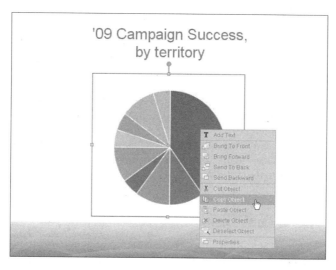

Figure 3.11
Right-clicking an object brings up a context menu that offers choices for working with the object.

Duplicating a Slide

You can copy a slide to use it as the basis for a new slide or to emphasize a point by returning to it later in a presentation. To make an exact copy of an existing slide, you've got a couple options:

- In the left slide sorter pane (or in Sorter View), right-click the slide and choose Duplicate from the context menu. Show inserts the duplicate immediately after the original, but you can move it (see upcoming section) to wherever you want.

- Copy the slide and then paste it where you want it. Right-click the slide you want. If you click the slide in the editing pane, select Copy Slide; if you click it in the slide sorter, select Copy. Next, choose the slide that will come before the copy you're pasting in. In the toolbar above the slide editor, click Actions, Paste Slide.

 Another way to duplicate a slide is to copy and paste it. In the left slide-sorter pane, click a slide to select and choose Actions, Copy Slide (or right-click and choose Copy). Then click the slide just before where you want the new slide to appear; select Actions, Paste Slide.

Moving a Slide

Some people like to rearrange the living room furniture; others like to try out different arrangements of slides in their presentations. But you won't strain your back moving a Show slide: In the slide sort pane (or Sorter View), select the slide you want to move. Holding down the mouse button, drag the slide to its new location. Let go of the button to drop it in place. (When you do, Zoho automatically changes the slide numbers to reflect the new arrangement.)

Adding Notes

Presentation notes keep you on your toes and let you make sure you're not forgetting anything. During a presentation, the notes are visible only to the presenter, so nobody will think you're cheating.

In the slide editor's Normal view, just below the current slide, is a pane where you can type notes for your presentation. Just click inside the text box and type away.

 Not enough room for your notes in that little pane? Hover your cursor over the border between the current slide and the Notes pane. When the cursor changes to a two-headed arrow, click-and-drag to resize the Notes pane.

Changing Your Presentation's Theme

When you create a new presentation, you choose a theme for it. But you're not stuck with that theme forever. You might decide, for example, that you want a lighter background color or that pink flowers don't really work with your gloomy sales report.

You change a presentation's theme using the pane on the right. Click the Themes tab (shown in Figure 3.12). From the drop-down list of themes, choose a category. Show displays all the themes in that category. Click one to apply it to the presentation. Show applies the theme and saves the presentation.

Figure 3.12
The Themes tab (circled) is where you choose a new theme for a presentation.

Deleting a Slide

If there's a slide that's just not working out, you can delete it from the presentation with a mere click or two. Right-click the slide. From the context menu, choose Delete Slide (if you're in the slide editor) or Delete (if you're in the Sorter View or pane). Show doesn't ask you to confirm the deletion—it just gets rid of the slide.

Saving a Presentation

Whether you're just taking a break or the presentation is finished, you want to be sure to save your work. You can save a copy right in Show, or you can export it using a range of file formats.

Saving a Copy

To save a copy, click the upper-left Save button. Then choose one of these options:

- **Save**—This saves a version of this presentation as it exists at this moment in time.
- **Save As**—Choose this option to save a duplicate version of the presentation with a new name. When you choose Save As, Show asks you to name the duplicate presentation. Give the copy a name and then click OK.

 Here's another option for creating a copy of a presentation: In the upper-right part of the toolbar, select More, Duplicate Presentation. As when you click Save, Save As, Show asks you to name the presentation. When you've done that, click OK to save your new copy.

Exporting a Presentation

When you export a presentation, you save a version of it in a format that works with other programs, such as Microsoft PowerPoint or OpenOffice.org Impress. This can be helpful when you want to snazz up a presentation with some animation, or when you want to print out paper copies of your slides as a handout.

When you're ready to export a presentation, click the Export button in the top row of buttons above the slide editor. That opens a menu from which you choose the type of file you want to export:

- **HTML**—For display on the Web
- **PPT**—To open, edit, and save in Microsoft PowerPoint
- **PPS**—For PowerPoint or the PowerPoint Viewer (Microsoft's presentation viewer)
- **ODP**—To open, edit, and save in OpenOffice.org Impress
- **PDF**—To view or print the file using Adobe Acrobat

If you select HTML as the file type, your presentation opens in a new browser window. If you want to save it, do so using your web browser. (The process will vary, depending on your browser.)

If you select any of the other file types, your computer asks you where you want to save the file; you can open it using the appropriate program or save it to your computer's hard drive.

 At this writing, you can't print a presentation directly from Zoho Show. If you want to print a presentation, export it as a PDF, open it in Adobe Reader or Adobe Acrobat, and then print from there.

Deleting a Presentation

If you're done with a presentation and you know you'll never use it again, you can delete it from Show. The easiest way to do this is to open the Show home page, which lists all your presentations. Find the presentation you want to delete and click its Trash link. This moves it to the Trashed Presentations section of Show. (You can get it back if you want; click the Trashed Presentations link, find the banished presentation, and click Restore.)

To delete a presentation completely, you need to dump it from Trashed Presentations. On the Zoho Show home page, click the Trashed Presentations link, find the presentation you're getting rid of, and click its Delete Forever link. Saying farewell forever is serious stuff, so Show asks if you're sure. Click Delete to confirm, and the presentation is gone for good.

Sharing a Presentation

When you're on a team that's creating a presentation together, Show enables you to invite others to work on the presentation you created. Everyone edits the same version, so when a colleague makes changes to your presentation, you (and everyone else you've invited) see those changes the next time you open the presentation.

To get more people on board—whether as viewers or full collaborators—open the presentation you want to share and click Share to open the dialog box shown in Figure 3.13. You can invite people to view your presentation without the ability to change it (Read Only Members) or give them full editing privileges (Read/Write Members). Type or paste in individual email addresses (use commas to separate them). Alternatively, you can click Add Contacts to choose from a list of your Zoho contacts. If you're inviting a group, click the Add Groups link and choose from the list that opens. To create a brand-new group, click Add Group, Manage Groups, Create New Group. Then follow the instructions in Chapter 1 for creating a group.

If you want Zoho to shoot you an email when a collaborator has made changes to your presentation, make sure the Notify Me box is checked.

You can send Zoho's standard email or add a custom message of your own. Click the Edit Invitation Email button to expand the Share This Document dialog box. A new text box appears on the right where can type your message.

When everything's all set, click Share to send out your invitations and add these people to your presentation.

 To send yourself a copy of the invitation email, click the Share This Document dialog box's Edit Invitation Email button and enable the Send a Copy to Me check box.

Show lets just one person at a time edit a presentation. So when a collaborator signs in and starts editing a presentation, it's locked to everyone else. On your Zoho home page, the presentation is listed as "locked for editing"; if you try to open it, Zoho tells you who's working on it right now and gives you the option to view the presentation (read only) as a slideshow (see the next section).

Figure 3.13
Invite individuals or groups to share a presentation.

 To see a presentation's history, go to Normal View's right-side pane and click the Version Details tab. This displays all the saved versions of the presentation; you can view, delete, or revert to any version.

Viewing a Presentation on the Web

Can't get everyone in the same room at the same time to view your presentation? No problem. One of the big advantages of creating and storing your presentation online is that you can share it over the Internet with an audience that accesses the presentation from wherever it happens to be.

Setting up a remote presentation involves two steps:

1. Inviting participants.

2. Giving the presentation.

Inviting Others to Your Online Presentation

A presentation isn't a presentation without an audience. So before you give your presentation online, you need to invite the people who'll view it. To send out invitations to audience members, open the presentation and select Remote. This opens the Remote URL dialog box, shown in Figure 3.14.

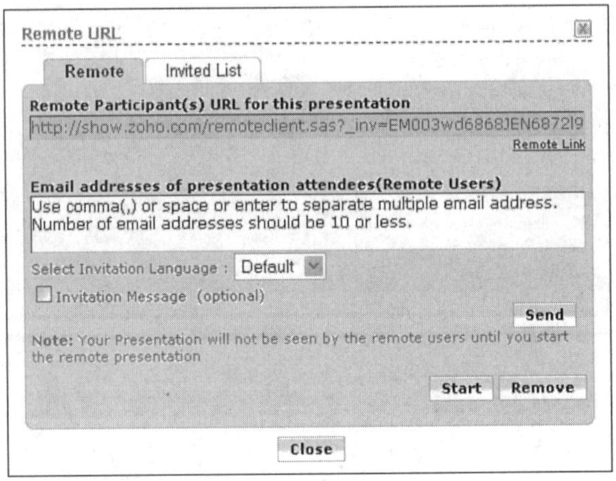

Figure 3.14
Invite others to view your online presentation.

The top section of this dialog box shows the web address for the presentation; this is where people can view the presentation when you show it.

The middle section is where you type in the email address of the people you're inviting to see your show. Be sure to include a comma between multiple addresses to separate them.

You can add a message to the standard one Zoho sends; this is a good way to let people know when the presentation will be. Check the Invitation Message box, and the section expands to show a text box where you can type in your message (up to 250 characters, so be concise).

Tip 4U To see whom you've already invited, click Remote and then choose the Invited List tab. Click Re-Invite to send no-shows a quick reminder email.

When you've listed all the people you're inviting, click Send. Your invitations zip off through cyberspace to land in invitees' Inboxes. The email Zoho informs each recipient that you've invited him or her to attend a presentation and gives a link to the presentation's web address. When it's time to see the show, each attendee clicks the link, gives his or her name, and clicks another link to see the presentation.

Info 4U The presentation doesn't start until you, as the creator, begin it, so you don't have to worry about anyone showing up early and paging through your slides.

Giving a Remote Presentation

When you're ready to give the presentation, sign in to Zoho Show, open the presentation, and click Remote to open the Remote URL box shown in Figure 3.14. Click the Start button to get things going.

The presentation view opens in a new window. Click the Start Remote link to start the show. When you click this link, a couple of things happen, as Figure 3.15 shows. The presentation becomes visible on your screen, as well as on the screens of any audience members who've already arrived. You also see the names of signed-in audience members in the Participants List on the right. Below this list is a chat window; type in the text box at the bottom to send a message to all signed-in participants.

 Tip 4U To hide the Participants List and chat window, click the right-pointing arrow immediately to the left of this pane. This expands the presentation pane on your screen only. (Participants can click the arrow on their own screens, if they want.) To reveal the right-side pane, click the arrow again. (When the pane is hidden, the arrow points left.)

Presenter's controls

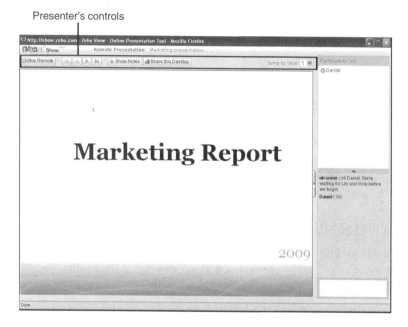

Figure 3.15
Zoho Show presentations appear in this viewer.

When you're the presenter, you see some controls across the top of the screen (refer to Figure 3.15) that participants don't have:

- **Stop Remote**—When the presentation's over, click this button to end the show, on your screen and your viewers' screens alike.

- **Navigation buttons**—Move forward or back by one slide, or jump to the last or the first slide of the presentation.

- **Show/Hide Notes**—If you've included notes on your presentation's slides, click this button to show (or hide) them. Notes appear on your screen, but not on your viewers' screens.

- **Share this Desktop**—Clicking this button installs the Zoho Meeting plug-in in your web browser if it's not already installed. (You may have to instruct your browser to allow the plug-in by listing show.zoho.com as a trusted site.) When you have Zoho Meeting installed, you can share your computer's Desktop with the presentation's viewers. Chapter 10, "Zoho Meeting: Web Conferencing Made Simple," explains everything you need to know about Zoho Meeting.

- **Jump to Slide**—If you want to skip a couple slides or go back to a previous one, choose the slide number to jump right to the one you want.

 A participant can leave the presentation by clicking the upper-right X to close the browser window. Before the browser window closes, Zoho puts up a warning box saying that closing the window ends the remote presentation; the participant must click OK to leave. When someone leaves a presentation before the presenter ends it, that person's name disappears from the Participants List.

Publishing a Presentation

Those who can't be there for the group presentation are not completely out of the loop. (Or maybe the presentation is something you want to share with the world—an overview of your company, for example.) When you publish a presentation on the Web, anyone who has the URL can view the presentation at his or her leisure. You can also embed a presentation on an existing web page. This section tells you how to do both.

Publishing a Presentation on the Web

When you publish a presentation on the Web, Zoho embeds your presentation in a web page where people can view it at their own pace and, if they want, leave a comment on it. Viewers can find your presentation via its URL or (if you want) through Zoho's list of public presentations.

To publish a presentation on the Web, follow these steps:

1. In Show, open the presentation you want to publish. Click Publish to open the Make Public dialog box shown in Figure 3.16.
2. The Make Public dialog box requires a couple decisions. To update the public presentation every time you make changes to it in Zoho Show, make sure that the box labeled Automatically Re-Publish When Document Is Modified is checked. And if you want the presentation to be included on Zoho's massive list of public presentations (at http://show.zoho.com/latest), leave the Show in Zoho Public Presentation List box checked.
3. Click Make Public & Continue.

Zoho publishes your presentation to the Web and changes the Make Public dialog box to reflect this. To view the presentation, click the This Presentation Is Publicly Available at the Following URL link, or copy the link in the box below it and paste it into the address bar of your web browser. The link looks something like this:

    http://show.zoho.com/public/yourZohoID/Presentation%20Name

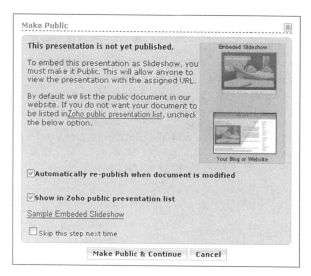

Figure 3.16
Publish a presentation on the Web with the Make Public dialog box.

You can email that link to others right from Zoho. (Click the Email link and provide addresses separated by commas.)

 To remove your presentation from Zoho's public presentation list, open the presentation and click Publish. In the Make Public dialog box, click the Change to HIDDEN Mode link. If you want a hidden presentation to appear on Zoho's public list, click Publish, Change to SHOW Mode.

 To remove a published presentation from the Web, open the presentation in Show and then click Publish, Remove Public. Click OK to confirm.

Embedding a Presentation in an Existing Web Page

You may have a website where you want to show the presentation to anyone who visits the site. For example, you could feature a presentation about new products on your company's home page. The first step in doing this is to publish the presentation, as described in the previous section. When you've done that, the Make Public dialog box changes to give the URL of the published presentation. It also gives you HTML code that you can use to embed the presentation in your own web page.

Open the published presentation in Show and then click the Publish button. In the top section of the dialog box is a snippet of HTML code that looks something like this:

```
<iframe src="http://show.zoho.com/embed?USER=yourZohoID&DOC=
Presentation%20Name&IFRAME=yes" height="335" width="450"
name="Presentation Name" scrolling=no frameBorder="0"
style="border:1px solid #AABBCC"></iframe>
```

Copy the code snippet and paste it into an HTML document. Upload the document to your site, and the presentation appears there.

Track Data with Zoho Sheet

If you've ever used Excel, Lotus 1-2-3, Calc, VisiCalc, or Quattro Pro, you'll feel right at home with Zoho Sheet. It's got the familiar rows-and-columns grid for entering data. You can create charts, sort data, use formulas and functions—everything you expect (and require) from a spreadsheet. What might surprise you is how powerful Sheet is, helping to make your job easier by giving you the ability to record and use macros, grab external data, and create pivot tables. Not only that, but because Sheet is web-based, you can share, collaborate on, and publish your spreadsheets—all with just a few clicks.

Getting Started

Sheet's spreadsheet editor, shown in Figure 4.1, is where the action is. The left side of the screen organizes your spreadsheets; the rest of the screen is taken up by the spreadsheet itself. Above the spreadsheet are a couple toolbars for working with the spreadsheet. And at the bottom of the screen, you'll find tabs for moving between sheets in a workbook, as well as buttons for adding comments and opening a chat window to discuss the spreadsheet as you work with collaborators.

If you've ever worked with a spreadsheet program, such as Microsoft Excel or OpenOffice.org Calc, Sheet will look familiar. You can get right down to business: Click inside the first cell and start entering your data.

Creating a Spreadsheet

The first time you open Sheet, Zoho has already created a spreadsheet for you. This spreadsheet is named Untitled, so one of the first things you'll want to do is give the spreadsheet a name. Above the spreadsheet is a text box that holds the current title. In Figure 4.1 no title has been assigned yet, so it reads "Untitled." Click inside the text box and type the title. When you hit Enter or click outside the box, the spreadsheet is named or renamed.

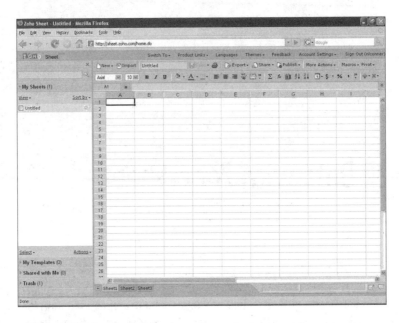

Figure 4.1
Zoho Sheet's spreadsheet editor gives you plenty of room to enter data.

To create a new spreadsheet, click the New button and then select Blank Spreadsheet. Sheet sets up a brand-new, untitled spreadsheet. Give it a name and start filling it in.

 The New button also lets you create a new template or choose from your list of existing templates to start a new spreadsheet. The upcoming section "Working with Templates" tells you more.

Importing Spreadsheets

Chances are that you probably have some existing spreadsheets in a program such as Excel that you'd like to get into Sheet. Doing so is simple. You can import a spreadsheet directly from your computer (using any of several file formats) or from the Web.

Whichever method you use, the way to start is to click the upper-left Import button, opening the dialog box shown in Figure 4.2.

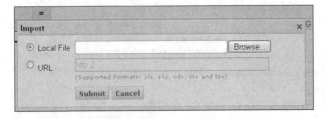

Figure 4.2
You can import a spreadsheet into Sheet from your computer or from the Web.

Importing a Spreadsheet from Your Computer

When you're importing a spreadsheet from your computer into Sheet, you can use any of a bunch of formats:

- Microsoft Excel 97–2003 (.xls)

 Note that Sheet doesn't currently let you import Excel 2007 (.xlsx) files.

- OpenOffice.org Calc (.sxc or .ods)
- Comma-separated values text file (.csv)
- Tab-separated values text file (.tsv)

 If you use a spreadsheet program whose format can't be imported into Zoho Sheet, such as Lotus 1-2-3 or Excel 2007, save your spreadsheet as a .CSV or .TSV file and then import that file into Sheet.

In the Import dialog box (shown in Figure 4.2), make sure the Local File radio button is enabled and then click the Browse button. In the window that opens, find the file you want to import. Click Open to get the file's name and location into the Import dialog box and then click Submit.

Zoho imports the file and opens it as a new spreadsheet.

Importing a Spreadsheet from the Web

If your spreadsheet is published on the Web, all you need to import the spreadsheet into Zoho Sheet is its web address (URL). Start by surfing over to the spreadsheet and then copying the URL in your browser's address bar. (Select the URL and then press Ctrl+C in Windows or Cmd-C on a Mac).

Next, go to Sheet, click Import, and in the Import dialog box (shown in Figure 4.2), select URL. Paste the spreadsheet's web address into the URL text box (press Ctrl+V or Cmd-V). Click Submit to import the spreadsheet into Sheet.

Entering Data

To enter data into a spreadsheet, click in any cell and start typing. Use the Tab key to jump to the next cell. You can also use your keyboard's arrow keys to move from cell to cell in the spreadsheet.

To select a range of cells, click the upper-left cell in the range you want, hold down the Shift key, and then select the lower-right cell in the range—or you can simply click-and-drag. You can also select a range by holding down the Shift key and using your keyboard's arrow keys.

If you want, you can copy (Ctrl+C in Windows or Cmd-C on a Mac) or cut (Ctrl+X or Cmd-X) the range and paste it into a new location: Move the cursor to the first cell of the new range and press Ctrl+V or Cmd-V.

Saving a Spreadsheet

To save a spreadsheet you've been working on, click the Save button in the top row of buttons. To save a duplicate of the spreadsheet, click the arrow next to the Save button to open the Save As menu. From this menu, choose New Spreadsheet. The Save as New Spreadsheet dialog box appears, asking you to give the duplicate a name. Name the copy and then click OK.

 You can also save a spreadsheet as a template to serve as a model for new spreadsheets. Skip ahead to "Working with Templates" in this chapter to learn how.

You may want to distinguish a particular version of your spreadsheet with a label. This makes it easy to find in the version history. To add a description to a particular saved version, click the arrow next to the Save button to open the Save As menu and then select Mark as New Version. (Alternatively, you can click More Actions, Mark as New Version.) The Version Description dialog box opens. Type in your description and then click Submit.

Adding a description doesn't change the spreadsheet's name. Instead, when you look at the spreadsheet's version history (More Actions, View Version History), the description you wrote for this version appears in the Description column of the Version History dialog box. For more about working with a spreadsheet's version history, see "Viewing a Spreadsheet's Version History" later in this chapter.

Exporting a Spreadsheet

To export a spreadsheet from Sheet to another program, open the spreadsheet you want to export and click the Export button. The menu that appears lists the formats and programs you can use for the export:

- MS Excel Workbook (.xls)
- OpenDocument Spreadsheet (.ods)
- Open Office Spreadsheet (.sxc)
- Gnumeric Spreadsheet
- Comma Separated Values (.csv)
- Tab Separated Values (.tsv)
- XML File (.xml)
- XHTML (.xhtml)
- HTML (.html)
- PDF Document (.pdf)

Choose the kind of file you want to export and then select whether you want to open it with the appropriate program or save it to your computer. Click OK to export the file.

 Zoho offers a plug-in for Microsoft Office that lets you work with spreadsheets in Excel and save them directly to Sheet. Chapter 1, "Have Your Say with Zoho Writer," tells you how to get the plug-in.

Deleting a Spreadsheet

To delete an old spreadsheet that you no longer need, look in the list on the left under My Sheets. (If necessary, click My Sheets to expand that section.) Find the spreadsheet you want to delete. To the right of its name is the Actions icon, a little picture of a gear with a downward-pointing arrow. Click it. From the menu that appears, select Move to Trash. And that's exactly what happens—Zoho moves that spreadsheet to the Trash.

If you accidentally trashed a spreadsheet and want to bring it back, click Trash in the left-side list to expand that section. To the right of each file's name are two symbols: a curved arrow and an X. Click the curved arrow to restore the spreadsheet to your My Sheets list. To delete a file forever, click the X.

 Zoho doesn't ask for confirmation before it deletes a file from the Trash. So check twice to make sure you've got the right file before you click that X.

 To move all the files in the Trash back to My Sheets in one fell swoop, click Restore All and then OK. To dump all the files out of the Trash forever, click Empty Trash and then click OK to confirm.

When someone else shares a spreadsheet with you, it's that person's spreadsheet, not yours—so you can't just toss it in the Trash. What you can do, however, is decide not to share it. This removes the spreadsheet from your Sheet account without affecting anyone else's ability to view or work with it.

When someone has shared a spreadsheet with you and you aren't interested in working with it, click Shared with Me in the list on the left to see the list of files others have shared with you. Find the file you want to get rid of and click its Gear icon (which symbolizes Actions). From the Actions menu, select Remove Sharing. Zoho asks whether you're sure; if you are, click OK, and the spreadsheet disappears from the list.

 When you remove a shared spreadsheet, that spreadsheet doesn't go into the Trash. Instead, you lose access to it. So be careful not to remove sharing on a spreadsheet you might need later. (If you do, you'll have to ask the spreadsheet's owner to share it with you again.)

Formatting Your Spreadsheet

Sheet's work area is easy to use, but as you work, you'll want to format your spreadsheet in various ways—adding a new column or deleting one you don't really need, making a numeric column hold a specific currency, highlighting specific data. This section shows you how to do all that and more.

Adding and Deleting Rows and Columns

Often, as you work on a spreadsheet, you need to add new rows or columns to hold your data. Piece of cake. Select a row or column. (Click the number at the left to select a whole row or the letter at the top to choose a whole column.) From there, you have two options, as Figure 4.3 shows:

- Right-click the letter or number that labels the row or column and, from the context menu that appears, choose to insert a row above, a row below, a column before, or a column after.

- Click the plus sign on the right side of the toolbar. A menu appears; choose where you want to insert the new row (above or below) or column (before or after) in relation to the cells you chose.

To add multiple rows or columns, follow the same procedure. Instead of selecting just one row or column, however, select the same number you want to add. Now, when you add the new rows or columns, Sheet inserts the same number you selected.

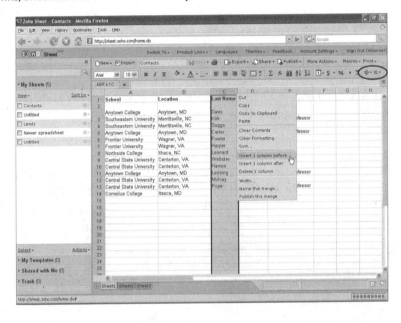

Figure 4.3
Select a row or column. Then, click the plus sign (circled) to add another row or column. Click the X (also circled) to delete your selection.

Deleting columns is pretty much the same thing. Select the range you want to delete and then either right-click or click the fat red X on the right side of the toolbar. From the menu, choose Delete Row or Delete Column.

 Tip 4U If you want to clear the contents of a row or column (rather than deleting the range of cells along with their contents), select the range you want to clear, right-click, and then select Clear Contents.

Formatting Data

Across the top of the spreadsheet is a row of formatting buttons, as shown in Figure 4.4. Use these to format the contents of your spreadsheet's cells:

- **Text Formatting**—Choose a font style, size, color, or background fill (highlighting). Apply boldface, italics, or underlining.

- **Border**—Select a range of cells and put a border around it. You can also use the Borders button to emphasize the gridlines between cells.

- **Alignment**—Keep your columns looking neat by centering text or lining it up on the left or ride side of each cell.

- **Wrap Text**—Click this button to prevent text from overflowing into neighboring cells.

- **Merge Cells Across**—This button removes the vertical lines between the cells in a range you choose. Merging cells can be helpful when you want to create a subheading in your spreadsheet.

- **More Format Options**—Click this button to align cells' contents vertically (bottom, middle, or top of cell) or to split cells across.

 Tip 4U To apply formatting to a range of cells—for example, to make all the column headings bold and center-aligned—select the range and then click the formatting buttons you want. If you select an entire column or row (such as row 1 for headings), subsequent data that you enter in that column or row appears with the formatting already applied.

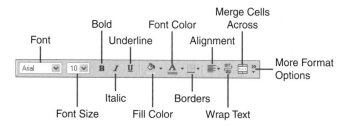

Figure 4.4
Use these buttons to format text and cells in your spreadsheet.

Depending on what you're using your spreadsheet for, you'll want to format its numbers in various ways. For example, if you're tracking sales or product prices in different countries, you want to use the relevant currency for each region. There are other ways you can format numbers, as well: Take a look at the number-formatting buttons on the right side of the toolbar shown in Figure 4.5:

- **Date/Time**—If you've got a column that shows a date or time (or both), use this button to select your preferred formatting. Date formats include 31-12-09, 12/31/2009, December 31, 2009, and a whole bunch of others. For time formats, choose the 24-hour clock or the AM/PM system.

- **Currencies**—As Figure 4.5 shows, you can choose from a variety of currencies to format amounts. Click the arrow next to the dollar sign (or whatever currency is displayed there) to choose from the list shown in Figure 4.5.

- **Percent**—To show numbers as percentages, click this button.

- **Comma**—To put a comma separator between sets of zeros in big numbers, showing (for example) 20,000 instead of 20000, click this button. (The button toggles, so if you're seeing comma separators you *don't* want, click it to remove them.)

- **More Format Options**—Click this button to increase or decrease the number of zeros after a decimal point or to treat numbers as text.

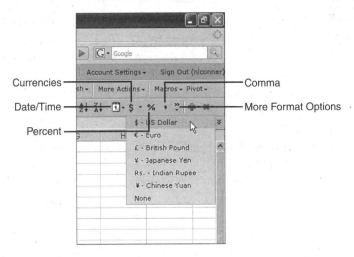

Figure 4.5
You can format numbers in a variety of ways, such as in different currencies.

Working with Sheets

A spreadsheet can be made up of multiple sheets (similar to what Excel calls a workbook). As you can see in Figure 4.3, individual spreadsheets are represented by tabs at the bottom of the screen. Click a tab to move to the spreadsheet it names.

When you right-click a tab, a context menu appears, giving you these options:

- **Insert**—Choose this option to insert a new sheet to the left of the tab you right-clicked.

- **Delete**—This deletes the selected tab. Click OK to confirm the deletion.

- **Rename**—Choosing this option opens a dialog box where you can type in a new name for the sheet; then click OK to apply that name.

- **Copy This Sheet**—This option makes an exact copy of the selected sheet. When you select it, the Copy This Sheet dialog box opens. Give the sheet a name in the Sheet Name field (or use Zoho's suggestion: Copy of *<current sheet name>*) and choose a location from the Place It drop-down list. Click OK to insert the copy.

- **Move This Sheet**—When you select this option, the Move This Sheet dialog box opens. Choose a new location for the sheet from the drop-down list and then click OK.
- **Share This Sheet**—This option lets you share just this sheet with others. See "Sharing a Spreadsheet" for details about sharing and collaborating in Sheet.
- **View Code**—For advanced spreadsheet users and developers only, this option opens a VBA editor, where you can view and edit the spreadsheet's code.

Working with Templates

When you've created and formatted a spreadsheet that makes a good pattern for future spreadsheets, you can save that spreadsheet as a template. Later, when you create a new spreadsheet from that template, it has all the formatting already applied. Just clear its data and start filling it in.

 Tip To clear all the data from a spreadsheet, select the whole sheet. (Press Ctrl+A or click the upper-right rectangle above the numbers and to the left of the letters.) Right-click and then click Clear Contents. Voila! You've got a fresh, clean spreadsheet to work with.

Saving a Spreadsheet as a Template

To save a spreadsheet as a template that you can use for creating new spreadsheets in the future, click the arrow next to the Save button. From the Save As menu, select New Template. In the Save as New Template dialog box, give your template a descriptive name and then click OK.

Zoho saves the spreadsheet as a template and adds it to your My Templates list.

Creating a Template from Scratch

If you know that you're going to be creating multiple spreadsheets with the same basic format, you can set up the formatting in a blank template and then use that template whenever you need to create a new spreadsheet with that formatting.

To set up a template from scratch, click New, Spreadsheet Template. Zoho creates the template with the name Untitled Template. Set up the formatting you want, along with any content (such as column headers) that will be helpful to have in new spreadsheets created from this template. Click Save, name the template, and then click OK. Now, you've got a new template in your My Templates list that you can use for creating a new spreadsheet.

Creating a New Spreadsheet from a Template

When you want to use a template to create a new, preformatted spreadsheet, you have two paths:

- Click New, From Templates List. In the Templates List dialog box, choose the template you want to use. When you make your selection, Zoho fills in the template's name as the new spreadsheet name. If you want, change the spreadsheet's name in the New Spreadsheet Name text box. To create your new spreadsheet, click Create.

■ Click My Templates to expand the section and see your list of templates. Find the template you want and then click the Gear icon to its right. A menu appears; select Create as New Spreadsheet. The Save as New Spreadsheet dialog box opens; name the spreadsheet you're about to create and then click OK.

Sorting and Displaying Data

A spreadsheet is useful for holding tons of data. But just holding that data isn't a whole lot of help unless you can (a) find the data you need and (b) use it to show trends, patterns, and so on. In this section, you learn how to sort your spreadsheet's data and display it as a chart. Sheet offers nine chart styles, so you can show off the data to its best advantage.

Sorting Data

When you sort data, you organize it in a particular order:

■ **Ascending**—From lowest number to highest number or alphabetically from A to Z.

■ **Descending**—From highest number to lowest number or alphabetically from Z to A.

 If the data you're sorting contains both letters and numbers, numbers come before letters in an ascending sort. Conversely, numbers follow letters in a descending sort.

To sort your data in one of these orders, first select the range of cells you want to sort. (If you've got a row of column headers, don't include those—Sheet will sort them just like any other content.) To do a quick sort, click the toolbar's Sort Ascending or Sort Descending button, shown in Figure 4.6. When you do, Sheet sorts the cells you chose based on the far-left column. For example, in Figure 4.6, clicking Ascending Sort organizes the spreadsheet's records in A-to-Z order based on school name.

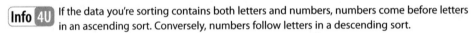 When you choose a single column and then click one of the Sort buttons in the toolbar, Sheet asks if you want to "expand the selection." Click OK to select complete records and continue the sort, based on the column you originally chose. Click Cancel to sort *only* the column you chose, without changing the order within other columns in the same rows (which means that you can no longer read across rows because the data in one column is sorted differently from the others). Careful, though—if you've got column headers in your spreadsheet, they'll be included in the sort.

But what if you don't want to sort by the leftmost column? Take a look at Figure 4.6—maybe you want to sort the data by each contact's last name. In that case, instead of clicking one of the Sort buttons in the toolbar, right-click the cell range you want to sort, and choose Custom Sort from the context menu. This opens the Sort dialog box shown in Figure 4.7. In that box, make these choices:

■ **Sort By**—Select the column you want to sort by. (In our example, you want to sort by last name, so you'd select Column C.) If you want to sort by more than one column, choose the additional columns from the Then By drop-downs.

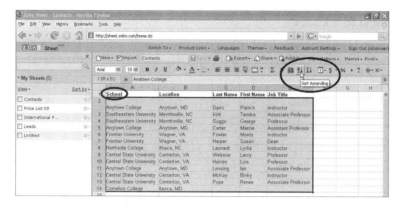

Figure 4.6
When you select a range and click one of the toolbar's Sort buttons (circled), Sheet sorts the data by the range's leftmost column (here, School).

- **Ascending/Descending**—Click the radio button that represents the order in which you want to sort the data.
- **List Options**—Choose whether you want to include column headers in the sort (you can't make that choice in a quick sort): If you want Sheet to ignore column headers, be sure there's a check in the Contains Header check box. Also choose whether you want Sheet to pay attention to upper- and lowercase letters.
- **Orientation**—As you prefer, you can sort the data vertically (by column) or horizontally (by row).

When you've made your choices, click OK to rearrange the data in your spreadsheet.

Figure 4.7
To fine-tune your sorting criteria, use the Sort dialog box.

Displaying Data as a Chart

The endless rows and columns of a spreadsheet make it hard to interpret the data it holds. When you convert that data into a chart, however, you get a lot of visual impact, so your audience can see at a glance how the data stacks up.

There are three steps to creating a chart from a spreadsheet:

1. Choose the type of chart you want.

2. Tell Sheet which data to use in the chart.

3. If you want, add labels, a title, and a legend.

Choosing a Chart Type

To create a chart from a spreadsheet, click the Add Chart button in the toolbar. This opens the Add Chart dialog box, shown in Figure 4.8. This dialog box shows the kinds of charts available in Sheet:

- Column Chart shows the data in vertical columns.

- Bar Chart shows the data in horizontal bars.

- Line Chart presents a series of connected points.

- Pie Chart shows the whole as a circle, divided into sections that represent different categories.

- Scatter Chart plots one piece of information along the x-axis and another piece of information along the y-axis.

- Area Chart is like a line chart with the area below the lines filled in.

- Web Chart looks like a spider web, plotting points based on their distance from the center of a circle.

- Bubble Chart is a type of scatter chart that shows numeric values as circles of varying sizes, which is good for comparing three kinds of data.

- Stock Chart, also called an OHLC chart (for Open High Low Close), compares four values. For example, in tracking the value of stocks, this chart would show the value of each stock at the opening of trading, its high and low values during trading, and its value at the end of trading.

 If you select the data and labels before you click Add Chart, you can click Done after choosing a chart type.

Select any chart type to get a preview of what it looks like. If the chart has subtypes (as in Figure 4.8), click the subtype you want. For example, you might prefer a 3D chart to a flat one.

When you've chosen the chart type and subtype you want, click Next.

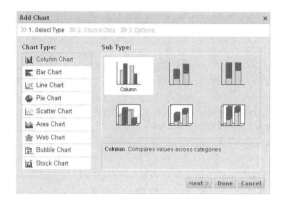

Figure 4.8
Sheet offers nine types of charts.

Defining the Source Data

The second step in creating a chart, shown in Figure 4.9, is to tell Sheet what data to use for the chart. One way you can do this is to select a range of cells before you begin to create the chart. If you've done this, the cell range appears in the Data Range text box of the Add Chart dialog box. If you didn't preselect the cell range, though, you can type it in here. Use this syntax:

    A4:E4

This example defines the range by telling Sheet to start with the cell at the intersection of column A and row 4 and to stop with the cell at the intersection of column E and row 4.

 Sheet looks in the first cell in the range for the chart's legend; it doesn't include this cell's contents in the chart itself. For example, if your range starts with a column's header, that header becomes the legend in a chart. Keep this in mind when defining your cell range.

 If you can't see the cells you want behind the Add Chart dialog box, put your cursor near the top of the dialog box so that the cursor becomes a four-way arrow. When it does, click-and-drag the box to a new location.

In addition, select a radio button to tell Sheet whether you're working with rows or columns. Click Next.

Adding Labels and Other Options

The final step in creating a chart, shown in Figure 4.10, is where you add these finishing touches, which are optional and vary according to the kind of chart you're making:

- **Titles**—You can give a title to the whole chart and the x- and y-axes (where applicable).
- **Data Labels**—If you want the chart's data to show values or percentages, for example, choose from this drop-down.

Figure 4.9
Define the range of cells whose values will be used to make the chart.

■ **Show Legend**—Checking this box shows a legend that labels the chart at the bottom. The first cell in the range you choose provides the legend.

To create your chart, click Done. Zoho whips up whatever kind of chart you chose and displays it on the spreadsheet, as shown in Figure 4.11.

Figure 4.10
The options for labeling a chart depend on the kind of chart you're creating. (These options are for a column chart.)

Editing a Chart

After you've created a chart, you can tweak it in just about any way you like: Try a different chart style, change the data, add or erase labels, and so on. When you pass your cursor over a chart, a frame appears around it (you can see this frame in Figure 4.11). Click Edit in the upper-left corner to open the Edit Chart dialog box, shown in Figure 4.12.

This box is similar to the Add Chart dialog box, except instead of moving you through sequential steps, it presents tabs: Type, Data, and Options. Click the tab that holds the info you want to revise. When you're done making changes, click OK to change the chart.

Moving or Resizing a Chart

You're not stuck with the placement Zoho uses to display the chart in your spreadsheet. To move the chart around, put your cursor on the chart to show the frame. Move your cursor to the bar at the top of the frame. When the cursor changes to a four-way arrow, click-and-drag the chart to its new location.

Chart title   Data labels

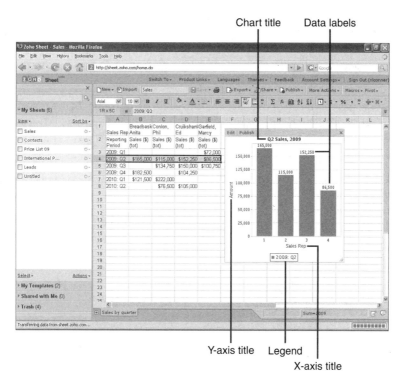

Y-axis title   Legend
               X-axis title

Figure 4.11
Here's a column chart created from spreadsheet data.

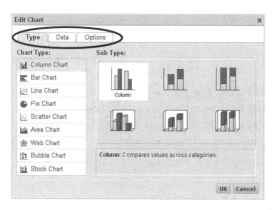

Figure 4.12
In the Edit Chart dialog box, tabs (circled) let you move straight to the part you want to edit.

If you want to make the chart bigger or smaller, place your cursor on the chart. When the frame appears, move your cursor to the frame's lower-right corner. (You'll see three diagonal lines marking the spot.) The cursor changes to a two-headed arrow; click-and-drag to make the chart bigger or smaller. When it's just the right size, let up on the mouse button.

Publishing a Chart on Your Website or Blog

Sheet lets you create a chart and then show it to the world on a web page or blog. To do this, you need a snippet of HTML code that tells web browsers where to find the chart so they can display it.

To get this code, pass your cursor over the chart to bring up its frame. At the top of the frame, click Publish. You'll see a Publish Chart dialog box like the one in Figure 4.13. The text box holds the snippet you need to publish your blog.

Click Select Snippet for an easy way to make sure you get the whole thing. Then press Ctrl+C or Cmd-C to copy the code. Next, paste the code into an HTML file and upload that file to your website or blog.

Later, if you need to find the HTML snippet again, bring up the chart's frame and click URL to see the same box shown in Figure 4.13. If you want to stop publishing the chart, bring up the frame and click Revert Publish.

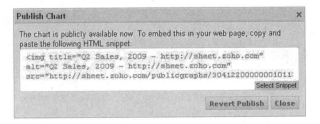

Figure 4.13
Copy and paste this snippet of code to display your chart on a web page or blog.

Deleting a Chart

When you're done with a chart, you don't want it hanging around and cluttering up your spreadsheet. You can get rid of an outdated chart by bringing up its frame (just pass your cursor over the chart) and clicking the frame's upper-right X. As soon as you click the X, Sheet deletes the chart. (There's no confirmation box, and Undo won't bring it back, so be careful not to click the X by mistake.)

Using Formulas and Functions

Any spreadsheet power-user knows the benefits of working with *formulas*, which take the numbers you've entered into your spreadsheet and work with them in various ways: adding, subtracting, multiplying, figuring percentages, and so on. You can write your own formulas from scratch, of course, but Zoho speeds up your formula writing by providing *functions*, prewritten formulas already programmed into Sheet. You can insert functions into your formulas, from commonly used functions (such as adding or averaging) to advanced engineering, statistical, and financial functions.

Entering a Formula

In a spreadsheet, a formula lives in a certain cell; the formula tells the cell what to display in that cell. As data changes, so does the result of the formula.

To write a formula, start by clicking the cell where you want the formula's result displayed. You'll see the cell displayed just above the spreadsheet, as shown in Figure 4.14. The text box to its right displays the cell's contents; this is where you write your formula. As you type, the formula appears in the selected cell. When you're done, hit Enter; Sheet goes to work calculating the formula and displays its results in the cell.

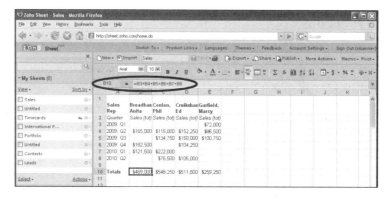

Figure 4.14
Choose a cell and then write a formula that tells Sheet what to display in that cell.

Basic spreadsheet formulas are easy to write. Here's the basic blueprint:

- **The equals sign (=)**—This tells Sheet that what you're typing is a formula; all formulas begin this way.

- **Numbers and/or references to cells**—You might tell the formula, for example, to add the contents of six cells and display the sum. (That's what the formula in Figure 4.14 is doing.) Or you might tell sheet to add a certain percentage to a number to calculate base price plus markup or price plus sales tax.

- **One or more operators**—Operators tell Sheet what to do with the numbers or cell references in the formula: add them, multiply them, and so on. Table 4.1 lists operators frequently used in spreadsheet formulas.

Figure 4.14 shows a simple formula that tells Sheet to add the contents of the cells in column B, beginning with B3 and ending with B8, and display the result in B10. Notice that the formula begins with an equals sign (=) and uses the add operator, which is a plus sign (+). If the contents of B3, B4, B5, B6, B7, or B8 change, the contents of B10 would change to reflect the new sum.

Table 4.1   Commonly Used Mathematical Operators

Operator	What It Does
+	Addition
-	Subtraction
*	Multiplication
/	Division
=	Equals

Working with Functions

Functions are built-in formulas that you can use to supercharge your own formulas, making complex formulas easier to write.

Functions consist of two parts: a function and an argument. The function comes first, and the argument immediately follows it, inside parentheses, like this:

function(argument)

The function tells Sheet what to do (such as SUM to add a series of numbers) and the argument tells Sheet what to work with (a cell or range of cells).

Here's a simple example: You could tell Sheet to add the numbers in a range of cells by writing a formula that uses the add operator between each cell, like the one shown back in Figure 4.14:

=B3+B4+B5+B6+B7+B8

Or you could use the SUM function and save yourself some typing:

=SUM(B3:B8)

Both ways of writing the formula produce the same result: add the contents of B3 through B8.

 Tip 4U For a list of functions and what they do, check out http://sheet.zoho.com/functions.do.
You can also get to this page by clicking the Reference link in the Insert Function dialog box (see Figure 4.15).

To insert a function, begin as if you were writing any formula—that is, click inside the cell that will show the formula's results. Next, click the toolbar's Insert Function button (the button with *fx* on it) to open the Insert Function dialog box, shown in Figure 4.15. Sheet starts off your formula for you by inserting an equals sign (=) in the formula bar; choose a function from the Insert Function box to start creating your formula.

Sheet offers lots of functions to choose from. Use the drop-down list in the upper-left part of the Insert Function box to browse function categories. When you choose a category (such as Date/Time, Mathematical, or Financial), the list changes to show functions in that category.

Click any function to insert it in your formula. If you choose SUM, for example (as in Figure 4.15), your formula looks like this:

=SUM()

Now, add the argument: Inside the parentheses, tell Sheet which cells you want the function to work on. For example, if you wanted to add up the numbers in column C of Figure 4.14, your formula would look like this:

=SUM(C3:C8)

Hit Enter when you're finished, and Sheet uses the function to make the calculation and display its results.

Tip 4U For one-click insertion of a function that adds a range of cells, select an empty cell that's immediately adjacent to the cells you want to add and then click the toolbar's Sum button. (It's the Greek letter sigma, Σ, and sits next to the Insert Function button.) Sheet inserts a SUM function that has the cells immediately to its left or above it as its argument. Check to make sure the function includes the correct range of cells; then hit Enter to get the sum.

Insert Function button

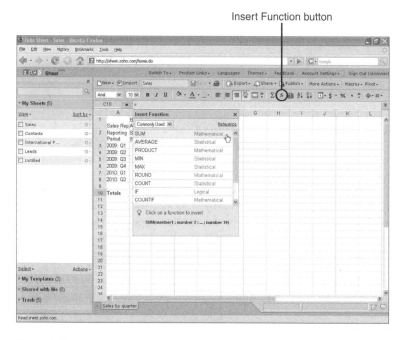

Figure 4.15
Choose a cell and then write a formula that tells Sheet what to display in that cell.

Tip 4U Make formula writing easier by naming a range of cells and then using the name in the formula. To name a cell range, select the range and right-click it and choose Name This Range. (Alternatively, you can select Name This Cell/Range.) This opens the Names List dialog box. Type the cell range name into the Add New Name box and then click Add. Sheet gives those cells the name you specified—and you can use that name in any formula you write.

Working with Macros

Macros save you time and effort on repetitive tasks. Instead of doing the same task over and over, you can record a macro for that task and then play back the macro whenever that task comes up.

Here's an example: Say you've got a set of column headings, formatted a certain way, that you use often. Instead of having to type those headings and then apply formatting every time you need them, you can perform those actions just once, recording them as a macro. Next time you need to insert those headings in a spreadsheet, play the macro and—presto!—there are your headings. You can then focus on the next task.

Recording a macro is just what it sounds like: Every action you perform, whether on the keyboard or with the mouse, is captured by Sheet. When you play back the macro, those actions are done all over again.

 When you record a macro, Sheet captures everything you do—the mistakes as well as the planned actions. So it's a good idea to write down the sequence of actions you'll record and use it as a script to make sure the macro does exactly what you want it to.

Recording a Macro

To create a brand-new macro, click the Macros button in the upper-right part of the screen. From the menu that appears, choose Record Macro to open the Create Macro dialog box, shown in Figure 4.16.

In the Create Macro box, make sure that the Record radio button is enabled. (The Write Macro option is for programming types who know VBA, or Visual Basic for Applications.) Give your macro a name (so you can find it later to play it back) and, if you want, a description. Check the Use Relative Reference box if you want to be able to play the macro on any part of the spreadsheet, not just the cells where you're recording the macro. When you're ready, click Start Recording.

Sheet displays a message above the spreadsheet that says "Macro Recording in progress," as you can see in Figure 4.17. Now, do the series of actions that you want to record. Take your time and make sure you get the sequence of actions just right. But don't worry about making a mistake— if you do, just click Cancel, click OK to confirm, and start over.

When you're finished, click Stop Recording (see Figure 4.17). If all went well, Sheet tells you that the macro was recorded successfully and adds the newly recorded macro to your Macros List.

When you're recording a macro, keep in mind that there are some actions you can't record:

- Creating a new spreadsheet or template
- Deleting a spreadsheet or template
- Using Save As options
- Importing
- Exporting

- Sharing
- Publishing
- Versioning
- Tagging
- Commenting
- Creating a pivot table or pivot chart
- Editing collaboratively

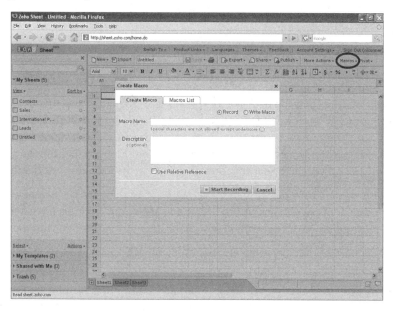

Figure 4.16
Naming your macro is the first step in creating it.

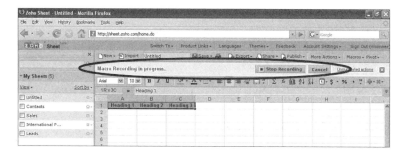

Figure 4.17
Sheet tells you when you're recording your macro; click Stop Recording when you're done.

Playing a Macro

When you're ready to put your macro to work, open the spreadsheet where the macro will do its thing. If you used a relative reference while recording the macro, select the cell or range where you want the macro to work. Click Macros, Run Macro. This opens a list of the macros you've recorded. Find and click the macro you want to run it.

 If you know VBA, you can edit your recorded macros or write a macro from scratch. To write your own macro, choose Write Macro in the Create Macro dialog box and click Write to open a VBA editor. (Or you can take the direct route by selecting Macros, VBA Editor.) To edit an existing macro, click Macros, View Macros. Then select the macro you want to edit to open it in the VBA editor.

Creating Pivot Tables and Charts

A *pivot table* sorts and sums the data in your spreadsheet, no matter how that data is arranged in the spreadsheet itself. This kind of table is particularly useful for summarizing data in database-style tables. Use pivot tables to cross-tabulate (summarize and analyze) your data, presenting it in easy-to-read tables and charts. Create a summary table simply by choosing the columns you want to compare. A *pivot chart* does the same thing, but in the form of a graph rather than a table.

To get the most out of pivot tables and charts (and to keep from tearing your hair out in frustration), keep these guidelines in mind for choosing the data that works best with these reports:

- Make sure the data includes some numbers. A pivot table or chart needs numbers to create subtotals.
- Make sure at least one column contains duplicate values. In the example we'll develop in this section, the spreadsheet tracks the amount of time employees have spent on two different projects. So the Project Name column repeats *Smith Project* and *Jones Project* for different weeks and for different employees.

Creating a Pivot Table

The first step in creating a pivot table is to click Pivot, Create Pivot Table and open the Create Pivot Report box shown in Figure 4.18.

In this dialog box, the Pivot Table radio button is preselected. Give your pivot table a title (required), a description (optional), and a data range (also required). The data range tells Sheet which cells to include in the pivot table (for example, A2:E25).

When you're ready, click Design Pivot to go to the next step.

In the Design Pivot dialog box, shown in Figure 4.19, drag the rows and columns you want into the appropriate boxes and then drop them there. If you want to filter the data, click the Filter tab and choose the values you want to filter. To see how your pivot table is shaping up, click the link Click Here to Generate Pivot. This displays a sneak peek of the pivot table in the Preview window, as shown in Figure 4.20.

When your table looks good, click Done. Sheet creates your pivot table and puts it on a new sheet in your spreadsheet.

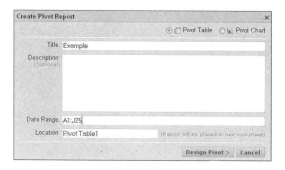

Figure 4.18
Name your pivot table and designate a range for its data.

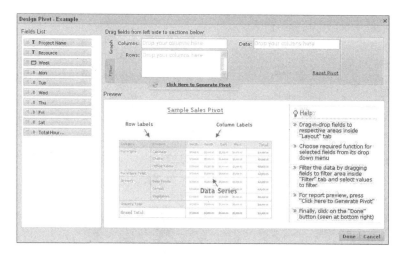

Figure 4.19
Drag fields from the Fields List into the Columns, Rows, and Data boxes.

Creating a Pivot Chart

If your data would display better in a chart, create a pivot chart instead of a table. The process is basically the same: Select Pivot, Create Pivot Chart. Name the chart and specify the data range. So far, so good.

When you're creating a chart, you need to tell Sheet what to use for the x- and y-axes. And if you want, you can also specify which data to use for different colors and text in the chart. Preview the chart to make sure it shows the data you want to display; click Done to create the chart on a new tab of your spreadsheet.

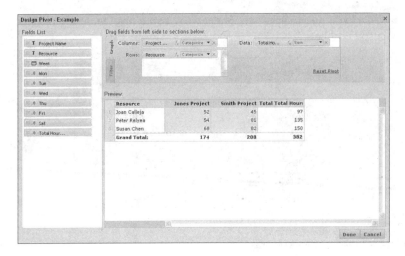

Figure 4.20
You can preview your pivot table before you create it.

Figure 4.21 shows an example of a pivot chart that compares hours spent by employees on two projects.

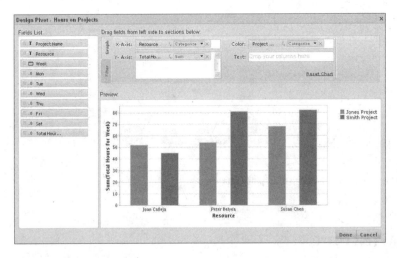

Figure 4.21
You can create pivot charts, as well as pivot tables, with Sheet.

Working with Pivot Tables and Charts

After you've created your pivot table or pivot chart, you can work with it in various ways. To see the table or chart, click the tab of the sheet that holds it. From there, you can perform these actions:

▪ **Change its name or description.** Click Pivot Properties, which opens a dialog box where you can rename the table or chart. You can also add or revise a description here. Click Update to save.

▪ **Edit its design.** To edit your table or chart, click the Edit Design button. This opens a dialog box that looks just like the one you used to create the pivot table/chart, with the choices you made filled in. Make your changes; then click Done to save them and revise your pivot table/chart.

▪ **Change the cell range.** To expand or contract the range of cells your chart or table uses to get its data, click Source Data. In the dialog box that opens, type in the new cell range and then click OK.

▪ **Refresh the data.** If you've made changes to the spreadsheet, click the Refresh Data button to update the pivot table or chart.

▪ **Delete a pivot table or chart.** To do this, delete the sheet that holds the table/chart you want to delete. Right-click the tab of the sheet you want to get rid of; from the context menu that appears, select Delete. Zoho asks for confirmation; click OK and it's gone.

Working with External Data

If you frequently update your spreadsheet with external data posted elsewhere on the Web, you're going to love this feature. Sheet can grab external data automatically—whether it comes from a CSV file, HTML page, or newsfeed—and insert that data into your spreadsheet. You tell Sheet what to fetch and how often to fetch it, and Sheet does the rest.

For example, say you want to know when a public calendar or stock price is updated. By linking to that external data, you can get the update and insert it in your Sheet spreadsheet, automatically. In fact, if you tell it to, Sheet will check the external data at a time interval you specify and automatically update your spreadsheet.

Linking to External Data

To link your spreadsheet to external data, the first thing you need to do is get the address of the feed, so you can tell Sheet where to get the external info you want.

Sheet can link to external data in three ways:

▪ **CSV Data**—This stands for *comma-separated values*, which is a common format for transferring data from one spreadsheet to another. Look for the site's public CSV feed to get the data.

▪ **RSS/Atom Feed**—RSS (really simple syndication) and Atom are two ways that programs can check for updates published on a website.

▪ **HTML Page**—If a website has a table that's periodically updated, you can grab the updated information by giving Sheet its URL (web address).

Open the page that has the data you want Sheet to fetch and choose one of these three methods for getting it. Copy the URL you need to export the data, so you can give that URL to Sheet.

Step 1: Point to the External Data

Back in Sheet, open the spreadsheet that will receive the external data. Select More Actions, Link External Data to open the External Data Dialog box shown in Figure 4.22. In that box, select the kind of URL you're providing and then paste that URL into the text box. Click Next.

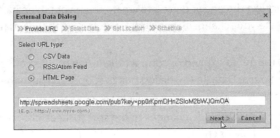

Figure 4.22
Let Sheet know where to find the external data you're linking to.

Step 2: Select the Data Your Want

Sheet goes to the URL you gave and presents a dialog box like the one in Figure 4.23. Look carefully at the tables and columns it shows, and check the box for the table and columns you want in your spreadsheet. When you've done that, click Next.

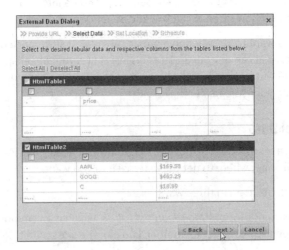

Figure 4.23
Check the boxes for the table(s) and column(s) you want to link to.

Step 3: Situate the Data in Your Spreadsheet

The next step is to tell Sheet where to display the external data in your Zoho Sheet spreadsheet, by sheet name and starting cell. Select a sheet from the drop-down (if you don't want the current one) and type the starting cell into the text box (Alternatively, you can click a cell in the spreadsheet.) Click Next.

Step 4: Schedule Updates

In this step, you tell Sheet how often you want it to check the external site for new data. To do this, enable the Now and Schedule Periodically radio button. When you do, the dialog box expands so that you can schedule updates, as shown in Figure 4.24. You can schedule updates to happen daily, weekly, monthly, or every x number of hours or even minutes. Or if you prefer, you can grab the data now and not worry about updates—just enable the Only Once and Now radio button.

Make your selection and then click Done to bring the external data into your spreadsheet, as shown in Figure 4.25.

 Some websites have limits on how frequently programs can poll them (that is, check their data). To make sure you're not exceeding these limits, check the site's terms and conditions, and keep your Sheet updates within those limits.

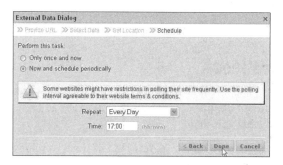

Figure 4.24
Tell Sheet how often to check for new data.

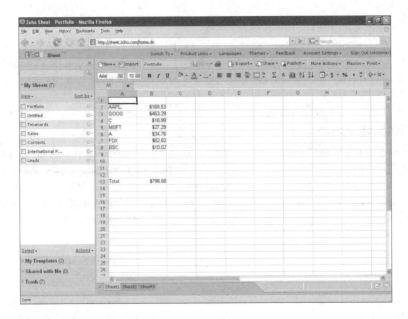

Figure 4.25
This data has been grabbed from an external spreadsheet and posted to Sheet.

Sharing a Spreadsheet

Sharing a spreadsheet in Sheet is almost exactly like sharing a presentation in Zoho Show—with one exception. So check out Chapter 3, "Presenting…Zoho Show," to get step-by-step details for sharing and managing what you share.

The exception? You can see it in Figure 4.26. You can tell Sheet to share an entire spreadsheet or just one sheet within it. So choose which you want to share. If you enable the Specific Sheets radio button, the Share This Document dialog box changes so you can select which sheet (or sheets) you want to share. Select the level of permission you want for each sheet (the options are Read Only, Read/Write, and Hide), tell Sheet whom you're sharing with, and then click the Share button.

Collaborating with Others

When you invite others to work on a spreadsheet with you, collaboration happens in real time. That means if Peter Relyea and Susan Chen are both working on the same spreadsheet at the same time, any changes Peter makes appear on Susan's screen, and vice versa. Because these changes happen as they're made, you don't have to refresh the screen to see them.

 When you're working in a spreadsheet and someone else either opens or closes the same spreadsheet, Sheet notifies you with a box the lower-right part of the screen.

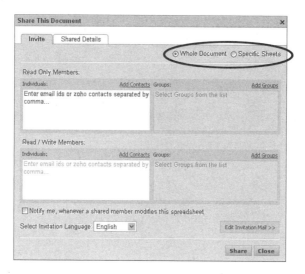

Figure 4.26
Share an entire spreadsheet or just part of it.

Discussing Shared Spreadsheets

When someone else is viewing or working on a spreadsheet at the same time you are, Sheet lets you know with a notification in the status bar at the bottom of the screen, as shown in Figure 4.27. In the figure, one other person is working on the spreadsheet, so the status bar shows "1 Viewing." When you click that [Number] Viewing link or the speech bubble to its right, Sheet opens a chat pane (shown in Figure 4.27) where you can discuss the spreadsheet with your collaborators.

Type in the text box at the bottom of the chat pane and hit Enter to display your thoughts to everyone else who's working on the spreadsheet right now.

 Sheet doesn't lock the cells you're working in when you and a collaborator are editing. So use the chat feature to let others know which section you're working on. Otherwise, your work could get overwritten by someone else.

Commenting on a Spreadsheet

When you and your collaborators are working at the same time, you can use chat to ask questions, make comments, and resolve issues. But if it's 2:00 a.m. and you're the only person who's working instead of sleeping, you can leave comments for others to read.

To add a comment, click the Comments button at the right side of the status bar to open the comments pane, shown in Figure 4.28. Any existing comments appear in this pane. Type your comment into the New Comment box and then click Add to post your comment.

To edit or delete a comment, click the Comments button to open the comments pane. Find the comment you want and then click its Edit link (to change the comment to an editable text box) or its Remove link (to delete it).

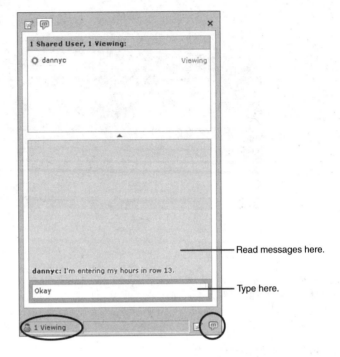

Figure 4.27
Click the circled link or button to open a chat pane.

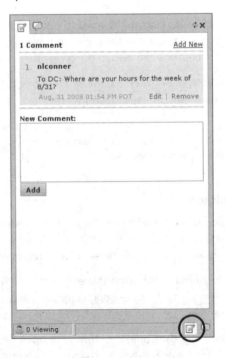

Figure 4.28
Click the Comments button (circled) to view comments or add one of your own.

Collaborators can delete only their own comments. If you created the application and shared it with others, though, you own that application and can remove anyone's comments.

Viewing a Spreadsheet's Version History

As with other Zoho applications, you can view a spreadsheet's past versions and, if you want, revert to one of those. To see previous versions, click More Actions, View Version History. This opens a dialog box like the one shown in Figure 4.29.

In the Version History dialog box, you can view, revert to, or delete any version of the spreadsheet. Click View to see a full-sized version of the spreadsheet. You can't edit this version (because it's a snapshot of a previously saved version), but you can revert to it, making it the current version of the spreadsheet. To revert to a version that you're viewing, click Actions, Revert to This Version.

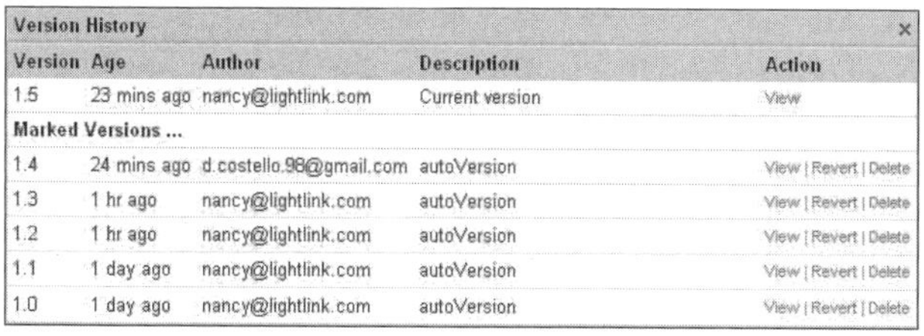

Version History					×
Version	Age	Author	Description		Action
1.5	23 mins ago	nancy@lightlink.com	Current version		View
Marked Versions ...					
1.4	24 mins ago	d.costello.98@gmail.com	autoVersion		View | Revert | Delete
1.3	1 hr ago	nancy@lightlink.com	autoVersion		View | Revert | Delete
1.2	1 hr ago	nancy@lightlink.com	autoVersion		View | Revert | Delete
1.1	1 day ago	nancy@lightlink.com	autoVersion		View | Revert | Delete
1.0	1 day ago	nancy@lightlink.com	autoVersion		View | Revert | Delete

Figure 4.29
Choose a previous version from the Version History list and click View to see it.

 You can export a previous version of your spreadsheet. View the version you want and click Export to export it just as you normally would (see the earlier section "Exporting a Spreadsheet").

5

Zoho Reports: Online Databases and Reports

Whether you're finally getting around to organizing your CD collection or tracking purchase order requests for your department, Zoho Reports can help you store, organize, and report on your data. Its spreadsheet-style interface, a grid of rows and columns, makes data entry a cinch. (You can also import data from an existing spreadsheet and create a new database that way.) Of course, storing your data on the Web means that you (and anyone you share with) can access it from anywhere: on the road, at home, in your favorite coffee shop, or waiting for a flight.

Perhaps the best thing about Reports is the wealth of ways you can report on your data: charts, tables, summaries, pivot tables, and more. You don't have to be a database expert to create these reports—just drag-and-drop the columns you want to report on.

Creating a Database

A *database* is a program that holds data, that is, information. A database is essentially like a big spreadsheet or table, with rows that represent *records* (complete information for one item in the table) and columns that represent *fields* (kinds of information). For example, imagine you're creating a database to keep track of contact information for members of your high school class. Fields would probably include name, street, town or city, state, ZIP code, phone number, and email address. You can think of these field names as column headings across the top of a table; each field collects one particular kind of information. If you read down the name column, you get a list of all names in the table. When you look at one of those names and read it as a single row across the table, you're looking at a record: You get a complete picture of each classmate's info by reading across.

When you're ready to try your hand at creating a database, Reports gives you several approaches, as Figure 5.1 shows. You can build the database from scratch, use a handy template, import existing data, or just start entering data and build the database as you go along. This section explains each method.

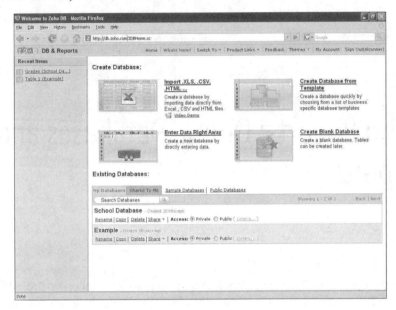

Figure 5.1
Create a new database (top of page) or open an existing one (bottom of page).

From Scratch

If you want to design your database from the ground up, sign in to Reports (reports.zoho.com). On the welcome page, shown in Figure 5.1, click Create Blank Database. The Create Blank Database dialog box asks you to name the database (50 characters or less) and add an optional description and tags. When you've done that, click Create to open the Create New Table page, shown in Figure 5.2.

Here, Reports asks you to set up the first table in your database. You've got four methods to choose from:

- **Import .XLS, .CSV, .HTML...Files**—Import existing data in one of these file formats.
- **Using Design View**—Name columns and specify data types and column properties.
- **Enter Data Right Away**—Start entering data, and let Reports create a table based on that.
- **Query Table**—Extract data from an existing table using the SQL SELECT query.

Choose a method for creating your table. (Skip ahead to the "Working with Tables" section to learn more about the ways to create a table.) When you save the table, your new database is up and running. Click the Home link at the top of the page to return to the Reports home page and see your new database in the My Databases list.

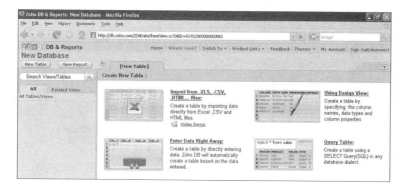

Figure 5.2
Choose a method for creating the first table in your new database.

By Entering Data

If you're one of those who takes the hit-the-ground-running approach, you can create a new database simply by naming the database and typing in data. It's just like creating a new database from scratch (previous section), but it skips the step of asking how you want to create the database's first table.

On the Reports home page (reports.zoho.com), click Enter Data Right Away. This opens a dialog box where you type in the new database's name and, if you want, a description and tags. Click Create.

Reports creates your database and presents a table where you can start entering data. For more on filling your table with data, see "Adding and Editing Data," later in this chapter.

From a Template

If you're new to Reports, a good way to get your first database up and running is to piggyback on someone else's hard work. Reports has several predesigned templates that offer a blueprint for your own database. Currently, Reports offers the following templates:

- **Project Manager**—For tracking tasks and progress in a project
- **Issue Manager**—To keep track of and deal with bugs and other issues in IT development
- **Google Adword Campaign Performance Analysis**—To track and analyze how your advertising campaign with Google AdWords is doing

If one of these templates meets your needs, sign in to the Reports home page (reports.zoho.com) and click Create Database from Template. This opens the dialog box shown in Figure 5.3.

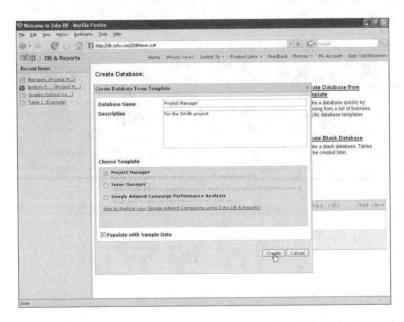

Figure 5.3
Choose a predesigned template to get a head start on your new database.

In the Create Database from Template dialog box, type in a name for your database (required) and an optional description. Next, select the template you want. If you want to see sample data in your new database (a good way to get a sense of how the database works), leave the Populate with Sample Data box checked. If you don't need to see any sample data, uncheck the box. Click Create.

Zoho sets up your new database based on the template you chose. Figure 5.4 shows an example of a database made from the Project Manager template. It displays a report in the center of the screen and a list of the database's existing tables and reports in the list on the left.

 If you choose to include sample data in a database you build from a template, you'll want to delete that data before adding your own. To do this, open a table (click its name in the left list) and select Delete, Delete All Rows. This saves the table's structure (for example, column headings) but gets rid of its records, that is, its data.

By Importing

If you already have data in a file and you want to use that data as the basis for a new database, you can import it, creating the new database as part of the import. To create a database using this method, start on the Reports home page (reports.zoho.com) and click the Import .XLS, .CSV., HTML link.

The Step 1 of 2: Create Database (Import) box opens, as shown in Figure 5.5. Start by giving your database a name (required), a description (optional), and any tags you want to label it with (also optional).

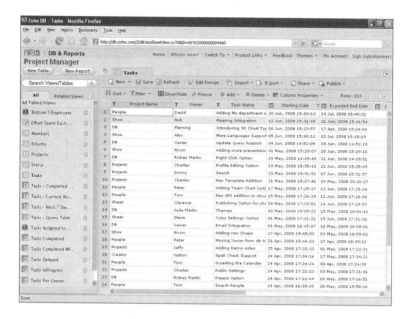

Figure 5.4
This database, complete with sample data, was created using Zoho's Project Manager template.

Next, use the File Type drop-down to choose the kind of file you're going to import:

- Comma-Separated Value (.csv). This option also works with tab-separated value (.tsv) files.
- Excel (.xls) or OpenOffice.org Calc (.sxc).
- HTML Content (which must have at least one table in it).

Info 4U When you're importing a file to create a database, the file should be smaller than 3MB and have fewer than 100,000 rows.

After you've chosen the kind of file you'll import, tell Reports where to find it by choosing one of these Data Location options:

- **Pasted Data**—When you enable this radio button, Reports provides a roomy text box. Copy your source data and paste it into the text box.

Info 4U Pasted Data is the only option available for importing an .xls or .sxc file.

- **Local Drive**—If the CSV or HTML file you want to import is stored on your computer, enable this radio button and then browse to the file's location on your computer. Select the file and click OK to insert the file's location in the File text box.
- **Web**—When you're importing or a CSV or HTML file that lives on the Web, click this radio button. In the Url box, paste in the web address of the file.

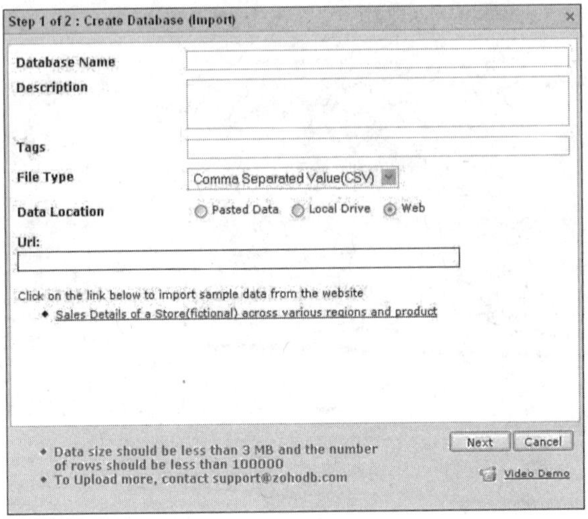

Figure 5.5
Tell Zoho what kind of file to import and where to find it.

Tip 4U If you've got a table in a document, such as a Word document, you can easily import it into Reports—no need to convert the table to text or save it as a separate file first. Copy the table. In the Step 1 of 2: Create Database (Import) dialog box, select CSV as the file type and Pasted Data as the data location. Paste the table you copied into the text box and then continue with the import.

When you've filled in the info needed for step 1 of the import, click Next. This takes you to the second step in a new database via import: creating a table based on the data you imported. As Figure 5.6 shows, in this step Reports looks at the imported data and turns it into a table. Here, you fine-tune the table so it will appear the way you want it in the new database.

In the Step 2 of 2: Create Database (Import) box, take a look at these settings:

- **Table Name**—You've already given your database a name; here's where you type in the name of your first table. Give it a name that suggests the kind of records it holds, such as Contacts, Orders, Timecards, or whatever.

- **First Row Contains Column Names**—Take a look a the table preview in the bottom half of the dialog box. The first row (shown in orange) holds the contents of the first row of the file you imported. If this first row will become column headers in your table, select Yes. Otherwise, select No, and Reports moves the contents of that row down, changing the column headings to Column 1, Column 2, and so on. (You can rename the columns later.)

- **Date format of the column(s)**—If one of the columns holds dates, this section shows the formatting for those dates. To select a different format, click Choose Matching Date Format and make your choice from the box that opens.

- **Preview**—This section shows what the new table will look like. If you don't want to import a column, uncheck its box. If you want to change a column heading, double-click that heading to change the column's name to a text box. For each column, choose a format from the drop-down list:

    - Text includes plain text, multiline text (which is roomier than plain text), and email field types.

    - Numeric includes number, positive number, decimal, currency, and percent field types.

    - Others includes date and decision box (check box) field types. If you're designating a column as a Date column, be sure to select a date format that matches your data. (Click the Choose Matching Date Format link.)

- **On Import Errors**—If there's a problem with the import, Reports needs to know how to handle it. Choose one of these options:

    - Set Empty Value for the Column continues with the import but leaves the troublesome column empty—so you may not get all your data.

    - Skip Corresponding Rows jumps over any rows that present a problem with the import.

    - Don't Import the Data cancels the import if there's a problem.

When you're ready, click Create. Zoho imports your data and gives you a summary to show how many columns and rows were successfully imported. Click Close to see the imported data in your shiny new database.

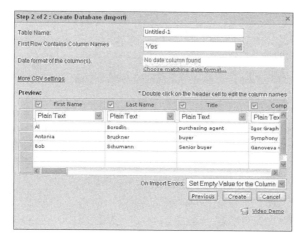

Figure 5.6
Use the Preview section to fine-tune your new table before you import the data to create it.

 Zoho has created a video demonstration to walk you through the process of creating a new database by importing an existing file. Look on the Reports home page, under the Import .XLS, .CSV., HTML link; click Video Demo to launch the demo in the current window.

Working with Data

After you've created a database, the next thing you'll probably want to do is work with its data. You can add new data, edit existing data, save tables, and export data to other applications. Read on to learn more.

Adding and Editing Data

As you can see in Figure 5.7, a Reports table looks like a spreadsheet—and it works much like a spreadsheet, as well. Double-click any cell to type in it. Use the Tab key or arrow keys to move between cells.

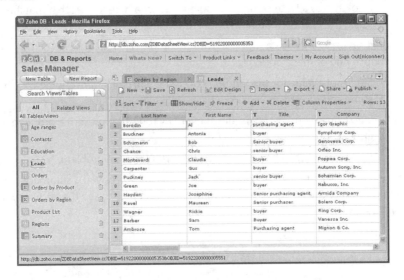

Figure 5.7
A database looks a lot like a spreadsheet: Columns represent fields and rows represent records.

 To see at a glance what kind of data a column holds, look at the symbol to the right of the column's header. For example, the Ts in Figure 5.7 tell you that these columns hold text. Other symbols for common datatypes include # for numeric, $ for currency, a calendar icon for date, an envelope icon for email address, and so on.

Saving Data

When you've made some changes to a table, click the Save button or press Ctrl+S. If there are unsaved changes and you try to sign out or navigate away from the table, Zoho pops up a box that warns you that you haven't saved some data. Click Cancel (to stay on the current page), save your table, and then you can leave the page.

Exporting Data

There are two ways you can export data from a Reports table:

- As a CSV file (a text file that uses commas or other markers to separate pieces of data)
- As a PDF (to be viewed using Adobe Acrobat or Adobe Reader)

The steps of the export vary according the kind of file you choose.

Exporting as a CSV File

To export data as a CSV file, open the table whose data you want to export and then click Export, Export as CSV. This opens the Export Data: Settings dialog box shown in Figure 5.8.

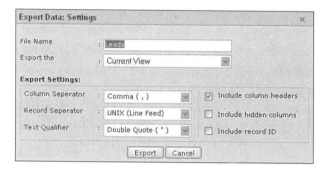

Figure 5.8
One option for exporting data from a Reports table is to export it as a CSV file.

In this box, name the file and choose the view you want to export. (For more on the kinds of views, or reports, you can create with Reports, see "Viewing Your Data" later in this chapter.)

Next, choose the settings for your export. The Export Settings section has these choices:

- **Column Separator**—Use this drop-down to choose the marker that separates pieces of data for each record in the CSV file you're creating: commas, tabs, semicolons, or spaces.
- **Record Separator**—This indicates when a row ends, using one of these platform-specific choices: Windows (Carriage Return + Line Feed), UNIX (Line Feed), or Macintosh (Carriage Return).
- **Text Qualifier**—A *text qualifier* indicates that certain text belongs to a cell, even if it has a column or record separator in it. For example, the quotation marks around "August 31, 2009" indicate that the comma in that phrase is text, not a marker of a new piece of data. You can choose double or single quotation marks for text qualifiers. (Excel uses double quotes for this purpose.)

Optionally, you can include or exclude the table's column headings, hidden columns, and a unique ID for each record in the export. Check or uncheck these options as you prefer.

Click Export. A dialog box opens, asking how you want to deal with the file you're exporting. You can open it with a spreadsheet program or save it to your computer. Choose the option you want and then click OK to export the file.

Exporting as a PDF File

This is a great way to email or print a nicely formatted table from a table in your database. Simply export it as a PDF (Portable Document Format) file and open it in Adobe Acrobat or Adobe Reader (available for free download at www.adobe.com). Unlike CSV files, you can't edit PDF files, so use these when you want a read-only view of your data.

Click Export, Export as PDF to open the Export as PDF – Settings dialog box, shown in Figure 5.9. This dialog box has two tabs: one for formatting and other options; the other for setting the margins, header, and footer of the final PDF file.

Format & Options

This tab, shown in Figure 5.9, has several sections:

- **Options**—Here's where you name the file and choose a paper size (letter, legal, A4, and so on).
- **Orientation**—Choose portrait (vertically oriented) or landscape (horizontally oriented).
- **Title and Description**—You can have these items appear at the top of the PDF, at the bottom, or not at all.
- **Select Columns to Export**—You may not want every single column in your table to appear in the PDF—or you may find that not all columns fit. Use this section to tell Zoho which columns to include.

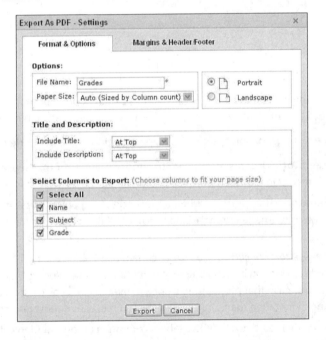

Figure 5.9
Export data to a PDF file.

Margins & Header/Footer

You have some options about margin size and what appears in your PDF file's header and footer, as Figure 5.10 shows. Whether you're adjusting the top, bottom, left, or right margin, keep the settings between zero and one inch. (Between 0.25 inches and 0.5 inches looks good for many purposes.)

This tab is also where you determine what, if anything, goes in the PDF file's header and footer. The drop-down lists here let you decide what (if anything) to put in the left, center, and right sections of header and/or footer. Each drop-down contains these options: blank, title, date/time, page number, page # of #, and custom (so you can type in your own text).

When you've set up both tabs the way you want them, click Export. Tell your computer whether you want to open the file using Adobe Acrobat (or Reader) or save it to your computer and click OK.

After you've exported the data as a PDF file, you can save that file, print it, attach it to an email—just as you would for any PDF. Figure 5.11 shows an example of a PDF file exported from a Reports table.

Figure 5.10
Set the PDF file's margins, header, and footer.

 You can export multiple tables, views, or both, in a single PDF file. When you click Export, Export Multiple Views (PDF), a new section appears on the Format & Options tab of the Export as PDF dialog box. This section, Select Views to Export, has a list of all the tables and views in your database. Select the ones you want by checking their boxes (or simply check the Select All box) and then continue with the export. Zoho exports all the files you chose into one PDF file—and even throws in a table of contents as a bonus.

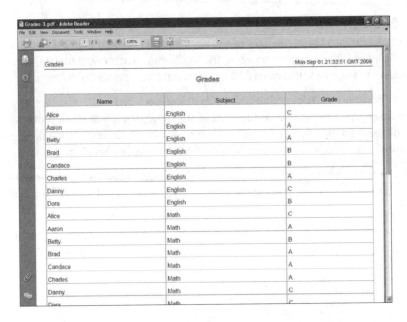

Figure 5.11
This table was exported in PDF format from Zoho Reports.

Working with Tables

In a database, a table is what holds your information; it provides the structure into which you put your data. A database can have multiple tables; for example, a database that manages your sales force could have separate tables for leads, customers, and orders. Looking at those tables, you can probably see that some tables are related—such as customers and orders—and you can create a relationship between such tables so that one table can draw relevant information from the other. In fact, there's lots you can do with tables in Reports, and this section gets you up and running.

Creating a New Table

As mentioned earlier in this chapter, in the section on creating a new database from scratch, you've got a bunch of options for setting up a new table. This section describes each method in detail. To get started, open the database that will hold the new table and click the New Table button. (Alternatively, if you prefer, you can click New, New Table.) This opens the Create New Table page (shown back in Figure 5.2).

Importing Data

When you have data in a spreadsheet or table that you want to use as the basis for a new table in Reports, you can import that data from a Microsoft Excel or OpenOffice.org Calc spreadsheet, an HTML file, or comma- or tab-separated value (CSV, TSV) file.

Click New Table and then choose Import from .XLS, .CSV, .HTML files to open the Step 1 of 2: Create Table (Import) dialog box. From there, the process is the same as creating a new database by importing a file, except that you name the new table in step 1 rather than in step 2. Flip back to the section on creating a new database by importing data to get step-by-step instructions on how to set up a new table by importing data from another program.

Using Design View

When you choose this option for creating a new table, you design your new table from the ground up, creating columns and defining various properties (such as the kind of data the column will hold) for each. To get started with do-it-yourself table design, click New Table and select Using Design View. The Edit Design dialog box, shown in Figure 5.12, opens.

In the Edit Design box, each row defines a column in the table you're creating. Start by typing in the name of the column; then for that column (moving from left to right), set up this information:

- **Data Type**—What kind of information will the column hold? Double-click a cell in this column and choose a data type, such as plain text, email, date, currency, decision box, and so on.

- **Mandatory**—To specify that a field must contain data, double-click in this column and choose Yes from the drop-down list. No (the default) means that it's okay to leave the field empty.

- **Default**—If you want a standard value to appear in this column when a user adds a new record, type that value in here. (Be aware that users can double-click the cell to overwrite it.)

- **Lookup Column**—A *lookup field* creates a relationship between two tables in the database by looking up data from one table and automatically inserting it another. Double-click this cell and choose a table and column from the drop-down list. Read the "Creating a Relationship Between Tables" section of this chapter to learn more about how relationships work.

- **Formula**—You can insert a formula here that determines the field's contents. For example, you might have a Total Price column whose contents are determined by adding the contents of the Price column and the Markup column.

 For more on formulas, see Chapter 4, "Track Data with Zoho Sheet."

- **Description**—You can write a description to explain what the column's about. The description appears in the Edit Design box.

When you're done, click Save. To close the Edit Design box, click its upper-right X.

Entering Data to Create a Table

This is a fast-and-easy way to get your new table started. When you click New Table, Enter Data Right Away, you see a brand-new, blank table. All of the columns are numbered rather than named. (To rename a column, right-click it and select Rename Column from the context menu.)

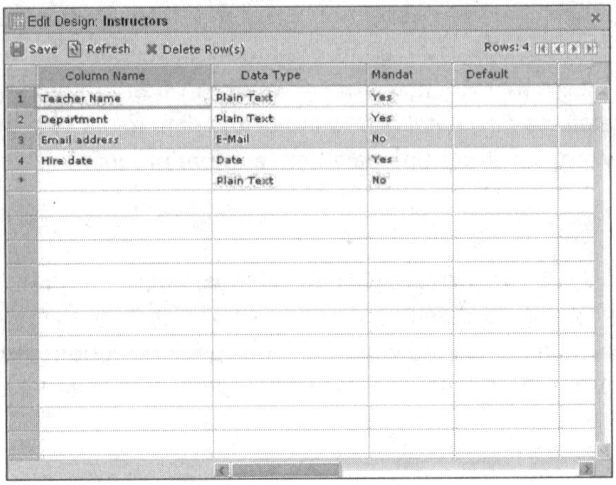

Edit Design: Instructors				✕
📄 Save 📄 Refresh ✕ Delete Row(s)			Rows: 4	◄◄ ◄ ► ►►
Column Name	Data Type	Mandat	Default	
1 Teacher Name	Plain Text	Yes		
2 Department	Plain Text	Yes		
3 Email address	E-Mail	No		
4 Hire date	Date	Yes		
*	Plain Text	No		

Figure 5.12
Each row you design here becomes a column in the new table.

Double-click inside a cell and start entering data; hit Tab or an arrow key to move between cells. As you type, Reports guesses each column's type based on what you entered—so make sure your columns line up, containing the same kind of data. For example, *Joe Smith* would become a plain-text column, and *09/02/2009* would become a date column. To adjust a column's data type, see the upcoming "Editing a Table's Design" section.

Click Save to give to name the table and give it an optional description. Click OK to save the table you just named.

Fetching Data from an Existing Table

Even if you think SQL stands for *South Queensland Library* or *specified quality level*, you can still use it to create a new table by fetching certain data from an existing table. (In case you were wondering, SQL stands for *structured query language*, and it's a standardized language for accessing the info in a database.) You'd create a new table in this way when you want to use a subset of data as the basis for its own table. For example, say your sales management database lists all sales reps for all regions, but you want a table listing only those sales reps in one particular region.

 What's your favorite flavor of SQL? Zoho Reports probably supports it. Currently, you can use SQL Server, MySQL, Oracle, Sybase, Informix, PostgreSQL, and ANSI SQL.

To create a new table by grabbing some of the columns from an existing table, start by opening the database that holds the existing table and selecting either New Table, Query Table or New, New Query Table. Either way, a tab that looks like the one in Figure 5.13 opens.

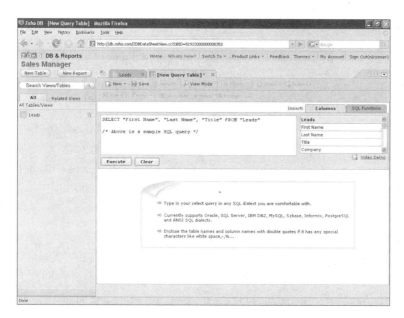

Figure 5.13
If you're not familiar with SQL, study Zoho's sample query and use it as a model for your own.

The [New Query Table] tab is where you write a query to create your new table. Zoho helpfully includes a sample query, so you can get an idea of what your query will look like. A simple SQL query for creating a new table looks like this:

```
SELECT "First Column Name", "Second Column Name", "Third Column Name"
FROM "Table Name"
```

In other words, you're telling Reports to *select* specific columns *from* a specific table and then use those columns to create the new table. Notice that the names of the columns and the name of the table are enclosed in double quotation marks. Also, a comma separates column names.

Now that you know what goes into a SQL SELECT query, you can easily write your own. Zoho makes it even easier for you: You don't have to type in table and column names—just click a name in the Columns list (on the right), and it appears in the query you're writing, double-quotes and all. (But don't forget to put commas between multiple names.)

 In the Columns list, column names have a white background; table names are both shaded and bold.

When you've selected the columns from the table (or tables) you want, click Execute to preview the new table. The preview appears in the lower half of the [New Query Table] tab.

Tip 4U To select columns from different tables in the same database, structure your query like this: SELECT "First Column Name", "Second Column Name", "Third Column Name" FROM "First Table Name", "Second Table Name".

If you want, make adjustments to your table by revising the query you wrote. When the preview table looks good, make it a real table by clicking Save, naming the table, and clicking OK. To see your new table, click the View Mode button near the top of the tab.

 If you're adept at writing SQL queries, the [New Query Table] tab has a list of functions you can use to fine-tune your queries. Click the SQL Functions tab to see what's available.

Editing Tables

As you work with your database, you'll probably find you need to tweak a table or two, such as adding a new column, renaming an existing one, changing a data type, and so on. Reports gives you several options for editing a table, as this section explains.

Editing Columns

The quickest way to make changes to a column is to right-click its header. This brings up the context menu shown in Figure 5.14. Here's what the context menu lets you do:

- **Sort**—For more on sorting data, read the upcoming "Sorting and Filtering Data" section.
- **Hide Column**—This option removes the column from the table's display but doesn't actually delete the column and its data. (The Delete option is at the bottom of the menu.)
- **Freeze Column**—To keep a column out of a sort, choose this option—and read the section "Sorting and Filtering Data" to find out more.
- **Add Column**—Choose this menu item, give the new column a name, pick its data type, and then click OK. Zoho adds the new column at the far right of your table.

 Don't like where Zoho put your new column? To move a column, click its header, drag it to the new location, and let up on the mouse button to drop it there.

- **Add Formula Column**—When you choose this option, a new menu flies out that contains possible formulas you might want, based on the column's data type. You can select one of these options or create your own custom formula. Either way, Zoho adds the new column as the rightmost column in the table.
- **Format Column**—Choosing this option opens a dialog box where you can set the columns alignment: left (which is the standard), center, or right.
- **Rename Column**—Click this option to get a dialog box where you can change a column's name as well as revise (or add) its description.
- **Change Datatype**—Use this option to choose the kind of data the column holds, such as making cells in a text column roomier by changing from Plain Text to Multi Line Text or changing a numeric column from Positive Number to Currency.

 Be careful when you're changing a column's datatype. When a column contains data (for example, email addresses) and you try to change that column to a type incompatible with that existing data (for example, currency), you may lose the data.

■ **Delete Column**—Choose this option to remove a column and all its data from your table. Zoho checks to make sure you really want to delete the column; click Yes to proceed.

Figure 5.14
When you right-click a column, you get these options for editing it.

Editing Rows

To edit a row, right-click its number and choose one of these options:

■ Add Row puts a new row at the bottom of the table.

■ Delete Row(s) removes the chosen row or rows, including the data, from the table. When you select this option, Zoho doesn't ask you to confirm. It immediately deletes the row, so don't be too quick on your mouse button!

■ Delete All Rows clears the data from a table while keeping its structure. Zoho asks you to confirm before deleting; click Yes to clear the data out of the table.

 You can also add or delete a row or column using the Add and Delete buttons in the toolbar at the top of the table.

Editing a Table's Design

To change the way a table is set up, open the table and click Edit Design. The Edit Design dialog box looks just like the one you used to create the table. For most tables, it looks like the box shown in Figure 5.12; for query tables (that is, tables created from queries, as with the SQL code you learned about earlier in the chapter), it looks like the tab shown in Figure 5.13. Editing a table is just like the table creation described in the "Using Design View" section and the "Fetching Data from an Existing Table" section (for query tables).

Creating a Relationship Between Tables

When two tables are *related*, it means that one table gets some of its data from the other. It does this through a lookup field; when you create a lookup field, you're telling the table, "For values in this column of Table A, look at a particular column in Table B."

Here's an example: Say that you're creating a database to keep track of the courses taught at your school. You start by creating a table that has columns called Course, Instructor, Department, Instructor Email, and Instructor Phone. Soon, though, because each instructor teaches several courses, you get tired of typing in the same information over and over again. It would be a lot easier if you had two tables: one for data about courses and another for data about instructors. And it would be easier still if one of those tables could draw its information from the other—instead of typing in a teacher's name, for example, you could choose a name from a drop-down list.

To relate two tables so that one can look up data from another, start by creating the table that has the source data. In the example, you'd create the Instructors table first, with columns such as Last Name, First Name, Department, Email, Phone, and so on—whatever data you want to collect and track about instructors.

When that's set up, create the Courses table. This table might have columns named Course Name, Number, Department, Instructor, Maximum Size, and so on. Among these columns, you've got two possibilities for lookup fields—Department and Instructor—because they have counterparts in the Instructors table.

To make Instructor a lookup field, open the Edit Design dialog box. (Click New Table, Using Design View if you're building a new table; open the table and click Edit, Design if you're working on an existing table.) Find the name of the column you want to designate as a lookup column and then scroll to the right to the Lookup Column field. Double-click in that field, and the field turns into a drop-down list, as shown in Figure 5.15. On that list, find the table and column whose values you want to appear in the lookup field. (In the example, you'd select the Last Name field from the Instructors table.) Click Save.

Now, when you're entering data about courses into the Courses table and you come to the Instructor field, double-click that field. A drop-down appears, listing all the values in the Last Name column of the Instructors table, as shown in Figure 5.16. Click a name to insert it and then move on to the next column.

Sorting and Filtering Data

After you fill up a table with lots of info, you want to be able to organize that data and find whatever parts of it you may need.

Sorting Data

Organizing data by sorting it is easy. Select the column you want to sort by; then click the toolbar's Sort button and choose either Sort Ascending (*A* to *Z* for words, lowest to highest for numbers) or Sort Descending (*Z* to *A*, highest to lowest). In a flash, Reports rearranges your records according to the criterion you chose. To put the records back in their original order, click Sort again and select Remove Sorting.

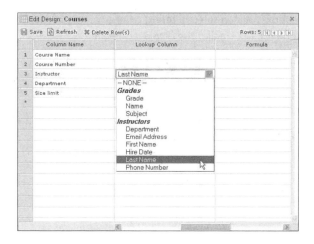

Figure 5.15
Choose the table and column that hold the data you want this table to look up.

Figure 5.16
A lookup field in action—the choices on the drop-down list come from the Last Name field of the Instructors table.

 Tip 4U You can also sort records by right-clicking the column you're sorting by, choosing Sort, and then choosing Sort Ascending, Sort Descending, or Remove Sorting.

Filtering Data

When you want to find a particular set of records—for example, all the employees in a particular department or all the accounts opened on a certain day—create a filter that finds and displays only those records that fit your filter's criteria.

To create a filter that shows only certain records, open the table you want to filter and click Filter. The table changes to look like the one in Figure 5.17. Above each column are a drop-down list and a text box. Use these to tell Reports what to look for. For example, you might want all last names that begin with the letter *B*. In that case, you'd select Starts With from the drop-down and type **B** in the text box. You can select filtering criteria for one of more columns—the more columns you set criteria for, the smaller the displayed results.

When you've set your filtering criteria, click Apply to see all matching records. To erase the current criteria and start again, click Clear. To save this filter, click Save, give the filter a name, and click OK. Click Close to restore your table to its usual appearance.

 Tip 4U To find a filter you've saved, click the down arrow next to the Filter button and choose the filter from the menu that appears.

Figure 5.17
In this example, the filter will show all records where Department is English and the Email field is empty.

Viewing Your Data

All that data in your database is just a mishmash of bits and pieces of information until you can organize your records into a report that lists important info, shows trends and patterns, or gives an at-a-glance overview. And that's what Reports' views are all about. In Reports, the terms *view* and *report* are pretty much interchangeable: A view reports on the data using criteria that you set up. And you won't believe how easy it is to set those criteria—it's as simple as choosing a report style and then dragging-and-dropping the columns you want. You tell Reports what to display and how to display it—and Reports takes care of the rest.

Creating a Tabular View

Tabular view presents your data in a table format. What makes this view powerful is its capability to group and summarize data. To create a tabular view, open the table whose data you'll be working with and click New, New Tabular View. Alternatively, you can click the upper-left New Report button and then select Tabular View.

Grouping Records

When a column has repeating values, you can group related records by those values. For example, imagine a table listing teachers that has a Department column. You can create a table view that groups together all employees by their department, as shown in Figure 5.18.

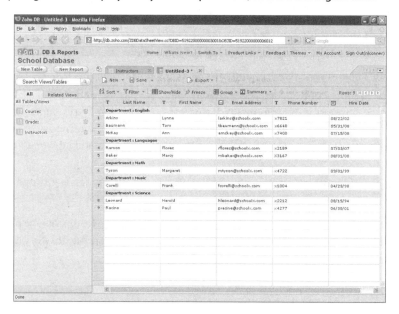

Figure 5.18
This view shows sectional grouping based on the Departments field.

To group records, click a column's header to select the column you want to group by. In the example, you want to group teachers by department, so select the Department column. Next, click Group and choose one of these grouping styles:

- **Group – Block**—Moves the column you selected to the far left of the table, shading it and making each cell large enough to be an umbrella for all the records it contains. For example, if three teachers work in the English department, *English* is a block the height of three rows; if two teachers work in the Science department, *Science* is a block the height of two rows.

- **Group – Sectional**—Creates shaded subheadings that give the field's name and contents, such as *Department: English* and *Department: Math*, and groups relevant records beneath each subheading. Figure 5.18 shows an example of this style of grouping.

You can also ungroup records: Select the column you want to ungroup and choose Group, Ungroup. Alternatively, you can select Group, Ungroup All. Either way, the table returns to its original format.

Summarizing Data

When you've got a long column of figures that you want to add up, average, or perform another operation on, Tabular View can create a summary report. Here's how:

1. Open the database that contains the table you want and click New Report, Tabular View. (In a database that has more than one table, you'll next choose the table you want.) You can alternatively take this route: Open the table you want to summarize and click New, New Tabular View. Either way, Reports opens a new tab in Tabular View.

2. Select the column you want to summarize by clicking its heading.

3. Click the Summary button. Reports shows a menu that has the options available for the kind of data you selected. If the column holds text, for example, Summary counts records in that column. If the column holds numbers, the Summary menu lets you choose to add or average the numbers; count records; or find the minimum, maximum, standard deviation, or variance.

4. Select the functions you want by checking their boxes. (You can select just one or as many as appear in the menu.) Click OK.

Reports creates a new row, titled Grand Summary, and displays the results of whichever function or functions you chose. If you want to save this view, click Save (or press Ctrl+S), give the new view a name, and click OK.

Creating a Pivot View

As Chapter 4 explains, a pivot table offers ways to summarize and analyze the data in a table. Creating a pivot table in Reports is just like creating a pivot table in Sheet. In Reports, open the table you want and select New, New Pivot View. Alternatively, in the appropriate database, click New Report, choose Pivot View (Matrix View), and (if you're in a database with more than one table) choose the table you want to use. This opens a tab where you create the pivot table.

Create the pivot table in the same way you'd create one from a spreadsheet. (Flip back to Chapter 4 to read all about that.) When you're done, click Save (or press Ctrl+S), name your new pivot view, and click OK.

Creating a Chart View

Chapter 4 gives the basics for making charts from spreadsheet data. The process for creating a chart from a table in a database is similar. So if you need to brush up on the different kinds of charts, flip back to Chapter 4.

In Reports, you create a chart from a table by selecting New, New Chart View. Alternatively, you can click New Report, choose Chart View, select the table you're working with (in a multitable database), and click OK. This opens a tab that looks like the one in Figure 5.19.

If you've created a chart from a spreadsheet, this tab should look familiar. To create your chart, select fields from the list on the left and then drag-and-drop them into the aspects of the chart where you want to display each one.

When you want to see how your chart is coming along, click the Click Here to Generate Graph link. Reports looks at the selections you've made and chooses the best kind of chart to display them. As Figure 5.19 shows, though, you can choose a different kind of chart. The toolbar displays a series of buttons, each representing a different kind of chart. Reports activates any buttons that will work with the current data; those that won't work with the data you've chosen remain grayed out. Click any active button to generate that kind of chart.

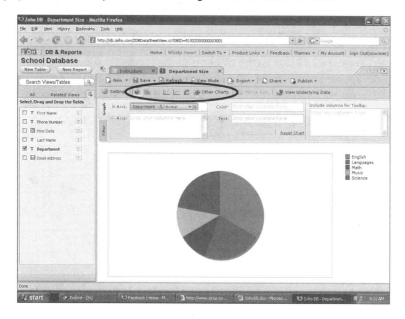

Figure 5.19
Reports chooses a chart style based on the data you've chosen; click a chart button (circled) to display the data in a different kind of chart.

If you want to filter the data that goes into the chart, click the Filter tab and then select, drag, and drop any columns you want to filter. Depending on the columns you choose, you have different options for filtering. For example, you might create a filter to show only those employees hired within a specific date range. To see how any filters you've applied affect the chart, click the link Click Here to Generate Graph.

To save a Chart View, click Save, give the view a name and optional description, and then click OK. Reports saves the chart and adds it to the list of tables and views.

Creating a Summary View

As its name suggests, a *summary table* lets you group data in various ways and then summarize the table's values. Summary tables are helpful when you want to look at the data in various ways to find trends and patterns. For example, in a table that tracks purchase orders, you may want to see the most popular products for different geographical regions, age groups, education levels, and so on. A summary table can do that.

When you want to group and summarize a table's data, open the table and click New, New Summary View. Alternatively, in the appropriate database, click New Report, select Summary, and then select the table you're summarizing. Reports opens a tab like the one in Figure 5.20.

Start by dragging the column you want into the Group By box. The column you group by appears in the summary view's leftmost column (*Product* in the example). Next, drag the subtotals you want to see into the Summarize By box. In the example, you'll see the relevant subtotal for Quantity and Amount for each product. Click the Click Here to Generate Summary link to see a preview of your summary view. When things look good, click Save and name your view to save it.

As the preview in Figure 5.19 shows, the contents of the Product column, the column by which we're grouping, appear at the left. Reading across each row gives you two subtotals: the quantity ordered for each product and the total dollar amount for each product's orders.

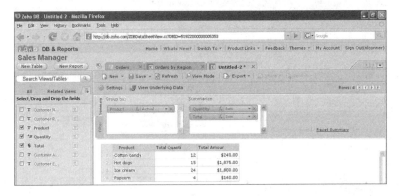

Figure 5.20
Use a summary view when you want to group and summarize data in a table.

Opening a Saved View

When you save a view you've created, Reports adds it to the list of tables and views. You can find and open a view by scanning the list and clicking the name of the view; Reports opens it in a new tab.

In a database that has lots of tables and applications, it may be tough to zoom in on one particular view. In this case, the easy way to find what you're looking for is to do a search. At the top of the left pane, type in a word or phrase from the view's name. Reports lists the results below.

 Tip 4U If you're working on a table and want to find one of its views, go to the left pane and click the Related Views tab. The list changes to show only those views that were created from the data in the current table.

To see the table used to create the view, click the View Underlying Data button.

Editing a View

Editing a view is a lot like creating it. Open the view you want to edit and then click Edit Design. The view changes to show the interface you used to create the view. (Tabular View doesn't have the Edit Design button.)

Make whatever changes you want and then click Save to keep those changes. Click View Mode to close the editing tools and switch back to a display of the view.

Changing a View's Name

To rename a view, open the view and change its name in one of these ways:

- Double-click the name in the view's tab. The name changes to a text box that you can edit.
- Click Settings. Then, in the dialog box that opens, type the view's new name into the Title text box and click OK.

Sharing Your Data

As with other Zoho apps, it's easy to share your data with others, inviting them to take a look at the data (but not change it) or to become a full-fledged collaborator with the ability to see, add, and edit data. In Reports, you can share one or more views (that is, reports) based on your data or an entire database.

Sharing a View

To share a particular view, open the view you want to share and click Share, Share this view. This opens the Invite Users dialog box shown in Figure 5.21. Type in the email addresses of those you want to share with, separating multiple addresses with commas. Add your own comments to the invitation email if you want and then click Share.

 If you've created a group with which to share this database (see the upcoming section), check the Share with Group box to share with the entire group. This way, you don't have to enter individual email addresses.

Zoho sends the invitation email to the addresses you listed. When a recipient clicks the link in the email, the view opens in a browser window in read-only mode.

 In Reports, shared views (that is, reports you've created from a table's data) are read-only; shared tables can be read-only or read/write.

Sharing a Database

Sharing a database is a lot like sharing a view, except you've got more flexibility in what you share and how you share it. In the database you're sharing (whether the whole database or just part of it), click Share, Share This Database. This opens the Invite Users dialog box shown in Figure 5.22, which has three steps:

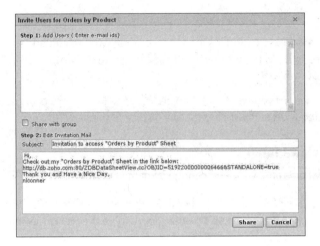

Figure 5.21
Give Zoho the email addresses of those you want to invite to share a view.

1. **Add users.** Type or paste in the email addresses of those who'll be sharing the database. If you're entering more than one email address, make sure you separate addresses using commas.

2. **Select tables and views and set permission levels.** The upper-right part of the dialog box has a list of all tables and views in this database. Check the ones you want to share. Select All shares the entire database (all its tables and views), or you can select only some of the tables and views. This step is also where you set permissions; click the down arrow next to the current permission level (Read Only in Figure 5.22) and choose Read Only or Read/Write. You can set the same permission for all the tables you've chosen by using the permission level at the top of the section, or you can set permissions on a table-by-table basis. Note that views are read-only.

3. **Edit the invitation email.** The lower half of the Invite Users dialog box displays the email Zoho will send to the recipients you specified. You can edit this as you like, or just leave it the way it is.

When you've got sharing set up the way you want it, click Share. Zoho fires off the invitation emails and adds the recipients to the list of those sharing this database.

 You can share a database right from the Reports home page. Find the database in your My Databases list; under the database's name, click Share, Share This Database. This opens the Invite Users dialog box shown in Figure 5.22.

Sharing with a Group

If you're part of a team working on a project and you don't want to type or paste in everyone's email address every time you create a new report to share, you can create a group and then share with that group. Creating a group means you only have to enter email addresses once; after that, just check Share with Group in the Invite Users dialog box when you want to share a report or table.

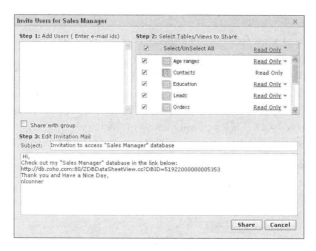

Figure 5.22
Share a database (all or just part of it) in three quick steps.

To create a group, select Share, Add/Edit Group. This opens the Add Group dialog box. In the top half of the box, enter the email addresses (one address per line) for everyone in the group you're creating. In the bottom half, you can read the invitation Zoho sends to potential group members and edit it if you like. Click Add to create the group and send out the invitations.

Later, if you want to edit the group, just click Share, Add/Edit Group again. Zoho opens the Add Group dialog box, with current group members filled in. Make your changes and then click Add to edit the group's membership.

 Zoho doesn't tell you when more than one person is editing the same database. If you and a colleague are both adding data to the same table at the same time, you won't see the other person's ID. When you save or refresh the table, though, the other person's additions appear, along with your own.

Managing Sharing

After you've shared all or part of a database, you may need to tweak the details of what you've shared, such as changing permissions, deleting tables or views, and removing users from sharing. You do all this from the Shared Details dialog box, shown in Figure 5.23. To open it, click Share, Edit Shared Details.

In the Shared Details box, you can do these things:

- **Remove users from sharing**. At the top of the dialog box, turn on the Users radio button. Find the user or group you no longer want to share with, and click the red X to the right of that user's or group's name.

- **Remove a table or view from being shared**. Enable the Views radio button. (Or, if you're looking at Users, click the plus sign next to a user or group to see what they're sharing.) Find the table or view you want to remove from sharing and click the red X to its right.

- **Change the permission level**. Enable the Views radio button and find the table or view you want. Click its Shared to [Number of] Users link. The section expands, listing users and the permission level for each. Click a permission level (such as Read Only) and select the new level (such as Read/Write) from the menu that appears.

- **Share with new users**. Click the Share to New Users button to open the same Invite Users box you use to set up sharing with an individual or group (see Figure 5.22).

After you've edited the database's sharing settings, click Save to keep the changes.

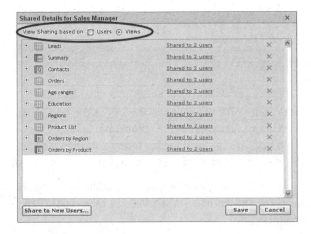

Figure 5.23
Choose to look at current sharing settings by Users or by Views (circled).

Publishing a Table or View on the Web

Publishing a view can make it easy for coworkers to see a snazzy pie chart or bar graph you've created. It's also a handy way for the public to see information you've drawn from your database, such as a product list or a list of teachers or courses at your school. As the information in the database changes, so does the published information.

Public Versus Private Databases

Tables and views you create in Reports are private by default, which means that people who surf to a table or view that you've put on the Web need to sign in to their Zoho account before they can see it.

If you make the database public, however, its views become available to anyone who surfs to a web page that contains the view. You can choose to make all the views in a database public, or you can decide on a case-by-case basis.

 Making a database public doesn't let just anyone come along and start changing your data. The public views of the database are read-only.

To make a database public, click Publish, Public Settings for Reports. The Public Settings dialog box opens, looking something like the one in Figure 5.24. As the box explains, when you make a database public, anyone can view it. Also, the standard setting for making a database public is that the database gets added to Zoho's public database listing at http://reports.zoho.com/ ZDBPublicDatabases.cc (where it can be found by search engines such as Google and Yahoo!). If you *don't* want the database in Zoho's list, uncheck the Show in Zoho's Public Databases Listing check box.

In the bottom half of the Public Settings box, choose the tables and views you want to make public by checking their boxes (or just check Select All). Click Make Public, and the tables and view you chose are no longer private.

 To make a public database private again, click Publish, Public Settings for Reports, Make Private.

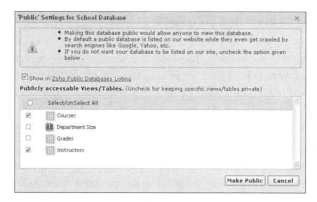

Figure 5.24
When you make a database's tables and views public, anyone can see them (but not edit them).

Publishing a Table or View

To put a table or a view on the Web, simply open the table or view and click Publish, URL for this view. This opens the Access URL dialog box, shown in Figure 5.25, which gives the URL (web address) for the table or view. Copy the URL; then you can email it to those who might want to see what you've published, or you can use it to create a hyperlink in a document or on a web page.

If you've made the table or view public (see previous section), the URL shows the view to anyone who finds his or her way to the web page. If, however, the view is private, viewers can't see it unless they sign in to their Zoho account.

 To get a public URL for a private table or view, look for the sentence "To access this view/table without login, Click Here," and click where indicated (circled in Figure 5.25). Zoho generates a URL that allows people to see the view on that web page only, while still keeping the database private.

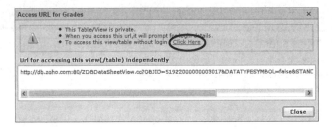

Figure 5.25
Copy the URL and use it to direct others to this view.

Embedding a Table or View in a Web Page or Blog

There are lots of reasons you might want to post a view or table on your web page: Maybe your company is growing, and you want customers and investors to see a graph that shows the good news. Or maybe you want to provide a list of your sales team members and their contact information. A local sports team might want to track its stats for its fans. Whatever you want to put on your web page or blog, you need to embed it there. To do that, you need a snippet of HTML code that points web browsers to the view, so they can display it on your web page.

To get that code, open the view you plan to embed and select Publish, Embed in Website/Blog. This opens the Embed Snippet dialog box, where you can set the height and width (in pixels) of the view you're embedding and copy the HTML code you need to embed it.

After you've copied the code, paste it into an HTML file and upload the file to your blog or web page. Now, the view shows on the page. And when you update the underlying data, the view updates as well.

 Embedded views can be either public (anyone can see them) or private (viewers must log in to a Zoho account to see them). See the previous section for how to make a view public or private.

Do-It-Yourself Applications: Zoho Creator

Whether you're tracking monthly household expenses or collecting customer feedback, you know the kind of information you need to gather, store, and analyze. It'd be great to create your own forms for collecting that information. But unless you're a programming pro, designing your own database application can seem daunting.

But who says you need to know how to program to create an application? With Zoho Creator, if you know how to use a mouse, you can create your own database applications. A database application is a table (or set of tables) that holds data, organized as records. You can add new data and view, update, or delete existing data. To receive data, each application is made up of one or more forms. And you can relate the application's tables to each other and view your data in different ways, such as in grid or chart form. So in a database application, forms collect the data, tables hold it, and views display it. And by the way, if you like to program, Zoho offers Deluge, an easy-to-use scripting language.

Zoho Reports or Zoho Creator: Which One's for You?

Zoho Reports and Zoho Creator are both database applications where you can store, organize, and analyze data. So which one's right for you? Why choose one over the other? This checklist may help you decide:

- **Do you need to generate reports using the data?** Zoho calls it *Reports* for a reason—flexible, in-depth reporting. If you frequently need to group your data or use pivot tables, for example, Reports offers the reporting capabilities you need.

- **Do you use SQL queries?** Reports supports SQL querying in many SQL dialects. Zoho Creator, on the other hand, uses a scripting language called Deluge, which was designed by Zoho to make it easy to create database applications (as you'll see in this chapter).

■   **Do you want to create forms to gather data?** If forms are a big priority, go with Creator. At this writing, Reports doesn't support forms.

■   **How much do you want to pay?** Reports is free. Creator, on the other hand, lets you build and use a maximum of five database applications for free. After that, you can upgrade to a business edition. Business editions range from free, $25/month (for up to five users, 10 applications, and 200MB of storage) to $300/month (for up to 100 users, unlimited applications, and 12GB of storage).

Zoho says that it will integrate Creator and Reports in the future. The first phase will be to make data from a Creator application automatically available as a database in Reports—where you can use the reporting features of Reports. Later, further integration will let you set up a form in Creator, embed the form on your website, and feed the data it gathers into a Reports database. By the time you read this, maybe some of this integration will already have happened. In the meantime, you can export data from Reports as a CSV file (Chapter 5, "Zoho Reports: Online Databases and Reports," tells you how) and import that data into Creator (see "By Importing Data," coming up in this chapter).

Creating an Application

As its name suggests, Creator is all about creating applications—designing databases. You (or users you share with) can input data through a form that you design. Then, you can display that data in various ways—such as in a chart or a spreadsheet-style grid—that Zoho calls *views*.

To get started, go to http://creator.zoho.com. If you're not already signed in to your Zoho account, do that now. Zoho signs you in and opens the Creator home page, shown in Figure 6.1. The first time you open Creator's home page, instead of an application list, you see a message that you don't yet have any applications. You're about to change that; click Create New Application. The Create Application page, shown in Figure 6.2, opens. From the list on the left, choose your method for creating your new application. You can also click the Marketplace tab to create an application from a template. The rest of this section walks you through each method.

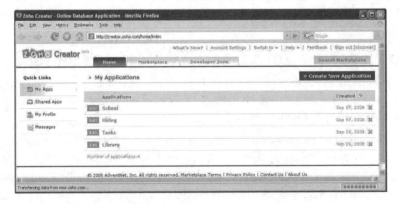

Figure 6.1
Creator's home page lists the applications currently in your account.

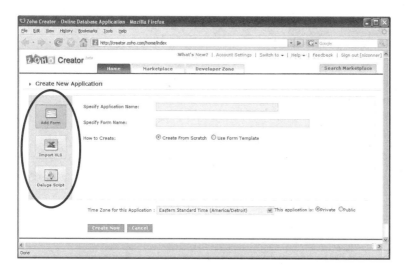

Figure 6.2
Choose how you want to create a database application.

By Adding a Form

One of Creator's big advantages is that you can use forms to get data into your database. A great way to create that database is to start by designing the form used to input data. On the Create Application page (shown in Figure 6.2), select Add Form from the left menu (if it's not already preselected) and start by giving both your new application and the form a name. For an example, we'll create an application for cataloging all the books in a library. So in this first step, we type in **Library** for the name of the application and **Books** for the form's name.

 Tip 4U As a guide, Zoho has created a form template. This template, for creating a database that stores information about people, has such fields as First Name, Last Name, Gender, Mobile Number, Birthday, Address, and so on. If your new application will hold similar information, enable the Use Form Template radio button and take two giant steps forward in creating your form. (You can always tweak the fields later: See "Adding and Editing Fields" later in this chapter to find out how.)

After you've named the application and the form, click the Create Now button.

Zoho creates your form and opens Creator's Forms tab, shown in Figure 6.3. The Insert Fields section, on the left side of the tab, lists the different field types you can use for your form. (The *field type* determines the kind of data a field will hold, such as single- or multiline text, a currency amount, a multiple-choice list, a check box, and so on.)

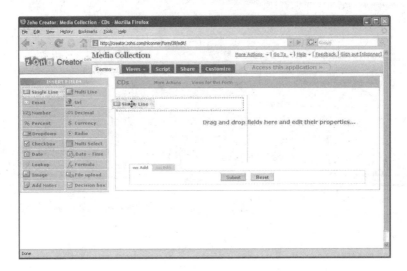

Figure 6.3
Drag-and-drop fields to create a form.

Start designing your form by clicking a field type and dragging it to the right. When you let go of the mouse button, a box like the one shown in Figure 6.4 appears. (Click Options to make the box appear as it does in the figure.)

The first field we want to create in our Books form is a single-line text field called *Title*. So we type `Title` into the Label Name box. After we've named the field, we could click Done to create it, but we want to see what other properties the new field can have. Click Options to find out. The settings available under Options vary, depending on the field type you've chosen, but most of them have these:

- **Validation**—Check the This Is Required Field box to force users to enter data or a value for the field. In the example, all books have a title, so we'd make sure this box is checked.

Info 4U Required fields show an asterisk in the form.

- **Permission**—If you want to keep this field all to yourself—for example, in a human resources application, you'd want to keep employee information such as Social Security numbers or salary private—check the Hide This Field to Others box. By default, this box is unchecked.

- **Field Name for Script**—This setting is for any scripts you write for the database (more on scripts later in this chapter); the name becomes the field reference in the script. Let Zoho pick the name, or type in the one you want.

- **Appearance**—If you want a field to have a default value, specify it here. You can also include instructions for the field.

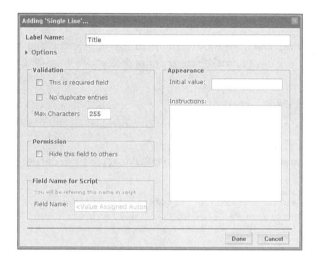

Figure 6.4
For each field you add, type in a name and, if you want, set options such as whether to require the field or how many characters a text field can have.

When you're done naming the field and tweaking its properties, click Done to add the field to your form.

 Don't like the way the fields are arranged? Simply drag-and-drop any field you want to move into its new location.

Add as many fields as you need. For our sample library application, you might add fields named Author, Publication Year, Edition, Genre, and so on. (Don't worry about coming up with every single field you might ever need now—you can always come back and add new fields later.) When you've finished adding fields to the form, click Access This Application to see how the new form looks (see Figure 6.5 for an example) and to start entering data into your application.

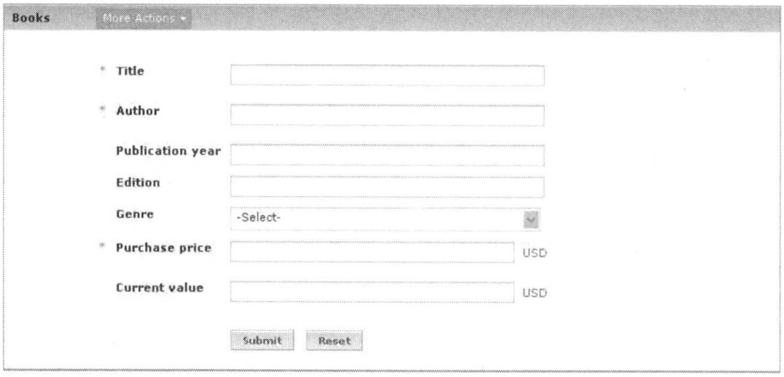

Figure 6.5
After you've created a form, it's ready to receive data.

By Importing Data

With Creator, importing data from another program is as easy as copying and pasting. Well, *almost* as easy. First, you have to make sure that the data you're importing is in one of these formats:

- **.xls**—A Microsoft Excel spreadsheet
- **.csv**—A comma-separated values file, in which individual pieces of data are set apart from each other by commas
- **.tsv**—A tab-separated values file, in which individual pieces of data are set apart from each other by tabs

 Tip 4U If you have data in Zoho Reports that you want to get into Creator, you can export the data from Reports in as a CSV file (see Chapter 5) and then import it into Creator.

Open the appropriate file, select the data, and copy it. Next, from Creator's home page, click Create New Application to get to the Create Application page (refer to Figure 6.2). On the left side of the page, click Import XLS. This changes the Create Application page to look like the one in Figure 6.6.

At the top of the page, give the application a name. Beneath that, in the large text box, paste in the data you copied from the .xls, .csv, or .tsv file. If the data you're importing contains any dates, use the drop-down in the bottom-right part of the screen to choose a date format that matches what you're importing. For example, if dates are formatted 05/31/09, choose MM/dd/yy from the drop-down. Changing to a different format will only confuse Creator during the import. Click Create Now.

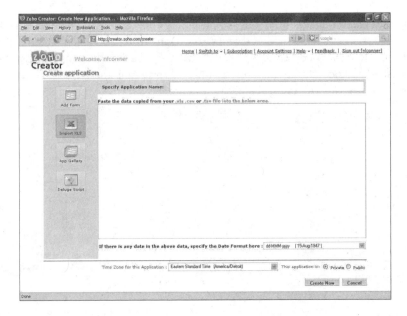

Figure 6.6
Paste the data you've copied into the large text box to start the import.

Creator analyzes the data and opens the Importing Data page, like the one shown in Figure 6.7. On this page, Zoho shows the columns that will make up the fields in your new application. Each column has a field type (which Creator chose based on what was in the columns you pasted in), a label (taken from the first row of your data), and data for the first five rows. To see how many rows Creator has imported in total, look at the top of the page.

Check each column to make sure the field type and label name (column heading) are correct and then make any necessary adjustments. When everything looks good, click Finish to create the application and open a form, based on this data.

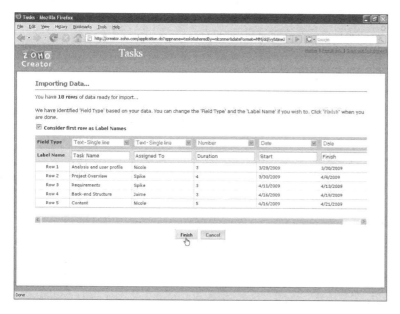

Figure 6.7
Before you create the application, make sure your data has imported correctly.

 To switch from the form to a table showing the data you imported, click <Tablename> View in the application's left list. In Figure 6.5, for example, you'd click Books View to see a table holding all the books in the database.

By Writing or Importing Deluge Script

Deluge is an online scripting environment created by Zoho to work with Creator. This means you can write your own applications from scratch. But you don't have to be a programmer who dreams in code to create your own application this way. Zoho has deliberately kept things simple, so that anyone can use Deluge to create an application.

Writing Your Own Script

When you create an application using Deluge, you tell Creator how to set up the application, step by step:

- The application's name.
- The name of the tab that will hold the form and any associated views.
- The names and types of the fields that make up the form.
- If you're creating a view to display the data, what you want in that view. (You can always create new views later.)

Tip 4U You can have more than one form or view (or both) on a tab.

Here's a simple example that creates an application for a school, collecting information about students:

```
Application "School"
{
    page "List of Students"
    {
        form  student_list
        {
            displayname  =  "Students"

            last_name
            (
                displayname = "Last Name"
                type  =  text
            )

            first_name
            (
                displayname = "First Name"
                type  =  text
            )

            grade_level
            (
                displayname = "Grade Level"
                type  =  radiobuttons
                values  =  {9,    10,    11,    12}
            )

            gpa
            (
```

```
            displayname = "GPA"
            type    =   decimal
        )

        comments
        (
            displayname = "Comments"
            type    =   textarea
        )
    }

    table   "All Students"
    {
        show  all  rows  from  student_list
        (
            last_name
            first_name
            grade_level
        )
        filters
        (
            gpa
            comments
        )
    }
  }
}
```

Let's take this apart to see how it works. The first line names the application. (Note that the name, School, is inside double quotation marks.) Next, the page—the tab on which this form will appear—is named, also inside double quotes.

After that, the form is created and named, and fields are defined, one by one. For each field, you give its name, such as last_name, its displayname (that is, the name that will show on the form) enclosed in double quotes, such as "Last Name", and its field type (type = text). The displayname and type of each field are enclosed in parentheses. Larger elements, such as pages, forms, and views, are enclosed in braces.

The form collects this information for each record: Last Name and First Name (both text fields), Grade Level (four radio buttons that display 9, 10, 11, and 12), GPA (a number field that accepts decimals), and Comments (a multiline text field).

This script also tells Creator to display a view on the List of Students tab, in the form of a table named All Students. This table will display the Last Name, First Name, and Grade Level fields for each record, while filtering out GPA and Comments.

Figure 6.8 shows the application created by the sample script.

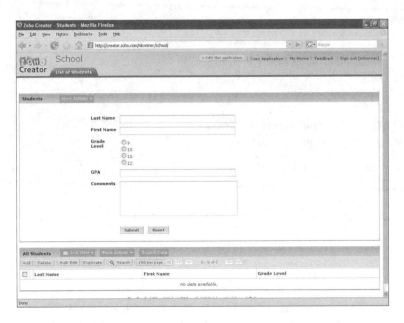

Figure 6.8
Creator made this application based on the sample Deluge script in this chapter.

 Zoho has created a script builder to help you get up to speed with Deluge. You can find it at http://creator.zoho.com/help/deluge/index.html?url=what_is_deluge.html, where you can read it online or download it as a PDF.

Importing a Deluge Script

You can save an existing application as a Deluge script, as the Tip in this section explains.

Info 4U Deluge scripts end with the file extension .ds.

If you've saved an application on your computer as a Deluge script file, you can import that script, using it as the basis for a new application. On the Create Application page (refer to Figure 6.2), choose Deluge Script on the left, and then enable the Import Script radio button.

The page changes to show a text box and a Browse button. Click Browse, find the .ds file on your computer, and click OK to put the file path in the text box. Click Create Now. Zoho opens a page that displays the application's script. Click Save Script, and Creator uses that script to create a new application.

 To save an application (minus its data) on your computer, open the application you want to back up. Click More Actions at the top of the screen and then choose Save as Script to download the application (in the form of a .ds file) to your computer. Save the file to your computer, specifying where you want to save the file. Click OK, and you have a copy of the application on your computer.

By Choosing from the Marketplace

You don't necessarily have to build your own application from the ground up. Zoho has given you a head start by collecting sample applications in its Marketplace. Choose an application and use it as the basis for creating your own. Then, tweak that application however you like to customize it to your needs.

 Many of the applications in the Marketplace are free, but some charge a licensing fee. Look for License in the application's description to see the cost (if any) of an application.

On the Zoho Creator home page (shown earlier in Figure 6.1) or on the Create New Application page (shown earlier in Figure 6.2), click the Marketplace tab. The page changes to show the Marketplace's featured applications. Each application shows a name and a brief description. Browse the left-hand list of categories, or scroll down the Featured Applications list to see what's available. You can also search for a specific kind of application by clicking the Search Marketplace tab and typing a search term, such as *employee*, into the Search Apps box. Choose a category (if you want to limit the search), and then click Go to see a list of applications with your search term in their name or description.

In the Marketplace, you'll find applications that range from Project Tracker and Expense Tracker, to Recruitment, to Help Desk and CRM. There are even fun applications to catalog your favorite albums and set up your friends with dates.

 Want to see what's in a sample application before you use it to create your own? Click View Demo to open a demo version of that application in a new window.

When you're ready to create your application, click the Install This Application link for the application you want. Zoho creates the application for you, a process that may take a couple of minutes. When the installation is complete, Zoho adds the application to your account and sends you an email to tell you it's been installed. (You can also see this email in the Messages section of your Creator home page.)

After Zoho has installed the new application, click the Access This Application button to open your new application and start adding your own data. (Or if you're in the market for another application, click Go to Marketplace.)

Putting Your Application to Work

Creating an application is just the beginning. The next step, of course, is adding data. From Creator's home page, click the name of an application. Zoho opens the application. If the application has more than one tab, click the tab you want and then start entering data into the form. For each record you enter, click Submit. Creator adds the record to your database.

Adding and Editing Fields

One of the great things about Creator applications is their flexibility—when you find you need to add a field or change the properties of an existing one, you can do so with just a few clicks.

You add and edit a form on the Forms tab, shown previously in Figure 6.3. For an existing form, the current fields already appear on the page. The path to get to the Forms tab depends on where you're starting from:

- **From the Creator home page**—Click the Edit button to the left of an application's name.
- **From an application**—Click the Edit This Application button at the top of the screen.

Once you're on the Forms tab, you can perform these actions:

- **Add a new field**. Choose a field type from the list side of the screen and then drag it into the form and drop it where you want it to appear.
- **Edit a field**. When you move the cursor over a field, the field is highlighted. Move the cursor to the down arrow next to the pencil icon on the left, and a menu appears (as shown in Figure 6.9). Select Edit This Field. This opens an Editing box that looks just like the one in Figure 6.4; make your changes there and then click Done.
- **Create a rule for the field**. You can write a script that creates a rule for the field, specifying something that should happen when data in the field is submitted or updated. (Read the next section to learn about creating rules using scripts.) Move the cursor over a field's Edit icon to make the Edit menu appear; then choose either Actions on User Input or Actions on Update.
- **Delete a field**. If there's a field that's not getting much use or that's no longer relevant to the application, put your cursor over the field, moving left until the Edit menu appears (see Figure 6.9). From the menu, choose Delete. A confirmation box appears; click OK to delete the field and all its data.

 When you delete a field, any and all data it held is gone forever. So when Creator asks if you're sure you want to get rid of the field, think twice (or even three times) before you click that OK button.

Using Scripts to Create Form Rules

Data entry gets a lot easier—and more accurate—when you have some control over what happens when a user enters or edits a value in a certain field. For example, when a user selects a certain value in a particular field, you might want to show or hide another field. Imagine a customer feedback form, for instance, in which customers rate service as Poor, Fair, Good, or Excellent. If the customer selects Poor or Fair, you want to know what the problem was, so you can show a required multiline text box and ask for an explanation.

Let's develop a simple example in an application that lists students at a high school. The form collects each student's name, address, grade level, grade-point average, and any comments a teacher may have. Freshmen who are just coming into the school don't have a grade-point average yet, so when a user selects 9 as the grade level, you want the form to hide the GPA field.

To begin, on the Forms tab of your School application, put your cursor over the Grade Level field to highlight it. Click the Edit icon (the pencil) to open the Edit menu (refer to Figure 6.9) and then select Actions on User Input. This takes you to the Script tab's ScriptBuilder for that field, shown in Figure 6.10.

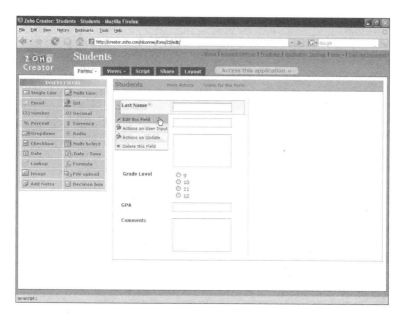

Figure 6.9
Creator's Edit menu lets you change a field's properties, create rules, or delete the field.

When you first open ScriptBuilder, you see a sample script that looks like this:

```
if(<condition>)
{
        hide field1;
        show field2;
}
```

The sample sets up the syntax you need: If some condition inside the parentheses (which you'll specify) is in place, you'll hide one field and show another (both of which you'll also specify).

To specify the condition and the results, put your cursor on the line of the script that you want to change; note that Edit and Delete buttons appear. Click Edit. A dialog box appears that lets you specify the condition, as shown in Figure 6.11. Choose the field you want to create the rule for— in the example, it would be grade_level—and click it. Creator puts the field in the text box at the bottom of the dialog box, where you're building the *if* condition. Next, use the buttons just above that text box to define the condition.

In the example, you want something to happen if a user chooses 9 as the grade level, so you use the Equals button to insert the equals operator (==). Finally, you finish the condition by typing in **"9"** (including the quotation marks around the digit). When you click Done, Creator inserts the following as the first part of the script:

```
if((input.grade_level == "9"))
```

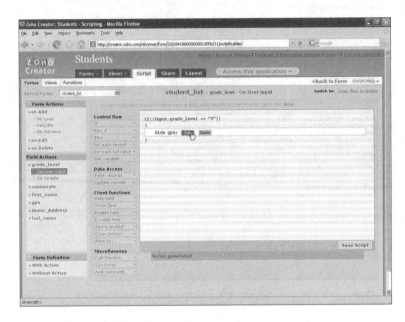

Figure 6.10
ScriptBuilder helps you write a script, step by step.

This says, "Okay, Creator, when someone enters a new record and chooses 9 as the Grade Level, I want you to do something special." In the next part of the script, you tell Creator what that something special is. So hover over the line that reads "hide field1" and then click the Edit button.

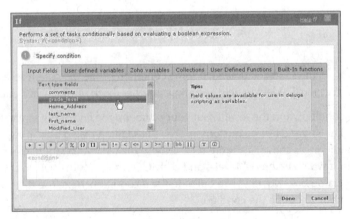

Figure 6.11
Use this box to complete the if condition.

Now, Creator opens a dialog box that holds a drop-down list. Click the list and select the field you want to hide. For the example, that's gpa. Click Done, and the script now looks like the one in Figure 6.10:

```
if((input.grade_level == "9"))
{
    hide gpa;
}
```

Click Save Script. Now, when a user adds student data via the form, enabling the Grade Level field's radio button labeled 9 will make the GPA field vanish.

 Tip Need help figuring out what you're doing with your script? Click the upper-right Script Help link for detailed assistance with formulas, functions, filters, and more.

This example shows one kind of rule you can write, but there are many others. ScriptBuilder breaks the process down into steps:

1. Choose an action from the left list; then drag-and-drop it into the script editor.

2. Edit that action so it affects the appropriate fields in your form.

3. Repeat as necessary.

4. Save the script.

 Tip If you'd prefer to write your own script, rather than using ScriptBuilder's drag/drop/edit approach, click the Free-Flow Scripting link in the upper-right part of the screen.

Creating a New Form

Even if you started your application with a single form, you're not limited to just one. When you need to collect related data that's different from what you get through your current form, open the application and put your cursor on the Form tab. A list of the forms currently in this application appears. At the bottom is an item called New Form. Click that to open the New Form page, shown in Figure 6.12.

Figure 6.12
Creator gives you two ways to create a new form.

On the New Form page, pick one of these ways to add another form to your application:

- **Add Form**—This method, shown in Figure 6.12, requires you to name the new form, indicate whether you want to create a view based on this form automatically, and (if your application has more than one tab) designate which tab it will appear on. When you click Done, Creator takes you to the Forms tab, where you can start stocking up the new form with fields.

- **Import XLS**—Click this button to create a new form by pasting in existing data from a Microsoft Excel (XLS), comma-separated values (CSV), or tab-separated values (TSV) file. Creating a form in this way is just like creating an application by importing data, so flip back to "By Importing Data" earlier in this chapter to learn the specifics.

Whichever way you choose to create your new form, click Done when you're ready to create the form.

Setting Email Notification for a Form

As you'll learn later in this chapter, you can share an application with others. If you give other users permission to add records, you might want to know when new data appears in your application. Just have Zoho send you a quick email when somebody submits a form, and you'll always be on top of your data.

You set up email notifications from the Forms tab. If you have more than one form in the application, place your cursor over the Forms tab and then (from the menu that appears) choose the form you want. When it opens, click More Actions, Set Email Notification. This opens the Set Email Notification dialog box shown in Figure 6.13.

Here, give Zoho the email address where you want the message sent, add a subject line, and write the message itself. If you want the email to include the data that was just submitted, check the Include User Submitted Data box. Click Done, and from now on Zoho will send an email to the specified address when someone adds new data through the form.

 Too many emails landing in your Inbox? You can turn off any email notifications you've set up. On the Forms tab of the appropriate form, click More Actions, Set Email Notification to get back to the box shown in Figure 6.13. At the bottom of the box, turn on the Disabled radio button and then click Done to stop the flood of emails.

Creating a Relationship Between Two Forms

In an application that holds several tables, the information in those tables is likely related. For example, if your application catalogs your CD collection, you might have one table that lists CDs and another that lists information about record labels. These tables hold different information: The CD table might have fields for Album, Artist, Genre, Release Date, Label, Live or Studio Recording, and so on; the Record Labels table might hold such information as Name, Address, Kinds of Music, Web Site—whatever. Because you already have a table that lists record labels, wouldn't it be easy if you could pull label names from that table as you're entering data about a new CD?

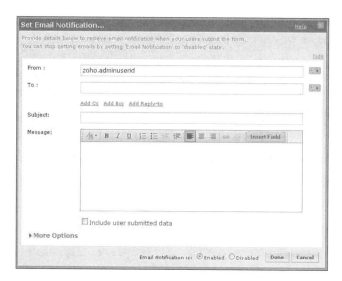

Figure 6.13
You can be notified by email whenever someone uses a form to add data to your application.

You can, by creating a relationship between the forms. When you create a relationship, you can take information from Table A and import it into a field in Table B. When Table B gets updated with new information or has an obsolete record deleted, the new info is automatically reflected in the choices in Table A. So, for example, when you add a new record label name to your Record Labels table, that new name automatically appears as a choice in the Label field of the CDs form.

 You can relate two forms whether they're in the same application or in different applications.

To show how relating forms work, we'll develop an example for our School application, creating a relationship between a form called Teachers and a form called Courses. When we're adding information about new courses, we want to be able to get the current teachers' names from the Teachers table, so that we can just choose a name from a drop-down list instead having to type in the same names over and over.

Start by creating a form called Teachers. For each teacher, create a field for Last Name and First Name. (You could also include other fields, of course, such as Department, Phone Number, Email Address, and so on.) Use the form to create a Teachers table by filling in and submitting teacher information.

Next, create a second form; call this one Courses. Create a single-line text field for Course Name. When you create the Teacher field, choose Lookup as the field type. The dialog box that opens looks like the one in Figure 6.14. Here's where you tell Creator where to find the data it's looking up:

- In the Import Data From section, select the application and the field that Creator will use to look up the data. In the example, you'd choose School as the application. In the Select Field box, find the table you want and look under it for the field you want. Because we're looking up teacher names, we want the Last Name field of the Teachers table.

▪ In the Display As section, tell Creator how users will select data in the lookup field. If you want users to be able to select only one option, choose either Dropdown or Radio Button. If you want users to be able to make multiple selections, choose either Checkboxes or Multiple Select (which creates a dropdown list).

When you've made your choices, click Done.

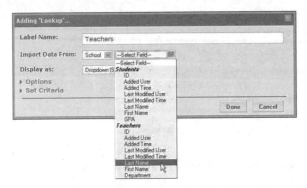

Figure 6.14
Choose the application and field that supply data to the lookup field.

To see how your new lookup field works, click Access This Application and open the Courses form. As Figure 6.15 shows, the Teachers field has a drop-down list showing all the names in the Teachers table. When you add a name to the Teachers table, that name is also added to the drop-down. If a teacher's name changes in the Teachers table (for example, if a teacher gets married and changes her last name), it automatically changes in the drop-down and any relevant lookup fields. And, of course, if you delete a name from the Teachers table because a teacher has left the school, that name is also deleted from records in the Courses table.

Viewing Data

If you checked Generate Auto-View for This Form (refer to Figure 6.12) when you created a form, you already have one way of viewing the data in your application. In Creator, *views* are reports that present an application's data in various ways. The most common view is a tabular report (in table format, with rows and columns), but you have other options, including showing the data as a spreadsheet, calendar, chart, and more. This section gives you the lowdown on creating, editing, and working with views in Creator.

Creating a New View

You create views on the Views tab. If you're working in an application, click Edit This Application, put your cursor over the Views tab to see its menu, and then click New View. (If you're on Creator's home page, click the Edit button for the application you want; then hover over the Views tab and select New View.) The New View page, shown in Figure 6.16, is the place to start designing your view:

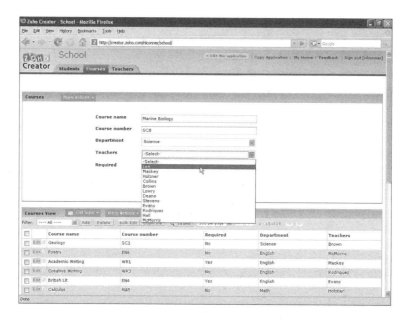

Figure 6.15
Creator looks up information from one table and imports it to another.

1. Choose the kind of view you want from these options: List (which is a table), Grid (which looks like a spreadsheet), Summary, Calendar, Chart, or HTML Page. (The options you see here depend on the data in the form you've chosen.)

2. In the View Name box, type in a name for the new view. Choose something descriptive so that later you can easily find the view you want.

3. If there are several forms in your application, choose the form you want to use as the basis for the new view in the View Based On drop-down list.

4. For applications with several tabs, select the tab or section where you want the view to appear. (To find out how to create a new tab, see "Creating a New Section" later in this chapter.)

5. Set access permissions for the view by checking the boxes to let others add, edit, or delete records. (These check boxes are off by default.) If you check Add, Zoho gives you another option: Duplicate Records. If you check Edit, Zoho asks whether that includes bulk editing (the ability to update multiple records at once).

6. Click Done to go to a page where you can edit the new view.

Creator opens a page like the one in Figure 6.17, which shows a preview of your view. Here, you can tweak the view with a number of actions in the View Configuration bar on the left side of the screen (the options you see here depend on the kind of view you're creating):

■ **Set Display Type**—If seeing the preview makes you want to try a different kind of view, click this button to choose the new view style.

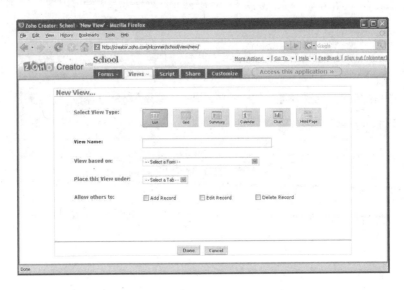

Figure 6.16
Tell Creator which data you want to display and how you want to display it.

- **Properties**—This option may say "Chart Properties" or "Column Properties," depending on the kind of view you're creating. Here, you tell Creator which aspects of the data you want to display: x- and y-axes in charts, and columns in tables and lists.

- **Set Criteria**—The standard for new views is to display all data. Here, you can set specific criteria that tell Creator which records to display. To do that, enable the Restricted Records radio button and then tell Creator which records you want. For example, in the School application, you could choose to display only those records where the Department field contains English.

- **Set Filters**—Create a custom filter, telling Creator which columns you want to show and whether there are any specific conditions for displaying those columns. To create a custom filter, click the Custom Filter button and set your criteria. For example, you could create a filter for the School application's Courses table so that the view displays only required courses (that is, those courses that have Yes in the Required field).

- **Set Grouping**—Organize a list or other table-style view by selecting a criterion for grouping its records. For example, the Courses list might group courses by department, so that all records with, for example, English in the Department field would be grouped together, as would all records with Science in that field, and so on.

- **Set Sorting**—Usually, Creator sorts records by when they were added. But you're not limited to chronological order. To sort, select a field and click Add to move it to the box on the right. Make sure the field you want to sort by is selected; then click Sort Asc/Desc to toggle between ascending and descending order.

- **Set Permissions**—If you want to change the permissions that were in place when you created the view, select this option. On the Set Permissions page, check or uncheck the boxes that give users permission to add, edit, or delete records.

- **Custom Actions**—This option is where you can define a function using a Deluge script to perform custom actions, such as sending an email notification when a record is edited. Give the custom action a name and configure the function here.

 If you're not into writing scripts, there's an easier way to set up email notifications. See the previous section "Setting Email Notification for a Form" for the how-to's.

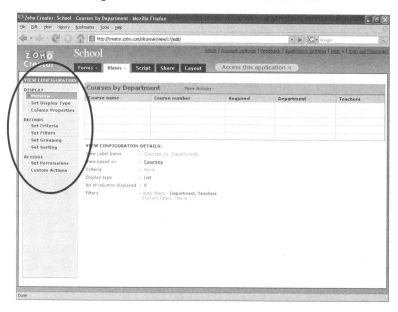

Figure 6.17
Use the options on the View Configuration menu (circled) to adjust your new view.

Combining Views

Your data doesn't have to live in isolation, restricted to views generated from a single form. When you have two related forms in the same application (see the earlier section on creating a relationship between forms), you can combine their data in one view.

When you want to create a combined view, start by selecting the form you want from the Forms tab. (Choose one that has a lookup field, such as the Courses form from our School application example.) Name the view and choose a display type and other options, as you would when creating any view (see the previous section). Click Done to move to the next page, where a preview of the new view appears.

On this preview page, choose Column Properties from the View Configuration menu. Your lookup field has the notation "(related fields)" to its right. Click this to expand the section, showing fields from the lookup field's related form, as shown in Figure 6.18. Check the boxes of any fields from that table you want in your combined view. Click Done to create the view.

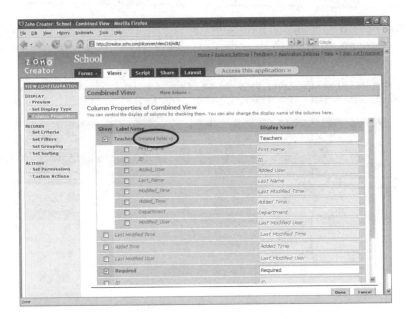

Figure 6.18
A table with a lookup field lets you select fields from the related table to create a combined view.

Deleting a View

If you no longer need a particular view and you don't want it cluttering up your application, you can delete it from the Views tab. Hover your cursor over the Views tab; then select the view you want to delete. When it opens, choose More Actions, Delete This View. Click OK to confirm, and Creator gets rid of that view.

Changing an Application's Layout

Creator gives you some options for customizing the look, feel, and organization of your application. Choose between Tab Layout (the standard layout—you can see an example in Figure 6.15) and Pane Layout (shown back in Figure 6.5) or pick a new design and color scheme, called a *theme*. And whichever layout you choose, you can add new pages to organize your forms and views.

Changes to an application's layout happen on the Customize tab. For the application you want, click Edit (if you're on the home page) or Edit This Application (if you're working in the application). An example of the Customize tab appears in Figure 6.19.

Choosing a Layout Style

With Creator, there are three ways to arrange the forms and views in an application—choose the one that best suits your working style:

- Pane layout shows forms and layouts as a list in a pane, organized by sections, that can be displayed on the left or the right side of the page. Use this list to navigate the application.

- Tab layout lets you create tabs, which appear across the top of Creator's pages, and then place forms and views on those tabs. Users navigate the application by clicking a tab and then scrolling down to find the view or form they want. This layout style also includes a pane that lets you choose different forms or views—put the pane on the left or the right side, as you prefer.

- Drop Down Menu layout shows a menu bar at the top of the page. When you click an item on the menu bar, it displays a menu of related options.

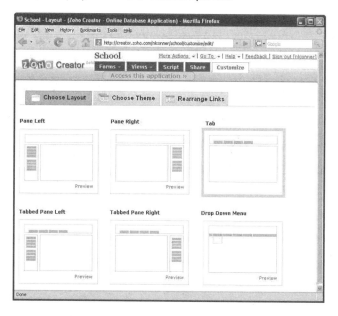

Figure 6.19
The Customize tab gives an overview of your application's layout and lets you move things around.

When you're editing an application, click its Customize tab (see Figure 6.19). The Choose Layout tab shows Creator's different layout styles, with your current layout selected. To choose a different layout, hover your mouse pointer over the style you want; the word Apply appears. Click Apply, and Zoho changes Creator's layout for you.

Tip 4U It can be hard to picture what Creator will look like from the outlines on the Choose Layout tab. To get a better look at a particular layout, click its Preview link. Zoho opens a full-fledged preview of that layout. Use the drop-down menus at the top of the page to try a different layout or color scheme. When you find a layout you like, click Apply (in the upper-left part of the screen) to apply it to your Creator account.

Choosing a Theme

Picking a layout is just one way you can tweak Creator's appearance. You can also choose an appearance and color scheme, called a *theme*. Pick a theme that's more pleasing to your eye—or that doesn't clash with your office décor.

To choose a theme, click the Customize tab and then click its Choose Theme tab to open the page shown in Figure 6.20. This page shows the themes that Zoho has designed for Creator; your current theme, along with its main color, is selected. To pick a different main color for your theme, just click the color you want. The preview changes to show how Creator will look using that color. Click Preview to get a full-sized look at the new color or Apply to use this color in your Creator account.

To choose a different theme, hover the mouse pointer over the theme you want. Color options appear; click a color to preview that theme with that color. Click Apply to apply this theme and color scheme to Creator.

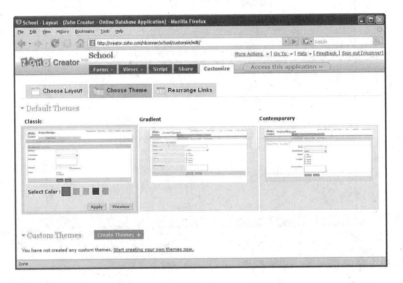

Figure 6.20
Redesign your Creator pages by choosing or creating a theme.

 If you don't like any of Zoho's themes, you can create your own. On the Choose Theme tab (see Figure 6.20), click Create Themes. This opens a page where you name your theme, pick a Zoho-designed theme to base it on, and then go to town choosing options for fonts, tabs, heading and styles, and so on. (Click the plus sign next to any theme element to preview its options.) When you're done, click Save, and Zoho adds your custom theme to the Choose Layout tab.

Creating a New Section

If you're adding a new form or a new kind of data to the application, keep things organized by adding a new section to the application. The new section appears as a tab (in Tab layout), as a section within a pane (in Pane layout), or on the menu bar (in Drop Down Menu layout).

Start on the application's Customize tab (refer to Figure 6.19) and then click Rearrange Links to open the page shown in Figure 6.21. At the top of the page, click Add a New Section. In the dialog box that opens, name the section, click Add, and you're all set.

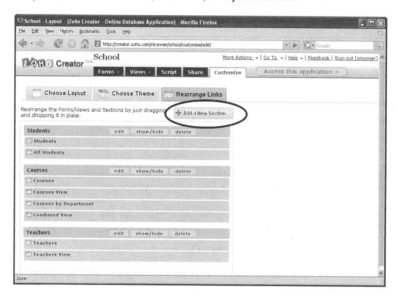

Figure 6.21
Rearrange an application's sections or add a new section (circled) on the Rearrange Links tab.

Rearranging an Application's Contents

You can move around the forms and views that live in your application. Move them to a new location on their current section, or put them in a different section. Depending on the layout you use, "section" can refer to a tab, pane section, or drop-down list.

As you can see in Figure 6.21, the Rearrange Links tab shows all the forms and views in an application; each form or view is listed under its current section. To move a form or a view, hover your cursor over the name of the form or view you want to move; the cursor becomes a four-way arrow. Click-and-drag the rectangle to a new location; then let go of the mouse button to drop it in place.

Working Sections

On the Rearrange Links tab, each section has three small icons to the right of its name. Here's what each does when you click it:

- **Edit**—Opens a dialog box where you can rename the section.
- **Show/Hide**—Displays the section or prevents it from being displayed in the application. Hidden sections have a dark gray background on the Rearrange Links tab. If a section is currently shown, this button hides it. If the section is currently hidden, this button shows it.
- **Delete**—Gets rid of the section and moves its contents to the previous section. Click OK to confirm.

Sharing Your Application

For personal applications, like the one organizing your CD collection, you probably won't need to share with anyone else. However, other kinds of applications—such as an application where on-the-road sales reps submit their expenses through a form—require that numerous users have access.

Creator gives you a lot of flexibility in sharing an application: You can share an entire application, a section or tab (and all its contents), or a single form or view.

Sharing happens on the Share tab, shown in Figure 6.22. To get there from Creator's home page, click the Edit button of the application you're sharing and then click the Share tab. If you're in the application, click Edit This Application, followed by the Share tab.

On the Share tab, select the application, section/tab, or view/form you want to share. Next, add the users you want to share with. Click the blue Add Users button to open a dialog box where you can add the email addresses of people you want to share with (one address per line). Click Add.

Back on the Share tab, click Share to Users. The screen changes to show a list of users with whom you've shared the application. Choose the ones you want. (Hold down Shift or Ctrl to select multiple users, or check Select All to choose everyone.) If you want to email a notification to the people you're adding, check the Send Invitation box (and, if you like, add an optional custom message). When you're ready to share your application (or the part of it you've chosen), click Share Now.

 When you share an application with someone else, it's still your application. It's not added to sharers' Creator home page, and even if sharers can add, edit, and delete records, they can't edit the application as a whole.

Going Public

By default, all applications are private, which means that no one can see the application or any part of it unless you share it. To share an application with the whole world, so that anyone can fill out a form or view the application's data, enable the Public radio button at the top of the application's Share tab. To make just part of the application public, such as a single form, make a selection from the Select menu on the left. At the top of the Share tab for your selection is a sentence that reads, "This form/view is private." Click the change link to make it public.

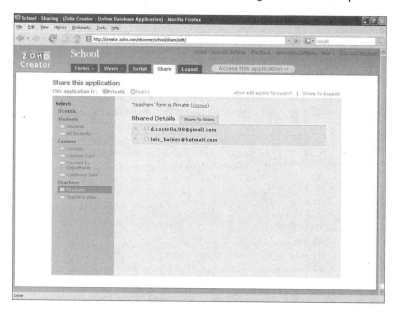

Figure 6.22
The Share tab lets you share with others and shows current sharers.

Editing Permissions for Views

It can be convenient to let users work with records right from a view, so they can correct typos, for example, or delete obsolete records. Creator has three kinds of view permissions for your application's users: add, edit, and delete. You can grant none of these, all of them, or any combination for each view.

You can set permissions when you create a view (see the earlier section "Viewing Data"). You can also set or change them from the Views tab, shown back in Figure 6.18. On the tab, select the view you want and then choose Set Permissions from the left pane's View Configuration menu. The page that opens has a check box for each kind of permission. Check or uncheck these, as you prefer, and then click Done to set the permission.

Removing a User from Sharing

If someone has left your business and you no longer want that person to have access to your application, you can stop sharing the application with that person with just one click. On the application's Share tab, click the X to the left of the person's name. Just like that, Zoho stops sharing the application with that person.

Publishing an Application

Putting a form on your website can be a great way to collect information—such as customer feedback or email addresses for a newsletter. Similarly, putting a view on your website can keep people informed with up-to-the-minute product lists, personnel rosters, and upcoming events. You can publish a form or view by embedding it in your web page. This displays the form or view on the page and keeps it current with changes made in the application.

Embedding requires an HTML snippet. To get that, open the application you want. (If you're in edit mode, click Access This Application.) Find the form or view you want to embed, and in its title bar, click More Actions, Embed in Your Website. This opens a dialog box like the one shown in Figure 6.23.

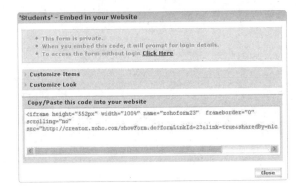

Figure 6.23
Copy the code from the box and paste it into an HTML file to embed the form in a web page.

Pay attention to the information at the top of the box, which tells you whether the form or view is public or private. *Public* means that anyone can see it; *private* means that users have to log in to their Zoho account before they can see or work with the form or view. To switch from private to public (or vice versa), click the Click Here link.

The text box holds the snippet of code you need to embed the form or view in a web page or blog. Copy that code, paste it into an HTML file, and upload it to your site. Voilà! Your form or view is on the Web.

 You can customize the form or view before you put it on your web page. In the Embed in Your Website dialog box, as shown in Figure 6.23, are sections you can click to expand: Customize Items and Customize Look. Click them to see what your customization options are.

7

Zoho Mail: Web Mail Redux

Dozens of web-based email programs are available today, most of them free and all of them vying for your attention. So why should you use Zoho Mail? For starters, it's super-easy to use: You'll be shooting off emails using your default @zoho.com email address within seconds of opening the program. It has both labels and folders to help you organize your messages in a way that makes sense to you. You can fine-tune your spam protection, and chat with your contacts without leaving Mail. And as your Inbox fills up (at this writing, Zoho Mail offers *unlimited* storage space for your messages and attachments), Mail's powerful search feature will help you find the exact message you're looking for. You can also configure Zoho Mail to send and receive mail from other POP email accounts you already have.

Best of all, though, is Mail's integration with other Zoho programs. When someone attaches a document, for example, you can open it in Writer—no need to worry about macro viruses messing up your desktop word processor.

This chapter gets you started and up to speed with Zoho Mail. Soon, you'll be using it like a pro (and wondering why you tried all those other email programs).

Touring Zoho Mail

To start using Zoho Mail, go to http://mail.zoho.com and sign in to your Zoho account. This takes you to Mail's home page, shown in Figure 7.1. A welcome message appears there, sent to your default Zoho email address. As a Zoho user, you already have a Zoho email address, consisting of your Zoho username and @zoho.com. This account is preconfigured in Zoho Mail. You'll learn to add your other email accounts to Zoho Mail later in this chapter.

A quick look at the home page shows you how things are organized. The left pane gives an overview of your Zoho mail account: folders that hold your messages, labels you can create to mark messages, and views, which filter messages to show, for example, only those messages you haven't read or only those you've flagged as important.

Most of the home page is devoted to a list of messages—the messages in your Inbox appear here, for example, when you first open Zoho Mail. If you click a different folder, such as Outbox, the list changes to show messages in that folder. Click any message, and a pane opens below the message list, displaying the contents of the message. In the status bar at the bottom of the screen are icons that let you chat in real time right from Zoho Mail (more on chatting at the end of this chapter).

 Tip 4U When you open Zoho Mail, the Inbox shows a list of all unread messages. If you'd rather see a full list of messages (both read and unread messages) when you sign in to Zoho Mail, click Settings, My Preferences and the change the By Default Show My setting to Inbox.

Across the top of the Inbox is a toolbar with these buttons:

- **Compose**—Opens a new window so you can write an email.
- **Fetch**—Checks for new messages.
- **Labels**—Lets you create a new label or apply an existing one to an email message (see the upcoming section).
- **Delete**—Sends the selected message (or messages) to the Trash.
- **Move**—Gives you a choice of other places to put the selected message (or messages): Inbox, Spam, or Trash. If you've created one or more folders, these folders also appear here.
- **Mark As**—Offers ways to flag an email, such as Read, Unread, Archive, Important, Follow up, and more.
- **All**—Filters messages to show either all messages, unread messages only, or flagged messages only. The name of this button changes depending on which filter you've chosen.

To read a message, just click its subject. Mail splits the mailbox into two panes: The top pane shows the list of messages; the bottom shows the content of the message you clicked.

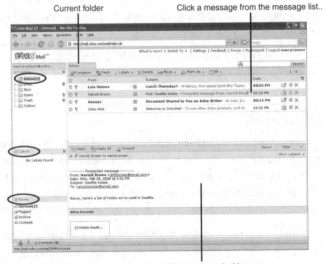

Current folder   Click a message from the message list...

...to read the message in this pane.

Figure 7.1
It's easy to find your way around Zoho Mail's home page.

Getting Started with Zoho Mail

If you've ever used a web-based email program before (and even if you haven't), you'll find Zoho Mail easy to use. Click Zoho's welcome message to read your very first message (and get a few tips about using Zoho Mail), or click Compose to get busy sending emails to friends, family, and colleagues. This section covers the basics of using Zoho Mail.

 If you want to set up your own POP email accounts in Zoho to send and receive email, skip to "Setting Up Other Email Accounts with Zoho Mail" later in this chapter, which tells you how to configure other email accounts.

Composing a New Message

To send someone an email, click the Compose button in the toolbar above the list of messages. A new window opens, like the one in Figure 7.2. Here's where you write your email.

 Many web browsers (such as Internet Explorer) block pop-up windows by default. If you click the Compose button and nothing happens, tell your browser to allow pop-ups from www.zoho.com. (If you're not sure how to allow pop-ups, check your browser's Help files.)

Figure 7.2
Zoho Mail's Compose window has lots of space for you to type your message.

This window will look familiar to anyone who's ever written an email. In the From line, your email address is already filled in. If you have more than one mail account set up in Zoho Mail, you can choose a different account from which to send from the drop-down list associated with the From line.

Type the recipient's address in the To line (if you're writing to multiple recipients, use commas to separate email addresses); add another address in the Cc line if you're sending a copy of the email to someone else.

In the Subject line, type a subject for the email. Then jump down to the big text area and start writing your email.

 You can also send a blind copy of the email to another recipient—meaning that the people in the To line and in the Cc line don't see the address of the other recipient. To do this, click Add Bcc in the Compose window's upper-right corner. This inserts a Bcc text box just below the Cc box. Use the Bcc box to type in the "secret" recipient's email address.

You can optionally format your email with the same type of font attributes, colors, and paragraph settings that you use in Writer. The formatting toolbar has these buttons, going from left to right:

- Bold (Ctrl+B or Cmd-B) toggles the bold attribute on/off.
- Italic (Ctrl+I or Cmd-I) toggles the italic attribute on/off.
- Underline (Ctrl+U or Cmd-U) toggles the underline attribute on/off.
- Background Color highlights the text you've selected.
- Font Color changes the color of your text.
- Font Family lets you select a font, such as Arial or Verdana.
- Font Size offers seven sizes for your text, from tiny to shouting for attention.
- Insert Web Link inserts a hyperlink to a URL that you specify. Type some text and select it first, before clicking this button. That text will then become the hyperlink.
- Remove Web Link removes the hyperlink from the selected text, reverting it to regular text.
- Decrease Indent (Ctrl+D or Cmd-D) moves the left edge of the paragraph closer to the left margin. This works only if the paragraph is currently indented; you can't move it further to the left than the left margin.
- Increase Indent (Ctrl+T or Cmd-T) moves the left edge of the paragraph farther away from the left margin.
- Bulleted List indents the text and adds a bullet character to its left.
- Ordered List indents the text and adds a sequential number to its left.
- Justify Left sets the paragraph's horizontal alignment to left-aligned.
- Justify Center sets the paragraph's horizontal alignment to centered.
- Justify Right sets the paragraph's horizontal alignment to right-aligned.
- Spell Check goes through your message, looking for misspelled words. It highlights all questionable words at once; click a highlighted word to see suggested alternatives, or click Ignore to leave the word as is. You can turn off Spell Check's highlighting by clicking Cancel, above the message area and on the right.
- HTML Editor turns off the message area's formatting buttons, so you compose your email using HTML tags.

After you've typed your message, click the Send button, located in the upper-left corner of the window. Off whisks your email through cyberspace. A confirmation box appears in the lower-right part of the Mail home page to let you know that the message has been sent successfully.

 When you send an email to someone, Zoho automatically adds that person's email address to your Address Book. You can use the Address Book to choose an email address (or several at once) to insert in the To line. Click Address Book and then find and check the boxes of all recipients. Then click To, Cc, or Bcc to put the addresses in one of those sections. Zoho has already added issues@zohomail.com and support@zohomail.com to your Address Book, making it easy to contact someone there when you need help.

Saving Your Draft

Interruptions happen—the phone rings, the baby cries, your boss summons you from your cubicle, *now*. If you get interrupted in the middle of writing an email, you won't have lost the work
you've done. Just save the draft you're working on until you can come back to it.

Click Save Draft. Zoho saves your in-progress email and puts it in the Draft folder. When you've
got time to continue the email, click Draft to open that folder; then click the subject of the message to open it in a Compose window.

 Zoho automatically saves a draft of your message every few minutes. But if you want to be
extra-sure you've got the latest version, do a manual save before you close the Compose
window.

Getting and Reading Email

When you sign in and open Zoho Mail, any new messages appear in your Inbox's message list (as
shown in Figure 7.1). Mail periodically checks for new messages, but you can tell it to check right
now by clicking the Fetch button above the message list. Click any message's subject to open it
in a pane below the message list. If the message pane doesn't feel roomy enough, click the
Popout icon to the left of the message's name. (It's a square with a diagonal arrow pointing
upward.) Zoho opens the message in a new window.

 If you prefer always to read each email message in a separate window, go to Settings, My
Preferences. Then set the Open Mails In option to A Popup.

To move through the emails and read them one at a time, click the Older and Newer links in the
upper-right part of the message pane.

Replying to a Message

To respond to an email you've received, open that email and, in the message pane, choose one
of these options above the message pane on the left:

■ **Reply**—Opens a Compose window, quoting the message you're answering and filling in the
recipient's address in the To line.

■ **Reply All**—This is handy when you're replying to an email that was sent to multiple recipients; when you choose this option, your reply has all recipients' addresses already filled in.

■ **Forward**—Sends an email you've received to a new recipient.

 When you've replied to an email, a speech bubble icon appears next to the sender's name
in your email list. Click the speech bubble to open a new tab that shows the conversation
in progress, including all emails and responses in that thread.

Working with Attachments

An email message isn't always just about the text in the message body. Often, you'll want to attach a document, photo, or other file to your email. This section tells you everything you need to know to send and receive attachments using Zoho Mail.

Adding an Attachment

When you're writing an email in the Compose window and you want to attach a file to the message, click Attach at the top of the window. This opens a File Upload window, where you can browse through the files on your computer and find the one you want to attach. After you've found the file, select it and then click Open.

Zoho attaches the file to your message. You can see attached files in the upper-right part of the Compose window, as shown in Figure 7.3.

To attach another file, repeat the process. To remove a file you've attached, click the X next to the file in the Attachments box.

Figure 7.3
Files you've attached appear in the Attachments box (circled).

Opening an Attached File

When an email message with an attachment lands in your Inbox, you know there's an attached file because a paper-clip icon appears next to the message preview, as Figure 7.4 shows.

When you open the email to read it, Mail puts an Attachments section after the body of the email (see Figure 7.4). The Attachments section shows the name and type of the file, and if the attachment is an image, a preview is provided.

To download an attached file, click its Download link. Tell your computer where to store the file (or which program to use to open it) and then click OK.

 If a message has several attachments that you want to download at once, enable the attachments' check boxes and click Download as ZIP in the upper-right part of the email's Attachments section. This creates a compressed archive file on your hard disk that contains all the attachments. Windows XP and Windows Vista have built-in support for the ZIP format; double-click the ZIP file to open it. Otherwise, use a program such as WinZip or StuffIt to extract the attachments from the ZIP file.

Files that can be opened using a Zoho Docs app, such as documents or spreadsheets, also have a link that lets you open the file in the appropriate Docs program. By clicking the link, you can open a document, for example, in Zoho Writer.

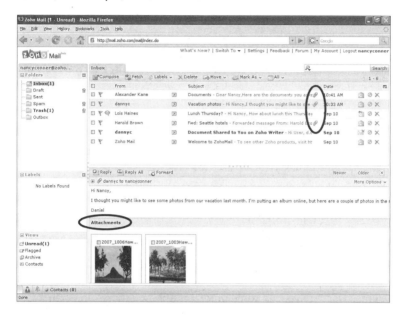

Figure 7.4
A paper-clip icon (circled) indicates that an email message has one or more attachments, which appear in the message's Attachments section (also circled).

Working with Zoho Mail

Now that you've mastered the basics of sending and receiving messages, you can take Zoho Mail to the next level. This section covers intermediate-to-advanced topics for Mail users.

Setting Options for Sending Email

Sure, you can type out an email, maybe attach a file or two, and send it on its way. But Zoho Mail lets you do more than that, such as set a priority level and receive notification when a recipient has opened your email.

Setting a Priority Level

When an email message is urgent, you want to let the recipient know. You can do that by setting a priority level, a mark that appears with the email in the recipient's Inbox. When you open a new Compose window, the priority level setting is always Medium. This means that no special priority mark is added to the email.

To set a different priority level, look at the top of the Compose window for the current priority level (for a new email, that will be Medium). Click the down arrow next to the priority level to open a menu showing your choices: Highest, High, Medium, Low, and Lowest. Choose the one you want, and Mail gives your outgoing message that priority level.

 Not all email programs display a priority level. This includes many web-based programs (even Zoho Mail itself). So if your message is going to an address at, for example, gmail.com or hotmail.com, the recipient may not see the priority level you've set. In addition, some email programs (such as Outlook) have three priority settings, not five, and may not recognize the level you chose.

Requesting a Receipt

When you send an important letter through the postal service, you want to make sure it reaches its destination, so you may request a signed receipt by return post. When you need to be sure that an email's recipient read your message, you can do the same thing electronically—you can request notification when the recipient opens (or, in some cases, closes) the message.

You request a receipt by return email in the Compose window: Check the Ask Receipt box in the upper-right corner before you click Send. That's all there is to it.

When the recipient opens the email, a dialog box appears saying that you've requested notification that the email was received. (In some programs, this box shows up when the recipient closes the email after opening and reading it.) The box gives the recipient a choice: This person can tell his or her email program to send or not to send the receipt. So even if a recipient has received and read your email, you may not get a notification.

Choosing Plain Text or HTML

You have two choices for sending email in Zoho Mail:

- **Plain text**—This is just what it sounds like: plain ol' text. No fancy formatting or flashy displays. Images appear as attachments.
- **HTML**—Hypertext markup language is the language that web browsers use to interpret and display web pages. In email, enabling HTML means you can see images and formatting that don't display in plain text.

Many people set their incoming email to plain text because of security issues: HTML emails may contain viruses or ways to let spammers know that you looked at the email they sent, thus resulting in more spam. HTML emails also take longer to download than plain-text messages.

On the other hand, plain text is, well, boring. And people may get tired of seeing a message that the email they just received holds images that can't be displayed, or they may get frustrated trying to decipher a bunch of HTML gobbledygook that looks something like

```
<div dir="ltr">I've got some <b>great </b>news that you're going to <i>love </i>
hearing!<br></div>
```

when what you wrote looked more like this:

> I've got some **great** news that you're going to *love* hearing!

You can choose whether to send an email as plain text, HTML (if your email has formatting), or both. When you open a new Compose window, the standard choice is both: At the top of the window is the current choice, which initially says Plain Text & HTML. To change that setting, click the down arrow to its right and choose from one of these menu options: Plain Text, HTML, or Plain Text & HTML. Mail sends your outgoing email according to your choice.

Creating a Signature

When you send a letter on paper, you can sign it with a flourish, adding your personal mark. For email, you can also create a signature, which appears at the end of messages you send. An email signature isn't the legal signature you'd use to sign a check or a contract; it's one or more lines of text that might give your title, company name, and phone number, or it might be your favorite saying—anything that says a little more about who you are.

To create a signature, click Settings and then click the Personalize <Your Account> tab and choose Signature. A text box opens, complete with formatting buttons, for you to write up your signature. If you want the signature to appear automatically on every email you send, check the box labeled Add My Custom Signature at the End of All Mails. When you're finished, click Save.

 Tip It's embarrassing to find a typo in your signature after you've appended it to a bunch of emails. So click the Spell Check button at the right side of the formatting toolbar before you save your signature.

Setting a Vacation Reply

Your vacation is a time to relax and have fun—not to drive colleagues and contacts crazy because they can't figure out why you're not answering their emails. Don't let this happen to you. Instead, set a vacation reply that automatically gets sent to everyone who emails you while you're away from the office.

When you want to set up a vacation reply, click Settings and choose the Personalize <Your Account> tab. Click Vacation Reply. On the page that opens, configure these settings:

- **Enable Vacation Reply**—The default for this setting is No. Selecting Yes means that your autoreply is ready to go.
- **Send Vacation Reply To**—Your choices are All (the default), My contacts, and My non-contacts.
- **From/To**—Set the start and end dates for which you want your autoreply to be in effect.
- **Subject**—Write the autoreply's subject line, which might be something like "Out of the office."
- **Content**—What do you want the autoreply to say? Type it here. Usually, a message like this tells recipients when you'll be back and whom to contact in the meantime.

■ **Sending Interval**—This setting, in days, is how long Zoho Mail waits before sending another autoreply to a particular email address.

After you've set up your autoreply, click Save.

Setting Options for Receiving Email

In Zoho Mail, receiving an email is as easy as clicking the Fetch button, and reading that email is as easy as clicking its subject. But you can do more with the email you receive than just read and reply, as this section explains.

Reporting Spam

Nobody likes getting junk email, popularly known as *spam*—it's a waste of your time, attention, and Inbox space. When you get an email promising you big winnings in a foreign lottery you never entered or peddling anything from cheap medications to bogus university degrees, you can get rid of it with a single-click.

To report an email as junk and move it to your Spam folder, click the far-right "No" symbol (a gray circle bisected by a diagonal line). The junk email disappears, and you can get on with reading the rest of your email.

Managing Your Spam Filter

Reporting an email as spam puts the email's sender on your Black List, automatically blocking future emails from that sender. You can also add both email addresses and domains to your Black List. (The domain is the part of the address that comes after the @ symbol—in spammer@spamyou.com, *spamyou.com* would be the domain.)

Your Zoho Mail account also has a White List. Emails from addresses and domains on this list bypass Zoho's spam filters, which means that such emails will always get through to your Inbox.

To manage your Black and White Lists, click Settings (at the top of the page) and then click AntiSpam. This opens the page shown in Figure 7.5. Your Black List is on the left; your White List is on the right. To add an email address or domain to either list, type the address or domain into the text box at the top. Click the plus sign to the right of what you just typed; Zoho moves the address or domain onto the list. When you're done adding to the lists, click Save.

 To remove an address or domain from a Black List or White List, click the red X to the right of its name.

Flagging an Email

When an important email comes in and you want to be able to find it easily later on, you can "flag" it, which marks an email in your Inbox by turning its flag (to the left of the sender's name) red, so it stands out from others in the list. To flag an email, enable its check box. Then, above the list of messages, click Mark As, Important. The message's flag turns red.

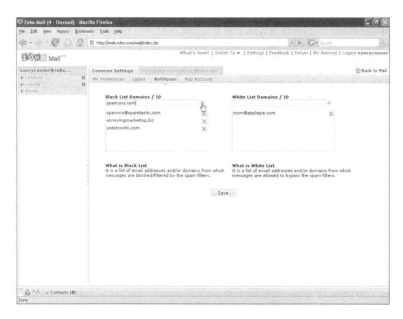

Figure 7.5
You can tell Zoho to always block or always allow messages from particular senders or domains.

To look at only those emails you've flagged as important, look in the left pane under Views and click Flagged. This displays a list of all emails that you've flagged—and no others. This way, you can easily find important emails without digging through a long list of everything else.

Info 4U Flagging an email adds it to Flagged View but doesn't remove it from the Inbox.

You can also mark an email in other ways. When you select one or more emails by checking their boxes and then click Mark As, you can select from these options:

- **Read/Unread**—In your mailbox, unread emails are bold, and emails that you've read appear in normal font. You can set an email that you've already read to Unread (or vice versa) with this option.
- **Archive**—This option removes an email from your Inbox and puts it in the Archive view. This is the virtual equivalent of taking a memo out of your desk's inbox and putting it away in a filing cabinet.
- **Spam**—The previous section tells you one way to report junk emails and dump them in your Spam folder. This is another option for doing the same thing.
- **Info**—Choosing this option turns a message's flag blue and adds it to the Flagged View.
- **Important**—As already described, this option makes a message's flag red and adds it to the Flagged View.

- **Follow-Up**—If an email requires action on your part and you don't want to forget, choose this option. It changes a message's flag to green, reminding you to follow up on the message's contents. Messages flagged "Follow-Up" also appear in Flagged View.

- **Clear Flag**—When a flag is no longer relevant, choose this option to gray out the flag and remove the message from Flagged View.

Saving an Email to Your Computer

You can leave your emails safely stored on Zoho's servers pretty much forever, where you can always find them. But if you want to save an email on your own computer for future reference, you can do that, too.

If you're not already reading the email, click its subject to open it. In the top-right part of the reading pane, click More Options, Save. This downloads the email as a ZIP file. A window opens asking how you want to handle the download. Choose to save the file to your computer and select the location where you want to save it. (You can also open it with a program such as WinZip or StuffIt; if you take this route, remember to save the file after you've looked at it.) Click OK, and your computer downloads the file.

Printing an Email

Often you'll want to print out an email so you can refer to it when you're away from your computer. To do that, open the email you want to print and click More Options, Print View. This opens a new window that shows how the message will look when printed. Click Print (upper right) to open a dialog box where you can choose a printer, specify a page range, and set the number of copies. When you're all set, click OK to print the email.

 If the email you're printing has an attachment, this method prints just the email message, not the attachment. To print an attachment, open it with an appropriate program (such as Zoho Sheet for a spreadsheet) and then print it from there.

Viewing an Email's Header and HTML Code

When you read an email, you're not necessarily seeing everything. The email reader hides some information that simply clutters up the message. If you want, you can see the message in its "raw" form, including its full header (which describe the path the email took to reach you) and the HTML code that provides its layout and formatting.

Why would you need to see the full header? Looking at the header can help you determine whether your friend really sent you that email—or whether someone else is faking the From address. And spam-fighters such as Spam Cop (www.spamcop.net) and the Federal Trade Commission (spam@uce.gov) need the full header to analyze where the email came from. Similarly, when you look at the message's HTML code, you can detect when a link points to a website other than where it claims to be pointing, thus saving yourself from clicking a link to a site that could harm your computer.

To see a message in its raw form, open the message and click More Options, Show Original. This opens the email in a new window that looks like the one shown in Figure 7.6. Notice how much more information you see before you even get to the message itself—that's the full header.

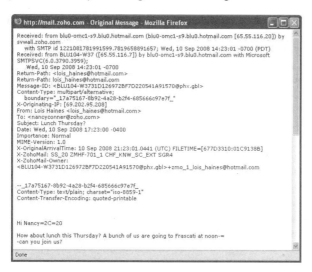

Figure 7.6
Looking at an email's full header can reveal where an email really came from.

Creating Filters

In an email account, setting up filters is like having a kid in the mailroom who sorts incoming letters into the right mailboxes. With filters, you can have emails from your mom land directly in the Family folder, flag all messages from your boss as Important, or label all messages from your team with the *Smith Project* label. You can filter messages based on other criteria, too, such as a particular word or phrase in the Subject line or whether a message is Cc'd to a particular person.

To create a filter, click Settings; on the page that opens, click the Personalize <Your Account> tab. Next, click Add Filter, which opens the page shown in Figure 7.7. From there, follow these steps:

1. Name your filter in the Filter Name box.

2. Set your filter criteria in the For Incoming Messages That section. In this section, you might select Sender Is mom@applepie.com or Subject Contains smith project. Whatever you want Mail to watch for, specify that here. If you set multiple criteria for this filter, tell Mail whether messages must meet all the criteria you set, or just any of them.

3. Set the action you want Zoho Mail to take. As Figure 7.7 shows, you can send the email to a particular folder, flag or tag it, mark the message as read, or send it straight to the Trash.

4. Click Save to create the filter.

Later, if you need to edit or delete a filter, click Settings, Personalize <Your Account> to see a list of filters. Click Edit to open a page that looks just like the one in Figure 7.7, with this filter's info already filled in. Click Delete; then (in the confirmation box) click OK to delete the filter.

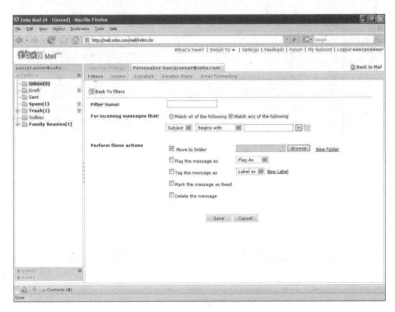

Figure 7.7
Filters make it easier to manage your incoming email.

Setting Up Other Email Accounts with Zoho Mail

These days, many people have more than one email account. For example, you might have one account for work and another that you use for personal emails. You can use Zoho Mail as a central location for accessing email from other accounts.

To set up another email account with Zoho, first make sure that the other email account is POP-enabled. POP, which stands for *post office protocol*, is a method for transferring messages from a centrally located email server to your computer. You don't need to know how POP works to set up another email account with Zoho, but you do need to enable POP access to that account. How you do that depends on the email program you use. As an example, here's how to enable POP access in Gmail:

1. Sign into your Gmail account.

2. Click Settings and then click Forwarding and POP/IMAP.

3. In the POP Download section of the page that opens, select Enable POP for All Mail (to send all your messages to Zoho Mail) or Enable POP for All Mail That Arrives from Now On (to send messages that arrive from this point forward to Zoho Mail).

4. Tell what to do when Zoho fetches your messages using POP: keep Gmail's copy in the Inbox, archive Gmail's copy, or delete Gmail's copy.

5. Click Save Changes.

After you've enabled POP access in the other email account, you need to set up Zoho to use POP to fetch messages sent to that account and deliver them to your Zoho account. Sign in to Zoho Mail and then follow these steps:

1. Click Settings, which opens to the General Settings tab.

2. Click Mail Accounts and then click Add Mail Account to open a page that looks like the one in Figure 7.8.

3. Fill in the General Information section: Type your name in the Display Name field and the address of your other email account in the Email ID field. (For example, for the Gmail account you configured earlier, you'd type yourname@gmail.com.)

4. The Mail Server Information section collects information that lets Zoho fetch mail from your other account. So type in the username and password you use to sign in to that account. The name of the incoming mail server, which handles the mail you receive, will probably begin with *pop*. (For Gmail, it's pop.gmail.com.) The name of the outgoing mail server, which handles the mail you send, will probably begin with *smtp* (for Gmail, it's smtp.gmail.com). For the port numbers, try Zoho's defaults of 110 for incoming mail and 25 for outgoing mail.

Info 4U If Zoho Mail can't access your other email account, check with your email account administrator to see if you need to use different mail server names or port numbers for incoming or outgoing mail.

5. Tell Zoho whether to use a secure connection, which encrypts the data that passes over it. If your email server requires a secure connection, check the box marked Use Secure Connection (SSL). If you're not sure whether this is necessary, ask your email administrator.

6. Some mail servers need authentication (checking your username and password) before they'll send your outgoing email. If yours does, check the box labeled Outgoing Mail Server Requires Authentication. (Again, if you're not sure, check with your email administrator.)

7. Click Save.

Zoho sets up POP access to the other account and adds it to the list of your mail accounts on the Common Settings tab. At this point, it's a good idea to send a test email to your other email account. If the text message lands in your Zoho Inbox, you're all set. If it doesn't, go back to the Common Settings tab, click Mail Accounts, and then click the Edit icon next to the new email account to edit its settings.

Reading Your Email When You're Offline

Because Zoho Mail is web-based, you can access your email messages from wherever you have an Internet connection and a web browser: at home, at your favorite coffee shop, from your hotel room when you're on the road. That's convenient—until you need to review an email message and you *don't* have an Internet connection.

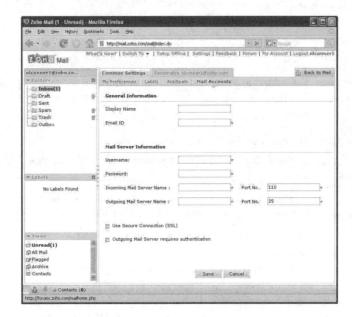

Figure 7.8
Set up Zoho Mail to work with your other email accounts.

Don't worry. Zoho Mail has you covered. Now you can read your Zoho Mail messages even when you're not online. (You can't get new messages or send messages, though—those activities still require an Internet connection.)

Getting offline access to your stored email messages is thanks to Google Gears, which works with your web browser to store and display messages. Chapter 1 "Have Your Say with Zoho Writer," discusses how Google Gears works with Zoho Writer, so flip back to that chapter to learn how to install Gears on your computer.

After you've installed Gears, you need to set up offline access for Zoho Mail. Sign in to Zoho Mail and then click the Setup Offline link at the top of the page. This opens the Offline Settings dialog box shown in Figure 7.9. Here, set up these options:

- **Number of Mails to Download Initially, to Setup Offline Mode**—Choose the maximum number of emails you want to download to get started with offline access: the most recent 50, 100, 150, 200, or 250.

- **Number of Sent Mails to Be Available Offline**—Tell Zoho how many of the most recent emails from your Outbox you want to be available initially: 0, 15, 20, or 25.

- **Download Images and Attachments in Mail**—If you want emails' pictures and attachments available, check this box. If you want just the messages, leave it unchecked.

- **Create Desktop Icon**—Checking this box puts a shortcut on your computer's Desktop to give you one-click access to Zoho Mail.

When you've made your choices, click Setup Offline.

Figure 7.9
Before you can view your email messages while offline, you need to set up offline access.

Now, the next time you're offline, you can open your Web browser and go to mail.zoho.com. (You don't have to sign in.) A message at the top of the screen says that you're currently offline, but you can read and compose messages just like you would when you're connected and signed in to Zoho. (If you compose a new message, make sure you save it as a draft, so you can send it the next time you're online.)

 When you enable offline access, anyone can open and read your email messages in offline mode—no password required. So if you have sensitive messages in your Zoho Mail account and someone might snoop, offline access probably isn't for you.

Organizing Your Email

As your Inbox begins to fill up, you'll want to make messages easier to find by organizing them. Zoho Mail gives you a lot of flexibility in how you organize your messages: You can use folders, labels, or both—whatever makes sense to you. Read through this section to get a sense of the possibilities.

Organizing with Folders

When you want to move a message out of your Inbox and store it elsewhere, you can create a folder and put the message there. Zoho Mail starts you off with a number of standard folders, such as Inbox, Draft, Sent, Spam, Trash, and Outbox; you can also create your own. For example, say you're planning a family reunion and you want to keep all correspondence related to the event in its own folder. Create a folder called Family Reunion; then select the messages you want to store there and click Move, Family Reunion. Neat, organized, efficient.

To create a folder, go to the left pane's Folders heading and click the blue-and-white plus sign symbol to the right of the word *Folders*. This opens the New Folder dialog box, shown in Figure 7.10. Name your new folder in the Folder Name text box.

If you want, you can make the folder you're creating a subfolder of an existing folder. In the family reunion example, you might want to create a separate folder to hold all the RSVPs you receive—it makes sense to create RSVPs as a subfolder of the Family Reunion folder. As Figure 7.10 shows, when you select Family Reunion from the top-level folders list, it appears in the Location box like this:

/Family Reunion

This tells you that the new folder, RSVPs, will be a subfolder of the Family Reunion folder.

When you're ready to create your new folder, click OK. Zoho creates the folder and adds it to the Folders list. (If the new folder is a subfolder, Zoho puts it inside the main folder; click the plus sign to the left of the main folder's name to see its subfolders.)

 It's annoying to create a folder and then discover a typo in its name. To rename a folder, find the folder in the Folder's list and right-click it. From the context menu, select Rename. This opens the Rename Folder box, where you can correct the typo (or give the folder a whole new name). Click OK to make the new name official.

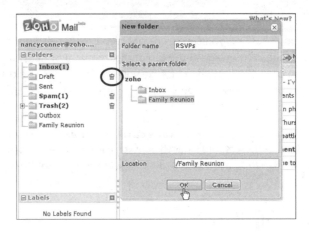

Figure 7.10
When you add a new folder by clicking the circled plus sign, you have the option to make it a subfolder.

 If you're done with a folder and the emails it holds, you can delete it by right-clicking the folder and then choosing Delete. Mail asks for confirmation; click OK to move the folder and its contents to the Trash. If you find later that you deleted something you meant to keep, check the Trash folder.

Organizing with Labels

Another option for organizing your messages is to label them. A *label* is a tag you create that marks email messages. When you create a label, you give it a name and a color. When you apply that label to a message, a tag icon with that label's color appears in the list of messages. Labels also appear in the left pane's Labels section; click any label to see a list of messages with that label.

The big advantage of labels is their flexibility. You can apply the same label to as many messages as you want, and you can stick several labels to the same message. Unlike folders where you store messages (and then may have to dig around a bit to find them again), labels "stick to" messages, wherever those messages happen to be. You can use folders and labels together for maximum efficiency.

In the family reunion example, you might want different labels for correspondence about venues, bands, caterers, and so on. You could make the venues label pink, the bands label blue, and the caterers label green (or whatever colors strike your fancy). As emails accumulate, you can spot the label you're looking for with a glance. And, to create a super-fast filter, you can view a list of only those emails with a particular label.

Creating a New Label

Creating a new label is as easy as assigning a color and a name. Click Labels, New Label to open the New Label dialog box shown in Figure 7.11. Type in a name, assign a color, and then click OK. Zoho creates the label and adds it to the Labels menu and the left pane's Labels section.

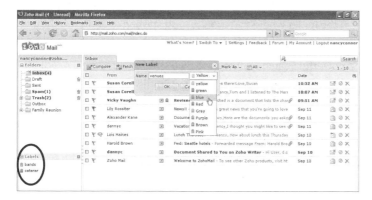

Figure 7.11
Assign a color and a name, and your new label appears in the Labels section (circled).

Assigning a Label to a Message

You can stick a label on one message or on several at a time. From the message list, select the message (or messages) you want by checking the box to the left of the sender's name. Click Labels. From the Labels menu, choose the label you want to apply (or create a new one; see the previous section). Mail applies the label; you'll see a tag icon in the label's color to the left of the subject (Figure 7.11 shows an example).

Viewing Labeled Messages

Any label you create appears in the left pane's Labels section. Simply click a label to open a list showing all emails with that label—and no others.

Removing a Label

To remove a label from a message (or from multiple messages), select any messages you want (use the Labels list to find them easily) and then click Labels, Clear Label. Zoho peels off the label and removes the messages from the Labels list.

When a message has several labels, Clear Label removes them all, so you may have to reapply some labels.

Deleting a Label

To get rid of a label, removing it from the Labels list, the Labels menu, and all emails to which it's attached, right-click the label's name in the left pane's Labels list. From the context menu, select Delete Label. Mail asks you to confirm; click OK, and the label is gone.

Searching Email

No matter how well organized you are, an occasional email message will probably fall through the cracks—it's not in the folder where you thought you stashed it, and even though you could swear you labeled the message, it's not in the list of emails with that label. So how can you find it?

Thanks to Mail's powerful Search feature, finding a stray email is not a needle-in-a-haystack task. If you can remember who sent the email, a word from the subject line, even a word or two from the body of the email, you can easily find the message you're looking for.

Mail's Search box is in the upper-right part of the page. You can search everything in all folders by typing in your search term and clicking Search. Alternatively, as Figure 7.12 shows, you can instruct Mail to search more narrowly, focusing only on subject lines, for example, or in the current folder. To restrict your search in this way, click the down arrow next to the magnifying glass at the left side of the Search box.

After you click Search, Mail performs the search and returns the results on a new tab. The tab's name reflects your search term. Putting search results on their own tab is useful, letting you return to the list of results as necessary.

Figure 7.12
You can search broadly or narrowly for the word or phrase you're looking for.

Chatting in Zoho Mail

Even though email has sped up twenty-first century communications (remember the days when you had to stick a stamp on a letter, drop it in a mailbox, and wait days for a reply?), sometimes even email isn't fast enough. Sometimes you need an answer and you need it *now*—not when Mary or Joe finally gets around to it.

You can speed up your communication by using Mail's built-in chat feature. Open a chat window right from Zoho Mail. If the person you want to chat with is online, you can get a conversation going simply by clicking his or her name.

At the bottom of the screen, on the left side of the status bar, are three buttons that relate to chatting:

 ▧ View Your Profile looks like a person wearing a green coat. Clicking it shows your username, a photo (if you've included one; see the following tip), and your current status: Available, Busy, or a custom status message that you write.

 Adding a photo to your Zoho account lets your friends and colleagues see who they're chatting with. To add a photo from Zoho Mail, click My Account (at the very top of the screen) to open your Zoho Accounts page. If you haven't yet added a photo, the top-left part of the page shows a silhouette. Under the silhouette, click Upload Your Photo. A box opens that lets you browse through files on your computer; when you find one you like, select it and click OK to upload it to your Zoho account. If your photo doesn't show up in Zoho Mail right away, sign out and sign back in to see it.

 ▧ Notifications looks like a bell and tells you whether you have any saved chats that you haven't read, as well as any pending requests to add you to someone's Buddies list.

 ▧ Contacts lists your buddies—those people you've chatted with or have agreed to chat with.

This section explains these buttons and more—everything you need to know to chat from Zoho Mail.

Adding Someone to Your Contacts List

Before you can chat with someone, you need to get his or her okay, confirming that this person is willing to chat with you. And to do that, you add the person to your chat Contacts list:

1. In Zoho Mail's status bar, click Contacts to open the Contacts box shown in Figure 7.13. This box lists existing and invited contacts.

2. Click the box's upper-right Invite icon. The box changes to let you enter someone's Zoho email address or username.

3. Type in the Zoho ID of the person you want to chat with; then click Add.

Zoho sends a notification to the person you added, saying you've added him or her to your Buddies list and displaying buttons that let your invitee accept or reject your invitation. When the invitee clicks Accept, you've got a new chatting partner in your Contacts list.

When someone invites you to join his or her Contacts list, you see the request in two places: the Notifications button in Zoho Mail and on your Zoho Account page. Click Accept if you want to be able to chat with the person who's inviting you. If you don't know the person who issued the invitation (or you simply don't want to chat with that person), click Reject.

Figure 7.13
You'll find chat-related buttons (circled) in the status bar. To invite someone to chat, click Contacts and then click the Contacts list's Invite icon (also circled).

Launching a Chat

When one or more of your contacts are online, the status bar's Contacts button displays a number. Click Contacts to see who's online.

The Contacts list shows a list of names and their current status: Available (green circle), Busy (red circle), or Offline (gray circle). You can start a chat with anyone who's online, regardless whether this person has set his or her status as Available or Busy—although your contacts might get a bit annoyed if they've set their status to Busy and you launch a chat about last night's *American Idol*.

If the person you want to chat with is shown in your Contacts list as available, click his or her name to open a chat window, as shown in Figure 7.14. Type your comment into the text box at the bottom of the chat window; hit Enter when you're done.

Your message appears in a similar chat window on the other person's screen. When that person answers, the message appears below yours in the chat window. A message just above the box where you type your text lets you know what your chat partner is doing, such as typing or being idle.

 If you find yourself squinting at a too-small chat window, click the up arrow in the chat window's upper-right corner. This pops out the chat window, so you can make it as big as you like. Popping out the chat window also adds a row of formatting buttons so you can add bolding, italics, underlining, and emoticons to the chat.

When you're done chatting, close the chat window by clicking its upper-right or lower-right X.

Figure 7.14
When you launch a chat, a small chat window opens next to your Contacts list.

Setting Your Status

To set your chat status, click the far-left View Your Profile button on the status bar (the one that looks like a person in a green jacket). The My Profile box shows your current status. At the bottom of the box, click Change Status. As Figure 7.15 shows, your current status changes to a text box. You can click inside the box and type your own status message, such as *Working on final edits* or *Away from computer* or *Ran away to Tahiti*. Alternatively, you can click the list arrow to choose a status message. The default messages are Available and Busy, but if you've written any custom messages, these also appear on the list. Choose your status message and then press Enter; Zoho displays your new status.

To erase custom status messages, click View Your Profile, Change status. Click the list arrow and then select Clear Status Message. This gets rid of *all* your custom status messages (not just one).

 Tip You can read transcripts of past chats in Zoho Chat. Chapter 8, "Instant Communication with Zoho Chat," tells you all about it.

Figure 7.15
Click Change Status (circled) to write or select a new status.

8

Instant Communication with Zoho Chat

In this high-speed world, people want instant communication—and Zoho Chat delivers. There's no software to download, so you can chat from anywhere there's a computer and an Internet connection. You can chat one on one or in groups, transfer files through the chat window, and save a transcript of the conversation. You can even embed Chat in your website or blog.

Chat is a timesaver for busy professionals. If you need a quick answer and the person who can give it to you is online, you can pop open a chat window and have your answer faster than you could dial the phone. Group chats keep you in touch with your team, even when everyone's not in the same room. And, as teenagers everywhere know, chatting isn't just for business—saying a quick "Hi, how ya doin'?" to a friend or family member can offer a moment of fun in a busy day.

Zoho Chat works similarly to the instant-messaging feature you may have used with Zoho Mail, but as you'll see, Chat offers more: more features, more styles, more flexibility. This chapter tells you everything you need to know to use Zoho Chat—from creating a Contacts list, to starting a chat, to chatting in groups, to putting Chat on your own website.

The Zoho Chat Home Page

When you sign in to Zoho Chat, at http://chat.zoho.com, the home page looks something like the page in Figure 8.1. On the right is a floating window, My Lists, which holds your contacts, any groups you've created, and transcripts of previous chats. After you've added some contacts (see upcoming section), this is where you'll launch your chats.

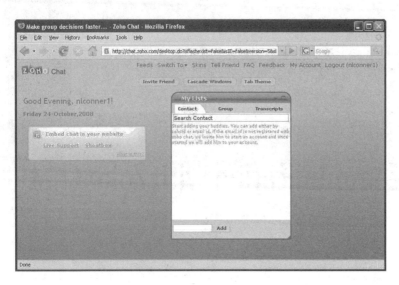

Figure 8.1
The Zoho Chat home page is your starting point for adding contacts and creating groups.

Changing the Home Page's Look

You've got your own personal style—and Zoho knows it. So you've got the option to change the look of Zoho Chat. You can choose between two themes:

- **Tab Theme**—Shown later in this chapter in Figure 8.2, this theme shows your lists (Contacts, Groups, and Transcripts) on the left. When you initiate a chat (or someone starts a chat with you), the chat opens on a new tab.

- **Desktop Theme**—This theme, shown in Figure 8.1, has a sleek look and feel. Your lists initially appear on the right side of the screen, but you can click the My Lists title bar and drag the box to a new location. When a chat starts, it opens as a new window. You can also drag-and-drop these windows around the screen, arranging them as you like.

To switch from Tab Theme to Desktop Theme, click the Desktop Theme link at the top of the page. To switch from Desktop Theme to Tab Theme, click the Tab Theme button near the top of the page.

Info 4U Switching from one theme to the other won't interrupt any chats you have going on.

Besides themes, you can also change Chat's color scheme. (Maybe a nice pink theme feels most soothing when you're chatting with the boss about why your project is late.) Click Skins at the top of the page and then pick from these options:

- **Tab Theme**—Blue, Brown, Dark Blue, Grey, Olive, or Pink
- **Desktop Theme**—Blue or Black

For Tab theme, as soon as you choose an option, Zoho applies it to Chat. For Desktop theme, choose the color you want and then click OK. You can change themes and skins as often as the mood strikes you.

Adding Contacts

Before you can start chatting, you need to add people to chat with. Zoho calls these people *contacts*, and adding a new contact is a two-step process:

1. You add a person to your Contacts list, automatically sending that person an invitation to become one of your chat partners.
2. That person accepts the invitation, becoming a full-fledged contact.

Until the other person accepts your invitation, Zoho lists him or her as *invited*, and you can't initiate a chat with that person. After an invitee has accepted, either of you can start a chat with the other person.

To add a new contact, go to the Chat home page:

- In Tab Theme's left pane, click Add (next to My Contacts). This opens the Add Contact section in the My Contacts pane. Enter the contact info (Zoho ID or email address) and click Add.
- In Desktop Theme, click the Contact tab in your My Lists box. At the bottom of the box is the Add text box. Type in a Zoho ID or email address and then click Add.

Zoho zips off a message to the person, giving your Zoho ID and providing a link that he or she can click to accept your invitation. Invitees who already have a Zoho account must sign in to accept your invitation and chat. (If they're already signed in, a notice pops up asking them to respond to your invitation.) Invitees who don't yet have a Zoho ID of their own must create a Zoho account before they can accept your invitation. (If you don't want to make them do that, see the next section, "Inviting Guest Users," where you'll learn about guest chatting.) After they've created an account and signed in to Chat, your invitation is there, waiting for them to accept or reject.

When an invitee accepts your invitation, Zoho adds that person to your Contacts list. From there, click the contact's name to launch a chat.

 To find a particular contact in a long list, just start typing the contact's Zoho ID or email address in the Search box at the top of your Contacts list. As you type, Zoho guesses which contact you might be looking for and shows a list of results that match the letters you've typed so far.

Inviting Guest Users

Although people on your Contacts list—your regular chat partners—must have a Zoho account to chat with you, it's also possible to set up a chat with guest users, people who don't have a Zoho account. Zoho allows guest users to join you in a chat—no sign-up required. This might be useful for a one-time meeting, for example.

If you're using Tab Theme, make sure you're on the Home tab (see Figure 8.2). In the Invite Your Friend to Chat with You section, write a message explaining what you want to chat about (this is optional) and type in your friend's email address. You can type in more than one address—just be sure to type a comma or hit Enter between each address. When you're done, click Invite.

If you're using Desktop Theme, click the Invite Friend button near the top of the screen. This opens the Invite Your Friend dialog box. Although the look is different from Tab Theme, the process is the same: Type in an optional message, enter recipients' email addresses, and click Invite.

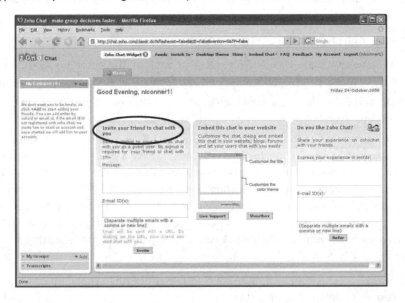

Figure 8.2
You can chat with people who don't have a Zoho account by inviting them as guests.

Zoho sends an email to the addresses you specified. The email contains a link to a guest chat room, shown in Figure 8.3. First, your guest types in his or her name. When the guest clicks the CHAT button, Zoho launches a chat with you. Your chat appears as a tab (in Tab Theme) or a window (in Desktop Theme) in Chat.

Figure 8.3
This is what a guest chat room looks like: a chat window on the left and button to sign up for a Zoho account on the right.

Basic Chatting

Chatting, of course, is the main event. And launching a chat couldn't be easier. Your Contacts list lets you know who's online by showing a symbol next to each contact's name:

- A green sunburst means that the person is online and available.
- A red sunburst means that the person is online but busy.
- A gray sunburst means that the person is offline.

To initiate a chat, click an online contact's name. (You can launch a chat with someone even if his or her status is Busy.) This opens the chat in a new tab (in Tab Theme) or a new window (in Desktop Theme, shown in Figure 8.4). At the bottom of the chat area is a text box; type your message there. If you like, you can use the formatting buttons to add emphasis, color, or an emoticon (smiley face) to your message. To send the message, either press the Enter key or click Send.

As Figure 8.4 shows, your message appears in the chat area, identified by your Zoho ID and a date/timestamp. When your chat partner responds, his or her message appears just below yours.

Managing Multiple Chats

If you have a lot of friends, or even just a few, you might find yourself involved in several chats at once. When that happens, each chat takes place in a new tab or window, depending on the theme you're using. (Figure 8.5 shows multiple chats in Desktop Theme.) Each chat is separate and self-contained, and you can move back and forth between multiple chats by clicking the tab or window of the chat you want to switch to.

Figure 8.4
Type in the bottom of the chat window and then press Enter or click Send to make your comment appear in the chat area.

When you get a new message, the tab or window's title bar turns orange to let you know there's a new comment in that chat. When you switch to that chat, the normal color returns.

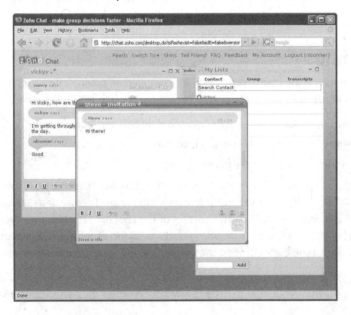

Figure 8.5
Desktop Theme showing multiple chats open in multiple windows, with the active chat in the foreground.

Multiple chats can make Desktop Theme look a bit messy. You can neaten up the screen by clicking the Cascade Windows button, which stacks the windows while letting you see the title bar of each. Click any window to bring it to the front and make it the active window.

Sending a File Through Chat

As you chat, you may want to send your chat partner a file—a spreadsheet needed by a colleague who's compiling a report, for example, or a photo from your cousin's wedding. Perhaps you want to send your chocolate cake recipe to a friend who can't stop raving about it. Regardless, you don't have to open up an email program or make a note to yourself to remember to send the file later. You can transfer the file immediately using Chat.

In the lower-right part of the Chat window, just above the Send button, is Send File. In Tab Theme, it's a link; in Desktop Theme, it's a button that looks like a sheet of paper. When you click Send File, the text box where you normally type messages changes to box with a Browse button, as shown in Figure 8.6. Click the Browse button to open a File Upload window. Find the file you want to transfer, select it, and click OK. The file path appears in your Browse box; click Send.

Chat transfers the file as a link, which appears in your chat area and your partner's. Your chat partner can click the link to download the file or open it in an appropriate program.

Figure 8.6
Click Send File (circled) to choose and transfer a file from your computer.

Sending an Offline Message

When a contact is offline, you obviously can't chat with that person. But you can use Chat to send him or her a message. The next time your contact signs in to Zoho Chat, your message is waiting as an unread message.

The way to send an offline message is to act as though the other person is online; click the ID you want (even though that person is offline) to open a chat tab or window. Type in your comment and click Send (or press Enter). The other person isn't signed in to Zoho, so you won't get a response right now. You might as well close the window or tab.

Later, when the other person signs in to Zoho Chat, he or she will see a new unread message. When that person reads the message, if you're online, he or she can initiate a chat that begins with the offline message you sent. If you're not signed in to Zoho, the other person can send you an offline message in return. This message, which appears in your Unread Messages, shows your original comment and the response.

 Unread Chat messages also appear in the Notifications area of Zoho Mail's status bar. When you click Notifications, Unread Messages, Chat opens in a new window, where you can read and respond to those messages.

Group Chats

Think of a group chat as a conference call—one that uses instant messaging instead of a telephone. Instead of chatting one on one, you carry on a single conversation with multiple participants. Start by creating a group, a list of people you want to have group chats with. After you've created a group, click the group's name to start a chat with any and all group members who are online. (Any group member who misses the chat gets a transcript of it.) You can edit a group (adding or deleting members) or delete it at any time.

Creating a Group

If you want to chat with a group—whether it's family members, your circle of friends from high school, or the members of your project team—the first thing you need to do is create the group, adding members you can chat with en masse with a single-click.

If you use Tab Theme, go to the left pane and click Add (to the right of My Groups). If you use Desktop Theme, in your My Lists window, click Group; at the bottom of the window, click the Add button. This opens Add Group (as a section of My Groups in Tab Theme, or as a new window in Desktop Theme, shown in Figure 8.7).

Give your group a name. This is how you'll find the group in your Groups list, so make it descriptive. Your contacts appear in the Existing Contact List box. Select a name to move it to the Added List box, thus adding that name to the group you're creating. When you've selected all the members you want, click Add to create the group and add it to your Groups list.

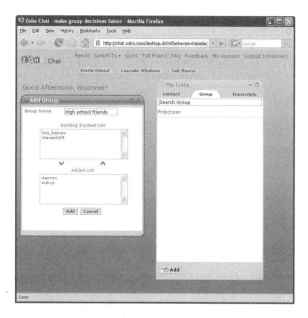

Figure 8.7
Move contacts from the Existing Contact List (top) to the Added List (bottom) to add those people to your group.

After you've created a group, you can find it in My Groups (Tab Theme) or on the Group tab of the My Lists window (Desktop Theme). Click a group's name to open a group chat. When you type in a message, it goes to all group members who are currently signed in to Zoho. Those who miss the chat get a transcript of it as an unread message the next time they sign in.

Managing Groups

Groups aren't chiseled in stone. After you've set up a group, you can modify its membership. If you no longer need a group—a project has ended, for example, and the team disbanded—you can delete it.

Editing a Group

To change a group's membership, click My Groups (Tab Theme) or the My Lists window's Group tab (Desktop Theme). Place your cursor over the group you want to edit and then click the Edit icon that appears. (It looks like a pencil poised over a sheet of paper.) This opens the Update Group section (Tab Theme) or the Modify Group window (Desktop Theme).

This window looks just like Add Group; contacts who aren't group members appear in the top box, and current group members appear in the bottom box. Click any contact to move it to the other box. When you're finished, click Update, and Zoho saves the changes you've made.

Searching for a Particular Group

To search for a group by name, click My Groups (Tab Theme) or in the My Lists window click Group (Desktop Theme). At the top of the list of groups is a search box. Type all or part of the group's name into the box, and as you type, the list narrows down to close or exact matches.

Deleting a Group

When you no longer need a group—the project is finished, the class reunion was a big success—you don't want it cluttering up your Groups list. To delete a group, click My Groups (Tab Theme) or the My Lists window's Group tab (Desktop Theme) to display the list of groups. Move your cursor to the group you're getting rid of so that a red X appears to the right of the group's name. Click the red X. Zoho asks you to confirm that you want to delete the group; click Yes to finish the deletion.

Inviting Others to Join an Ongoing Chat

When you're having a discussion in a chat, from time to time you'll likely wish to bring somebody else into the conversation—to get a third opinion, answer a policy question, or give a new perspective. During an ongoing chat, even if the chat is one on one, you can invite others to join you. This saves you the trouble of having to start the chat from scratch when you want to include more members.

Adding a Contact or Group to an Ongoing Chat

When you're chatting and you want to bring in another participant from your Contact list, click Add Participant. In Tab Theme, click Add (to the right of Participants in the pane on the right). In Desktop Theme click the button that shows a person and a plus sign in the lower-right part of the chat window. This opens a box that looks like the one in Figure 8.8, with three tabs: Contact, Group, and Invite Guest.

To select an existing contact or group, click the appropriate tab and make your choice from the list. Click Add. The chat shows that you've added someone new to the chat, and a chat tab or window opens in the contact's screen.

 When someone joins a chat already in progress, that person's chat window or tab shows everything that has been said in the chat so far.

Inviting a Guest to an Ongoing Chat

Just as you can invite guests who don't have a Zoho account to chat with you one on one, you can also invite a guest to join a chat that's happening right now.

When you start a chat with one of your Zoho contacts, that chat, by default, blocks non-Zoho guests from participating. So the first step in inviting a guest is to unblock guests. To do this in Tab Theme, look at the bottom of the Participants pane, where it says "Guest Blocked" (see Figure 8.8). Click the Allow link to open up the chat for guests. In Desktop Theme, you need to make the chat window show current participants to allow guests; click the Show Participants button in the lower-right part of the chat window, and a pane opens inside the window that shows who's participating in the chat. Click Allow at the bottom of that pane.

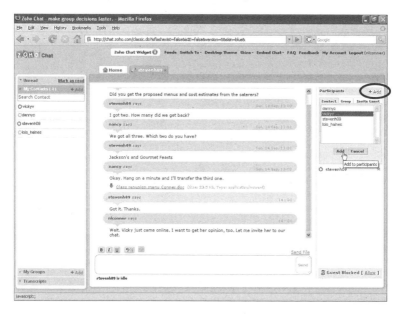

Figure 8.8
Click Add (circled) to bring someone else into an ongoing chat.

Info 4U When you allow guests to be invited to the current chat, a message appears in the chat tab or window notifying participants that you've turned on guest access.

After you've unblocked the chat, the next step is to invite a guest or two. Click Add in Tab Theme's Participants pane or the Add Participants button in Desktop Theme. This opens the box shown in Figure 8.8. Click the Invite Guest tab, as shown in Figure 8.9.

On the Invite Guest tab, type in the email address of the person you're inviting. If you want, you can supplement the brief invitation message Zoho sends. Click Add. Zoho sends a message to the email address you entered; in the email is a link. When the guest clicks the link, it opens a window like the one shown back in Figure 8.3. As soon as your guest types in a name, he or she joins the chat already in progress.

Info 4U Guest users appear in the Participants list only after they've joined the chat.

Blocking and Unblocking Guest Access

Any Zoho-registered Chat participant can block guests during a chat. All it takes is clicking Block at the bottom of the Participants pane. When you block a guest, the guest's chat window displays this message: *Guest access has been temporarily blocked.* To unblock guest access and let your guest back in on the discussion, click Allow.

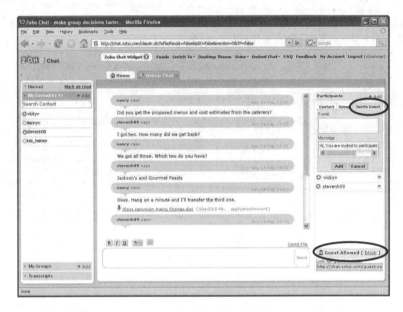

Figure 8.9
Make sure guest access is allowed; then click the Invite Guest tab to send out an email invitation to join the chat.

 After you reenable guest access, your guest can see what was said in the chat while access was blocked.

Saving Your Chats: Transcripts

Ever half-recall something from a conversation and wish your memory was better? There are days when life would be easier if you had your own personal secretary to follow you around and take notes on all your conversations. Zoho Chat offers the next best thing: It records your chats and saves a transcript of each one. You can view, delete, and search these transcripts. You can even continue the conversation by using the transcript to launch a new chat.

You don't have to do anything to save transcripts of your chats—Chat saves a transcript auto-matically when a chat ends. Any transcripts you haven't looked at are called "unread" messages, as shown in Figure 8.10. In Tab Theme, Zoho adds any unread messages to the top of your list in the left pane. If you don't need to read them, mark them as read (in Tab Theme); Zoho transfers them to your Transcripts list. Each transcript is identified by the name or Zoho ID of the person you chatted with, as well as the date or (for today's chats) the time.

 Transcripts of Zoho Mail chats also appear in your Zoho Chat Transcripts list (see Chapter 7, "Zoho Mail: Web Mail Redux").

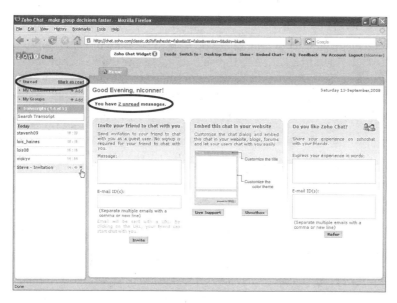

Figure 8.10
Click Unread or the "x unread" link to see transcripts of past chats or messages sent to you while you were offline.

Searching Transcripts

If you chat a lot, those transcripts pile up pretty quickly. If you're looking for a particular chat, the sheer volume of transcripts can seem daunting. So it's a good thing that Chat has a Search box that's just for transcripts. (You can see it in Figure 8.10.)

When you type in a search term, Zoho starts searching the content of all your transcripts. As you type, Zoho returns results—so you may not even have to hit Enter to find the chat you're looking for. To open a transcript from the results list, click the chat you want, and Chat opens it on a new tab or in a new window (depending on your theme).

Continuing a Saved Chat

This is a nice feature if you have a question about or a response to something particular in a previous chat: You can use the transcript of that earlier chat to launch a new one.

When you click a chat to open it in a new tab or a new window, the text box appears at the bottom of the tab or window, just as it does in an active chat. If your chat partner is online, type something into the text box and then click Send or press Enter.

The chat launches on the other person's screen, showing not just your new comment but the transcript of the previous chat. Handy if you have to quit a chat in the middle of an argument or a juicy gossip session.

Deleting a Transcript

If you want to delete a transcript from Chat, you have to be using the Tab Theme. (So if you're using the Desktop Theme, click the Tab Theme button.) Locate the transcript you want to delete in the Transcripts section of your Lists pane. When you move the cursor over a transcript, the transcript gets highlighted and a red X appears to its right. Click that X. Zoho asks whether you're sure you want to delete the transcript; click Yes to finish it off.

 Keep in mind that each chat has at least two transcripts: yours and transcripts of other participants. Even if you delete your transcript, your chat partner still has another one. So be careful about what you say in Chat—don't say anything that could get you fired, make your best friend hate you, or drive your spouse to file for divorce. There's probably a record of your words.

Embedding Zoho Chat in Your Website or Blog

On your website or blog, you probably already provide a way for visitors to contact you via email. But how about letting them chat with you, right from your page? This can be a great way to connect, quickly and easily, with potential customers, fans, friends, family—anyone who visits your site or blog. As long as you're online and signed in to your Zoho account, visitors can initiate a chat with you.

Embedded Chat comes in two flavors:

- Live Support lets you do one-on-one chats with visitors to your site or blog.
- Shoutbox allows multiperson chats, so visitors can chat with you and with each other, as well. With Shoutbox, a message sent by one visitor is visible to all the others.

The first steps in embedding Chat in your website or blog depend on the theme you use:

- **Tab Theme**—Start at the top of the page. Click Embed Chat and then choose Live Support or Shoutbox. Alternatively, you can click the Live Support or Shoutbox button in the Home tab's middle section.
- **Desktop Theme**—Start on the left side of the page, under the greeting and date. In the Embed Chat in Your Website box are two links: Live Support and Shoutbox. Click the one you want.

A box (Embed Chat in Tab Theme) or window (Configure Embed UI in Desktop Theme, shown in Figure 8.11) opens that lets you preview the Chat gadget you're embedding as you tweak its design just a bit. You can give the chat box a title and adjust its colors so it won't clash with the colors already on your site. Click a color to apply a predesigned color theme, or use hexadecimal values to design your own color scheme.

 Don't speak hexadecimal? Go to www.htmlhelp.com/cgi-bin/color.cgi for a table that lists popular colors and their hexadecimal values.

As you try out titles and colors, the preview on the right changes to show how your chat window will look. When it looks good, copy the HTML code snippet that appears in the box labeled Copy and Paste the Code.

Next, paste the snippet into an HTML file and then upload that file to your site or blog. The window appears on your page, just as you designed it, ready for visitors to start chatting with you.

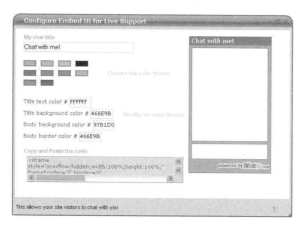

Figure 8.11
As you adjust the chat window's settings; the preview shows how the embedded window will look.

 You don't have to go to chat.zoho.com to chat with your friends, family, and colleagues. Go to http://widget.zoho.com/downloads/download.htm to download the Zoho Chat Widget and install it on your computer. With the widget, you can chat, see your contacts, and view their current status, even if you don't have your web browser open. Currently, the Zoho Chat Widget is available only for Windows users.

Zoho Planner: Your Online To-Do List

List makers get things done. When you organize your tasks, events, and appointments by writing them down, you're more efficient. And there's something satisfying about checking off those tasks as you accomplish them.

Zoho Planner is an online to-do list that lets you keep track of the things you have to do, the people you have to meet, the places you have to be. It's simple, streamlined, and easy to use. In Planner, you create pages to hold your lists and appointments (as well as any notes). You can create one big master page, or break things down into different pages for different areas of your life—your work schedule, the kids' activities, a "honey do" list for your spouse—and then relate those lists through tags.

This chapter covers everything you can do with Planner—from creating your first page, to filling it with content, to sharing it with others.

Filling Your Page with Content

Start by going to http://planner.zoho.com and signing in. Zoho Planner opens with one list that's waiting for you to start filling it up with items: your Home Page, shown in Figure 9.1. All Planner pages have a list along the left side where you can navigate your pages, take a look at reminders you've set for yourself, and get an overview of upcoming tasks. But before you can do any of that, you have to create content for your first page.

Creating a To-Do List

A Planner To-Do list is just what it sounds like: a way to jot down errands, chores, and other tasks that you need to work your way through, as shown in Figure 9.2. As you complete a task, you can check it off as completed—and enjoy the satisfaction of watching that long list of *to-do's* become a long list of *dones*.

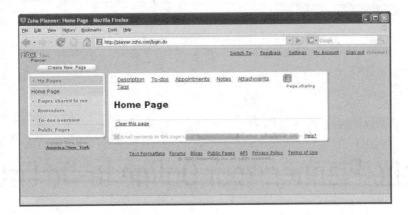

Figure 9.1
Planner's Home Page has a simple, streamlined design.

As Figure 9.2 shows, a To-Do list consists of specific headings, such as Errands, Household Chores, and so on—whatever categories best express the things you need to get done. After you've created a category, you can add specific tasks to that category, keeping your hectic life organized.

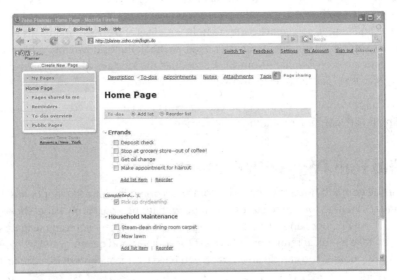

Figure 9.2
A To-Do list puts tasks into categories that you create.

To create and fill in a To-Do list, follow these steps:

1. Open the Zoho Planner page that will hold the list and click To-Dos at the top of the page. The page expands to look like the one in Figure 9.3.

2. With To-Dos, a *list* is a category, which shows up on your page as a heading. In the text box, type the name of the list you want to create, such as *Errands*, and then click the Add List button. (Each list name shows up on the page as a heading.) The section expands so you can add your first item to the list, as shown in Figure 9.4.

3. In the To-Do Description text box, type in the first task that belongs in the list you just created. In the Errands list, for example, you might create a task such as *Pick up drycleaning*.

4. If desired, add a due date for the task. Click the calendar next to the Due Date box to select and insert a date.

5. If you want, set a Remind Me option, so that Zoho sends you a reminder about the task. You can choose to get a reminder one day before the scheduled task, on the same day, when the task expires, or every day. (For more about reminders, see "Getting Reminders" later in this chapter.)

6. Click the Add List Item button (or press Enter). Zoho adds the task to your To-Do list and opens another To-Do Description text box so you can add another task.

7. When you're finished adding tasks to the list, click the Close link to return to the page, or click Add List in the To-Dos title bar to create another new list.

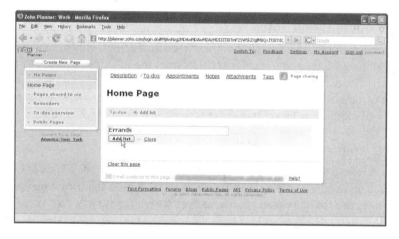

Figure 9.3
Create a category for tasks on your To-Do list.

Tip 4U Want to change Planner's color scheme? Give Planner a different skin. Click Settings. On the page that opens, the Choose a Skin section has five color choices. Pick one to update Planner's look.

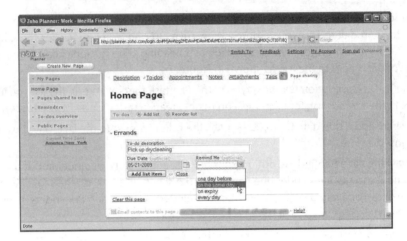

Figure 9.4
When you add items to your To-Do list, you have the options of adding a date and getting a reminder about the task.

Adding Appointments and Notes

An online planner wouldn't be complete without sections for appointments and notes. Planner keeps appointments in their own section, separate from the To-Do list, because to-do tasks can often be put off for another day, but when you have an appointment, you have to make sure you're there on time. And notes, which also get their own section, provide helpful reminders when you need a little extra info about where you're going or what you're doing.

Adding an Appointment

Missed appointments waste time, cause inconvenience, and cost money. Planner helps you make sure you remember and keep your appointments. It'll even send you a nudge anywhere from 15 minutes to a full day ahead of time, so the time won't get away from you.

To create an appointment and add it to your page, open the page you want and click Appointments at the top. The page expands to look like the one in Figure 9.5. Fill in this info:

- **Appointments**—Give your appointment a name so you'll know whom the appointment's with or what it's for.

- **Scheduled On**—In this section, pick a date (click the calendar to choose) and time (use the drop-downs). Minutes are in 5-minute increments.

- **Remind Me**—Based on the time of your appointment, Zoho will send you a reminder at the specified time: 15 minutes or half an hour before; 1, 2, 6, or 12 hours before; or a full day ahead of time.

- **Repeat**—For recurring appointments, such as your daughter's weekly ballet lesson, select the interval between appointments from this drop-down. For more on standing appointments, see "Recurring Appointments" later in this chapter.

■ **Notify to Shared Mail ID's**—If you've shared this page with others (covered in "Sharing Planner Pages" later in this chapter), check this box to send notification of this appointment to those you're sharing with.

After you've set up the appointment, click Add Appointment to put it on your page.

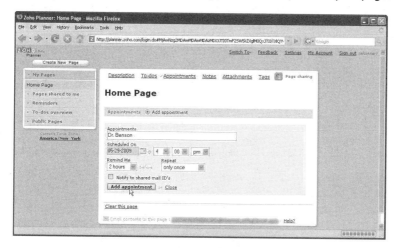

Figure 9.5
Schedule an appointment—and also reminders to give you a nudge as the time approaches.

Jotting Yourself a Note

Notes are the virtual equivalent of scrawling information on a sticky note and affixing it to a page in your planner, your cubicle wall, or your computer's monitor—only a lot less messy. A note can be any information that would be helpful to add to your page: the street address and phone number for an appointment, the names and subjects of your kids' teachers for a meeting at school, points and questions you want to include in an email or memo—anything at all.

Writing yourself a note and adding it to your page takes just a few quick steps:

1. Open the page where you want to put the note. At its top, click Notes, and the page expands to look like the one in Figure 9.6.

2. Give the note a name in the Title text box. On your page, this functions as a heading for the note.

3. Type your note in the Body box.

4. Click Add Note, and the note appears on your page.

Tip 4U A fast-and-easy way to add a note to a page is to email it. At the bottom of each of your Planner pages is an email address; send a message to that address, and the message is added to the Notes section of that page. Add the email address for each page to your address book to make sure your note lands where you want it to.

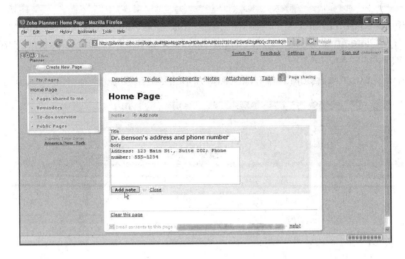

Figure 9.6
Write yourself a note to appear on your page.

Attaching a File

If something on your To-Do list requires a file, such as reviewing a spreadsheet or report or sign-ing off on a specification, you can attach that file to your page, so it's right at your fingertips when you're ready to tackle its associated task.

Attaching a file to a Planner page is easy. On the page where you're attaching the file, click Attachments at the top of the page. The Attachments section expands to look like the one in Fig-ure 9.7. Click the Browse button to open a window where you can find and select the file you want to attach; when you've done that, click OK and, back in Planner, the file path appears in the Browse box. If you want, add an optional description. Click Upload Attachment to attach the file to your page.

Info 4U   Make sure the file you're uploading is 10MB or less. Zoho can't transfer larger files.

After you've attached a file (such as the Sales.xls file that has been attached in Figure 9.7), click its name to download it or open it in the appropriate program.

Info 4U   If you've uploaded an image, Planner shows you a thumbnail of that image.

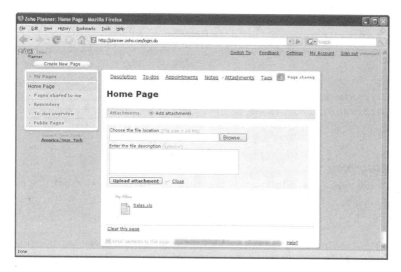

Figure 9.7
Tell Zoho where to find the file you want to upload; click a file's name to open it.

Working with Pages

After you've filled your home page with to-do lists, appointments, notes, and attachments, you know how useful Zoho Planner can be. But providing content is only the beginning. You might want to create more pages: one for work, one for your personal time, one for keeping track of the kids' schedules, and so on. Or you might find yourself reordering your priorities—and you want your To-Do list to reflect the changes. You can share a page with others or tag pages to make them easier to find. This section moves beyond the basics to help you get the most out of Planner.

Creating a New Page

To create a new page, click the Create New Page button. When you do, a Name Your New Page text box appears right below the button. Type in a name and click Create.

Zoho creates the page, opens it, and adds it to the left menu's My Pages list.

 Tip To rename a page, open the page you want to rename and click its title. The title changes to a text box. Give the page its new name and click Save Title to rename the page.

Describing Your Page

Adding a description to a page is a good idea for public or shared pages: When you create a page, *you* know what it's for, but others who view it may not. A page's description appears at the top of the page, beneath its title. So when someone else views the page, its purpose is clear.

To add a description to a page, open the page you want and click Description at the top. This opens a big text box where you can write the description. When you're finished describing the page, click Save Desc. Zoho displays your description at the top of the page, below the page's name and above your To-Do list.

 You can insert web addresses (URLs) into your description. When a URL in a description begins with http://, Zoho automatically turns it into a link that opens the web page in a new window.

Editing a Description

If you want to change a description you wrote, click the Edit Description link that appears just above the description. This opens a text box like the one you used to write the description, with the current text filled in. Make your changes and then click Save Desc to update.

 To delete a description, click Edit Description. When the text box opens with the current description, delete all the text from the box. Click Save Desc, and the description section disappears from the page.

Reordering Pages

As the list of pages under My Pages grows, you might want to change their order on that list, so that the pages you use most often are easy to open. To change the order of pages in the My Pages list, put your cursor over the My Pages bar; a Reorder link appears.

Click Reorder, and the page changes to list all your pages, as shown in Figure 9.8. Move the cursor over a page you want to move. When the cursor changes to a four-way arrow, click and then drag-and-drop the page where you want it. Click Save Page Order when you're done moving pages.

 The first page in your list is always your Home Page. You can give the Home Page any name you like, but you can't delete it.

Working with To-Do Lists

Earlier in this chapter, "Creating a To-Do List" took you step by step through creating a new To-Do list. Once you've created a list and added some tasks to it, you can work with that list in various ways.

Collapsing and Expanding Lists

When your To-Do list is made up of several different lists, each crowded with tasks, opening the page can seem daunting. To make your page less unwieldy, you can collapse any of your lists, hiding its individual items and showing only its title.

To collapse a list, click the small down arrow to the left of the list's name. To expand it, revealing all its individual items, click the arrow (which is now pointing right) again. Figure 9.9 shows what the collapse and expand arrows look like.

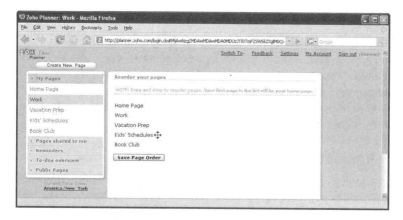

Figure 9.8
Drag-and-drop a page to change the order in the My Pages list.

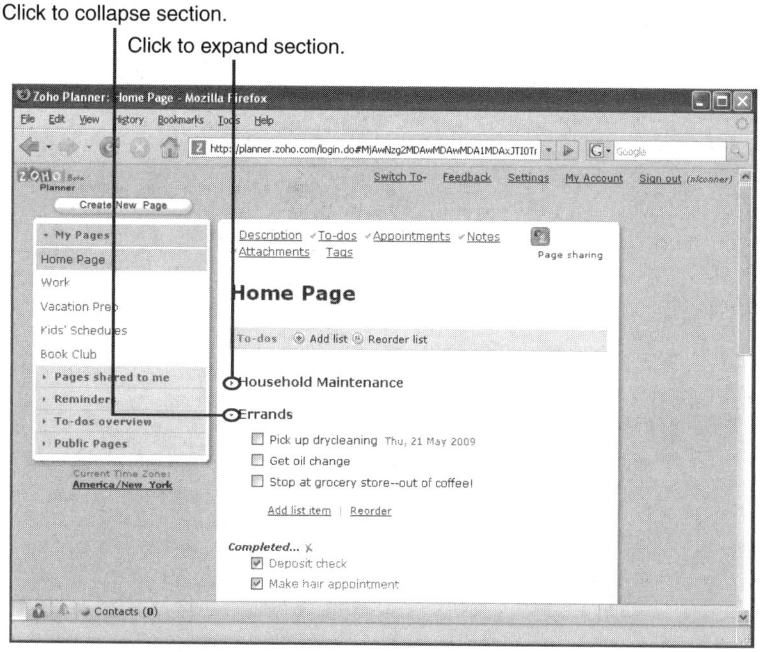

Click to collapse section.

Click to expand section.

Figure 9.9
You can show or hide items in a list by clicking the circled arrows.

Checking Off an Item as Done

One of the most satisfying things about keeping a to-do list is checking off items as you complete them. It conveys a sense of accomplishment to see the number of to-do's shrink. You can get that sense of accomplishment in Planner—when you've done something on one of your

To-Do lists, simply check the box next to that item. Zoho moves it to the Completed section of the list and places a green check inside the box. (Figures 9.2 and 9.12 show examples.)

If you want to remove an item from a To-Do list's Completed section, put the cursor over the item so that a red X appears to the item's right. Click the X to delete the item. To remove all items in the Completed section, click the red X to the right of the word *Completed*. Whether you're deleting one item or the whole Completed section, you get a dialog box asking you to confirm the deletion. Click OK to remove the item(s) from the list.

Rearranging Items on a List

It's easy to overlook an item that sits at the bottom of a long lists of tasks, chores, and to-do's. To make sure a particular item catches your eye, you can move it to the top of the list.

Click the Reorder link at the bottom of the list whose items you want to rearrange. Put the cursor on the item you want to move; the item is highlighted, and the cursor changes to a four-way arrow, as shown in Figure 9.10. Click-and-drag the list item to its new location and then drop the item there.

When you've finished moving items around, click Save Order to save your changes.

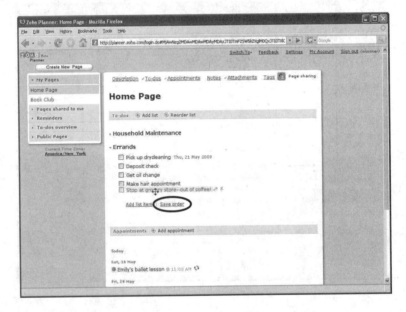

Figure 9.10
Drag-and -drop a list item and then click Save Order (circled).

 Tip 4U   You can also rearrange the lists that make up your To-Do list. To the right of To-Dos, click Reorder List. Zoho collapses all your lists, so you can click, drag, and drop to move them around. When you're finished, click Save List Order.

Recurring Appointments

Some appointments happen at recurring intervals, such as soccer practice, yoga studio, the weekly progress meeting at work, and so on. In fact, a recurring event doesn't have to be an "appointment." It can be anything that happens on a regular schedule: Think birthdays and anniversaries or medication that requires you to take a dose every 4 hours.

When you set up a new appointment, one of the settings is Repeat, a drop-down where you set the interval for how frequently the appointment or event recurs. The default is Only Once; you'd choose this setting for something like a job interview or a doctor's appointment. For events that happen over and over again at regular intervals, though, you can choose an interval such as 1 hour, 4 hours, 12 hours, every day, every week, every month, or every year.

With a recurring event, after the clock has ticked past the start time of that event, Zoho automatically schedules the event again, according to the interval you set. For example, say you have a meeting every Thursday at 2:00 p.m. You add the meeting as an appointment, choosing "every week" from the Repeat drop-down. When it's Thursday, as soon as the clock ticks past 2:00 p.m., Zoho moves the appointment from Today to next Thursday. This way, your recurring appointment is always up to date.

Tagging Pages

Putting tags on your pages can help you stay organized. A *tag* is a label that you create and apply to a Zoho Planner page, helping you stay organized. In particular, it can help you find other pages with content similar to the page you're looking at now. When you have only one or two pages, this is not an issue, but if you use Zoho to manage dozens of projects, for example, and each one has its own page, tags become a very useful way of grouping and organizing pages.

Adding Tags to a Page

To add a tag (or more) to a page, open the page you plan to tag and click its Tags link. This opens a text box where you can type in as many tags as you want. Use tags that describe the content of the page. For example, a page that helps you track tasks at work might have tags such as Smith project, Jones project, training, meetings, and so on. When you've added all the tags you want to (for now, anyway), click Save Tags. Zoho puts your new tags in a section at the bottom of the page, as shown in Figure 9.11.

Using Tags to Find Related Pages

After you've applied tags to a number of different pages, you can use those tags to help you find related pages. For example, say you added the tag *family* to several pages—those tracking the kids' schedules, your spouse's schedule, your parents' activities in their retirement community, preparations for the upcoming family reunion, and so on. When you open one of those pages, scroll down to the Tags section and click Family. Zoho shows you a section called Pages Tagged as Family, which lists all pages that share that tag. Open any page from the list by clicking its name.

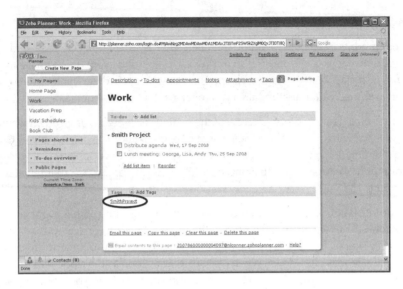

Figure 9.11
Zoho adds tags as links at the bottom of your page.

Editing To-Do Lists, Appointments, and Notes

If you need to change a To-Do list or task, an appointment, or a note that's on your page, you can. Whether you're correcting a typo or changing an appointment that the doctor's office called to reschedule, simply hover your cursor over the element you want to edit. As Figure 9.12 shows, the element becomes highlighted and two icons appear to its right: Edit (a pencil) and Delete (a red X). Click the Edit icon.

The element changes to a form just like the one you used to create the element, with the current information filled in. Make your edits and then click the button to save your changes. (The name of this button depends on the element you're editing: Save List Item, Update Appointment, and so on.)

Deleting an Element from a Page

When you want to remove some element from your page, whether it's a To-Do list, a task, an appointment, a note, or an attachment, place your cursor on the element you want to delete and then click the red X that appears to its right (see Figure 9.12). You see a confirmation box asking whether you're sure you want to delete the element; when you click OK, it's gone from your page.

 Deleting a To-Do list, such as Errands, deletes all the items on that list.

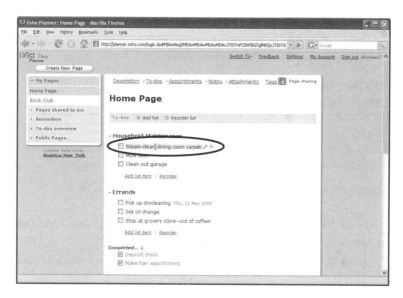

Figure 9.12
Hover over an item to make its Edit and Delete icons appear.

Deleting All Elements from a Page

Ready to make a clean sweep? You can clear everything from a Planner page with two clicks. Open the page you want to clear and scroll down to the bottom. Click the Clear This Page link. Zoho asks whether you're sure that you want to delete everything on the page. Click OK, and the page is empty.

 Clearing a page doesn't delete the page—just its content.

Deleting a Page

When you no longer need a page, you can delete it from Planner. Just open the page you want to delete and scroll down to the bottom. Click Delete This Page and then click OK to confirm. Zoho deletes the page and its content and removes the page from your My Pages list.

Sharing Planner Pages

When you create a list, it's private by default—which is great when you don't want others peeking over your shoulder at your schedule. But sometimes you want to share a Planner page: You might want members of your project team at work to be able to pencil in meetings, for example, or let students in a class you're teaching stay current with assignments and due dates. If you've created a page for an organization you belong to—such as a neighborhood association or a reading series at the library—you can publicize events by sharing the page with anyone who has Internet access.

When you want to share a page, whether it's with a select few or with the whole world, open the page you're sharing and click its upper-right Page Sharing link. The page changes to look like the one in Figure 9.13, giving you three options for sharing:

- **Public Sharing**—Check the Share This Page Publicly box to put the page on the Web so that anyone with its address can view it. Public pages are also listed here: http://planner.zoho.com/public/index.jsp. When you turn on public sharing, you have the option of letting viewers comment on the page; if you want viewer comments, check the box labeled Allow Comments to This Page. Click Share, and Zoho makes your page public. Click the Publicly Shared Page link to view it and get its public web address.

Info 4U When you make a page public, others can view the page but not edit it.

- **Private Sharing (Read Only)**—This option lets people you select view your page but not make any changes to it.
- **Private Sharing (Read/Write)**—This option allows others to view and edit your page. People with this level of access cannot share the page with others.

For private sharing, whether you're giving Read Only or Read/Write access, type or paste in the email addresses of those you want to share with. (For multiple addresses, put a space or a comma between addresses, or put each address on its own line.) Click Share. Zoho creates a new section on the page, showing the email addresses of people you've shared with.

Zoho sends a notification email to the addresses you entered. When recipients click a link in the email, they can sign in to Zoho. In Planner, your page appears in their Pages Shared to Me list.

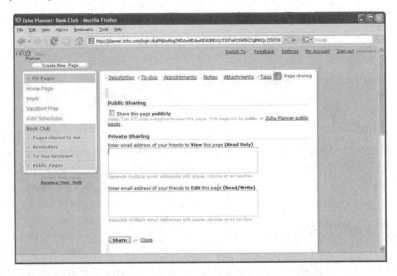

Figure 9.13
Make a page public or share it privately with a list of people you specify.

Staying on Track

Busy lives can feel overwhelming. And when you have multiple Planner pages with multiple To-Do lists, it may feel easy to lose track of what you have to do and when. Therefore, Planner has a couple features that help you stay on track:

■ **To-dos overview**—Shows you, in a calendar view, upcoming scheduled tasks from all the To-Do lists in all your pages.

■ **Reminders**—Use reminders to give yourself an extra nudge, making sure you don't forget things you have to do. Although you can link reminders to tasks and appointments, you can also create free-standing reminders.

To-Dos Overview

When you want an at-a-glance overview of how busy your schedule looks, click To-Dos Overview in the left list. The list expands to show a calendar view, as shown in Figure 9.14. Days that have scheduled tasks on a To-Do list (from any of your pages) are highlighted; a superscript number shows how many to-do's you have scheduled for that day. Click a date to see what its tasks are; Zoho displays them on the right.

Info 4U   To-Dos overview shows only scheduled items from your To-Do lists. It doesn't show appointments or notes.

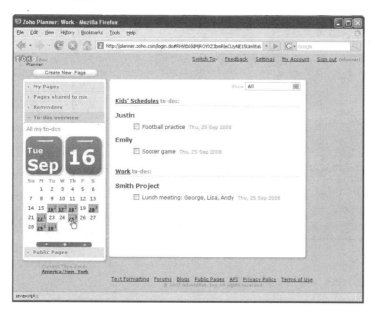

Figure 9.14
Click a date on the left to see that day's to-do's on the right.

Getting Reminders

As earlier sections of this chapter explain, you can schedule reminders for To-Do tasks and appointments when you create or edit them. But you can send yourself other reminders as well—reminders that aren't tied to a particular task or appointment. Maybe you have an important appointment coming up and you want extra reminders to make absolutely sure you don't forget. When you create a reminder, that reminder appears in your My Reminders list, under Reminders on the left side of the screen. You also receive the reminder at your registered email address.

To create a reminder, click Reminders, My Reminders in the list on the left. This opens a page that displays a list of any current reminders and when they'll be sent. Click Add New Reminder, and the page changes to look like the one in Figure 9.15, containing these settings:

- **Reminder**—This is the message that Zoho will email to you.
- **Scheduled On**—Tells Zoho the date and time to send the reminder.
- **Repeat**—Lets you set multiple reminders. Only Once means you'll get just one reminder at the time you specified. If you want more, choose a time interval between reminders, from every hour to every 12 hours, or every day, week, month, or year.

Click Add Reminder to create the reminder. Zoho adds the reminder to your My Reminders list and queues up the email (or emails) you requested.

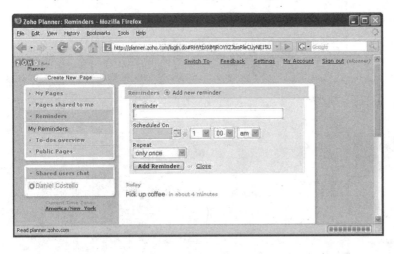

Figure 9.15
Create a reminder to email yourself a note that's not linked to a To-Do list or appointment.

 You can edit or delete a reminder in the same way you'd edit or delete an element from one of your pages: Place your cursor on the appropriate reminder and then click the Edit or Delete button that appears.

Zoho Meeting: Web Conferencing Made Simple

With people's busy schedules, it can be tough enough finding a time when everyone can attend a meeting. But getting everyone in the same room? Nearly impossible. When Dan is on the road visiting clients, Laura is at an industry conference on the East coast, Nick is setting up a new branch office on the West coast, and Steve is working from home, you might despair of ever getting them together for a meeting.

The answer, of course, is web conferencing. As long as they have a web browser and access to the Internet, participants can attend your meeting from wherever they happen to be. Zoho Meeting makes web conferencing simple—when you set up a meeting, Zoho automatically emails invitations to all participants and adds your meeting to their Invited Meetings list. So when you start the meeting, everyone can join you with just one or two clicks. During the meeting, you can chat with or talk to participants (via Skype), show what's on your Desktop, share presentation duties, and even let a participant take temporary control of your computer to illustrate a point or question. Whether you're inviting half a dozen people to a strategy meeting, troubleshooting a customer's technical problem, or helping your faraway college student with homework, Zoho Meeting is an easy way to meet up online.

Introducing Zoho Meeting

Zoho Meeting is a web-conferencing application that lets you get together with others over the Internet and share what's on your Desktop—those attending the meeting see on their screens what you're doing on yours. So you can give a slideshow presentation, discuss spreadsheet charts, demonstrate software, or go page by page through a report. If you're running the meeting, you need to download an ActiveX viewer that lets you share your Desktop; participants don't need to download anything, because they can choose to attend the meetings using a Java or Flash viewer, which runs right in their web browser. In fact, participants don't even need to have a Zoho account.

Like Zoho's other business-related apps, Zoho Meeting is available at a range of subscription prices, depending on your needs:

- For one-on-one meetings (that is, you and one other person), Zoho Meeting is free.
- For $12 a month, you can invite up to 5 participants to a meeting.
- For $18 a month, you can invite up to 10 participants.
- For $24 a month, you can invite up to 25 participants.

Whichever plan you sign up for, there's no limit on the number of meetings you can hold. And Zoho offers a 20% discount if you sign up for an annual subscription, rather than paying month by month. (For details, or to see whether these prices have changed, visit the Zoho Meeting pricing page at http://meeting.zoho.com/pricing.do.)

 If you want to try Zoho Meeting before you commit to a subscription plan, set up and run a couple of free one-on-one meetings. You'll get a good sense of how Meeting works and what you can do with it.

The Meeting Home Page

The Zoho Meeting home page (sign in at http://meeting.zoho.com) appears in Figure 10.1. Across the top of the page are four tabs:

- **Create Meeting**—Where you set up and schedule new conferences.
- **My Meetings**—Lists meetings you've created.
- **Invited Meetings**—Lists meetings in which you've been invited to participate.
- **Remote Assistance**—Lets you launch a troubleshooting or training session in which you control another person's computer remotely—helpful when you're training a colleague in using new software, for example.

The first time you sign in to Meeting, you'll probably want either to create a meeting or to check out the details of a meeting you've been invited to, so take a look at the Create Meeting or Invited Meeting tab.

Technical Requirements

Before you can use Zoho Meeting, make sure your computer and browser meet its minimal technical requirements. (Most do, but it's always a good idea to make sure.)

You can participate in a Meeting conference with any operating system (Windows, Macintosh, Linux) and of these web browsers:

- Internet Explorer 5.5 or higher
- Firefox 1.5 or higher
- Safari

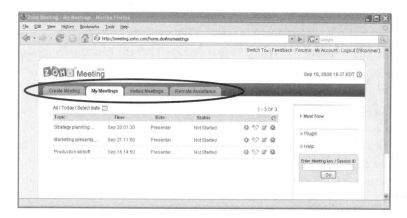

Figure 10.1
Use Meeting's tabs to find your way around.

If you're the meeting's presenter (that is, if you're running the meeting and sharing your Desktop with participants), you have to be using Windows 2000, XP, or Vista on a PC.

Info 4U Zoho promises that Mac support for presenters will be available soon—watch for it.

Creating a Meeting

You can start a spur-of-the-moment meeting by signing in to Meeting and clicking Meet Now, but most of the time you'll want to set up a meeting in advance. That way, your participants know when the meeting takes place, what's on the agenda, and what they need to do to attend.

To set up a meeting, click the Create Meeting tab, shown in Figure 10.2, and then provide the following info:

- **Meeting Topic**—Already filled in with your Zoho ID and the word *meeting*, but you can change this to reflect the actual subject to be discussed.

- **Date and Time**—Already filled in with today's date and the next 5-minute increment from the current time—handy when you're setting up an impromptu meeting. To schedule a future meeting, click the calendar to select the date and use the drop-down lists to choose a time.

Tip 4U If you're traveling and want to match the meeting time to your destination's time zone, click the time zone abbreviation after the time (EDT in Figure 10.2). A dialog box opens, letting you choose a time zone to associate with this meeting.

- Agenda, which is optional, is where you can type in a description of the meeting or a list of topics it will cover. The agenda appears in the email invitations you send out. To type an agenda, click Add and use the text box that appears. You can't format the agenda in this box or attach a copy of it to the invitation email. Instead, publish the agenda on the web (Chapter 1, "Have Your Say with Zoho Writer," tells you how to do that with Zoho Writer), and include its URL in the Agenda field. Participants can click the link to view the agenda.

- Presenter E-Mail ID is prefilled with your registered email address. If you're not the meeting's presenter, though, you can change this.

 A meeting's *presenter* is the person who shares his or her Desktop with the meeting's participants.

- The Skype check box lets you add Skype IDs for the presenter and participants. Skype uses VoIP (Voice over Internet Protocol) technology to let you make free phone calls over the Internet to other Skype users. As an upcoming section explains, Skype works with Meeting, so you can talk to other participants in a meeting.

- Participants E-Mail has several text boxes where you can invite participants when you create the meeting; enter one email address per box. (You can also invite people later, as the next section explains.) If there aren't enough text boxes to enter all participants, click Invite More.

Info 4U People you invite do not have to have a Zoho account to participate in a meeting.

- Control Transfer lets you specify whether a prompt appears during a meeting when control is transferred to a participant. (See the upcoming section "Giving a Participant Remote Control of Your Desktop.")

After you've set up the meeting, click Create. Zoho creates the meeting and adds it to your My Meetings list. It also emails a notification of the meeting to you and to any participants you listed. (In addition, Zoho adds the meeting to the Invited Meetings tab of participants who have a Zoho account.) A chat window also pops open. You can use this to chat with participants who are online and find out whether they have any questions. (For more about chatting in Zoho, see Chapter 8, "Instant Communication with Zoho Chat.")

Viewing a Meeting's Details

After you've created a meeting, you can review and edit its details. On the My Meetings tab, click the name of the meeting. This opens the Meeting Details page for that meeting, shown in Figure 10.3.

As Figure 10.3 shows, the Meeting Details page lists details you provided when you created the meeting: title, scheduled date and time, agenda (if any), and presenter of the meeting. In addition, you can see the current list of participants (click the View link) or add new participants (click the Invite link). Meeting Key is the code that lets people join your meeting once it's underway. This key is included in the email Zoho sends to all participants. The Status field lets you know whether a meeting has started yet. Given that you're running the meeting, that's not exactly news to you, but it's helpful for participants to know.

You can also perform these actions from a meeting's Meeting Details page:

- Click Start to start the meeting.
- Click Cancel to cancel the meeting.

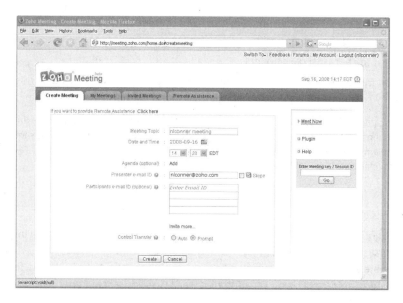

Figure 10.2
Create and schedule a meeting on this tab.

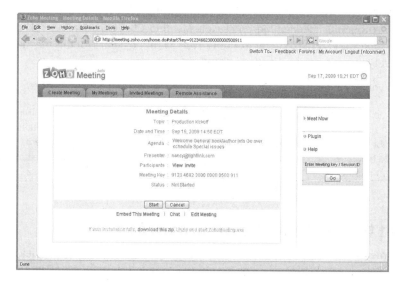

Figure 10.3
View or edit any meeting's details.

- Click Embed This Meeting to embed the meeting in your website or blog. After you've started the meeting, clicking Embed This Meeting opens the Embed Zoho Meeting dialog box, where you can adjust the size of the meeting viewer if you want, as well as choose whether you want the viewer to open in the same window as the web page or in a new window of its own. Then you can copy the code snippet, paste it into an HTML page, and upload that page to your website.

- Click Chat to chat with participants.

- Click Edit Meeting to open the Create Meeting tab, prefilled with info about this meeting. Make any changes you want and then click Save to update the meeting's details.

 Participant in a meeting, not a presenter? You can click the meeting's name on the Invited Meetings tab and view its details. But because you're not running that particular show, there are fewer details to see. For example, you can't edit or start a meeting or invite new participants.

Inviting Participants

As the "Creating a Meeting" section explains, you can invite people to participate in a meeting when you first set it up on the Creating Meeting tab. Often, though, things happen between the time you create a meeting and the time it begins—your boss asks to be included, for example, or Cindy from Accounting will be on vacation that week, so Todd is taking her place.

You can add new participants on your My Meetings tab (refer to Figure 10.1) or from the Meeting Details page (refer to Figure 10.3). On the My Meetings tab are several buttons to the right of each meeting on the list: From left to right they are Start/Stop Meeting, Join Meeting (if the meeting is in progress), Edit Meeting, and Delete Meeting. Click Edit Meeting. This takes you back to the Create Meeting tab (refer to Figure 10.2), with the details for this meeting already filled in. Just type in a new email address and click Save.

Zoho saves your changes and emails an update notice to you and all participants.

 You can also invite participants once a meeting is underway. On the Presenter toolbar, which appears in the meeting space while the meeting is underway, click the Invite Participant button to open a dialog box where you can type in the invitee's email address. This can be helpful when someone has lost his invitation email or wants to join the meeting at the last minute.

Preparing to Run Your First Meeting

Now we come to the main event—starting and running a meeting. It's a good idea to download and try out Zoho Meeting before you have an actual meeting about to start. This lets you get comfortable with how a meeting works and make sure that you don't have any kinks to work out in installing the Meeting software.

To get Zoho Meeting (for presenters) up and running on your computer, click Meet Now on the right of any page. (You don't have to invite any participants or fill in any details about the meeting.) The Meeting Details page opens, along with a chat window. When you're prompted to install Agent.jsp, click Install (or Install Now).

If nothing seems to happen when you try to start a meeting, look at the top of your browser window for a message in the Information Bar. You may have to grant explicit permission before the browser will proceed.

After the download, your Zoho Meeting software installs automatically and starts the meeting. You see a message box telling you the meeting has started, and the Presenter toolbar (flip ahead to Figure 10.5 to see what it looks like) appears on your screen. When this happens, you're all set up and good to go for running a real meeting.

 Having trouble with the automatic download? At the bottom of the Meeting Details page is a link that lets you download the Zoho Meeting software in a ZIP file. Click the Download This Zip link and download the ZIP file to your Desktop. Use a program such as WinZip or StuffIt to unzip the file and then run the file ZohoMeeting.exe.

Running a Meeting

Once you've installed Zoho Meeting on your computer, you're ready to set up and run a meeting. To launch the meeting (if you have not yet done so), display the My Meetings tab, find the meeting that's about to start, and click its name to open its Meeting Details page. Click Start to begin the meeting.

 If Meeting doesn't launch when you click Start, your firewall may be blocking the program. If a notice appears telling you that Meeting is blocked, tell your firewall to allow Meeting to connect to the Internet. If your firewall continues to block Meeting, contact your network administrator.

 Use Zoho Planner to schedule the meeting as an appointment (see Chapter 9, "Zoho Planner: Your Online To-Do List"). Share the page with the meeting's participants, and set up an automatic reminder to send an alert to everyone's Inbox an hour or so before the meeting begins.

When the meeting has launched, the page changes to look like the one in Figure 10.4, you get a notification that it has started successfully, and the Presenter toolbar (shown in Figure 10.5) appears. A chat box also opens—which can be useful for giving instructions if a participant has trouble joining the meeting.

As participants join the meeting, you get Participant Update notices in the lower-right part of the screen, and each participant is added to the Participant List on the left. (You can also see the Participant List by clicking the button with that name on the Presenter toolbar.)

Because you're the presenter, participants can see your Desktop as they join. If you prefer not to share your Desktop until everyone's there and the meeting is underway, click Stop Sharing in the upper-left part of your Meeting Details page. This makes participants' screens go blank in the Zoho Meeting window (showing only a message that you're not sharing your Desktop), until you're ready to share it and get things going.

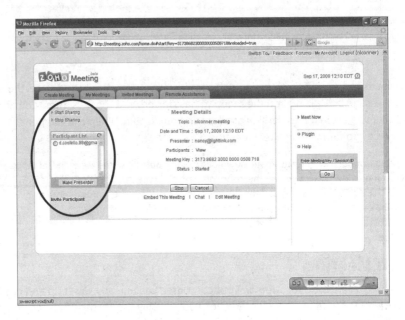

Figure 10.4
When a meeting you're running has begun, your Meeting Details page looks like this, with new options on the left.

Using the Presenter Toolbar

Once your meeting is underway, participants can see what's on your Desktop. Thus, you can give a slideshow presentation, demonstrate software, or go page by page through a report. What participants don't see is your chat window (if it's open)—they have their own chat window—or your Presenter toolbar, shown in Figure 10.5, which you use to control the meeting.

Figure 10.5
The Presenter toolbar lets you control a meeting-in-progress.

The Presenter toolbar has these buttons, from left to right:

- **Actions**—Click this button to choose from these options:

    - **Revoke Control**—When you've let a participant take temporary control of your Desktop, this option gets it back.

- **Connection Setting**—If your network administrator needs to tweak the settings you use to connect to Meeting, this is the place to do it.

- **Feedback**—This opens Zoho's feedback form in a new window, so you can submit comments about your Meeting experience.

- **Live Support**—Choose this option to open a new window where you can get one-on-one help from Zoho support staff via Chat.

- **Participant List**—Click this button to open a box that lists everyone who's currently attending the presentation. Click the down arrow next to a name to make that participant the presenter (so his or her Desktop becomes the one that's visible) or to give temporary remote control of your computer to that person. (You can get it back whenever you want.)

- **Invite Participant**—This button opens a dialog box where you can type in the email address of someone you want to join this presentation: Zoho shoots off an immediate email inviting that person to come on over.

- **Stop/Start Share**—Just as its name says, this button stops or starts sharing, depending on which one you're currently doing.

- **Chat**—Click this button to open the meeting's Chat window.

- **Minimize Toolbar**—This looks just like the familiar button you use to minimize a window, but when you click it, the Presenter toolbar closes entirely. The meeting is still going, but your Presenter toolbar is gone—and there's no obvious way to get it back.

 If you accidentally close the Presenter toolbar, transfer the presentation's control to another participant and then have that person transfer it back to you. Voila! Your toolbar reappears.

- **End Meeting**—Click the X button and then confirm to end the presentation.

Even when you allow a participant to take temporary control of your computer, the Presenter toolbar remains on your screen, so you're the one who stays in ultimate control of the meeting.

Communicating During a Meeting

It's not enough, of course, to show meeting participants what's happening on your Desktop—you need to *explain* to them what's going on. If you can set up a conference call for everyone to dial in to, you're all set—go ahead and skip this section. Same thing if you're doing a one-on-one meeting and can communicate via a simple phone call.

Otherwise, there are two ways you can communicate during your meeting: using text-based Chat or using Skype to talk over the Internet.

Chatting During a Conference

When a meeting begins, a Chat window automatically opens. During the meeting, participants and the presenter can chat to ask questions and make comments. When someone sends a chat message, the Chat window gets moved to the foreground on everyone's screens.

Talking via Skype

Skype is a service that lets you make voice calls over the Internet—free of charge if you're calling another Skype customer. To use Skype, you need a headset with a microphone or a Skype-enabled phone. You also need a Skype ID—for yourself and for each participant. (You can sign up at www.skype.com—it's free.)

To use Skype, you need to set the meeting up as a Skype meeting when you create it (as you learned earlier in the chapter); check the Skype box and add the Skype IDs of everyone attending as you are entering the meeting details.

Later, when it's time to start the meeting, you'll see a Skype Conference button. Click that to set up a conference call in Skype and dial in the presenter and all participants.

 When you're the presenter, use a headset with a microphone for your Skype conference call, so you can keep both hands free for your presentation.

Making a Participant the Presenter

Often, a meeting is run not by a single person but by a team, with several people responsible for one segment of the meeting. In that case, you may start off as the presenter; then someone else would take over for the next phase. When it's time to pass the baton, there are two ways to transfer the presentation to a new presenter:

- From the Presenter toolbar, click the Participant list button to open the box shown in Figure 10.6. Click the down arrow to the right of the participant who'll become the next presenter. From the menu that opens, select Make Presenter.

- From the Meeting Details page, in the Participant List, enable the radio button of the person who's taking over the meeting. Then click Make Presenter.

When you transfer the meeting to a new presenter, several things happen. Your Presenter toolbar disappears from your screen, replaced by a Participant toolbar. (See the upcoming "Using the Participant Toolbar" section for more about that.) The view on everyone's screens switches to show the new presenter's Desktop. And the change gets reflected in the Participants List: You're now shown as a participant and the new person appears as the presenter. Now, sit back and relax—someone else has responsibility for the meeting.

Figure 10.6
Use the Participant List to transfer control of the meeting.

Giving a Participant Remote Control of Your Desktop

During a conference, you may want to give one of the participants temporary control of your Desktop, so that person can ask a question or demonstrate a technique or procedure. Giving a participant control of your Desktop is not the same as making that participant the presenter (discussed in the previous section). In this case, you remain the presenter; you just let someone else use his or her mouse, for example, to point to something on your Desktop or perhaps use his or her keyboard to type in a document on your computer. You can take back control at any time.

To give a participant temporary control of your Desktop, go to the Presenter toolbar and click Participant List. In the Participant List box, click the down arrow next to the name of the person to whom you're giving control and then choose Give Control (refer to Figure 10.6).

Depending on the setting you chose when you created the meeting, the other person may see a notification box, saying he or she now has control (this is the default), or control just transfers. The other person can type, use the mouse, and so on, and the actions happen on your computer.

 When you give control to a participant, the Presenter toolbar remains active on your screen. The other person doesn't see it and can't use it, but you can.

When you're ready to take control again, click Actions, Revoke Control on the Presenter toolbar. Now you're back in charge of your own computer.

Ending a Meeting

All topics have been covered, all questions asked and answered, and now it's time to say goodbye and end the meeting. There two ways to end a meeting:

- From the Presenter toolbar, click the X button. Zoho asks whether you're sure that you want to end the meeting. If you want to save a transcript of the meeting's chat in your Zoho Chat account (see Chapter 9), check the Attach Logs box. Click Yes to end the meeting.
- From the Meeting Details page, click the Stop button. Zoho shows a confirmation box that asks, "Stop Meeting?" Click Stop.

When you've ended a meeting, participants' screens go blank, except for a message stating that you've stopped the meeting.

Joining a Meeting as a Participant

When somebody invites you to attend a meeting, you don't have to worry about creating the meeting, starting it, or running the show. All you have to do is show up at the right place at the right time to attend.

When someone creates a meeting and adds you as a participant, you get an invitation email that gives the name of the presenter; the meeting's topic, date and time, and agenda (if any); a meeting key for getting into the conference room; and a link you can follow to attend the meeting.

Invited participants can find meetings to which they've been invited on their Invited Meetings tab, shown in Figure 10.7.

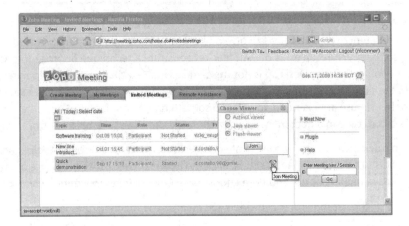

Figure 10.7
When you join a meeting (here, from the Invited Meetings tab), tell Zoho which viewer you want to use.

There are several ways to join a meeting in progress:

- Open the email that contains your invitation and click the Click Here to Join link. This takes you to the Meeting Details page for the meeting. Click Join.

- In the invitation email, copy the meeting key. This is a long number that looks something like this: *4187 8058 1000 0000 0403 336*. Go to http://meeting.zoho.com. Whether you land on the sign-in page or Meeting opens, there's a box where you can paste the meeting key. Paste in the key and click Go. On the Meeting Details page, click Join.

- On your Invited Meetings tab, find the meeting you want and click its Join Meeting icon (which looks like two people shaking hands).

- On your Invited Meetings tab, click the name of the meeting you're attending to open its Meeting Details page. Then, click Join.

Whichever method you use, you next have to tell Zoho which viewer you want to use to connect to the conference. Your choices, shown in Figure 10.7, are as follows:

- ActiveX viewer is the fastest viewer, but it doesn't work with Linux-based computers. This viewer (the default when you're running the meeting) installs software on your computer.

- Java viewer plugs into your web browser, so nothing gets installed on your computer.

Tip 4U For meetings where you're likely to be taking remote control of the presenter's computer, the ActiveX or Java viewer is your best choice.

- Flash viewer also runs on the browser, with nothing to download or install. (You do need to have the Flash plugin already installed.) This is probably the best choice when you're just sitting in on a conference and have no plans to present or take remote control.

Tip 4U If you're running into trouble joining the meeting with one viewer, try a different one.

Using the Participant Toolbar

In Meeting, presenters get one toolbar and participants get a different one. The Participant toolbar, shown in Figure 10.8, appears at the top of your screen. From left to right, here are its buttons:

- **File**—Click this to see all the other buttons as a menu.
- **Refresh**—This reloads the window in which the meeting is taking place.
- **Participant List**—Click this to see who has joined the meeting.
- **Meeting Details**—Clicking this button opens a box that lists the meeting's topic, key, and presenter. In the box is a View Participants button that opens the Participants List.
- **Chat**—This button brings the Chat window front and center (or opens it if you've closed Chat).
- **Request Control**—When you click this button, you don't just request control—you grab it! Clicking the button shifts control of the presenter's Desktop to you. Click the button again to give control back to the presenter. (Of course, the presenter can always use the Presenter toolbar to take back control if you're hogging the meeting.)
- **Zoom Out/In controls**—Use the buttons or the slider to make the image on your screen smaller or larger.
- **Fit to Screen**—Another way to adjust the image's size is to click this button, which makes sure the presenter's whole Desktop is visible on your screen.
- **Actual Size**—If you clicked Fit to Screen, this button returns the image on your screen to its original size.
- **Maximize Window**—This button does just what it says (but it only works in the ActiveX viewer).
- **Exit Meeting**—If you have to leave a meeting early, click the X to make your departure. (Or just close the browser window.)

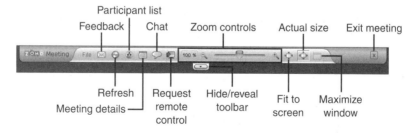

Figure 10.8
The Participant toolbar gives participants options during a meeting.

 Not all Participant toolbar buttons work in all viewers. You might have to play around with different viewers before you decide which works best for you.

Using Zoho Meeting for Remote Troubleshooting

If you've ever tried to explain how to do something on the computer using only words, you know how frustrating that experience can be. In fact, you were probably itching to jump in and *do* it. That's exactly what you can do with Zoho Meeting: Provide help remotely by temporarily gaining control of someone else's computer. Get in, make the fix, and get out—fast, clean, and simple.

 Meeting's Remote Assistance feature is equivalent to Remote Assistance via Windows Messenger in Windows XP and Vista. But if you—or the person you're assisting—doesn't have one of those operating systems, Zoho Meeting lets you provide the same service.

The Remote Assistance tab, shown in Figure 10.9, is the place to begin your remote session. On that tab, you can type in the email address for the customer or colleague you're going to help; then click Start. (Alternatively, if the other person is on the phone right now and doesn't need a formal invitation, you can just click Start to open a Remote Assistance session.)

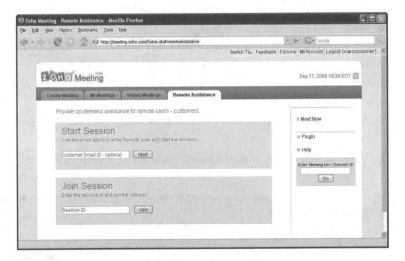

Figure 10.9
When you're troubleshooting a technical problem, type in the other person's email address (optional) and click Start to set up a Remote Assistance session.

Zoho creates a session ID (this is like a meeting key, to let others access the session) and, if you entered an email address, sends that address an invitation. Now, the Remote Assistance tab looks like the one in Figure 10.10. Click Start Session.

The invitation email contains a link that the recipient can click to join you in the troubleshooting session. Alternatively, you can give the person the session ID. When he or she signs in to Zoho and clicks the Remote Assistance tab, pasting the session ID into the Join Session box and clicking Join opens a window where your session is already in progress.

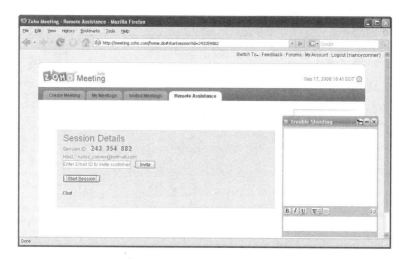

Figure 10.10
The session ID allows the other person to join you in a one-on-one meeting and get technical help.

In a troubleshooting session, you're the participant and the other person is the presenter. That may seem backward, but there's a good reason for it—you want to see the other person's Desktop on your screen. That's the only way you'll be able to take control, find, and fix the problem.

When you see the other person's Desktop on your computer screen, click the Remote Control button (you can see it in Figure 10.8). The button changes to the Give Up Control button, and a notification box lets you know you now have control of the other person's computer. Do your stuff and then click Give Up Control to return control to the other person.

 Just as in a meeting, in a Remote Assistance session the person whose computer you're controlling can take back control at any time through the Presenter toolbar by clicking Actions, Revoke Control.

Build Collaborative Sites with Zoho Wiki

A wiki is a website that people can edit collaboratively. You might create a page and add some text, for example, and then a collaborator might add some images or a video, while another collaborator puts in some links to relevant sites. You can invite just a few friends to collaborate—or you can let anyone in the world work on the site.

In the Hawaiian language, the word for quick is *wikiwiki*—and that's where the tech term *wiki* comes from, according to Ward Cunningham, who invented the first wiki. It's a good name: A wiki is a website that you (and anyone else you desire) can quickly build, edit, and update. You can create pages; fill them with content, images, and links; rearrange them; and share them with others. Zoho Wiki's easy-to-use text editor lets you see how your page will look as you write it; no need to learn HTML or guess whether your page will look the way you want it to. When you create a web page with Zoho Wiki, what you see truly *is* what you get.

Zoho Wiki is flexible, too. You can use it to create your own personal website, which others can see but not edit, or you can create a team site for a current project, a central place for team members to update progress, attach documents, and list their schedules and contact information. Teachers will find Zoho Wiki a great tool for creating class projects; students can post reports and comment on each other's work. Families, clubs, nonprofits, neighborhood organizations—whoever you are—Zoho Wiki provides a solution for any group that wants to set up a website that members can work on collaboratively.

Setting Up Your First Wiki

When you go to wiki.zoho.com and sign in, Zoho immediately gets you started in creating your first wiki, as Figure 11.1 shows. It takes less than a minute—here's all you need to provide:

- **Wiki Title**—Zoho fills this in with your Zoho ID, but you may want to change it. The wiki title appears in a web browser's title bar and the upper-left part of every page. So if your Zoho ID is jillfowler, you might want to display your actual name: Jill Fowler. Or you might want the name of your company or organization there.

- **Make This Wiki**—Choose one of these settings:
  - **Public**—Available to anyone and everyone on the Internet.
  - **Private**—No one else has access to the wiki unless you grant it.
  - **Group**—Members of a group, defined by you, have access to the wiki.
- **Select Wiki Skin**—Wikis come with a standard color scheme based on shades of blue and gray. To apply a different color scheme, make a choice from this drop-down. (Zoho previews the colors as you select an option.)
- **Choose Language**—It's a good idea to stick with the default here, which detects the language your browser uses.
- **Email Character Encoding**—This setting determines the character set used for emails. In most cases, the default choice of Unicode (UTF-8) is what you want. (The other setting is for Japanese characters.)

Click Save—and that's all there is to it. Zoho creates your wiki and takes you to your Dashboard, shown in Figure 11.2. You can return to your Dashboard at any time later by clicking Home in the upper-left part of any wiki page.

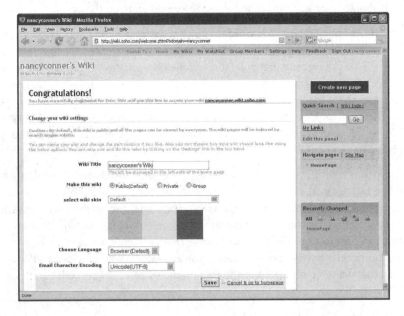

Figure 11.1
Create your first wiki as soon as you sign in.

 With a free account, you can create up to two wikis. Paid plans, which currently run between $5 and $75 per month, allow you to create more—up to 45 for the top-of-the-line Diamond plan.

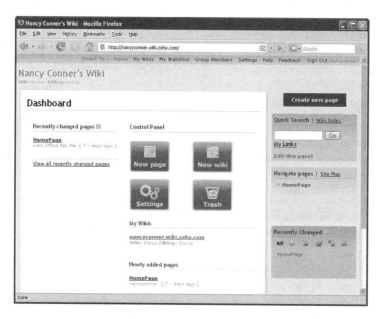

Figure 11.2
Your Dashboard is your Zoho Wiki control center.

The Dashboard (shown in Figure 11.2) is the overview page for all your Zoho wikis. It's your Zoho Wiki home page (unless you set a different home page, as described later in this chapter). It's also the place to go to create a new page or a whole new wiki, find a particular page, and view people's comments on your site.

The left side of the Dashboard shows recently changed pages. This list can be helpful for keeping an eye on the work your collaborators have done or finding a page you've worked on recently.

In the middle, you'll find four big, blue buttons for common tasks: New Page, New Wiki, Settings, and Trash (for restoring or permanently deleting pages). Below the Control Panel are lists of your wikis, pages you've recently added, and comments you've received.

The right side of the Dashboard has a Create New Page button (which duplicates the New Page button in functionality), a Quick Search box, a Navigate Pages section (which serves as a site map), and a Recently Changed box that makes it easy to find and work with pages, whether they're public, private, group, and so on.

Info 4U The right pane you see on the Dashboard appears on all Zoho Wiki pages as you create and edit them. You don't have to go back to the home page to create a new page or select a different one.

Of course, your Dashboard doesn't have much to show you until you've created some pages for your wiki. And that's what the next section is all about.

Working with Pages

The meat and potatoes of any website are the pages that work together to create the site as a whole. This section tells you how to create, fill, and edit your wiki's pages.

Creating a Page

When you first create a wiki, it has exactly one page—the HomePage. This page, created by Zoho staff, offers instructions for using Zoho Wiki. That's great, but you will want some pages for your own content. So go to your Dashboard and click either New Page (in the Control Panel) or Create New Page (upper right) to get started.

Whichever button you click, a text box appears, asking you to give the new page a name. Type in a name and then click Create. Zoho creates the page and opens it in the text editor, shown in Figure 11.3. Read on to learn about using the text editor to add content to your page.

Embed plugins

No wiki

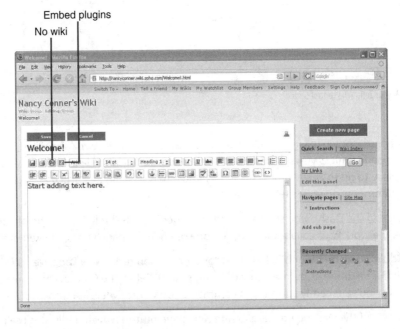

Figure 11.3
Zoho Wiki's text editor shows how your text will look on the page.

Adding and Editing Text

You've just created a new page—now you want to add some content. Because Zoho lands you in the text editor after it creates your page, all you have to do is start typing, as Figure 11.3 shows.

Of course, you want your text to look good—after all, it'll be on display on the Web. So Zoho gives you a formatting toolbar that contains the familiar formatting buttons you use with Zoho

Writer—or just about any word processor or text editor. If you want to review the formatting buttons, flip back to Chapter 1, "Have Your Say with Zoho Writer," for a list of buttons and what they do.

Zoho Wiki's text editor is a WYSIWYG editor. That stands for "what you see is what you get," and it means that the editor shows you how the text you're adding and formatting will look on the page (as opposed to showing, for example, HTML tags). WYSIWYG editors make it much easier to design a page, because you don't have to guess how the text will look as you're writing.

 If the formatting toolbar has too many buttons for your liking, you can hide the buttons that you never seem to use. Click Settings, My Editor to open a box that lets you show or hide groups of toolbar buttons. Uncheck the box of any buttons you don't want and then click Save to make them disappear from the toolbar.

Zoho Wiki has a couple of unfamiliar buttons that are wiki-specific. They're in the top row of the formatting toolbar, on the left side. (You can see them in Figure 11.3.) Here's what they do:

- No Wiki is a *W* with a red "no" symbol over it. This button disables automatic linking in this page. Automatic linking can be a helpful feature. For example, if you have a page named Contacts, whenever you type the word *contacts* in a different page, that word automatically becomes a link to your Contacts page. But there may be situations when you don't want that automatic linking—if you're talking about contact lenses, for example, you don't want the word *contacts* to link to a page listing names, phone numbers, and email addresses. Such situations are the reason this button exists. By clicking it, you can turn off automatic linking for this page only.

 Automatic linking is turned off by default. If you want to turn it on for an entire wiki, click Settings and then remove the check mark from the Disable Automatic Linking check box. When you've enabled automatic linking for a wiki, use the No Wiki button to disable it for a particular page.

- Embed Plugins (the red *Z* button) lets you choose any of your public Zoho documents and embed them in this page. More on that coming up in "Embedding a Zoho Document."

When you've typed in all the text you want (for now), click Save. Zoho closes the text editor and displays your text. To make further changes, click Edit to reopen the text editor, with your text filled in and ready for your changes.

Inserting Images and Tables

If web pages were nothing but text, they'd be pretty boring. This section tells you how to snazz up your page with some images or get your point across with a table.

Inserting an Image

If you've inserted an image into a Writer document, the process for getting an image into a wiki page is nearly identical, even though the dialog box looks a bit different. Start by positioning the cursor where you want the image to appear; then click the toolbar's Insert/Modify Image button, which shows the sun over a couple of mountains. This opens the Insert Image dialog box, shown in Figure 11.4.

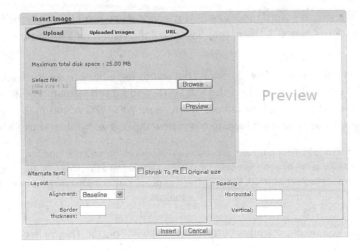

Figure 11.4
When inserting an image, use one of the three circled tabs to tell Zoho where to find the image.

 Any image you upload to Zoho Wiki must be 10MB or smaller. If you have an image file that's larger than that, open it in a graphics program and resize it to meet this restriction. Large pictures tend to make a web page load slowly, so keeping file sizes small is a good general practice, anyway.

The three tabs in this box indicate how to find the image you want to insert:

- Upload is where you select and transfer an image from your computer.
- Uploaded Images lets you select from images you've already transferred to Zoho Wiki.

 It's easier to figure out which file you want when you can see pictures instead of file-names. On the Uploaded Images tab, check the Thumbnails box to show the files as images—then just click to select.

- URL is the tab to use when the image you want already lives on the Web, in a service such as Flickr or Snapfish. Here, type or paste in the image's web address.

After you've chosen an image, Zoho shows a preview in the right side of the box. (You may have to click a Preview button to see it, depending which tab you're on.) Next, tell Zoho what you want for these settings (they're all optional):

- **Alternate Text**—This creates a label for your image that appears if the picture cannot load. It also is read by accessibility software, so that people who are visually impaired will know what the image is.
- **Shrink to Fit versus Original Size**—You can let Zoho Wiki size the image to your page, or you can upload it in its original size. Shrink to Fit is usually the better choice if you want viewers to be able to see the whole image at once, without scrolling.

- **Layout**—Specify the image's alignment (bottom, left, right, and so on) and the thickness of its border, if you want a border. The alignment options Texttop, Absmiddle, and Absbottom orient any wrapping text in relation to the image.

- **Spacing**—To adjust the horizontal or vertical spacing of the image on the page, use this section. You can resize an image once you've inserted it, but you can't drag-and-drop it.

When you've told Zoho where to find the image and specified the optional settings you want, click Insert to put the image in your page.

Editing an Image

Thanks to Zoho Wiki's WYSIWYG editor, you can see how your image will look on the page as soon as you've inserted it. If it doesn't look quite right yet, you can tweak it in various ways. Click the image to select it and then click the Insert/Modify Image button on the toolbar to reopen the Insert Image box (see Figure 11.4). Make your changes and then click Insert to see how the image looks.

Resizing an Image

When you click an image to select it, eight small squares, called *handles,* appear around its perimeter, as shown in Figure 11.5. Click any handle and then drag it to resize the image. Zoho resizes the image and repositions it. If you've centered the image, for example, the resized image remains centered.

Resizing handles

Figure 11.5
Click-and-drag a handle (circled) to resize the image. Each image has eight handles: one at each corner and one at the halfway point between two corners.

To keep your image in proportion, click-and-drag any of the corner handles. This adjusts the image's height and width together, so the picture won't look stretched or squashed horizontally or vertically.

If the image is so huge that it has scroll bars along the right side or the bottom, you probably didn't check Shrink to Fit when you uploaded the image. Click the image and then click Insert/Modify Image. In the Insert Image box, check Shrink to Fit and then click Insert. The image will be sized, proportionately, to fit on your page.

Deleting an Image

This one's easy. If an image doesn't work out, just click to select it and then hit your computer's Delete or Backspace key. The image disappears.

Change your mind about deleting the image? You can click Undo to reinsert the image, or you can find it on the Uploaded Images tab of the Insert Image dialog box.

Working with Tables

Inserting, formatting, and editing a table works the same way in Zoho Wiki as it does in Zoho Writer, so take a look at the "Working with Tables" section in Chapter 1 to learn everything you need to know about putting a table in a Zoho Wiki page.

 When it comes to tables, Zoho Wiki does have one advantage over Writer: the Quick Format box. Select the table and click the down arrow next to Format on the right side of the formatting toolbar. The Quick Format box opens with options for formatting your table. Click the Cell or Table tab; then add and format a border or adjust cell padding.

Embedding and Attaching Files

Besides typing in content using Wiki's text editor, you can embed a document, spreadsheet, or presentation you created using another Zoho program. You can also attach files to a web page, which is handy when you want to be sure everyone in your group knows where to find a particular document.

Embedding a Zoho Document

Zoho Wiki integrates with other Zoho applications, such as Writer, Sheet, and Show, so that you can take a document, spreadsheet, or slideshow that you created in one of those apps and embed it in a wiki page. The version you embed is read-only (so visitors can't mess with your data), and whenever you update the document in its original app, the embedded version gets updated, too.

The first step in embedding a document happens in the application where you created it: Writer, Sheet, or Show. Go to the program you want, open the document, and make it public. (See the appropriate chapter to find out how to do that.) Making a document public puts it on the Web, where anyone can view it. It also lets Zoho Wiki find that document for embedding in a page.

Back in Zoho Wiki, open (or create) the page where you'll embed the document. If the text editor isn't open, click Edit to open it. Click the Embed Plugins button in the top-left part of the format-ting toolbar. (It's a white *Z* on a red background.) This opens the Embed Plugins dialog box, shown in Figure 11.6.

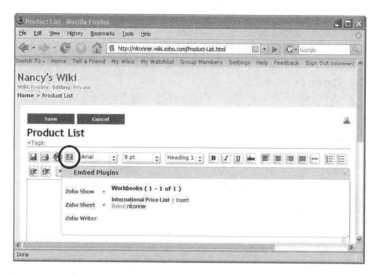

Figure 11.6
Click the Embed Plugins button (circled) to open this dialog box; click a Zoho app (here, Zoho Sheet) to see its public documents, which you can embed.

On the left side of the box is a list of your Zoho Docs applications: Show, Sheet, and Writer. Click the one that holds the document you're embedding, and a list of public documents in that app appears in the box. Next to the name of each document is an Insert link; click Insert to embed the document in the Wiki page.

 If you want to adjust the embedded document's size, click its name. The Embed Plugins box opens. Here, you can type in a new number for the width or height of the embedded document; click Insert to embed it.

Zoho embeds the document you chose. Click Save to make it permanent.

Editing an Embedded Document

If you want to edit the content of a document you've embedded, go to the app where you cre-ated the document—Writer, Sheet, or Show—and make your changes there. Those changes are automatically reflected in the document that's embedded in your wiki page.

If you want to change the size of the embedded document, you need to know your way around an HTML snippet. Open the page that holds the embedded document and click Edit. Then click the formatting toolbar's Toggle HTML Source button. (It's on the far right of the bottom row of buttons.) This changes the text editor from a WYSIWYG editor to an HTML editor.

Find the embedded document (the opening tag is `<iframe width...>`) and make your changes. When you're done, you can switch back to the WYSIWYG editor to see how they look by clicking the Toggle HTML Source button again. Click Save when you're done.

Embedding a Video

Want to embed a video in your page? You can easily embed a video from a site such as YouTube or Google Video. Start by finding the video you want; on its page should be a box labeled Embed. (On YouTube, for example, there's an Embed box to the right of the video that's playing.) Copy the code in the Embed box.

Back in Zoho Wiki, open the page you want, click Edit, and then take either of these actions:

- Click the Insert HTML button (angle brackets around a downward-pointing arrow). A dialog box opens. Paste the code you copied into the box; then click Insert. Zoho inserts the HTML into the page and closes the dialog box.

- Click the Toggle HTML Source button (< >). When the WYSIWYG editor becomes an HTML editor, paste in the code snippet you copied. Click Save, and you'll see the video embedded in your page.

Deleting an Embedded Document

If you want to remove an embedded document from a wiki page, your first impulse might be to stop publishing the document or even to delete it. And while either of those moves will stop displaying the document in your wiki, something else will appear instead: an error message. And that doesn't look good.

To remove the embedded document from your page, you have to root out the HTML snippet that put the document there in the first place. And that means you'll have to venture into the HTML that tells web browsers how to display your page.

Open the page and click its Edit button. Then click Toggle HTML Source to make the WYSIWYG editor switch to an HTML editor. Now, find the piece of HTML code that embedded the document. It'll look something like this:

```
<iframe width="480" scrolling="no" height="370" frameborder="0"
src="http://sheet.zoho.com/publish/yourID/spreadsheetname"
class="iframeapi"> </iframe>
```

Delete that piece of HTML. (If you're not sure you have the right code, use Ctrl+X to cut it, so you can paste it back in if necessary.) Click Toggle HTML Source again. In the WYSIWYG editor, the document (or error message) has disappeared. Click Save to keep the change.

Attaching a Document

An alternative to embedding a document is attaching one. By attaching documents, you can create a central repository for all documents related to a project or event—documents you want others to have access to but don't necessarily need to display on the page.

Attaching a document is basically the same process as uploading a file. On the page to which you're attaching the file, click the Attachments link. (It's below the page's content and comments.) This opens the Attach Your Files to This Page section, shown in Figure 11.7.

On the Attach New File tab, click the Browse button to find and select the file on your computer; click Open to put the file path in the Browse box. If you want, say a few descriptive words about the file in the File Description box. Click Upload to attach the file.

 Tip To attach a file that has already been uploaded to this wiki (and attached to another page, perhaps), click the Attach Existing File link. On the tab that opens is a list of all the files that have been uploaded to this presentation, including files that have been removed from a particular page. Click any file's Attach link (on the left) to attach it to the current page.

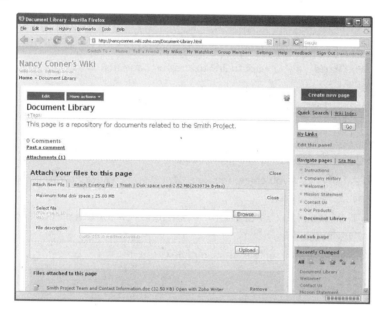

Figure 11.7
Attach files to a page by uploading them from your computer.

Viewing an Attached Document

To see a list of attached files, click the Attachments link and take a look at what's listed in the Files Attached to This Page section. Click a file's name to download it to your computer or open it with an appropriate program. Files that can be opened with a Zoho app, such as Writer, have an Open with Zoho <Application Name> link. Click Remove to detach the file from this page (but leave it in the list of existing files).

Deleting an Attached Document

When a document is no longer relevant to your wiki, you can delete it. That way, no one can mistakenly select an obsolete file from the existing files list. You can delete an attachment from any page in the wiki. Click Attachments, Attach Existing File. The tab that opens lists all files that have been attached to any page in the wiki. Find the file you want to delete, click its Delete link (on the right), and then click OK to confirm. This moves the file to the Trash.

From the Trash tab, you can either restore a file (putting it back on the existing files list) or delete it (removing it entirely from the wiki) by clicking the appropriate link. To sweep all files out of the Trash at once, click Empty Trash and then confirm by clicking OK.

Working with Links

There are six kinds of links in your Zoho Wiki, as shown in Figure 11.8:

- **URL**—This is a web link to a website beyond your wiki.
- **Existing Wiki Page**—If you want to link to another page that already exists in your wiki, use this kind of link.
- **Attachments**—Use this kind of link to attach a file to a wiki page. The page doesn't display the file; rather, viewers open the attachment when they click the link.
- **Email Address**—This kind of link opens a new email in the clicker's default email program, with a specified email address already filled in.
- **New Wiki Page**—When you create this kind of link, you create a new wiki page and link to that new page, all at once.
- **Anchors**—This kind of link is like a bookmark, letting you link to a particular section on a particular page in the wiki.

This section tells you how to create each kind of link.

Linking to a Web Page

When you want to link to a page outside of your wiki, start by selecting the text that will hold the link. Then click the toolbar's Insert Web Link button (which looks like some links of chain) to open the Insert/Modify Link box shown in Figure 11.8.

On the URL tab, provide this information:

- **URL**—Type or paste in the web address of the page to which you're linking.
- **Text**—If you've selected text to hold the link, it appears in this box. Otherwise, type in the text that will hold the link (such as *click here*). If you do not type anything here, the URL itself will appear on the page.
- **Title (tooltip)**—This optional text is what appears when a viewer hovers the mouse pointer over the link.
- **Target**—Choose from the list how you want the linked page to open. The standard option is to open the page in a new window.

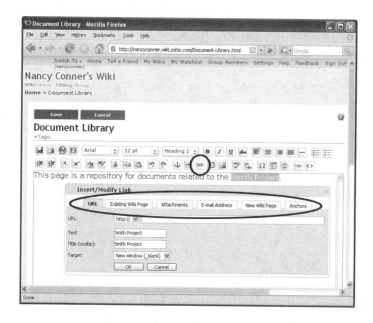

Figure 11.8
Click the Insert Web Link button (circled) to open this dialog box and select one of the tabs (also circled) to insert a particular kind of link.

When you're done filling in info and choosing your settings, click OK to insert the link.

Tip 4U To test a link you've inserted, click Save to close the text editor and then click the new link.

Linking to a Page or an Attachment Inside This Wiki

You can create an internal link to another page or attachment inside your wiki, making site navigation a breeze. To do this, select some text to hold the link and click the Insert Web Link button. In the Insert/Modify Link box (shown in Figure 11.8), choose one of these tabs:

- **Attachments**—To find and link directly to a file that has been uploaded and attached to a page in the wiki
- **Existing Wiki Page**—To find and link to a page that's currently in the wiki
- **New Wiki Page**—To create a page for this wiki and link to it at the same time

Each tab asks you for similar information: Tell Zoho which page or attachment to link to and then provide the link text (if you haven't selected it already), a title tooltip (if you want it), and a target (that is, whether to open the linked page in this window, a new window, or a frame). For existing pages and attachments, you can find and then select what you're looking for using the Search box at the top of the tab. For a new page, type a name in the Page Name text box. (The default name is New Page.)

Need to link to an attachment that hasn't been uploaded yet? You can upload it right from the Attachments tab. Just click the New Attachment link and, in the dialog box that opens, upload the file. Then, use the Search box to find and link to the file you just uploaded.

After you've filled out the tab, click OK to insert the link.

 Here's a no-effort way to create links between pages in a wiki. Click Settings to see the general settings for this wiki. In the Auto Linking section, turn off the Disable Automatic Linking section and then click the upper-right X to close Settings. This creates automatic links whenever you type the name of one of the other pages in the wiki. For example, suppose you have a page called Employee Handbook. When you type `Employee Handbook` on another page in the same wiki, Zoho automatically inserts a link to the Employee Handbook page. For the link to be inserted, the capitalization of what you type has to match the capitalization of the page title.

Linking to an Email Address

Make it easy for customers and clients to get in touch: Create a link that opens a new email, with your address (and an optional subject line) already filled in.

Select the text that will contain the link (such as *Contact us*), click the Insert Web Link button, and in the Insert/Modify Link box (shown in Figure 11.8), click the E-mail Address tab. There, fill in this information:

- **E-mail**—In this box, put the address to which emails will be sent.
- **Subject**—If you want, add a Subject line for emails, such as *Price quote* or *Customer feedback*.

The Text and Title (tooltip) fields are the same as in the previous section; Text specifies the text that serves as the hyperlink, and Title specifies the pop-up description that displays when a viewer hovers the mouse pointer over the link.

Using an Anchor to Jump to a Section of a Wiki Page

Anchors let you create section-specific links within your wiki. For example, suppose you have a human resources wiki that has a page containing the Employee Benefits Handbook. You can create one-click cross-references within the handbook using anchors. So if you have a reference to Section 3.b.2, for example, you can put in a link that jumps right to that section. This makes it much easier for viewers to navigate a long page with lots of information.

Before you can link to an anchor, you have to create the anchor point. To do that, follow these steps:

1. Open the page that contains the document for which you want to create linked cross-references. Click Edit to open the page in the text editor.
2. Select some text to anchor: This could be a chapter heading or subheading, a figure, a table, or any other content.
3. Click the Anchor button, which looks like (you guessed it!) an anchor. This opens the Insert/Modify Anchor dialog box.

4. Give the anchor a name. Make sure it's descriptive so that you can easily find it later in a long list of anchors. Click Insert to create the anchor.

After you've created an anchor (or a whole bunch of them), you can link text to that anchor:

1. Select the text that will hold the link and then click Insert Web Link. Zoho opens the Insert/Modify Link box (see Figure 11.8).

2. Click Anchors to open the Anchors tab.

3. On the Anchors tab, the Anchor drop-down lists all the anchors you've created for this page. Select the one you want to link to and then make your choices for the Text and Title (tooltip) fields (both explained earlier in the "Linking to a Web Page" section).

4. Click OK, and Zoho inserts the link in your page.

Rearranging Pages

A site's pages should be easy to find in the navigation bar, the sidebar that lists links to each page. So when you need to, you can rearrange the order in which pages appear here.

In the Navigate Pages box at the right, click Site Map. This opens a list of all the wiki's pages. To move pages around, hover your cursor to the left of a page's name (so that the cursor changes to a four-way arrow). Click a page and then drag-and-drop it in its new location.

Creating a Subpage

Not all wiki pages are created equal. To keep your growing wiki organized, you may want to make some subpages of other pages. A *subpage* is simply a page that appears underneath another one in the Site Map, as shown in Figure 11.9. For example, say your business wiki has a page called About Us. You might want to create several subpages for this page, such as Company History, Mission Statement, Officers, and so on.

To create a subpage, open the main page (the one that the new page will be a subpage of). Click the blue More Actions button. From the menu that appears, select Add Sub Page. To take an even shorter route, click Add Sub Page at the bottom of the right Navigate Pages box. A dialog box opens, asking you to name the subpage. Type in a name and click OK.

Zoho creates the subpage and opens the text editor so that you can give it some content.

Deleting a Page

In any website, pages become obsolete after a while. To delete a page from your wiki, open the page and then click More Actions, Delete. A confirmation box appears; click OK. Zoho deletes the page and takes you to the Zoho Wiki home page.

 If the page you delete has subpages, Zoho does *not* delete the subpages. Instead, it moves them up a level.

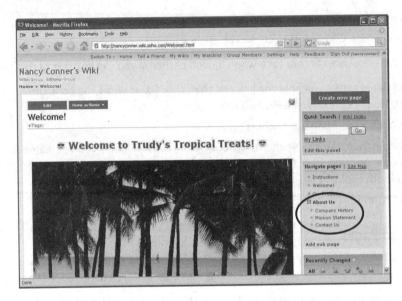

Figure 11.9
In this example, the About Us page has three subpages: Company History, Mission Statement, and Contact Us.

Customizing Your Wiki

It's your wiki—so you want it to reflect your organization's image or your own personal style. This section discusses ways you can customize your wiki, giving it the look and feel you want.

Choosing a Theme

When you first create a wiki, Zoho asks you to choose a color scheme, called a *theme* or a *skin*. If you're tired of the theme you chose when you created the wiki—or maybe it clashes with the logo you uploaded (see next section)—you can easily change it.

Click Settings—either the link at the top of any wiki page or the big blue button in your Dashboard's Control Panel. This opens the Settings box. On the left side of the box, click Wiki Skins. A drop-down menu appears, listing the five themes Zoho currently offers for wikis. Click Save to apply the new colors to your wiki.

Adding a Title and a Logo

Your wiki's title appears in the upper-left corner of every page in your wiki. Zoho gives you the opportunity to add a title when you create a wiki, but you can change it at any time. You can also add a logo or other image, which appears to the left of the title. Together, a logo and title make it clear that your wiki is an official company or organization site—or they add a little personality to an individual site.

You add or change a title and logo (or any image) by clicking Settings at the top of any page or in your wiki's Control Panel. In the box that appears, click Customization, and the box changes to look like the one in Figure 11.10. Look in the Change Your Wiki Title/Logo section and make sure that the Logo & Title radio button is enabled, so you can type in a title and upload a logo.

In the Wiki Title box, type the title you want to show at the top of each page. To include a logo, use the Browse button to select an image on your computer and upload it to Zoho Wiki.

 Tip 4U To keep your logo from overwhelming the page, keep it small: Zoho recommends 150 pixels wide and 50 pixels high as the maximum dimensions.

To see how the uploaded logo looks, click Preview. And if you want only the logo or image to appear in the upper-left corner—without any text—check the Logo Only box.

When your logo and title look good, click Save to apply them to your wiki. Click Close (or the upper-right X) to close the Settings box.

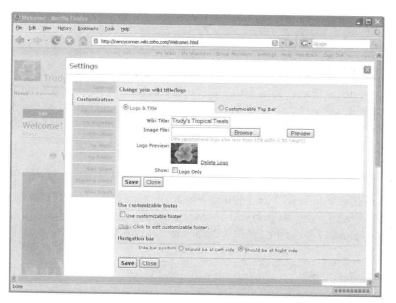

Figure 11.10
Customize your wiki's settings in the Settings box.

 Tip 4U For extra customization of your wiki's title, click Settings and then enable the Customizable Top Bar radio button. Click the Click: link to open a text editor that lets you choose a size and color for the title and insert the logo in a different position than to the title's left.

Adding a Footer

A footer appears at the bottom of every page in your wiki. It's a great place to put links to pages you want viewers to find easily, such as Contact Us or Help. You also might want to put a copyright notice there.

To create or edit a footer, click Settings, Customization to open the box shown in Figure 11.10. In the Use Customizable Footer section, check the Use Customizable Footer box. Then click the Click: link to open a text editor where you can type your footer, add links, and format it in any way you choose. Click Save when you're done.

Positioning the Navigation Bar

You have two choices for where to show the navigation bar that helps visitors find their way around your sight: left and right. To switch from one side to the other (or back again), click Settings, Customization. In the Navigation Bar section (refer to Figure 11.10), enable the appropriate radio button: Should Be at Left Side or Should Be at Right Side. Click Save to put the navigation bar where you indicated.

Sharing Your Wiki

Wikis are meant to be shared. Sure, you can set up a wiki and use it as a static website. But the real power of wikis comes from the ability to let others quickly and easily edit them. Why do all that work yourself? You can add other users (or whole groups) and set permissions so that they can edit the site as much—or as little—as you want. This section tells you how.

Setting Permissions

Before you go sharing your wiki with others, you should set the permission that those others will have in working with your wiki. And you do that by clicking Settings, Permissions to open the box shown in Figure 11.11. In the Set Permissions to This Wiki section are several kinds of permissions:

- **Reading**—This permission allows people to view the wiki.
- **Editing**—With this permission, people can change the content on the wiki's pages.
- **Creating Page**—This permission allows people to add new pages to the wiki.
- **Deleting**—People who have this permission can remove pages from the wiki.
- **Posting Comment**—This permission lets people leave a comment on any of the wiki's pages.

Each kind of permission has a drop-down list with these options:

- **Everyone**—This means that anyone and everyone on the Internet can do this action for your wiki.
- **Zoho Registered Users**—This means that anyone with a Zoho account (whether you explicitly made him or her part of a group) has permission to perform this action.

- **Group**—This means that only members of a group—people chosen by you—can perform this action. You will learn how to create the group in the next section.
- **Domain**—This means that anyone whose email address is part of a domain you specify—such as *yourcompany*.com or *yournonprofit*.org—has permission to perform this action.

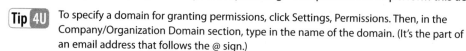 To specify a domain for granting permissions, click Settings, Permissions. Then, in the Company/Organization Domain section, type in the name of the domain. (It's the part of an email address that follows the @ sign.)

- **Only Me (Private)**—This means that you're the only person in the entire universe who can perform this action.

For each action, choose the desired setting. For example, if you're using your wiki as a static website and you want anyone who's surfing the Web to be able to see it—but not make changes to it—you'd set Reading to Everyone and all the other settings to Only Me (Private). On the other hand, if you were creating a company wiki that everyone could view but only your group could edit, you might set Reading and Posting Comment to Domain, and set Editing, Creating Page, and Deleting to Group.

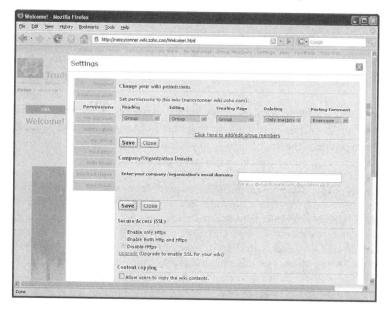

Figure 11.11
Tell Zoho who can do which actions in your wiki.

When you allow access to everyone on the Internet, all Zoho users, or another large group, you may occasionally run into someone who causes a problem on your site. For that reason, you can block specific users, as long as you know their email address or Zoho ID. Click Settings, Blocked Users, Block New User. Type in the person's email address or ID, along with the reason you're blocking that person (optional). Click Add to put the person on your Blocked User list.

Later, if that person promises to behave, you can return to the Blocked Users list, find the name, and click Delete to unblock the person and restore his or her access.

Creating a Group

If you have set any of the permissions to Group, you will need to create a group and populate it with one or more members. A group can have as many or as few members as you like. (There's currently no limit.)

To create a group, click the Group Members link at the top of any wiki page. (Alternatively, you can click Settings, Permissions, Click Here to Add/Edit Group Members.) This opens the Group Members box, which shows any group members you've already added. If the group has not been defined, only an Add Members hyperlink appears.

 If you do not see the Click Here to Add/Edit Group Members hyperlink, click the Save button under Change Your Wiki Permissions.

Click Add Members, and the box expands. In the Add Members text box, type or paste in the email addresses of people to whom you're giving wiki access (one address per line). If you want, type in an optional message for the invitation email in the Your Message box. Click Create to add these people to your wiki and send the invitation emails.

 To collaborate on your wiki, group members must have a Zoho account. The invitation contains a link where existing members can sign in and new members can sign up.

When you've added people to your wiki, they appear in the Group Members box. If a person's group membership is still pending, it means that person hasn't yet clicked the link in his or her invitation. (Zoho provides the link's address so you can send a reminder.) Group members who have accepted your invitation by clicking the link are listed as Subscribed.

 When other people change or comment on your wiki, Zoho assumes you want to know. So Zoho sends you an email to notify you of activity on your wiki: once a day for edits to the wiki and instantly for comments on a wiki page. If that's a little too much email for you, you can stop email notifications. Click Settings, Notification. The default settings for notifications are Daily Report (which sends a summary email of edits each day) and Instant Report (which fires off an email as soon as someone comments on one of your pages). To stop receiving either or both kinds of notifications, uncheck the relevant box. (You can always come back to this page later and re-enable notifications.) Click Save when you're done.

Comparing Previous Versions

When you have several people working on the same website (or even if you're simply trying things out on your own,) you'll probably run into a situation where you'll want to erase some changes and take a page back to an earlier version. Each and every time you save a page, Zoho treats it as a new version. Thus, you can compare versions and, if you want, restore a previous version to make it the current one.

When you want to take a look at some previous version of a page—or compare two versions—open the page and click More Actions, Show Version to open the Version box shown in Figure 11.12.

To see a previous version of this page, choose a previous version from the Show Version drop-down list. Versions are numbered and show how long ago each version was saved. If the first version you try isn't the one you want, keep choosing from the list. When you find the one you're looking for, click Revert Back to make it the current version.

You can also compare two versions. Choose the two versions you want to compare in the Show Changes In and the From drop-downs and then click Show. Zoho displays the page, highlighting the differences between the two versions you chose. If you want to revert to one of those versions, choose it from the Show Version drop-down and then click Revert Back.

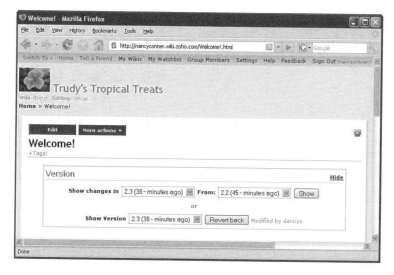

Figure 11.12
Compare two versions, or revert to a previous version in the Version box.

12

Manage Customers with Zoho Invoice and Zoho CRM

When it comes to dealing with customers, businesses want happy customers that pay on time. Zoho offers two programs to help you manage your customers: Zoho Invoice and Zoho CRM.

Which is better for your organization? It depends on the kind of solution you're looking for. If you want the ability to create, send, update, and process invoices, Zoho Invoice may be all you need. If you're looking for a full-service customer-relationship management solution that will help you track all phases of the sales cycle—planning a marketing campaign, generating and following up on leads, keeping in touch with contacts, sending out quotes, processing sales orders, sending and closing out invoices—CRM offers all this and more in a highly customizable program.

This chapter introduces you to Invoice and CRM, showing you everything you need to get started with these programs.

Getting Started with Zoho Invoice

Zoho Invoice gives freelance professionals, small-to-medium businesses, and other organizations the ability to automate their invoicing process—from creating a new invoice and sending it to a customer, to tracking overdue accounts, to processing payments.

It takes some setting up to get Invoice ready to use. But once you put Zoho Invoice to work for you, it'll save you tons of time and effort—in creating and sending invoices, tracking their status, and following up on overdue payments.

This is a question you don't need to answer right away, because you can use Invoice for free. On Zoho's free plan, you can create and send up to five invoices per month—and it won't cost you a cent. You get all the benefits of the paid plans (except for unbranded emails). These benefits include unlimited customers, invoice tracking, overdue reminders, multicurrency support, the ability to set up recurring invoices, integration with Zoho Projects (covered in Chapter 13, "Keep the Team on Task with Zoho Projects"), and more.

If five invoices per month isn't enough for you, Zoho lets you try any of the paid plans for 30 days with a money-back guarantee. If at any time during those 30 days you decide Invoice isn't for you, Zoho will refund your money.

Zoho offers these pricing levels for Invoice:

- **Free**—Create and send up to five invoices or estimates per month. The emails you send from the free account show the message "Powered by Zoho Invoice." (There's no Zoho branding on emails for any of the paid plans.)
- **Basic**—For $5 a month, this level allows you to send up to 25 invoices or estimates each month.
- **Standard**—This plan costs $15 a month and allows a maximum of 150 invoices or estimates.
- **Premium**—Send up to 500 invoices and estimates for $25 per month.
- **Elite**—If you need to send up to 1,500 estimates or invoices in a typical month, this plan will cost you $35 per month.

When you select a pricing plan, you're not tied down to it. Zoho lets you downgrade or upgrade to a new plan—even cancel Invoice altogether—whenever you want. No minimum subscription period, and no questions asked.

Setting Up Zoho Invoice

When you first sign in (http://invoice.zoho.com), Zoho Invoice lays out what you need to do to set up your account by showing you the page in Figure 12.1. This section walks you through the steps you need to take to set up your new Invoice account.

 After you've set up Invoice, you probably won't want to see the Welcome screen every time you sign in. To show the Dashboard at sign-in instead, check the Welcome page's upper-right Do Not Show at Startup check box.

Creating a Company Profile

To get started with Invoice, create a profile for your company. This profile provides information that will appear, nicely formatted, on your invoices.

If you're on the Welcome page, click the Setting Up Your Company Profile link. Alternatively, from anywhere in Invoice, click Settings at the top of the screen. This opens the Company Profile page, shown in Figure 12.2.

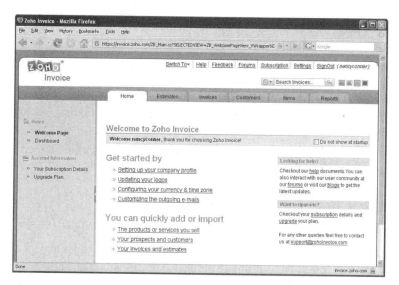

Figure 12.1
Zoho Invoice helps you get started with this Welcome page.

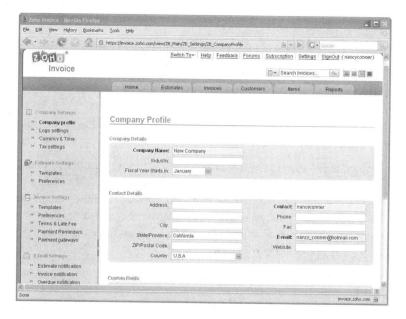

Figure 12.2
Invoice uses your company profile info on the invoices, estimates, and emails it creates.

The Company Profile page has three main sections:

■ **Company Details**—Type in your company's name (required) and your industry, and select the month when your fiscal year begins.

- **Contact Details**—In this section, a contact's name and an email address are required. You can also type in your business's address, phone and fax numbers, and website address.

- **Custom Fields**—Custom fields are optional but can be useful. A custom field can be anything you want to include on your invoices. If you need to show, for example, a tax ID, you can do so here. Type the kind of information the field will show (such as `Federal Tax ID#`) in the Label column; type the actual information (such as your company's actual ID number) in the Value column.

When you've provided the information for your company profile, click Save & Next to move to the next step of setting up Invoice.

Customizing Zoho Invoice with Your Logo

With Invoice, there are two places you can optionally display your company's logo:

- **System Logo**—This logo appears in the upper-left corner of all pages in your Zoho Invoice account. To display properly, the image should have a resolution of 72 dots per inch (dpi) and maximum dimensions of 60 pixels high by 140 pixels wide.

- **Invoice Logo**—This logo appears in the upper-left corner of your actual invoices. The file you use for the invoice logo can be up to 300 dpi, and the dimensions can be up to 250 pixels high by 580 pixels wide.

Info 4U The standard resolution for a computer monitor is 72 dpi, whereas 300 dpi is the standard resolution for printing. To make sure your logo displays properly, use two different image files with these resolutions: 72 dpi for your on-screen logo and 300 dpi for your invoice logo.

You can display either kind of logo, or both. (If you choose not to upload and display your own logo, the invoice displays no logo at all.)

To upload a system logo, make sure you're on the Logo Settings page. (If not, click Settings, Logo Settings.) In the System Logo section, click the Browse button and use the dialog box that opens to find and select the image you want to use as a logo. Click OK, and the image's file path appears in the Browse box. A preview appears in the System Logo section. (The preview may look a little more squashed than what you'll see on your pages. You can see what it looks like for real by glancing in the upper-left corner now.)

If you want to upload an invoice logo, go to the Invoice Logo section and click Change to make a Browse box appear. Browse to and select an image file, just as you did for the system logo. The preview for this logo is also likely to look smaller and more squashed than the way it will appear on your invoices.

When you've uploaded one or both logos (or chosen not to use either), click Next to move to the next setup step: choosing the currency you use, the time zone you live in, and the format you'll use for dates.

Choosing Your Currency and Time Zone

On the Currency and Time Zone page (Settings, Currency & Time), you can choose or adjust the following:

- **Currency Details**—In this section, choose a currency from the hundreds that are in the drop-down list. When you select a currency, its symbol (such as $ for dollars) appears in the symbol box. Choose the currency format you prefer, such as 1,000.00 (the standard format in the U.S., Canada, and many other countries) or 1 000,00 (the standard format in many eastern European countries, such as Poland and Estonia).

 Tip If you deal in more than one currency, click Add New Currency to insert another line where you can select a currency and a format. If you use multiple currencies, be sure to designate one as your base currency—the currency your company uses for its own accounting.

- **Time Zone**—Here, select your time zone from the drop-down list.
- **Date Format**—Click the drop-down list to choose a short, medium, or long format for the way Invoice displays dates. Each option on the list shows an example, so you'll know exactly how dates will look.

Everything all set? Click Save & Next to set up your tax info.

Entering Tax Information

If you're required to collect taxes on your product or service, you can set the tax amount here. In the Tax ID section, name the tax, such as *Sales tax*, and then put the percentage of the tax in the Percentage box. If you're calculating tax as a straight percentage of the item's price, choose ItemAmount in the Apply On column. If you have to calculate compound tax (that is, a second tax applied to the item plus the first tax), choose ItemAmount for the first line and then in the second line choose Item Amount + Tax 1. This calculates the second tax on the total of the cost of the item and the first tax combined. Click Save. (If you prefer, you can click Save & Next to choose a template for estimates. Keep clicking Save & Next to work your way through more than a dozen different settings categories. Clicking Save lets you end this process at any time; you can always come back and continue adjusting settings later.)

Managing Customers

After you've given Zoho some details about your company, you want to add details about your customers or clients. All Invoice plans (even the free one) allow you to add as many customers as you need to—there's no limit on the number.

Adding Customers

You can't send out invoices until you've let Zoho know whom to send them to. To add some customers to your account, click the Customers tab, which takes you to All Customers. After you've created some customers in your account, Invoice lists them here. The first time you visit the tab, however, Invoice tells you there aren't yet any customers in your account. Click the New Customer button to add your first customer.

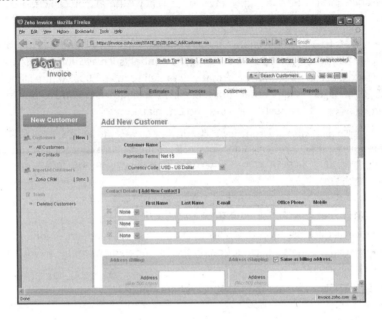

Figure 12.3
Use this form to add customers to Invoice.

The Add New Customer page, shown in Figure 12.3, collects this information:

- **Customer Name**—This field is required. It could be the name of an individual client or a company.

- **Payments Terms**—Your choices here are Net 15, Net 45, Net 30, Net 60, and Due On Receipt. The Net options specify the number of days before payment is due.

 If those payment terms don't reflect your company's policy, you can change them. Click Settings, find Invoice Settings in the list on the left, and then select Terms & Late Fee. On the page that opens, you can edit or delete existing payment terms or add new ones.

- **Currency Code**—If it's not already selected, choose the currency in which this customer pays.

- **Contact Details**—Choose a title (Dr., Mr., Ms., and so on) and type in the first and last names, email address, and office and mobile phone numbers for each contact related to this customer. If you need more than the three lines provided, click Add New Contact, and a new line appears.

 In Invoice, there's a distinction between a customer and a contact. Think of the customer as a company with whom you do business. A contact is a person you talk to within that company. So each customer you create may have several contacts—the buyer, the person you deal with in accounts payable, and so on.

- **Address (Billing) and Address (Shipping)**—Type in the customer's address here. If billing and shipping addresses aren't the same, uncheck the Same as Billing Address box (which is on by default), so you can enter the appropriate shipping address.

- **Custom Fields**—As with your Company Profile, you can create custom fields for any extra information you want to display on the invoice, such as a customer number.

Tip 4U For a repeating custom field, such as a Customer ID Number, check the Make These Fields Available for New Customers box. When you add another customer, Customer ID Number already appears in the Label column—which will spare you some typing if you're adding a lot of customers.

- **Notes**—Optionally, add any notes that are relevant to this customer, such as a special discount. Notes appear on the All Customer page's customer list.

Click Save Customer to add this customer to your customer list (see Figure 12.4) and clear the form so you can add another.

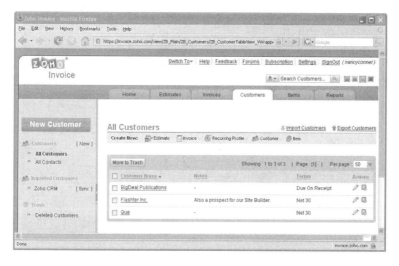

Figure 12.4
As you create customers, they appear on your All Customers list.

Importing Customers

You don't have to add customers one at a time using the Add New Customer page. If you have your customer info in a spreadsheet, you can import the whole shebang into Invoice all at once.

Info 4U For the import to work, your spreadsheet's headings must match the fields in Invoice's Add New Customer form. If they don't, the import will fail, and you'll get an error message telling you that some of the required fields are missing. So make sure your spreadsheet is set up so that Zoho will accept the imported data.

First, save the spreadsheet as either a CSV (comma-separated values) or TSV (tab-separated values) file.

Then, back in Invoice, click the Customers tab. From the All Customers page (shown in Figure 12.4), click Import Customers to open the page shown in Figure 12.5. Here, go to the section for the kind of file you're importing (CSV or TSV) and click its Import link. A box with a Browse button opens, as you can see in Figure 12.5. Click Browse, find and select your file, and click Open. The file path appears in the Browse box, and Zoho sets to work importing the file.

The records you've imported appear as new customers on the All Customers list. Click the name of any customer to open the record on the Customer Details page. From there, you can edit the file, add another contact for this customer, and so on.

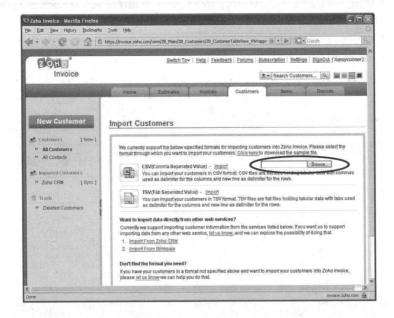

Figure 12.5
When you click the Import link in the CSV or TSV section, a Browse button appears so you can find the file you want.

 Tip 4U If you have customers in Zoho CRM, you can synchronize CRM and Invoice by clicking Sync in the Customer tab's left menu.

Importing Contacts

Just as you can import customers into Invoice, you can also import the contacts you have for those customers. (Remember, a *customer* is a company, and a *contact* is an individual person who works for that company. You can have multiple contacts per company.)

For example, if you get an email from a new contact with a vCard attached, you can use the vCard to import that contact directly into Invoice. A *vCard* is an electronic business card. You'll often find a vCard (a file ending in .vcf) attached to an email. Like a physical business card, a vCard holds a person's contact information: name, address, phone numbers, and sometimes a logo a photo or an audio clip.

vCards aren't the only way to import contacts into Invoice. You can also use CSV and TSV files that you have created by exporting from a spreadsheet, address book, or contact manager application.

To prepare to import contacts into Invoice, make sure you've saved them in one of the three supported formats: CSV, TSV, or vCard.

Next, import the contacts into Invoice. There are two ways you can do that:

- **From the All Contacts page**—Click Import Contacts to open the Import Contacts page. There, you can import your contacts in any of these formats: CSV, TSV, or vCard. The procedure is just like importing a list of customers: Find the kind of file you're importing and click Import. Use the Browse button to find and select the file. Zoho takes care of the rest.
- **From the Customer Details page**—If a new contact at an existing customer sends you an email with a vCard attached, import the vCard to quickly add that contact to the customer's Customer Details page. In All Customers, click the name of the customer you want. On the Customer Details page, click Import Contacts. A small dialog box opens, letting you browse through your computer to find the .vcf file you want. As soon as you select the file and click Open, Zoho imports the contact into Invoice.

Editing Customers and Contacts

To make changes to an existing customer or contact, go to the Customer Details page (refer to Figure 12.3). You can get there in one of two ways:

- Click the Customer Name, which appears for each listing on the All Customers or the All Contacts page.
- From the All Customers or All Contacts page, find the customer or contact you want and click its Edit This Customer icon (a picture of a pencil).

However you get there, the Customer Details page displays the current information for this customer and its contacts. Make your changes and then click Save Customer.

Deleting a Customer

With any luck, you won't have to delete a customer too often. But a company may go out of business or be so slow to pay that you decide not to deal with them again. (Remember, an individual contact is not a customer; the customer is the *company*. If you just need to delete a contact, see the following section instead.)

You delete customers from the All Customers page (refer to Figure 12.4). Check the box to the left of the customer you want to delete and then click Move to Trash.

If you *really* want that customer gone, such as when you know you'll never do business with that customer again, click Deleted Customers. (It's under Trash in the left menu of the Customers tab.) Check the customer's box and click Purge; then click OK to confirm.

If, on the other hand, you deleted a customer by mistake and want to restore that customer, click Deleted Customers, check the customer's box, and click Retrieve to restore that customer to your All Customers list. (You can't do this if you have purged the customer, as explained previously.)

Deleting a Contact

There's no point in keeping outdated contact information hanging around. When a contact leaves one of your customers or moves to a different job within the company, you can delete that contact by opening the appropriate Customer Details page. (Click the customer's name.) In the Contacts section, click the X to the left of the contact's name. There's no dialog box asking you to confirm the deletion, but you have to click Save Customer to make the deletion stick.

Creating Your Inventory

Whether you sell products or services, you'll want to set up an inventory of items in Zoho Invoice. Listing what you sell, item by item, is the next step in the process of getting ready to use Invoice; you need to have items in place before you can create and send an invoice or estimate.

You create your inventory on the Items tab. Click either the Items icon in the Create New line or the New Item button to open the Add New Item page. On this page, type an item name and specify the rate (that is, the price you charge for it). Both are required. You can also add an optional description of up to 500 characters and select a tax rate, if appropriate. (There are two tax rate boxes, Tax1 and Tax2, in case there are two different tax rates for the item.) Click Save Item to create the item and put it on your All Items list.

 The tax choices come from information you entered when you gave Zoho your company settings (see the earlier section "Entering Tax Information"). If you didn't set tax rates before you started creating items, you can do it now. Click New Tax to open a dialog box where you can set up the Tax ID, Percentage, and Apply On settings, as you learned earlier in the chapter.

After you've added some items to your All Items list, you can click its name or its Edit This Item icon to open the Item Details page and make necessary changes. Click Save Item when you're done.

 If you already have your inventory listed in a table or a spreadsheet, you can save yourself a lot of data entry by importing that info. Save the file holding the inventory items as a CSV or TSV file. Then, on the Items tab's All Items list, click Import Items. You import inventory items in essentially the same way you'd import customer info; flip back to "Importing Customers" earlier in this chapter to read up on the process.

Choosing a Payment Gateway

Zoho has set things up so that the email Invoice sends with your invoice has a convenient link that customers can click to make payment right away. Currently Invoice can insert either of two popular payment methods into your email: PayPal or Google Checkout. (If you don't accept online payments through either of these services, you can skip this section.)

If you use either of these services, do the following to make sure that Invoice can insert the appropriate payment method in your invoice emails. Click Settings. Under Invoice Settings, click Payment Gateways. This opens the Online Payment Settings page. Fill in the information for the service you use:

- **PayPal**—Your account's email ID
- **Google Checkout**—Your merchant ID and merchant key

If you want notification from Zoho when a customer makes an online payment, make sure the Notify Me on Online Payments box is checked. If you want to send an instant and automatic thank-you note when a customer pays online, check the Send Acknowledgment to Customers box.

Click Save when you're finished.

 Wondering whether it's safe for you—and your customers—to use online payment services? Zoho never stores your customers' credit card or bank account numbers; instead, Zoho simply forwards the information to the trusted payment service using SSL, which stands for *Secure Sockets Layer*. It's a method for sending data safely over the Internet by encrypting that data.

Setting Up Email Messages

Zoho uses the information you set up in your Company Profile and Customer Profiles pages to personalize the email messages you send. Each kind of message also has standard text that conveys its purpose. Before you create an invoice or estimate and send it out, make sure the message says what you want it to say.

Click Settings and, on the left side of the page under E-mail Settings, you'll see a list of the emails Invoice sends out. Figure 12.6 shows an example of an invoice notification email.

Zoho Invoice offers these email templates:

- Estimate notification
- Invoice notification
- Overdue notification
- Payment reminder
- Payment thank you

Click any email type to open the template. Templates use placeholders, a field name surround by percent signs (%), to indicate information that will be filled in later when you create and send the actual email. For example, if you're the informal type, you might start off your invoice notification emails like this:

Hi %FirstName%,

If the email were going to a contact named Cynthia Chan, it would begin like this:

Hi Cynthia,

If you're more formal in your business communications, you might start the email off like this:

Dear %FirstName% %LastName%:

That would open your email like this:

Dear Cynthia Chan:

Tip 4U When you view a template, common placeholders for that kind of template appear on the right side of the page. Click any placeholder to insert it into the template.

Figure 12.6
This is Zoho's template for an invoice notification.

As you look at the different templates, make sure they say what you need them to say and reflect your corporate or organizational culture (or, if you're a freelancer, your business personality). Be sure to click Save or Save & Next to keep any changes you've made to a template.

When you send an email, the email's signature is a few lines at the bottom of the message that can give (for example) your company's name, address, and customer service phone number. The signature gets attached to all outgoing emails from your Invoice account. So make sure it says what it should, before you sent out that first email. Click Settings; then under E-Mail Settings, choose Signature Settings. On the Signature Settings page, look over the standard signature, tweaking it as you like. For example, if you're a one-person operation or the only accounts receivable person in your organization, you might want to sign the email with your name, rather than Zoho's standard "Invoice Team."

When you're finished, click Save to apply your changes to the signature.

Creating and Sending Estimates and Invoices

Whether you're creating an estimate in hopes of gaining business or an invoice to charge for a completed transaction, the process is basically the same. Click the tab you want—Estimates or Invoices—and click the New Estimate or New Invoice button, respectively. Alternatively, from the Create New bar, click Estimate or Invoice. We'll look at the process for creating a new invoice.

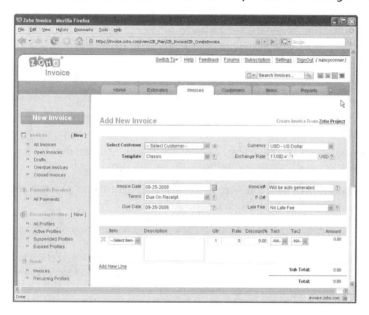

Figure 12.7
Create an invoice on the Add New Invoice page.

The Add New Invoice page, shown in Figure 12.7, asks for the following information:

- **Select Customer**—Choose the customer from a drop-down list of customers you've added to Invoice. If you don't see the customer you want, click the plus sign to open an Add New Customer box that collects essential details and creates the customer.

- **Template**—Zoho offers several different styles of templates in three invoice categories: Service, Product, and Fixed Cost. Select the template you want from the drop-down.

Tip 4U To preview Invoice templates, click Settings and, from the list on the left, find Invoice Settings and choose Templates. (There are also templates for estimates; under Estimate Settings, select Templates.) You can even create your own custom template; on the Invoice Templates or Estimate Templates page, click the Custom Template tab and then click Add Template. Now you can set up and format your template the way you want it, using placeholders such as %CompanyName% and %DueDate%.

- **Currency**—If the transaction is in currency besides your usual one, choose the currency from the list.

- **Exchange Rate**—For foreign-currency transactions, set the exchange rate you're using.

- **Invoice information**—In this section, choose an invoice date (if other than today), payment term (which determines the due date), an invoice number (if you don't want Invoice to assign one automatically), a purchase order number (if you have it), and the late fee, if any, that may be applied.

 To set your late-fee policy, click Settings and, under Invoice Settings, select Terms & Late Fee. There, you can specify whether the late fee is a percentage or a flat fee and how often to apply it if the invoice remains unpaid. Click Save when you're done.

- **Item or Service information**—The next section is where you select an item (from the list you've already created in Invoice). Add a description if you want, and provide or edit information about the quantity, any discount, and tax. If you need to add more items to the invoice, click Add New Line.

- **Customer Notes**—If you have any notes for the customer about the invoice, add them here. Zoho's standard note is a very polite: "Thanks for your business."

- **Terms & Conditions**—Whether they're standard or particular to a certain customer, you can add your invoice's terms and conditions here.

 No need to retype standard notes or terms and conditions every time you send an invoice. To set up or edit notes and terms/conditions that apply to all or most invoices, click Settings. Under Invoice Settings, click Preferences. In the Notes and Terms section, type in your standard text. Click Save, and what you've typed will be added to all your invoices.

After you've set up the invoice, click either Save as Draft or Save & Send. If you choose the latter, the next page shows the email that will be sent to the customer. Be sure to read the email carefully before you send it. If there's an empty placeholder, Zoho lets you know above the email. (In that case, click Cancel and provide the information the placeholder needs. Then come back to this page by clicking Invoices, finding this invoice in the All Invoices list, opening the invoice, and clicking Save & Send.)

When the email looks good to go, click Send, and off zips the email with your invoice attached.

 Invoices and estimates are attached to emails as PDF files, which your customers can open using Adobe Acrobat or Adobe Reader.

Setting Up a Recurring Profile

If you send out regular invoices for a recurring service, you don't want to spend precious time creating a new invoice for each billing cycle. You don't have to. Set up a recurring profile, and Zoho automatically creates and sends an invoice at the interval you specify.

Setting up a recurring profile is a lot like setting up any other invoice. In the Create New bar, click Recurring Profile. The page that opens looks a lot like the Add New Invoice page (see Figure 12.7). The difference is its profile information section, which contains these fields:

- **Profile Name**—This field is required, and lets you find this profile in the All Profiles list.
- **Start and End Dates**—Delineate the time period for sending recurring invoices.

 You must enter an end date; Invoice won't let you create a recurring profile that's open ended.

- **Late Fee**—This is where you choose a late fee policy that you added in Settings, Terms & Late Fee.
- **Terms**—This field has a drop-down list of repayment terms (which you can add or edit by clicking Settings, Terms & Late Fee).
- **Frequency**—This field tells Zoho how often to send a recurring invoice: a number of days that you specify, or every week, month, quarter, or year.

When you're finished, click Save Profile. Zoho adds the new profile to your All Invoices, All Profiles, and Active Profiles lists (all on the Invoices tab). From there, you can view the invoices related to the profile by clicking the far-right List Child Invoices icon. If there's a break in your services and you need to suspend sending invoices, check the box to the left of a profile and then click Suspend; the profile's status icon changes to a red square inside a circle. When things are back to normal, check the box again and click Resume.

Keeping Tabs on Your Customers

After you've created an invoice, Zoho adds it to the Invoices tab's All Invoices list, shown in Figure 12.8. Invoices that you've sent (but have not yet received payment for) also appear in Open Invoices; invoices that you've created but have not yet emailed appear on the Drafts list.

From any of these pages, you can take the following actions by clicking the appropriate icon in the Actions column:

- **Preview This Invoice**—Click this icon to open the Invoice Details page and see what your invoice looks like with all the placeholders filled in. The Details page also has a section that lists any payments received.
- **Edit This Invoice**—If you made a mistake in the invoice, click this icon to rectify it and send your customer the corrected invoice.
- **Add Payment for This Invoice**—The next section discusses how to mark an invoice as paid. Click this icon to start the process.

 Invoices you've created and sent also appear on customers' Customer Details pages in one of these categories: Overdue Invoices, Open Invoices, or Closed Invoices.

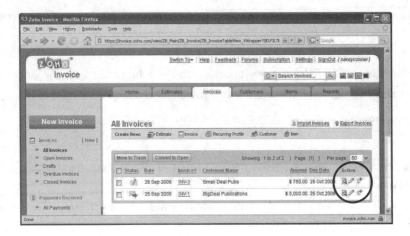

Figure 12.8
Take action on an invoice from the All Invoices list.

Processing Payments

Getting paid is the whole point of sending out invoices. As the money comes in, you want to keep Invoice up to date. How you process payments depends on how you accept them: online through PayPal or Google Checkout (both are integrated with Invoice) or by other methods.

Processing PayPal or Google Checkout Payments

If you use one of these online services to accept customer payments, you don't have to do a thing to process their payments in Invoice. When a customer pays using PayPal or Google Checkout, Invoice automatically updates their payment status, marking the invoice as closed. How easy is that?

Processing Other Payments

If your customers pay you by cash, check, credit card, or bank transfer, it takes just a second to mark a customer's invoice as paid and update your records. When you've received and processed a payment, go to the list of open invoices (Invoices, Open Invoices) and click the far-right Add Payment for This Invoice icon. The page changes to look like the one in Figure 12.9:

- **Received**—Lists today's date as the date you received payment; click the calendar to change it.
- **Mode**—Provides a list of different modes of payment. Select the one that applies to the payment you received.
- **Amount**—This is prefilled with the amount on the invoice. If you receive a partial payment or overpayment, you can change the amount to reflect that.
- **Description**—Provides a text box where you can add notes.

If you want to send the customer an email acknowledging payment, check the Send Payment Acknowledgment Email box. Click Add Payment to mark the invoice as closed.

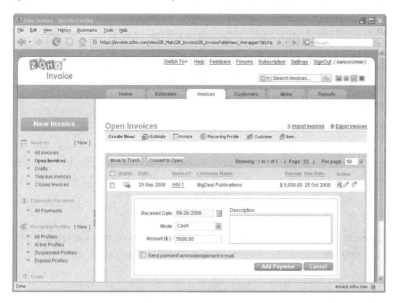

Figure 12.9
Provide payment info to mark an invoice as closed.

Setting Up Zoho CRM

Whether you're a freelancer working out of a home office or a multinational corporation, success in business is all about managing your relationships with your customers. You have to get out the word about your products or services, follow up on potential interest, close the deal, and process the payment—all while making sure your customers remain happy. CRM offers a complete marketing-through-invoicing workflow, along with case and solution management to help you solve customer issues before they become problems.

Choosing a Plan

You can try Zoho CRM for free, but it's worth taking a minute to look at the different payment plans and see which best suits your organization's needs.

As with Zoho Invoice, CRM comes with several different plans. Here's a quick overview of each to help you decide which works best for your business:

- **Free Edition**—This edition costs nothing to use. You can get up to three users and 100MB of space for storing your files. You also get sales force and marketing automation, inventory and workflow management, a calendar, dashboards and reports, and data imports of up to 1,500 records per batch.

- **Professional Edition**—For $12 per user per month, you get everything the Free Edition offers, plus a few more goodies: 250MB of storage space, up to 250 marketing emails per day, an import capacity of 10,000 records per batch, the ability to hierarchize roles, and SSL (Secure Sockets Layer) support for encrypting your data to keep it secure.
- **Enterprise Edition**—This edition charges a monthly fee of $25 per user. You get all the benefits of Professional Edition, along with these extras: 500MB of storage, batch imports of up to 20,000 records, autoresponders, and the ability to create groups and data-sharing rules for user profiles.

Info 4U Whichever edition you choose, the first three users are free.

If you want to discuss your organization's needs with someone at Zoho to help you decide which edition would be best for you, you can email sales@zoho.com or call 1-888-900-9646.

Signing Up

Even if you already have a Zoho account, you need to sign up again for Zoho CRM. So when you send your web browser to http://crm.zoho.com for the first time, click the Sign Up for FREE button.

On the Zoho CRM Sign Up Now page, provide your email address (this will also be the ID you use to sign in to CRM) and a password of six characters or longer. Choose the plan you want (see the previous section), and type in a verification code to prove you're a human and not some rogue program cruising the Internet. Check the box that indicates you agree to Zoho's Terms of Service and Privacy Policy; then click Sign Up Now.

Zoho sends a confirmation email to the address you used to sign up and takes you to the CRM home page, shown in Figure 12.10.

The home page is your centralized command station for working with CRM. It has tabs across the top so you can switch to pages related to various marketing, sales, and customer-management activities. Each tab represents a *module*, which is Zoho's term for a page that collects and displays records related to a particular aspect of customer-relationship management: Leads, Contacts, Accounts, Purchase and Sales Orders, Invoices, Cases, and so on.

Below the tabs is a button bar that gives you one-click ability to create a new lead, account, campaign, task, product—any kind of record you want to add to CRM. Down the left side of the page are a search box, a list of recently created or changed items, a drop-down list for creating new items, a calendar, and a clock. The main part of the screen has boxes that display items of your choosing, such as open tasks, today's events, sales by account, and so on.

Customizing CRM

One of CRM's strengths is that it can be customized to suit your needs and your work style. Before you take CRM live, adding users to the application and putting them to work, you need to set up CRM the way you want it. This section tells you how to customize CRM to suit your company's work style.

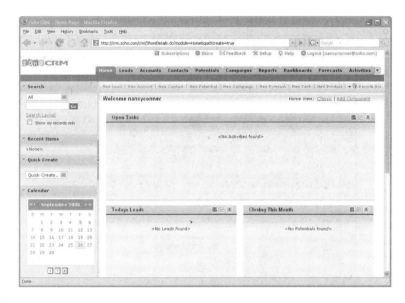

Figure 12.10
The home page is CRM's command central.

Customizing Tabs

Zoho CRM has more than a dozen tabs you can use to switch between pages and activities: ten across the top of the page and nine more on a menu. Click the far-right down arrow and choose the tab you want to make it appear.

You can customize these tabs in several ways:

- Hide tabs that you don't want CRM's users to have access to.
- Rearrange your tabs, customizing the interface to make it fit the way you work.
- Rename tabs so they reflect your organization's terminology.

The next three sections give you the steps for customizing CRM's tabs.

Hiding Tabs

If there's a tab or two that don't apply to your company's CRM workflow, you can hide that tab, so people using the program won't get confused. When you hide a tab, it means that no one using CRM, whatever their profile, has access to that tab. So before you hide a tab, make sure it's really not needed.

To hide tabs in CRM, click Setup at the top of the screen; on the page that opens, under Tab Settings, click Organize Tabs to open the page shown in Figure 12.11. This page has two boxes: Unselected Tabs on the left and Selected Tabs on the right. Initially, all CRM's tabs appear in the Selected Tabs box. Choose the tabs you want to hide (use the Shift or Ctrl key to select multiple tabs) in the Selected Tabs box. Click the left-pointing arrow to move them to the Unselected Tabs box. Click Save, and those tabs are hidden.

If it turns out later that you need to show some of those tabs after all, come back to the Organize Tabs page, find and select the tabs in the Unselected Tabs box, and click the right-pointing arrow to put them back in the Selected Tabs box. Click Save to make the tabs visible again.

Info 4U You can't hide CRM's Home tab.

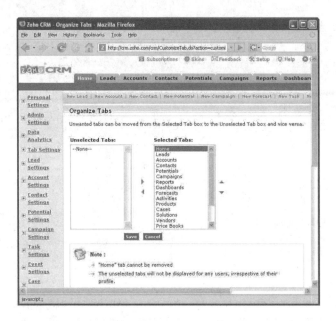

Figure 12.11
Hide or rearrange CRM's tabs on the Organize Tabs page.

Rearranging Tabs

If you're always hunting for a particular tab because it's never where you think it should be, you can move it to a new location. On the Organize Tabs page (click Setup, Organize Tabs to get there), visible tabs appear in the box on the right, as Figure 12.11 shows. The top-to-bottom order in this box reflects left-to-right order on your CRM pages.

In the Selected Tabs box, find the tab you want to move. Click it and then use the up and down arrows to move it to its new location. Click Save to make your new arrangement permanent.

Info 4U You can move only one tab at a time; you can't select a block of tabs and move them en masse.

Renaming Tabs

You might want to tweak the names of the tabs so they better reflect your organization's lingo. For example, maybe you deal in services instead of products, or there might be terminology specific to your industry that you want to use in CRM. You can change the name of a tab (and also any links and commands that contain the tab's name) by clicking Setup and then, in the Tab Settings section, clicking Rename Tabs.

On the Rename Tab page, find the tab's current name and click the Edit link to its left. This opens the Change Tab Name page for that tab. This page has two fields:

■ Name to be displayed in Tabs

■ Name to be displayed in Links/Commands

Type the new name in these boxes. (You can rename the tab only, but this might be confusing.) Click Save. Zoho applies the change and takes you back to the Rename Tab page. The tab you just renamed now displays two names:

■ **Module Tab Name**—What Zoho calls the tab (its original name)

■ **Display Label**—The new name you've just given the tab

> Currently, when you rename a tab and its corresponding links and commands, Zoho changes the name everywhere *except* in Dashboards and Reports.

Adding a Component

The main part of CRM's home page displays boxes, called *components,* that give information about your CRM tasks, leads, events, and so on. Components are highly customizable: Choose the components you want to include and the information each shows. You get an at-a-glance overview of important data right on your home page.

To add a component, go to the CRM home page and click the upper-right Add Component link. This opens the Add Component dialog box, which has a drop-down list of all the modules (that is, tabs) in your CRM account. Choose a module, and the dialog box expands to look like the one in Figure 12.12, so you can select what the component will display.

Give the component a name (this will appear at the top of the component on your home page), and specify whether it will contain one or two columns. Then, from the Custom View drop-down, choose what the component will contain. Your choices are based on the module you chose. Click Save to create the new component and add it to your home page.

Figure 12.12
Add a custom component to your CRM home page.

Changing a Component's Contents

When you first sign up for CRM, Zoho helpfully adds some standard components to your home page. But what you want to see there might be different from what the component shows. For example, rather than seeing *all* open tasks, you might prefer to see just those open tasks assigned to you.

When you want to change the contents of a component, click the Settings button in the upper-right part of the component box. This opens the Edit Component dialog box, which asks for the same information as the expanded box in Figure 12.12: Name the component, choose the number of columns, and select the information the component will hold. Click Save to update the component.

 If you don't want a particular component on your CRM home page, you can remove it by clicking its upper-right X and then clicking OK to confirm.

Choosing Custom Colors

If the standard CRM color scheme isn't to your taste (or if it simply clashes with today's outfit), you can pick a new one that's more to your liking. Click the Skins link at the top of the page. A box opens, showing Zoho's color-scheme offerings. Choose an option and click Apply to see how it looks, while leaving the dialog box open so you can try another. When you find a color scheme you like, click OK to keep it.

Working with Users and Profiles

After you've set up the home page, the next thing you'll probably want to do is add some users. (See "Choosing a Plan" in the previous section to find out how many users you can add.) After you've added other users, you can assign tasks and profiles—and put your team to work. Users you add to your CRM account can sign in and start working right away.

 When you first sign up for CRM, Zoho treats your account as a personal one. That's so you can take a look around before you commit to a subscription level. When you add your first user, you also upgrade to a company account, which allows multiple users.

Adding Users

To add a user to your CRM account, click Setup; in the Admin Settings section of the page that opens, click Users. The Users page lists any users associated with the account—in the beginning, that's just you. Click Create New User.

 If you haven't yet upgraded to a company account, clicking Create New User opens a page on which Zoho asks for your company's name. You need to provide this to add your first user.

Tip 4U After you've given Zoho your company's name, you can edit its details, change its currency, or add a logo from the Company Details page. Click Setup and, under Admin Settings, click Company Details. Click the Edit button to add or change information about your company.

The Create User page, shown in Figure 12.13, has these sections:

- General Information is where you give details such as the new user's name, email address, profile (default choices are Administrator and Standard; to create more profiles, see the next section), and role—all of which are required. Optional fields in this section include alias, contact info, website, and birth date.

- Address Information has the expected fields—street, city, ZIP Code, and so on. All are optional.

- Locale Information has three fields, all required: Language, Country Locale, and Time Zone. Choose each from a drop-down list.

- Password has a check box (checked by default) that tells Zoho to create a random password and send the new user immediate notification of being added to your CRM account. If you'd rather invite the new user later, uncheck this box.

Everything all set? Click Create New User to add this user to your account. If you told Zoho to notify the new user now, that person receives an email with login instructions and can start using CRM right away.

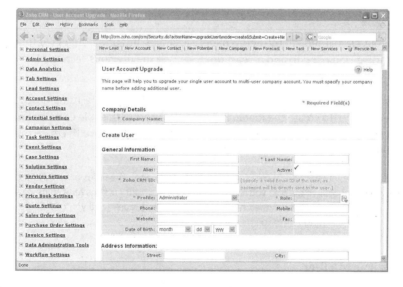

Figure 12.13
Name your company and then add details to create your first user.

If you unchecked the Generate a Random Password and Notify the User Immediately check box, you haven't yet notified the user you just added. When you're ready to send that notification, go to the Users page, check the box to the left of the user, and click Reset Password. Zoho asks for confirmation; click OK. Zoho sends the user his or her password and notification.

Working with User Roles and Profiles

Roles and profiles determine what users can do in your CRM account. *Roles* create a hierarchy, allowing higher-ups to access the records of those they manage. For example, sales reps don't have access to records belonging to other sales reps, but the sales manager has access to records of all the reps she manages. Regional sales managers don't have access to each others' records, but you (as CEO) have access to all managers' records.

 All CRM accounts come with two built-in roles: CEO and Manager. Free Edition users are limited to these two roles (although you can rename them; see "Editing or Deleting a Role"). Professional Edition accounts can have up to three roles, and Enterprise Edition accounts can have as many as 250.

Profiles, on the other hand, are created by you to allow or restrict access to certain modules (tabs), records, fields, and activities, such as importing, exporting, sending emails from CRM, and so on.

Creating a Role

To create a role, click Setup; on the Setup page, click Roles. (It's under Admin Settings—if you don't see it there, you need to add at least one user; see the previous section.) The Roles page opens, showing existing roles in a hierarchical tree. Click New Role.

On the New Role page, fill in the following information about the role: its name, the role immediately above this one (to create the hierarchy), whether users in this role can share data with others in the same role, and an optional description of the role. Click Save to create the role and add it to CRM's hierarchy.

 Here's a quick way to create a role: Click Setup, Roles to open the Roles page. Find the role that will be just *above* the role you're creating and hover your cursor over it to make some icons appear to its right. Click the Create Subordinate Role icon—and you can create a new role and slot it right into the hierarchy.

Assigning a Role to a User

When you create a new user, you assign a role to that user as part of the process. But users change jobs—a promotion, for example, might move a sales rep up the CRM hierarchy to sales manager. You want that user's role to reflect his new position.

To assign a role, open the Users page (click Setup; then in the Admin Settings section, click Users) and click the Edit link to the left of the user's name. This opens the Edit User Details page for that user, which looks just like the Create User page (see Figure 12.13) with the user's current details filled in. In the General Information section, click the Role Name Lookup icon to the right of the user's current role. A box opens, listing all the roles that exist in CRM. Click one to select it. Click Save to assign the new role.

Editing or Deleting a Role

Roles change—new management comes in and redefines the organizational hierarchy, a new job category is created, or an existing job gets renamed—and you need to make sure CRM can change with them.

Edit a role from the Roles page (Setup, Roles). In the roles hierarchy, place your cursor over the role you're editing; when icons appear to its right, click its Edit icon (a pencil poised over a clipboard). A page opens where you can rename the role and, if you want, write or edit its description. Click Save to save your changes.

If a job category is eliminated, you can delete the associated role from CRM. Click Setup, Roles. Put your cursor over the obsolete role, and click its far-right Trashcan icon. Zoho opens the Delete Role page, where you transfer this role's subusers to another role. For example, if you're deleting a middle management role, you'd transfer the subusers who currently report to that middle manager to a senior manager. Click the Role Name Lookup icon to find the role who'll take responsibility for the deleted role's subusers. Then click Transfer & Delete.

Zoho deletes the role and transfers any subusers to the role you specified, returning you to the Roles page.

Creating a Profile

Creating a profile helps you make sure that users have access only to the information—modules, records, even fields—that they need to do their jobs. The number of profiles you can create depends on your edition of CRM. With the Free Edition, you can have up to three profiles. Professional Edition allows up to 15 profiles and Enterprise Edition up to 25.

All new CRM accounts come with two standard profiles:

- **Administrator**—Users assigned to this profile have full permission to manage CRM. They can manage users, roles, profiles, groups, and data sharing. They can also customize CRM.
- **Standard**—This profile does not have the administrative permissions that the Administrator profile has.

To see the profiles in your account, click Setup and, from the Admin Settings section, choose Profiles. When you create a new profile, you start by "cloning" one of these existing profiles—copying its permissions to a profile with a new name. From there, you can edit the new profile to adjust its permissions.

Click the New Profile button to create a new profile. The New Profile page opens. Here, give the profile a name and pick the existing profile that will serve as the basis for the new profile. There's a field for an optional description of the new profile, as well. Click Save; Zoho creates the new profile and opens its Profile Details page, which shows the permissions for this profile. To tweak those permissions for your new profile, click Edit, which opens the page shown in Figure 12.14.

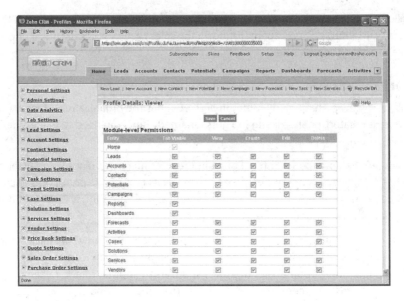

Figure 12.14
Edit a profile's permissions by checking and unchecking boxes.

Editing a Profile's Permissions

To grant or prohibit certain activities for a particular profile, open the editable version of the Profile Details page, shown in Figure 12.14. If you just created a new profile (see the previous section), you're already there. Otherwise, click Setup, Profiles. Then find the profile you want to tweak and click its Edit link.

Profiles have these permissions for you to set:

- **Module-Level Permissions**—For each module (such as Leads, Accounts, Contacts, Campaigns, Invoices, and so on), you can determine whether users in this profile can see the module's tab and view, create, edit, or delete its records.

 The Reports and Dashboards modules don't have their own records, so they don't have view, create, edit, and delete permissions available.

- **Reports and Dashboard Permissions**—In this section, the permissions are whether users with this profile can manage these modules and schedule reports.

- **Import Permissions**—Use this section to determine what kinds of records users can import into CRM, such as accounts, leads, vendors, cases, and so on.

- **Export Permissions**—This section is just like Import Permissions, except you're granting or withholding permission to transfer records out of (rather than into) CRM.

- **Tool Permissions**—This section allows users with this profile to perform certain actions on records *en masse*—or not. Examples of permissions in this section include sending mass emails to leads or contacts; mass transferring, updating, or deleting of records; and changing ownership.

- **Admin Permissions**—For regular users, you'll probably want to disable the permissions in this section, which are high-level permissions to manage users, the ability to customize your CRM account, and field-level access.

- **General Permission**—This catchall category has permissions for viewing data in Zoho Sheet or Print view; managing templates and rules; finding and merging vendors, leads, or contacts; and more. Take a look to see what's available here.

Each permission has a check box; a check in the box means this profile has this permission, and an empty box means the activity is off limits for this profile. After you've set permissions the way you want them, click Save.

Assigning a Profile

You associate a user with a profile using the same method by which you assign a role. From the Users page (Setup, Users), find the user you want and click Edit. This opens the Edit User Details page, where you can select the profile for this user from the Profile drop-down list. Click Save to assign the profile.

Deactivating Users

When you want to remove a user from your CRM account, whether you're suspending the user temporarily or removing him entirely from the account, start on the Users page (Setup, Users). Check the box of the user you're deactivating (you can select more than one) and then click the Deactivate Users button. Click OK to confirm, and the user's status changes from a check mark (active) to an x (deactivated).

 Using the Deactivate Users button works only for users whose profiles are something other than Administrator. So if you need to deactivate someone with an Administrator profile, change the profile first (see the previous section).

Deactivating a user does *not* remove that user entirely from your CRM account—you can always come back to the Users page and activate that user again by checking the user's box, clicking Activate Users, and then clicking OK.

Attention Professional and Enterprise Edition subscribers: Because deactivated users are still associated with your CRM account, you still pay for them. But you can remove a user from your account right after you've deactivated that user. From the Users page (Setup, Users), click the Manage Subscriptions button. The page that opens lists CRM's three plans, side by side, with your current plan identified. Scroll down and click Manage Your Plan to open the Manage Subscriptions page.

Check the Downgrade box and, in the Remove Subscription section, choose the number of users you want to remove from the account. Click Update Account to remove the user or users from your account.

Managing Your Customer Relationships

Zoho CRM is made up of a series of *modules,* tabs that contain and organize data related to a specific part of the customer-relationship management cycle—from creating a new marketing campaign, to closing the sale, to supporting customers. This section gives you a guided tour of CRM's modules.

 CRM offers nearly two dozen different modules to address a wide range of customer-relationship management practices. Depending on your industry or organization, you may find you don't need them all. You can hide any tabs that your users don't need. See "Hiding Tabs," earlier in this chapter, to find out how.

Marketing

The marketing–sales cycle usually begins with a marketing campaign. Marketing gets out the word about a product, and the sales team follows up. Get your cycle off to a good start by creating and keeping track of marketing activities:

- **Campaigns**—A new marketing campaign kicks off a new customer-relationship management cycle. This module helps you keep track of your organization's marketing activities so you can manage your marketing process: For each campaign, describe objectives, track expenditures, and compare them to projected costs.
- **Tasks**—Tasks happen, of course, in all phases of the marketing–sales life cycle. They're mentioned here because as you add marketing campaigns, you'll want to add marketing-related tasks. Tasks are your to-do list and include current status and due date. They appear on the Activities tab.
- **Events**—Like tasks, events appear on the Activities tab and happen in both the marketing and sales phases of the cycle. Events include the date, start time, and end time of whatever event you're planning.

 You can add tasks and events from the Campaigns tab; click the relevant button just below the list of campaigns.

Sales

Sales is the lifeblood of any organization. Keep your sales force on track by automating the tasks and information that managers and reps alike must juggle:

- **Leads**—Capture and organize contact information and product interests for leads generated by marketing campaigns, trade shows, networking, and other methods.
- **Accounts**—This module collects and organizes information about companies or departments that want to buy your products or services—now or in the future.
- **Contacts**—Whereas Leads represent potential business contacts, Contacts are those people with whom you currently do business. For each contact, you can provide contact information, track the campaign or lead that generated the contact, and associate the contact with a specific account.

- **Potentials**—Potentials are the same thing as opportunities. This module lets you track the sales cycle—from finding a lead, through demonstrating the product, to closing the sale. Keep track of success probability and expected revenue, as well.

- **Forecasts**—Sales managers can keep an eye on the bottom line by tracking sales numbers against individual quotas and expectations. Sales reps can use this module to see whether they're on track to meet their quotas.

- **Quotes**—Sales quotes are legally binding, so you want to make sure that you keep track of the quote a customer received, its terms, and its duration. This module also tracks the quote's status: Draft, Negotiation, Delivered, On Hold, Confirmed, Closed Won, or Closed Lost.

 If you have standard emails that you send at regular (or irregular) intervals, create an email template. Click Setup. Under Templates, click Email Templates. On the Email Templates page that opens, click New Template. Choose the record type the template is for (leads, contacts, invoices, and so on); then click Next to open a page where you can create and save the template.

Inventory and Orders

Whether it's coming in or going out, you have to keep track of the money: Where's it going? For what? Who owes it? What did they buy? For how much? When's it due? The modules in this section make life easier for those dealing with inventory and accounts, as well as purchasing and sales:

- **Vendors**—Whether you manufacture goods or resell products, you purchase supplies, goods, and services from people and companies outside your own organization. This module is like a virtual address book for keeping track of your vendors and what you purchase from them.

- **Purchase Orders**—When you're ready to place an order with one of your vendors, create a purchase order to track your organization's expenses and make sure the terms of the purchase are crystal clear. Tracking purchase orders also lets you check shipments and invoices against your own records.

- **Services**—Use the Services module to add products or services to your inventory. Keep the sales team up to date on current products and prices, and make it easy to create sales orders and invoices with one-click product selection.

- **Price Books**—Price books let you sell the same product for different prices, depending on the type of customer you're dealing with. For example, you may offer a better deal to customers who buy at a high volume than to one-off customers. A price book specifies both a unit price and a list price. The unit price, determined by the product's manufacturer, is a fixed price. The list price, on the other hand, is the price at which you sell the product. List prices can vary, depending on the deal you have with a customer.

- **Sales Orders**—When a customer agrees to a sales quote, you can create a sales order to formalize the deal. Sales orders look a lot like purchase orders, only you're the seller, not the buyer.

■ **Invoices**—Time to get paid! An invoice accompanies or follows shipment of a product or performance of a service. This module is where you create and track invoices.

 Check out CRM's inventory templates. Click Setup and, under Templates, click Inventory Templates. You'll find a range of templates that let you customize the print layout of inventory-related modules, including quotes, invoices, sales orders, and purchase orders.

Customer Support

Sales don't happen in a vacuum. To make sure your customers stay customers, you need to be ready to provide support throughout the sales and marketing cycle. You do this by creating cases to record and address customer problems, from the moment an issue arises until it's resolved.

■ **Cases**—Capture detailed information about a customer's issue by creating a case. Here you can specify the issue, account, origin, and status, as well as other information.

■ **Solutions**—Common customer issues don't need to be solved from square one each and every time they come up. Build a collection of frequently asked questions—and their approved answers—using the Solutions module.

Data Analysis

Throughout the marketing and sales cycle, managers need frequent reports to check on metrics and see whether goals are being met. CRM offers two ways to report on your sales and marketing data:

■ **Reports**—Reports show your data in various ways, letting you highlight successes or issues and spot trends. Use one of CRM's 40+ prebuilt reports or create your own (see the upcoming section).

■ **Dashboards**—Dashboards use charts to show a snapshot of your data from several different perspectives, giving you at-a-glance information: comparisons, patterns, and trends in all phases of the marketing–sales life cycle. For example, sales managers can compare reps' performance to their quotas, or you can look at trends in product sales from one quarter to the next.

 CRM Dashboards use Flash technology to build the charts that show your data, so make sure you have the latest version of Flash. You can get it (for free) at www.adobe.com/products/flashplayer.

Working with Modules

The previous section gives you an overview of the modules available in CRM—what they are and what you can do with them. In this section, it's time to roll up your sleeves and get to work.

Whatever kind of module you're working with, each works in pretty much the same way: You can create, edit, and delete records, find individual records in the module, and organize records to view the data in different ways. Although there are differences in the kinds of data each module collects and organizes, the procedures for working with the different kinds of data are similar across modules. So instead of repeating the same information for each module, we'll look at one example, drawn from one of the first modules you're likely to work with: Marketing Campaigns.

The first time you click a tab to open a module and start adding records, the page will look something like the one in Figure 12.15, which shows the Campaigns module. In this example, at the top of the page is the New Campaign button, along with links (on the right) to look at the data as a spreadsheet in Zoho Sheet and in Print view. Below those items, you can see an alphabet's worth of links, which help you find records by name. Moving down the page is a bar that relates to views, which let you filter and display the module's data in various ways. Below the Views bar is a list of records in this module. And at the bottom of the page are tools and reports related to the kinds of records this module holds.

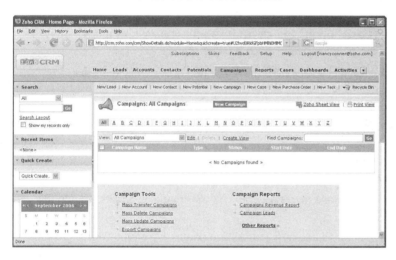

Figure 12.15
The Campaigns module's main page.

Creating a New Record

This section describes how to create a new campaign from the Campaigns tab, but you can create any kind of record by following these steps: Click the tab you want (or click a kind of record in the button bar) and then fill out the form to create the record. The fields on the form depend on the kind of record you're creating—for example, contacts and leads will have fields for name, address, email, phone number, and so on. Required fields have an asterisk and red field labels. When you're done with the form, click Save.

To go through the process of creating a new record, we'll create a new campaign. To do this, you can click the Campaigns tab and then click the New Campaign button. Alternatively, just click the button bar's New Campaign button, which is available no matter what tab you're on.

The Create Campaign page, shown in Figure 12.16, collects basic information about the new campaign:

- **Campaign Owner**—This field has your ID already filled in. To assign the campaign to someone else, click the Owner Name Lookup icon to the right of this field. The Change Owner box opens, where you can search for and select the person responsible for the campaign.

- **Campaign Name**—This required field is how you'll identify this campaign.

- **Type**—This drop-down lists common kinds of campaigns, such as direct mail, trade show, advertising, and so on. Click the list to select one.

- **Status**—The options in this drop-down are Planning, Active, Inactive, and Complete.

- **Start and End Date**—These fields determine how long the campaign will last.

- **Expected Revenue**—This is a currency field where you can enter how much money you expect the campaign to bring in.

- **Budgeted and Actual Cost**—These currency fields let you compare how much money has been allocated to the campaign and how much is being spent.

 Don't have a calculator handy? Click the calculator button next to any of this form's currency fields to open a calculator in a new window.

- **Num Sent**—Short for "Number sent." Use this field to record how many leads the campaign has targeted.

- **Expected Response**—This is a percentage field; use it to estimate what you think the campaign's turnout will be.

- **Description**—If you want, write a short description of the campaign and its goals in this text box.

Click Save to save this campaign and add it to your All Campaigns list (on the Campaigns tab). Alternatively, click Save & New to save this campaign and open another Create Campaign form.

Importing Data

For some kinds of records, such as contacts and accounts (to name just a couple), you can import existing data from an outside program, such as an Excel spreadsheet. This is a major time-saver when you have hundreds or thousands of records that you need to move into CRM.

To import data, you need to make sure the file holding the data is in a format that works with CRM: XLS, VCF, and CSV formats all work for 1,500 or fewer records. If you have more than 1,500 records to import, the file must be in CSV format. Here are a few other things to check for to ensure a successful import:

- Depending on your CRM edition, you have some limits on the number of files you can import in a batch:
    - **Free Edition**—1,500 per batch.
    - **Professional Edition**—10,000 per batch.

Figure 12.16
Use this form to add a new marketing campaign to CRM.

- **Enterprise Edition**—20,000 per batch if you use the Clone option for handling duplicate records. If you want CRM to skip or overwrite duplicate records, keep batches to 2,000 or fewer records.
- The file you're importing must be 5MB or smaller.
- The first row of the file should contain field names.
- If you're importing an Excel file, save it in Excel 1997–2003 format. At this time, CRM can't import Excel 2007 files.
- For check box fields, use TRUE and FALSE values.
- Make sure there are no embedded images or combination filters in your file.

When you're ready to import your file, open the tab for the module into which you're importing data. In the Tools section (near the bottom of the page), click an Import link. On the page that opens, use the Browse button to open a window where you can find and select the file you're importing. Click Open. Enterprise Edition users can also tell Zoho how to treat any duplicate records it finds during the Import: Skip, Overwrite, or Clone. (The last option is how CRM handles duplicate records in the Professional and Free editions.) After you've chosen the file you're importing, click Next.

CRM opens a page where you can map information in your spreadsheet to existing fields in the CRM module. For example, if you're importing contacts into the CRM Contacts module, you want to make sure name data goes into the name field, street address into the Mailing Street field, and so on. Use the drop-downs to tell CRM which data from your spreadsheet goes in which column in the CRM module. Click Next.

If you haven't mapped some of the data in your file to the CRM module's field, Zoho lets you know on the next page. Unmapped data gets left out of the import; so if there's any data that you need to move to CRM, click Previous and choose the field that will hold it. Otherwise, click Import. Zoho imports your data and uses it to create new records.

Organizing Your Records

As you create new records, CRM adds them to the All Records list on the module's tab. (The word *Records* will be replaced by the kind of records the module holds: Case, Purchase Order, Invoice, and so on.) That list can grow quickly, making it hard to find one particular record among all the others.

Searching for a Record

To find a record by searching the whole list, you have two options (both from the module's tab):

- **Search by keyword**—Type your search term into the Find Records box, above the list of records and on the right. Click Go (or press Enter) to find a list of records with your search term in the name.
- **Search by opening letter**—Across the top of the All Records page is a series of links: one for each letter of the alphabet. Click any letter to see all records whose names begin with that letter.

Viewing a List of Records

Maybe you don't want to find a single record by name; maybe you need to see a list of all the records that you own. Each module has a number of built-in views that filter records by a prede-fined set of criteria. For example, the Campaigns module has these views already built in: All Campaigns, All Active Campaigns, My Active Campaigns, and Unread Campaigns.

Click the View drop-down (on the left, above the list of records) and make your selection to apply the filter.

Creating a Custom View

If CRM's preloaded views don't meet your needs, you can create your own view of the data, using multiple criteria to create a very precise filter. You can also tell CRM how to display the results: which columns to show and which you don't need to see.

Using the Campaigns module as an example, here's how you create a custom view. Say you want a list of all active direct-mail campaigns whose expected response is greater than 10%. A custom view can find you all campaigns meeting those criteria. Then, specify which columns you want to see in the results.

On the Campaigns tab, click Create View. (The link is just above the All Campaigns list.) On the Create New View page, shown in Figure 12.17, follow these steps:

1. Name the view (required) and tell Zoho whether you want this view to be the default—that is, the first view you see when you click the Campaigns tab.

2. Specify your filtering criteria. These criteria tell Zoho which records to put in the view. As Figure 12.17 shows, you set the criteria by choosing a field, a verb (such as *is, is not, starts with, equals, is greater than,* and so on), and a value: either text or numeric, depending on the kind of field. To add another criterion, click the Add Criteria button, and a new line appears.

3. Select the columns the view will display. In the Choose Columns section, available columns are listed in a box on the left; selected columns (those that appear in the view) are listed in a box on the right. To add a column to the display, select a column's name in the Available Columns box and then click Add. To remove a column from the display, select its name in the Selected Columns box and then click the red X.

4. Tell Zoho who can see the new view. In the Accessibility Details section, choose whether the view is accessible to all users, to you and you alone, or to a group that you specify.

5. Click Save.

Zoho creates the view and adds it to the drop-down list of views on the Campaigns tab.

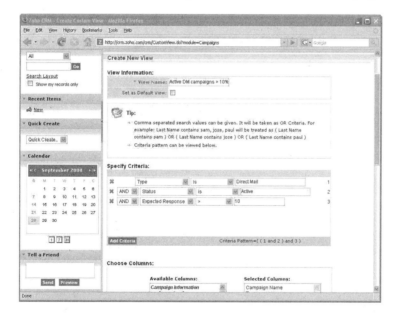

Figure 12.17
Create a view to show a list of campaigns that meet your criteria.

 Click the upper-right Zoho Sheet View link to open a module's records in Zoho's spreadsheet program (see Chapter 4, "Track Data with Zoho Sheet"). You can open a spreadsheet of up to 999 rows this way. Sheet view does not currently work with the Activities or Forecasts modules. Remember, too, that any new columns you add to the Sheet spreadsheet *won't* be added to the CRM module. (The next section tells you how to add custom fields to CRM modules.)

Working with Fields

You're not restricted to the fields that Zoho has created in CRM modules. As this section explains, you can add new fields or edit existing ones to make your CRM modules meet your organization's needs. To start, go to CRM's Setup page.

Adding a Custom Field

To add a field to a CRM module, click Setup. Then find the module you want, such as Quote Settings or Vendor Settings. In that section, click the Fields List link. Figure 12.18 shows the Fields List for the Campaign module.

To add a field, click the New Custom Field button. On the page that opens, choose a field type (text, integer, date, currency, and so on), give the field a label, and specify a length. Click Save (or Save & New to add another field) to create the field.

Info 4U CRM lets you add up to 100 custom fields to a module.

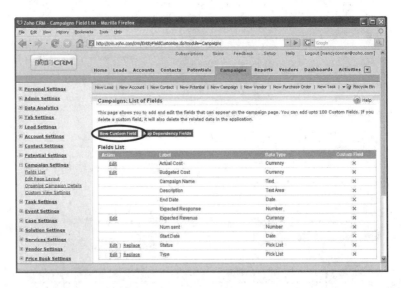

Figure 12.18
Create a new field or edit an existing one from the Fields List.

Editing a Field

As Figure 12.18 shows, you can edit many of the fields in a CRM module. What you can edit depends on the module, but the figure gives you an idea of some of the possibilities.

To edit a field, click its Edit link. CRM opens a page that shows what can be edited for that field. For example, in a currency field you can edit the number of decimal places, the length, and how to handle rounding. For a Pick List field, you can change what appears in the drop-down: Add a new choice, delete an existing one, change the order in which choices are displayed, or use the first value in the list as a default.

After you've made your changes, click Save to update the field.

 To replace a term on a drop-down list with one that's specific to your organization or industry, go to the Field List and click the Replace link. From the Select Value Changing From drop-down, choose the value you want to rename. In the Select Value Changing To text box, type in the term you're replacing it with. Click Save to replace the old term with your new one.

Mass Updating Records

When you have a whole bunch of records that you need to update—changing, for example, their status from Pending to Closed—it's the most boring kind of busywork to go through those records one at a time. You'll be glad to hear you don't have to—instead, you can select multiple records and update them all at once.

Click a tab to open the module you want. Optionally, you can choose or create a view (see the previous section) to show the records you want. Check the boxes of the records you're updating (or the box at the top of the list to check all records' boxes on the current page). Click More Actions, Mass Update.

A box opens, asking you to select the field you want to update. Choose a field from the drop-down list. When you do, another box opens where you can enter or select a new value for that field. For example, if a deadline has been extended, you'd type in the new end date. If you're changing records' status, you'd click the drop-down and select the new status from the list. When you've changed the field's value, click Save. Zoho updates all the records you chose in one fell swoop.

Printing Records

If you need a hard copy of your records (or a view containing a certain set of records), display the records you want and then click the upper-right Print View link. A new window opens, showing how the records will look when you print them. Click Print Page. A Print box opens where you can tweak the document's settings or choose a printer. When all looks good, click OK to print the list of records.

Deleting Records

There are two ways to delete a record; both take place on the tab of the module you want:

- To delete a single record, hover your cursor over the record you're about to delete. A trash-can appears just to the left of the record's name. Click the trashcan, and a box opens to ask if you're sure you want to delete this record. Click OK, and Zoho banishes the record to CRM's Recycle Bin.

- To delete multiple records, check the boxes of the records you want to delete. Click the Delete button (just below the list of records). Zoho asks for confirmation; click OK.

Deleted records—no matter which module they're from—all go to CRM's Recycle Bin. To see deleted records, click the upper-right Recycle Bin button. When the Recycle Bin page opens, you can restore or delete records or clean out the place by clicking Empty Recycle Bin.

In CRM, deleted records have a shelf life: After they've been in the Recycle Bin for 60 days, Zoho deletes old records.

Creating Reports and Dashboards

With all those modules, CRM collects a lot of information. After you've input or imported records into CRM, you'll want to use those records to create reports and charts that show trends, make comparisons, and reveal patterns. That's where reports and dashboards come in. A report shows your data as a table; a dashboard puts it in chart form. This section offers a primer on using reports and dashboards.

Creating and Customizing Reports

Zoho CRM comes with around 40 reports already built in. You'll probably find that some of these reports meet your reporting needs. Examples include Sales by Lead, Accounts by Industry, Campaigns Revenue, Cases by Status, Quarterly Sales Forecast Summary, Quotes by Stage, Products by Category—and a whole lot more.

 To browse the reports CRM offers, click the Reports tab. Here you'll find a list of reports by module; click any module name to expand its section and see its standard reports.

To see which reports already exist for a particular module, click that module's tab. Scroll down the page, below the list of records, and look for Module Reports. (The word *Module* will be replaced by the name of the module you're looking at, such as Contact Reports or Sales Order Reports.) This section lists standard reports for this module.

Click any report. A new page opens, showing the module's data in report form. At the top of the page is a filter you can use to narrow down the records shown in the report, if you want. You also have these options:

- **Export**—Click this button and then choose whether to export the report as an Excel file (XLS), a Comma-Separated Values file (CSV), or a Portable Document Format file (PDF).

 If you want to print the report, export it as a PDF. Then open the file in Adobe Acrobat or Adobe Reader and print it from there.

- **Save As**—This button opens a box where you can name the report and save it in a CRM folder.

- **Customize**—Click this button to tweak the current report. Choose tabular, summary, or matrix format; hide or show specific columns; group the data; specify columns to add or average; and apply additional filters.

- **Reload**—If new records have been added since you created the report, this button reloads the report with the new data included.

- **Hide Details**—This button does what its name indicates—hides detailed data from the report. Click Show Details to toggle back to a report that shows the data.

- **Create Chart**—Charts can make it easier for a viewer to make sense of a report's data. Click this button and then choose a chart type to convert the report into chart form. Current chart options include vertical bar, vertical stacked bar, pie, funnel, and line charts. Pick a style, tell Zoho which data you want displayed, and then click Save to create the chart.

Creating and Customizing Dashboards

A dashboard gives you a quick, summary-view snapshot of data that's currently in a module, from several different viewpoints. For example, the Leads dashboard shows leads by source, status, lead source, and industry. Dashboards usually show your data in chart form, as shown in Figure 12.19, although you can turn a chart into a table if you prefer.

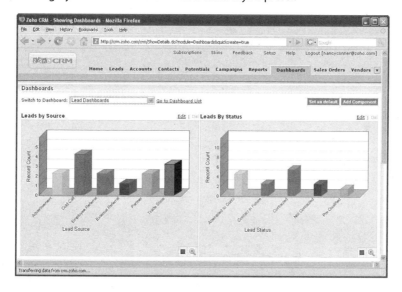

Figure 12.19
This dashboard shows bar charts for Leads by Source and Leads by Status.

When you click the Dashboards tab, CRM shows some dashboards that it's chosen for you as the tab's default: Pipeline by Stage, Pipeline Probability, and Potentials by Type. You can keep these, or you can open other dashboards and click the upper-right Set as Default button to make those dashboards the ones you see when you click the Dashboards tab.

To see other dashboards, make a selection from the upper-left Switch to Dashboard list, or click the Go to Dashboard List link to see a complete list, organized by module. Click any dashboard to see its charts.

You can switch between two-dimensional and three-dimensional views of the charts on a dashboard. For each chart, click the lower-right 2D View or 3D View link, which looks like a blue square.

If you want to tweak a chart (which CRM calls a *component*) on the dashboard, click its Edit link. This opens the Edit Component page. Editing a component takes just a few steps:

1. Specify the components details. This step includes whether you want to show the data as a chart or a table, as well as naming the component and choosing the report from which it draws its information. Make your choices and click Next.

2. This step depends on whether you selected Chart or Table in step 1. For charts, you specify the chart type and how you want the data displayed: what constitutes the x- and y-axes on a bar chart, for example. For tables, tell CRM which columns you want to use.

3. Click Finish to display the edited component on the dashboard.

13

Keep the Team on Task with Zoho Projects

Project management is a big job—and all too often a thankless one. When you're the project manager, you have to plan the schedule, assign tasks, set up meetings, track progress, and try to keep everything on time, in scope, and within budget.

Zoho Projects won't ensure that you get the thanks you deserve, but it will make your job run more smoothly—from a project's start to its final milestone.

Getting Started with Zoho Projects

As with Zoho's other business applications, Projects is offered by subscription, with pricing levels reflecting the needs of any business, from a single freelancer tracking personal workload to a large enterprise with many projects happening at once. Whatever the size of your business, you can take Zoho Projects for a spin around the block with a free version that lets you create and manage a single project. If you like Projects, you can upgrade to a subscription plan. The different Zoho Projects plans are shown in Table 13.1.

Table 13.1 Zoho Projects Pricing Plans

Plan	Cost (per Month)	Projects	Project Templates	File Storage
Free	$0	1	0	100MB
Personal	$5	3	1	500MB
Basic	$8	5	2	1GB
Standard	$12	10	4	2GB
Express	$20	20	8	3GB

continues

Table 13.1 Continued

Plan	Cost (per Month)	Projects	Project Templates	File Storage
Premium	$35	50	10	5GB
Elite	$55	100	15	10GB
Enterprise	$80	No limit	20	25GB

 All plans allow an unlimited number of users and clients. The Standard plan and higher have SSL support, which means that data you send to Zoho Projects is encrypted, to keep it from being intercepted by a third party as it travels across the Internet.

Signing In

To get started with Zoho Projects, point your web browser at http://projects.zoho.com and sign in using your Zoho ID. If this is your first time signing in, you're asked to choose a Project Portal URL. The Project Portal URL is the web address for your projects, and looks like this:

http://*yourname*.projects.zoho.com

Of course, you replace *yourname* with the name you choose. You might choose your company's name or your department's name, for example. After you've created your Project Portal, Zoho opens Projects, as shown in Figure 13.1. This opening page gets you started creating your first project, with links to common tasks and a list of Project's features.

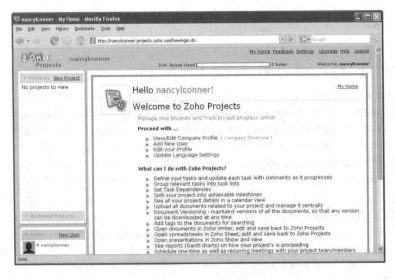

Figure 13.1
The Zoho Projects Welcome page lists features and offers links to start setting up Projects.

Your Projects Home Page

Projects gives you a page of your very own, which gives an overview of all your projects. Each member of your team gets one, too. From any page in Projects, click the upper-right My Home link to see a page like the one in Figure 13.2.

Your home page has sections that list your tasks, meetings, and milestones across all your projects, letting you know what's on your plate now and what's coming up, so you can prioritize your to-do list. Across the top of the page are some links that let you take a different view of your tasks and events:

■ **My Work Calendar**—Shows your tasks, meetings, and milestones in a calendar view.

■ **My Log Calendar**—Shows a calendar with the hours you've logged on all your projects. (See the upcoming "Tracking Time" section for more on keeping track of your hours.)

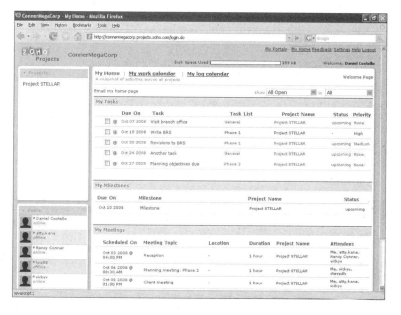

Figure 13.2
Your Projects home page gives you an overview of all your tasks, meetings, and milestones.

 Email yourself a reminder or what's coming up on your to-do list. Click My Home Page and then click the Email My Home Page link. (It's just above the My Tasks list.) Use the form that opens to set up a daily, weekly, or monthly reminder that sends your upcoming events right to your email inbox.

Choosing Your Settings

Before you start creating projects and adding users, you'll want to make sure that Projects Is set up the way you want it. Setting Up Projects now makes sure that the application is ready to go before you add users. This section explains both personal and applicationwide settings.

Click the Settings link at the top of any page. On the page that opens, click the General Settings tab or the Company Settings tab to start tweaking.

The General Settings Tab

This tab, shown in Figure 13.3, has these options:

- **Skins**—Skins are color schemes. Click a radio button to try out the colors you like.

- **Language**—Use this to set a language for the Projects interface. If you want links, buttons, commands, and so on to be in a language other than English, choose a language from the drop-down list (over a dozen are currently on offer) and then click Update Language Settings. Refresh your web browser to see the changes.

- **Profile**—This is where you can add or update personal information, including your name, job title, and phone numbers.

- **Password**—This is the place to go to update your Zoho Projects password. Type in your current password; then enter your new password twice and click Save.

- **Photo**—Lets you upload or delete a photo to associate with your Projects profile.

These options appear as large buttons down the left side of the General Settings tab. Click any one to change that setting.

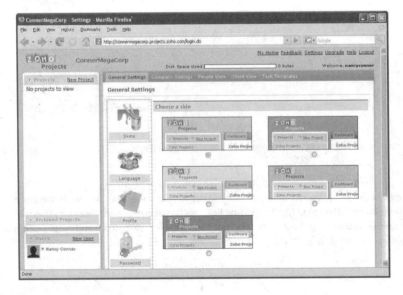

Figure 13.3
General Settings are your personal Projects settings.

The Company Settings Tab

The Company Settings Tab, shown in Figure 13.4, has the following buttons (down the left side of the tab) that let you set or tweak options:

■ **Profile**—This refers to your company's profile, and you can give information about your organization's name, website (required), address, time zone, email encoding (in most cases, you'll want to use the standard UTF-8), and the portal URL for this account.

Tip 4U Need to change the web address of your Projects portal? Only paying subscribers may do this. Send your request to support@zohoprojects.com.

■ **Date Format Settings**—This is where you choose both a time format (12- or 24-hour clock) and a date format (select from the drop-down) to use in Projects.

■ **Logo**—Lets you browse for and upload your company's logo, which appears in the upper-left corner of all pages in Projects (where the Zoho Projects logo appears in Figure 13.4).

Info 4U Some guidelines for your logo: Use the JPG, JPEG, GIF, or PNG format for your image file, and make sure the image is no bigger than 500KB. Maximum dimensions for a logo are 130 pixels wide by 50 pixels high.

■ **Powered By Logo**—This is a small image that appears in the lower-right corner of Projects pages, after the words *Powered by*. If you want to replace Zoho's logo here, keep your image small: 52–19 pixels is the max.

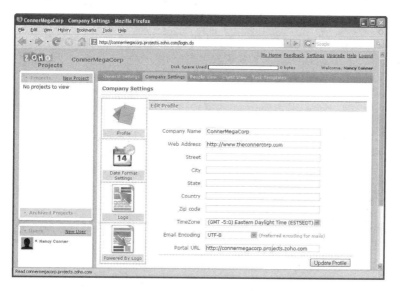

Figure 13.4
Adjust Company Settings as necessary.

Creating a New Project

Creating a new project is as easy as giving it a name. Click the New Project link in the upper-left corner of the page. The Add Project page opens, asking for the new project's name and an optional description. Type these in and then click Add Project. Presto! Like magic, you have a new project. Zoho adds the project to the Projects list and opens the new project's Dashboard (see Figure 13.5).

Now you can *really* get to work creating the project: adding the users and tasks that make a project happen.

The Projects Dashboard

You control a project from its Dashboard, shown in Figure 13.5. After you've created a project, its Dashboard appears. Across the top of the Dashboard are tabs related to different aspects of your project. The Week Ahead section shows upcoming tasks, milestones, and meetings, so you can stay on top of deadlines and appointments. The main part of the Dashboard shows recent activity related to the project: documents, forum posts and responses, and other activity.

To the left is a menu (shown on all pages in Projects) that lists projects, archived projects, and users. Click any project on the list to open its Dashboard.

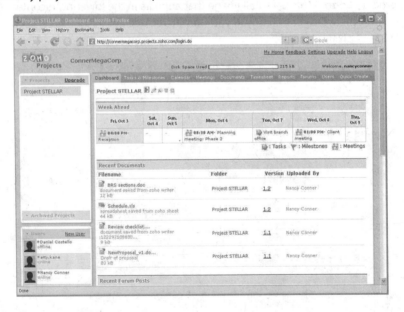

Figure 13.5
A project's Dashboard shows recent activity on the project.

Adding Users

After you've created a project, you want to add the members of your project team, so you can begin assigning tasks and scheduling meetings, and so they can add documents and discuss project-related topics in the Forum. There are two paths to the Add New User box, which lets you add a user to a specific project:

- Click the Users tab and then click the Add User button.
- Click Quick Create, New User.

Either path lands you on the Project Members page shown in Figure 13.6. This page lists existing project members (that is, users who have access to this project) and has a form for adding new users to the project. For each user you're adding, give an email address and choose a role: Contractor, Employee, or Manager. Contractors and employees have similar privileges; they can add, edit, or delete tasks, meetings, and milestones, as well as view reports and participate in forums. Managers can do all that plus a bit more: add and manage users and create categories on the Forums tab.

When you've filled out the form, click Add User. Zoho adds the user to the Users tab and sends an email to the address you gave, so the new user can sign in though your Projects portal. Users who already have a Zoho account just click the link and sign in using their Zoho password. If a user doesn't yet have a Zoho account, the email includes a password for his or her first sign-in— all users must have a Zoho account to participate in your Projects site. During the sign-in process, the person picks a username and a new password to create an account.

Users also appear, along with their online or offline status, in the Users list on the left. On the Users list, you can click any user's name to send him or her an email.

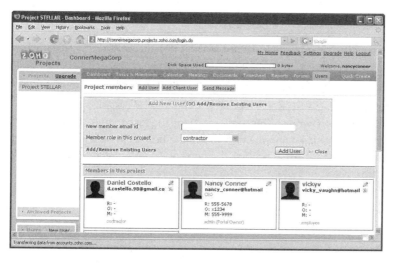

Figure 13.6
Add new users at the top of the page; view existing users at the bottom.

As the portal owner, you have administrative privileges for this Projects account; you can add and manage users or change Company Profile information, for example. Users you add have more limited abilities. For example, they can edit their own profiles but not the company's.

Adding a Client User

Sometimes, you'll want a project's client (that is, your customer) to have some access to what's happening in the project, so the client can keep an eye how things are progressing. Clients have limited access to the project; they can view and add tasks and milestones, see when meetings are scheduled, view and add documents, and participate in the project's forums.

To add a client user, click the Users tab and then click Add Client Users. The Project Members page changes to show a drop-down menu that lists all client users, organized by company. Choose one and click the Update Project Client Users button. Zoho adds the client user to the Client Users Accessing This Project section of the Project Members page.

If this is the first client you're adding, click Add Project Client. The page changes so you can add the client's company name and the email address of the client user you're adding. Click Update Project Client Users. Zoho adds the client user to the drop-down list and to the Project Members page.

Adding and Assigning Tasks

Now that you've added some users, it's time to put them to work. You do this by creating and assigning tasks. To create and assign a task, click the Tasks & Milestones tab and then click the New Task button. (You can take a shortcut by simply clicking Quick Create, New Task.) The page changes, as shown in Figure 13.7, so you can create the task.

Here are the basics for creating a new task:

- **Task**—Type the name of the task here. Make it descriptive, so it'll be clear what the task involves when it shows up on a list of many tasks.
- **Task List**—To assign this task to a particular task list (see the upcoming section), choose the list you want from the drop-down.
- **Project Members/Owner**—This section assigns the task to one or more team members. Choose the responsible team members from the box on the left (use the Shift or Ctrl key to select more than one) and then click the right-pointing arrow to move your selection to the Owners box.
- **Send Mail Notification**—Check this box to shoot off an email notifying users who've been assigned this task.

If you want, you can click Add Task at this point to create the task. However, because tasks usually have a priority and a deadline, you can click Advanced Options to add some more info about the task:

- **Start Date**—Make sure users know when to get started on a task by clicking the calendar and choosing a start date.

- **Duration or End Date**—To assign a task's due date, choose one of these two options and then enter the number of days the task should take or its expected end date. (Click the calendar to choose.)

- **Priority**—The choices here are None, Low, Medium, and High.

- **% Completed**—If a task has already begun when you add it (or if you want to edit the task to track its progress), choose a percentage from this drop-down. Percentages are in increments of ten.

Click Add Task to create the task and add it to the calendar. Tasks you've added are included in the owners' My Tasks list on their Projects home page.

 Tip To mark a task as complete, check the box to the left of the task's name.

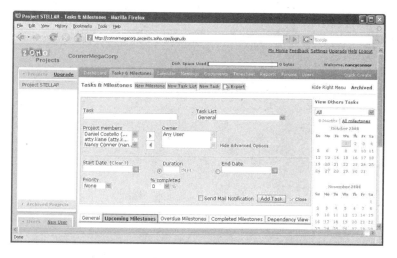

Figure 13.7
Using Advanced Options, you can schedule tasks as you create them.

 Tip If you need to make changes to a task you've created (reassign ownership, for example, or change an end date), place your cursor over the task's name so that icons appear to the left of that name. Click the pencil—that's the Edit Task icon—to reopen the Task box (see Figure 13.7), where you can make changes to the task. Click Update Task to save them.

Creating Project Milestones

A *milestone* represents a project phase, a goal that's reached when a specific set of tasks has been accomplished. Milestones help your team stay on track and create a sense of accomplishment over the long haul of a complex project.

Milestones are created on the Tasks & Milestones tab; click New Milestone (or from any page in the project, click Quick Create, New Milestone). The box for creating a new milestone, shown in Figure 13.8, appears. Give Zoho the following information:

- **Milestone**—Name the milestone here, such as End of Phase 1 or Specification Sign-Off.
- **Start Date/End Date**—Use these fields to choose when the project phase begins and when it ends (that is, the date you expect the milestone to be reached).
- **Owner**—Select from a list of the project members to indicate who's responsible for this project phase. A milestone's owner can delete the milestone; any team member can edit it.
- **Milestone Flag**—Choose Internal (only your team members can see this milestone) or External (client users with access to the project can see and edit the milestone).

Click Add Milestone to put the milestone on the project's calendar. Zoho also adds the new milestone to the Upcoming Milestones section of the Tasks & Milestones tab.

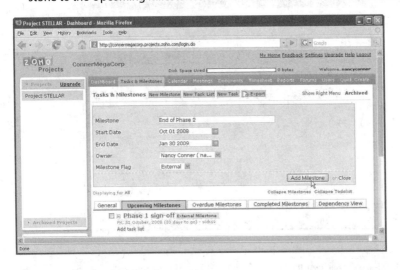

Figure 13.8
Set project milestones using this form.

Creating a Task List

To keep related tasks together, create a task list and add tasks to it. You can assign a task to a task list when you create the task, or you can move an existing task to a different task list (see the next section).

Create a task list on the Tasks & Milestones tab; click New Task List to start. Alternatively, if you're on a different tab, click Quick Create, New Task List. In the box that appears, type in the name of the task list and, if you want, choose a milestone to which you want to link the task list. Click the Add Task List button to create the list.

Depending on what you selected from the Related Milestone list, Zoho adds the task list to the appropriate milestone or, if you chose None as the related milestone, to the General section of the Tasks & Milestones tab.

 To add a new task directly to a task list, find the task list you want (in the General or Upcoming Milestones section of the Tasks & Milestones tab). Under the task list's name, click Add Task. The task you add appears on that task list.

Moving an Existing Task to a Task List

Maybe you created some tasks before you set up any task lists to put them on. Or perhaps milestones have shifted and you need to move some tasks to a different list.

Start by finding the task you want to move. It's either on the task list you chose when you created it or, if you didn't choose a task list then, in the General section of the Tasks & Milestones tab. Hover your cursor over the task's name so that some icons appear to the left of the name. Click the curved blue arrow; that's the Move Task icon.

A box opens that lets you choose a task list from a dropdown. Make your selection and then click Move Task to give the task a new home.

 Task lists associated with external milestones are also external. That means tasks on these lists are visible to external clients that you've added to your Projects account.

Managing Users

Managing people is tough enough—you don't want your project management program to make it any harder. Whether you're changing a user's role, blasting out an en masse email, or removing a user from the project, you can do it from the Users tab.

Reassigning Roles

To move a user from one role to another, go to the Users tab (shown previously in Figure 13.6). Each user is represented by a box with information about that user, including ID, email address, role, phone numbers (if the user has added these to his or her profile), and perhaps a photo. Find the user you want, and click the Edit Project Role icon (the pencil) in the upper-right corner of that user's box.

The user's role changes to a drop-down list. Pick the new role from the list and then click Update to give that user the new role.

Emailing Users

If you want to email a particular user, the quickest way is to click that person's name in the User's list on the left. Your email program opens, with the person's email address already in the To line.

But if you have bigger plans than firing off a quick email to one person, such as sending an email to everyone on your team, go to the Users tab and click the Send Message button.

The page changes so you can write your email right from the Users tab. Type in a subject and write your message in the Message box. Then, use the To list to choose the team members you want to email. Click the Send Message button. Zoho emails your message to the users you chose, and also sends a copy to you.

Deleting Users

If you need to delete a user from Projects, go to the Users tab. Find the user who's on the way out (this could be a team member or a client user) and click the red X in the upper-right part of that user's box. Zoho asks whether you really want to remove the user from this project. Click OK, and the user disappears.

Scheduling a Meeting

When you need to get the team together for a meeting, you want to make sure everyone know the date, time, and location. And it never hurts to send a reminder (or two) so no one forgets.

You create and schedule project-related meetings from the Meetings tab; click the New Meeting button. If you prefer, click Quick Create, New Meeting. The form for setting up a meeting is shown in Figure 13.9. Use the form to provide the following information:

- **Meeting Title**—Be specific here so it's clear to those attending what the meeting is about.
- **Scheduled On**—Use the calendar to pick the date; then use the drop-downs to select the time.
- **Meeting Location**—Type in the name of the conference room or auditorium where the meeting will take place. (You need to click Advanced Options to see this field.)
- **Duration**—It's always helpful if attendees have an idea of how long the meeting will take. If you know, use the drop-downs to indicate the likely duration in hours and minutes. (Duration is hidden unless you click Advanced Options.)
- **Remind All**—Nudge attendees with a reminder before the meeting starts—anywhere from a day to a few minutes ahead of time. You can even send a reminder as the meeting gets underway by choosing On Time.
- **Repeat**—If a meeting recurs at regular intervals, such as a staff meeting every Wednesday at 3:00, use this drop-down. Only Once means that just one reminder will be sent. Otherwise, choose every day, week, month, or year.
- **End After**—Use this drop-down to limit the number of reminders Zoho sends about the meeting.
- **Project Members/Meeting Participants**—Use these boxes to tell Zoho who's attending. Select one or more users in the Project Members box (use the Shift or Ctrl key to select multiple users); then click the right-pointing arrow to move them over to the Meeting Participants box.

When you have everything set up, click Schedule Meeting. As soon as you click that button, several things happen at once: Zoho adds the meeting to the calendar and to the My Meetings section of participants' home pages. You'll also find it in the Upcoming Meetings section of the

Meetings tab. Zoho emails a notification to the meeting participants and queues up reminder emails, so they'll be ready to go at the dates and times you set.

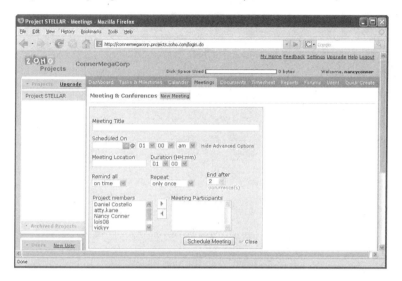

Figure 13.9
When you create a new meeting, fill in the meeting's details and set up reminders for participants.

You can also add notes to a meeting. Notes can be a helpful reminder, whether you're reminding attendees what to bring to an upcoming meeting or commenting on something that occurred during a meeting that's now over.

You can add a note to a meeting that you created or that you're attending. On the Meetings tab, find the meeting you want in the Upcoming Meetings or Elapsed Meetings section. Click the Add Note link. A text box appears, where you can type in your note. Click the Add Note button.

The note appears with the meeting's details on the Meetings tab. In addition, a Notes icon appears next to the meeting name in the My Meetings section of each attendee's My Home page. Hover the cursor over the Notes icon, and a box appears, showing any notes that have been added to that meeting.

Using the Calendar

Seeing a project's tasks, meetings, and milestones on a calendar gives you an overview of what's happening in the project. When you click a project's Calendar tab (shown in Figure 13.10), you get a bird's-eye view of the current month's schedule. Each day lists the tasks, meetings, and milestones that pertain to that day. Hover the cursor over any Tasks, Meetings, or Milestones link to see a description of that element. Click the link to change the calendar to show just that element—if you click a Tasks link, for example, the calendar changes to show just tasks.

Tip **4U** To move back to the previous month or forward to the next month, click the arrows on either side of the current month's name.

Figure 13.10
The Calendar tab gives you an overview of a project's events and deadlines.

Refining the Calendar View

On a big project with lots of events and looming deadlines, the standard Calendar view can be a bit overwhelming. You can filter what appears on your calendar in two ways:

- **Show only events related to a particular user**—When you open the Calendar tab, the default is to show all tasks for the current month. To restrict the calendar to a particular user, select the user you want from the drop-down list above the calendar. This is helpful when you want to focus on your own schedule, or when you're looking for a time you can schedule a meeting with another user.

- **Show only a particular kind of event**—By default, the calendar shows tasks, meetings, and milestones. By clicking one of the links above the calendar, you can choose to show All Tasks, All Milestones, or All Meetings.

Tip **4U** To narrow what's on the calendar even more, make the user and event filters work together. For example, if you want to see the times when your colleague Vicky has meetings scheduled, select Vicky from the drop-down and then click the All Meetings list.

Adding an Event from the Calendar

If you're looking at the Calendar tab and you spot a good time to, say, schedule a meeting, you can add that meeting right from the calendar. As Figure 13.10 shows (for Tuesday, July 7), when you put your cursor on any date in the calendar, three buttons appear at the top of that date's box:

- TD adds a new task to this date. (Think of TD as standing for *to-do*.)

- MS adds a new milestone.

- ME adds a new meeting.

Click the button that corresponds to the event you want to add. A box appears that lets you add the kind of event you chose. (Adding tasks, milestones, and meetings are described earlier in this chapter.)

Tracking Time

Time is money, as they say. On any project, you need to know how much time your team is spending on its tasks. Whether you're tracking time for an internal budget or to bill an external client, it's important to keep an eye on the clock.

That's what the Timesheet tab, shown in Figure 13.11, is for. As team members work on a project, they keep track of their billable and nonbillable hours. These hours appear on the Timesheets tab. Use the upper-right Show Timesheet For drop-down list to choose the team member whose hours you want to see. By default, the Timesheets tab shows hours using a calendar view, but you can see someone's hours in a more detailed list (which names the task related to the hours, its billing status, and task list) by clicking List View.

 Client users do not have access to your project's Timecards tab.

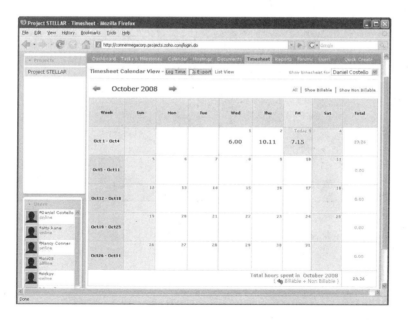

Figure 13.11
The Timesheet tab tracks users' hours.

Logging Time: The Basics

To input the hours you spent on a task, click the Timesheet tab and then click Log Time. The form shown in Figure 13.12 opens to collect the following information:

- **Date**—Today's date appears by default, but you can click the calendar to choose a different date—if you forgot to log yesterday's hours, for example.

- **Task**—Click the drop-down and choose the relevant task from the list.

- **Hours**—Type in the number of hours spent, using an *hours.minutes* format. So if you spent seven-and-a-half hours on a task yesterday, you'd type **7.30** (that is, 7 hours and 30 minutes).

- **Notes**—If you want to include a note about what you accomplished on the task, type it in here.

- **Billing Status**—Click this drop-down and choose Billable or Non Billable.

When you're finished, click the Add to Timesheet button to log your hours. Zoho puts the hours on the appropriate calendar date; when you're looking at the calendar, click the number of hours on a date to see the associated tasks.

 You can quickly add a new task right from the calendar. Put your cursor on a date, and a clock appears in the upper-left corner of the date box. Click the clock to open the form for logging time, with the date already filled in.

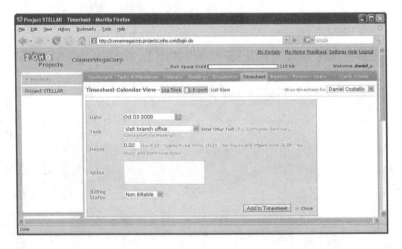

Figure 13.12
Use this form to record hours spent on a task.

Logging Time Automatically

Projects has a built-in timer that keeps track of the time for you—so you can focus on the task at hand. To turn on the timer, click My Home at the top of any page in Projects. This opens your My Home page (refer to Figure 13.8), which lists your tasks, milestones, and meetings. In the My Tasks section, find the task you're about to start working on and then click the green clock to the left of its name. When you click, the clock turns red, and the timer starts ticking.

When you've finished working on the task for now, return to your My Home page. Click the red clock. Zoho stops the timer and adds the hours and minutes you worked to the Timesheet tab.

Editing or Deleting Logged Hours

If you need to change or delete some of the hours that have been logged, click the hours for the date in question if you're in Calendar View. This opens a list of tasks for that day. (If you're in List View, each task already appears on the list.)

To the right of each task are two icons: a pencil (to edit the task) and a red X (to delete the task). Click the pencil to edit a task. You can add notes, change the number of hours logged, or change the billing status. Click Update to save your changes. Click the red X to delete the task. Zoho asks whether you're sure you want to remove the task from the timesheet log. Click OK to finish the deletion.

Creating and Sending an Invoice

Projects integrates with Zoho Invoice (see Chapter 12, "Manage Customers with Zoho Invoice and Zoho CRM") to create and send invoices for the hours your team worked. On the Timesheet tab, click Create Invoice. Zoho Invoice opens in a new window and displays the dialog box shown in Figure 13.13. To create the invoice, fill out the following fields:

- **Select Project**—Choose the relevant project from this drop-down.
- **Rate**—Type in the hourly rate for the project.
- **Choose Time Range**—Use the calendars to select a start date and an end date for the work to be billed.
- **Invoice Type**—If you want to break down the charges task by task, each task a single line item, enable the Task radio button. If you want to send the invoice with the project's name as the only line item, enable the Projects radio button.

Click Create Invoice to do just that. After you've created the invoice, you can save it as a draft or send it, just as you would any invoice in Zoho Invoice.

Figure 13.13
Projects links with Zoho Invoice, so you can create an invoice based on the hours you've tracked.

Working with Documents

Any project tends to generate pages and pages of documents: specifications, reviews, user guides, memos, meeting agendas and minutes, schedules—and that's just for starters. Projects lets you create a central repository for all documents related to a project, making it easy for your team to find and work on them. The Projects document repository is on the Documents tab.

Uploading a Document

To get a document into Projects, click the Documents tab and then click New Document. Alternatively, click Quick Create, Upload New File. This opens the box shown in Figure 13.14. From there, follow these steps:

1. Use the Browse button to find and select a file from your computer; click Open to put the file path into the Browse box.

2. Add a note or a tag, using the File Comment or File Tags box. A comment on the file is required. (More on tags later in this chapter.)

3. Select a folder for storing the document.

4. Choose any users you want to receive an email notification that the document has been uploaded.

5. Click Upload File. Zoho uploads the document to the Documents tab.

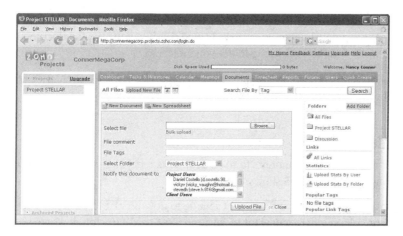

Figure 13.14
Upload documents to the Projects Documents tab using this form.

If you have a whole bunch of documents to upload, click the Bulk Upload link, just under the Browse box. This expands the dialog box with a new section that lists selected files. Select files to upload, and Zoho adds them to the Selected Files box. Keep selecting and adding files and then click the Upload File button to get them into Projects en masse.

 To see activity related to uploaded documents, click one of the links under Statistics on the right side of the Documents tab. Upload Stats by User shows which users have uploaded files, and how many. Upload Stats by Folder shows the number of documents in each folder. Both kinds of stats show how much space the documents are using.

Creating a New Document or Spreadsheet

Projects works with Zoho Writer (Chapter 1, "Have Your Say with Zoho Writer") and Zoho Sheet (Chapter 4, "Track Data with Zoho Sheet") so that you can create a new document or spreadsheet right from the Projects Documents tab. When you do, Writer or Sheet opens so you can create the document. Zoho adds the saved document or spreadsheet to the Documents tab in Projects.

 To create a new document or spreadsheet from inside Projects, make sure that your web browser's pop-up blocker allows pop-ups from Zoho.com. If you block pop-ups from Zoho, Writer or Sheet can't open in a new window.

To create a new Writer document or a new Sheet spreadsheet, click the Documents tab and then click either New Document or New Spreadsheet. In the box that opens, name the document and select the folder in Projects where you want to store it. Click Create New Document (or Create New Spreadsheet).

A new window opens, showing a blank Writer document or Sheet spreadsheet. Go to work on the document or spreadsheet as you normally would. When you save the document or spreadsheet, Zoho saves it in Projects, in the folder you indicated.

 When you create a document or spreadsheet through Projects, you won't find it in Writer or Sheet—it's on the Projects Documents tab.

Working with Documents

After you've added some documents to the Documents tab, you can work with those documents in several ways, as Figure 13.15 shows:

- **Download the file**—Click a document's name to download it to your computer. A dialog box opens, asking where you want to save the file. Choose the folder where you want to store the document and then click Save.

- **View versions**—As changes are made to a document, Zoho saves the document's different versions. Click a version number to see a list of versions, as shown in Figure 13.16, and to download a particular version or open it in Writer or Sheet.

- **Open in Writer or Sheet**—Click the folder icon to the right of any filename to open the file in Writer or Sheet.

- **Upload a new version of the file**—If you've been working on a document offline and you want your version to become the most recent in Projects, click this icon, which shows a green arrow pointing upward.

- **Move the file to a new folder**—Use this option to move a document to a different folder (such as Drafts to Final). On the page that opens, select the new file from the drop-down list and click Move File.

- **Delete the file**—To delete a file, click the red X to its right. A dialog box opens to confirm the deletion; click OK.

 When you delete a file from the Projects Documents tab, you can't recover that file. So make sure you really want the file gone before you click OK.

Organizing Your Documents

Projects makes your documents easy to find in two ways: folders and tags. You can use either or both to organize the documents that pile up in Projects.

Creating a Folder

The Documents tab has a list of folders on the right side of the page. To add a new folder to the list, click Add Folder. A box appears; name the folder and click the Add Folder button. Your new folder appears in the Folders list, ready to hold documents. To open the folder, just click its name.

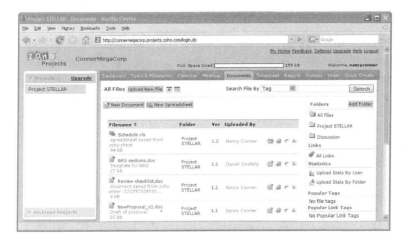

Figure 13.15
Documents attached to a project appear on the Documents tab.

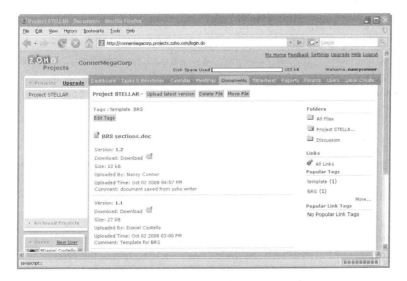

Figure 13.16
Open or download any saved version of a document from this page.

Tagging Documents

Tags are keywords you can use to group related documents together. For example, you might use the tag *Budget* to mark all documents, spreadsheets, memos, and so on related to a project's budget.

There are two ways to tag a document:

- When you upload a new file (see the earlier section), add some tags to the File Tag field during the upload process.

- For existing files, open a folder that holds the document and click its version number. A page listing the versions for that document opens (refer to Figure 13.16). At the top of the page is a list of tags associated with that file. Click Edit Tags to change the tags to a text box, where you can edit existing tags or add new ones. Click Update Tags to save.

Finding Tagged Documents

Tagging documents helps you find the document you're looking for, even when you can't remember which folder it's in. Tags give you these ways to find tagged documents:

- **Search by tag**—Use the upper-right Search box to find all files with a particular tag.

 You can also use the Search box to find documents by file extension. For example, you can look for a spreadsheet by searching for files that end with the extension .xls.

- **Browse popular tags**—Look in the Popular Tags list on the right side of the Documents tab to see if the tag you want is there; click it to see a list of files with that tag.

- **View the tag cloud**—The tag cloud gives a visual display of the popularity of different tags. Tags attached to many documents appear in a large font; tags attached to fewer documents are smaller in size. To see the tag cloud, click the More link under Popular Tags. When the cloud appears, click any tag to see a list of its associated documents.

Adding Links to a Project

Besides uploading and storing documents, you can also store links on the Documents tab. A link could be to a published Writer document or Zoho Show presentation, for example. You can also link to YouTube videos, online photo albums, other websites—if it lives somewhere on the Web, you can link to it in Projects.

On the Documents tab, click All Links and then click the Add Link button at the top of the page. Use the following fields in the form shown in Figure 13.17 to create the link:

- **Link Name**—This is how your link will be identified in the Links list, so make sure it describes what you're linking to.

- **Link URL**—Type or paste the link's web address here.

- **Description**—If you want, you can add a short description of the link and its purpose.

- **Link Tags**—You can tag links just as you tag documents, making a particular link easier to find.

Click Add Link to put the link on the All Links list. Now you can search for links by tag, view popular tag links, and see a tag link cloud, just as you can with document tags.

 Link tags are separate from document tags. Each kind of tags has its own list on the right and its own cloud.

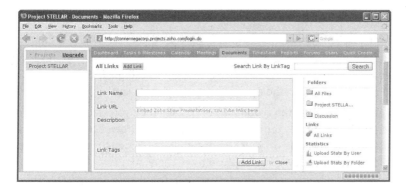

Figure 13.17
Link to web pages, videos, online photo albums, or published Zoho documents.

Editing or Deleting a Link

Each listed link tells you who added the link and when. In addition, each link on the list also has these options:

- **Edit Link**—Click to open the link's information in a form just like the one you used to create it (see Figure 13.17). Click Update to save your changes.

- **Delete Link**—Click to remove the link from the Documents tab. A confirmation box opens, warning that once you delete the link, you can't get it back. Click OK to delete the link.

Using Forums

Using email as your primary method of communication on a project can cause as many problems as it solves. When people's inboxes are overflowing, it's all too easy for an important email to get overlooked or accidentally deleted. Or you may find yourself answering the same question over and over again in one-on-one exchanges with individual team members.

Projects offers a different approach: Forums for each project. A forum is like an online bulletin board that all project team members can access simultaneously. Users can ask questions, get answers, and read each others' posts. You can post bulletins and instructions—and know that these are in a central location where everyone can find them. Messages that were posted or commented on most recently appear at the top of the page.

Posting to a Forum

Forums are located on a project's Forums tab, shown in Figure 13.18. To get the conversation started, click the Forums tab and then click New Forum Post. Alternatively, click Quick Create, New Forum Post. The form for creating a new post, shown in Figure 13.19, opens. To create a post and add it to the forum, follow these steps:

1. Give the post a title.
2. Write the content.
3. Choose a category. Categories work like folders to organize forum posts. Existing categories are listed in the Category drop-down. To create a new category, click the Add Category button, and a form for naming the category appears just above the post you're creating.
4. Add an attachment. This step is optional, of course, but if you want to attach a document, click the Attach link next to the Category drop-down. A Browse button appears, so you can browse to and choose a file on your computer. Files attached to forum posts do not appear on the Documents tab (unless you upload them there, too).
5. Notify team members. To send an email notifying some or all of your team members about your post, choose the users you want in the Notify This Post To box. (Use the Shift or Ctrl key to select multiple users.)
6. Click Submit to post your message on the Forums tab.

Tip 4U If you know HTML, you can use HTML tags in your forum posts. Use HTML to add emphasis, link to web pages, and embed slideshows, videos, or other web-based media to a post. Instructions for embedding a Zoho Show slideshow appear in Chapter 3, "Presenting…Zoho Show."

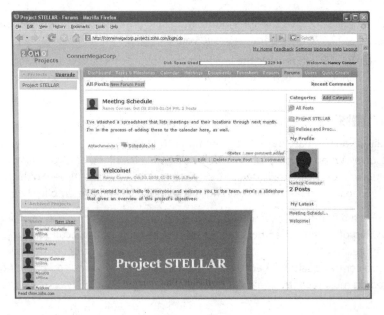

Figure 13.18
The Forums tab shows conversations related to a project.

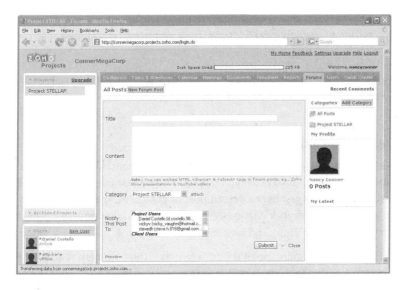

Figure 13.19
Write a new message to post on the Forums tab.

Replying to a Post and Viewing Comments

When you read a post and want to reply to it, you leave a comment on that post. To do so, click the Add a Comment link just below the post. A multiline text field, Post a Comment, opens. Type in your comment, choose any users you want to send a notification to, and click Post Comment.

Zoho adds your comment to that post, displaying a status of New Comment Added just below the original post. To view a comment, look just below the New Comment Added status; there's a link with the number of comments made on that post. Click the number to open the post with all its comments.

Editing or Deleting a Post

In any conversation, people sometimes backtrack, clarify, explain, or just plain change their minds. The same thing happens in forum discussions, so Zoho gives you the ability to go back and edit—or even delete—any message you posted. If you're an admin (that is, if you own the project portal), you can edit or delete any post that anyone makes in your project's forums—so you can deal with inappropriate posts and keep everyone on topic.

To edit a post, find the post you want on the Forums tab and, just below the post, click the Edit link. This opens a form similar to the one shown in Figure 13.18, with the current content of the post already filled in. Make your changes; then click Submit to post the revised message.

To delete a post, click the Forums tab and find the post you want to remove. Just below it is a Delete Forum Post link; click that. Zoho shows a box asking you to confirm; click OK to delete the post.

 Deleting a post deletes all associated comments. So make sure that you want to get rid of the whole conversation associated with a post before you delete it.

Editing or Deleting a Comment

Comments aren't chiseled in stone. You might notice a typo you'd like to correct, or you might want to elaborate on or explain a point you made. To edit a comment you made, click the Edit Comment link that appears just beneath your post or comment. The page changes, showing your post in a text box. Make your changes; then click the Update Comment button to post your revised comment.

If you want to delete a comment, open the post to which the comment is attached and click Delete Comment. A dialog box asks whether you're sure you want to remove the comment; click OK to finish the deletion process.

Generating Reports

Reports show how well you're managing a project and how your team is progressing with its tasks and milestones. On its Reports tab, Projects offers three kinds of reports:

- Task Graph View, shown in Figure 13.20, lays out a graph that shows tasks and their durations, as well as what percentage of a given task has been completed.
- Task List View shows a list of tasks, the start and completion dates, and the percentage of each task that has been done so far.
- Milestone Report shows when a project's phases begin and end.

To view a report, click the Reports tab. In the upper-left part of the tab, click the link for the kind of report you want to see. You can also use the upper-right Show drop-down to choose whether you want to see all tasks or milestones, those that are currently open, or those that are closed. For tasks, you can show only those tasks assigned to a particular person by selecting that person's ID from the Tasks Reports For drop-down.

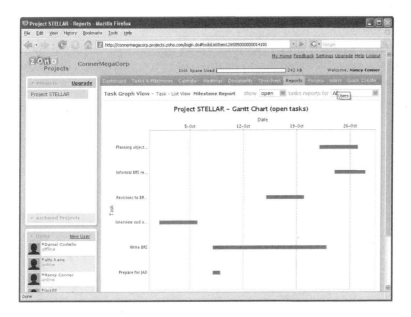

Figure 13.20
This report shows all open tasks.

When the Project Is Finished

After a project's over, feel free to pop open a bottle of champagne or two to celebrate with your team. In Projects, you can deal with a finished project in two ways: archive the project or delete it.

Archiving a Project

When you archive a project, you save all its data, but you clear the decks to start the next project; Zoho doesn't count archived projects as part of your subscription. To archive a project, click the Dashboard tab. To the right of the project's name, click the pencil icon (Edit Project Details). On the form that opens, change Project Status from Active to Archive. Click Update, and Zoho moves the project to the Archived Projects list.

Deleting a Project

To delete a project, head to the Dashboard tab. Click the Trashcan icon to the right of the project's name. You see a dialog box asking whether you're sure you want to delete the whole project. Click OK, and the project is gone.

 Deleting a project means that it's gone for good—you can't get the project or its data back. So be extra sure of what you're doing when you delete a project.

14

Zoho People: Your Online HR Office

Managing the people who work for your organization involves a complex set of tasks—from posting job openings, to identifying and hiring candidates, to managing your current employees. Employee management also involves keeping employees informed about company policies, processing requests for travel and time off, and offering training to keep skills up to date.

Zoho People lets you manage all that—and more—in a single application that meets all your Human Resources needs. (And if you have a need People doesn't address, you can customize the program.) With recruitment management tools, business process checklists, and a self-service tab where current employees can update their profiles and request travel, training, or time off, Zoho People is an ideal HR solution for small-to-medium businesses as well as large enterprises. When your business grows beyond, say, 25 or 30 employees, thus making it hard to keep track of your staff using spreadsheets, you should give People a try.

How Much Does It Cost?

Whether you're a mom-and-pop ice cream stand looking to hire summer help, a medium-sized nonprofit, or a multinational corporation, Zoho has a pricing plan to fit your needs, as Table 14.1 shows. (And if by some chance you don't see a suitable plan in the table, send an email to sales@zoho.com to discuss your organization's needs.)

Table 14.1 Zoho People Pricing Plans

Plan	Cost (per Month)	Employees (Includes Recruiters)	Recruiters	Custom Forms	File Storage
Basic Edition	$0	10	1	0	250MB
10-user pack	$19	10	1	2	500MB
25-user pack	$49	25	1	5	1GB
50-user pack	$99	50	3	10	2GB
100-user pack	$199	100	7	20	4GB
250-user pack	$295	250	7	50	10GB
500-user pack	$495	500	10	150	20GB
1,000-user pack	$850	1,000	20	Unlimited	40GB

Getting Started with Zoho People

To start managing employees with Zoho People, go to http://people.zoho.com and sign in using your Zoho ID and password. The first time you use People, Zoho asks you to choose a username, as shown in Figure 14.1. Type your name into the Username text box, take a look at People's Terms of Service and Privacy Policy (click either link to open the document in a new window), and check the box that indicates you agree to those terms and policies. Click Update, and Zoho opens People to the Getting Started tab, shown in Figure 14.2. As explained in the upcoming section "The Getting Started Tab," here's where you set up People, preparing it for use with your company's employees.

Tip 4U You can change your Zoho People username by editing your user profile. Click the Self-Service tab, then click My Profile, and click the Edit link.

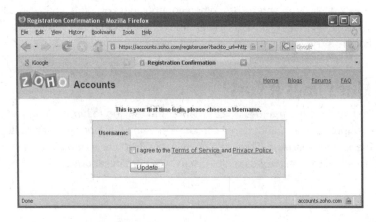

Figure 14.1
To get started with People, type in your name and agree to People terms and policies.

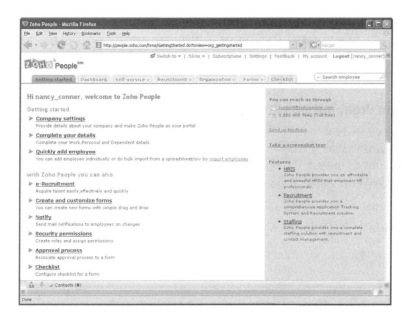

Figure 14.2
The Getting Started tab is the place to start exploring Zoho People.

Setting Up Zoho People

Two of Zoho People's strengths are found in the following tabs:

- **Self-Service tab**—Lets employees update their personal info, submit expenses, sign up for training, request time off, and so on
- **Recruitment tab**—Lets you manage the hiring process

Before you take People live in your organization, however, you have some setting up to do. You want to make sure the forms, roles, permissions, and processes will work the way your organization does business. This chapter shows you how to set up People for smooth running in your organization.

 When you set up a Zoho People account, you're automatically added as the first user and given Admin status, which means that you're able to view and edit all the fields in all the forms, as well as set up and edit People on an organizational level.

The Getting Started Tab

Zoho helps out administrators who are new to People with the Getting Started tab, shown in Figure 14.2. This tab contains links to common activities in People, such as creating a company or personal profile, setting up email notifications, customizing forms, setting up an approval process, and creating checklists for forms.

Below the links are introductory videos (not shown in Figure 14.2) you can watch to get acquainted with People and what you can do with it. And below the videos is a chart that shows the hierarchy of roles in People and what each role can do. ("Managing Employees," later in this chapter, tells you more about that.)

Creating Your Organization's Profile

After you've created a new Zoho People account, a good place to start is to set up information about your organization. To do this, click Settings (at the top of any page) and then click Organization in the list on the left. This opens the Organization Settings page, shown in Figure 14.3, where you type in information about your company:

- Organization name and website.
- Address. In this section, First Address and Second Address refer to two lines in the same address, such as this:

  123 Main St.

  Suite 104

- Contact person and contact info.
- Email encoding. (You probably want to stick with the default: UTF-8.)
- Currency locale. (This is used to determine the currency your company uses.)
- Administrator's email address.

When you've entered information about your organization, click Update to save the profile.

Figure 14.3
Administrators can set up an organizational profile.

Tip Replace the upper-left Zoho People logo with your organization's own logo. On the Organization Settings page (shown in Figure 14.3), click the Change Logo link above the form
to open a Browse box. Find and select the image file you want to use as a logo. Click Open
and then click Update to upload the file. For best results, use an image that's 80 pixels
wide by 55 pixels high.

Adding Departments

After you've added basic information about your organization, you may want to set up its structure by listing the departments that make up your company. This will let you assign employees
to departments as you add them.

You add departments to People on the Organization tab. Put your cursor on that tab and, from
the menu that appears, select Department, Add to open the Department Details form.

The only required field on this form is Department Name. Optionally, you can add a mail alias,
choose its parent department, and select a department lead from a list of users. (If you haven't
added any users yet, you can click the plus sign and add one now. Or you can create the department without a lead and then come back and edit the department's information after you've
added a list of users.)

For each department, click Save or Save & New to add the department to People's department
list. You can see the department list by clicking Organization, Department, List.

Importing a List of Departments

If you have a long list of departments to get into People—but you have neither the time nor the
inclination to add them one by one—you can import an existing list of departments into People.
Choose Organization, Department, Import Data and then follow these steps:

1. Choose a Microsoft Excel (XLS) file to import. Click the Browse button, find the file you want
   on your computer, and click Open. Back in People, click Import File.

2. Map the details of your imported file to People's form. In this step, People shows the fields for
   adding a new record. Next to each field is a drop-down list. For each field, click the list to
   choose the column heading from your spreadsheet that corresponds to that field in People. For
   example, if you have a column called Department Name in your spreadsheet, you'd choose
   that from the Department drop-down, so that records in the spreadsheet's Department Name
   column are imported into People as departments. Click Next to move on to step 3.

3. Confirm the mapping. In this step, Zoho lets you know whether there are columns in your
   spreadsheet that aren't mapped to a field in People, and whether there are any fields in
   People that don't have a corresponding column in your spreadsheet. If you see a problem,
   click Previous to go back to step 2 and fix it. Otherwise, click Import.

4. Check for duplicate entries. As Zoho imports the data from your spreadsheet, it notes any
   duplicate records it finds. In this step, tell Zoho whether you want to overwrite existing
   records with the data you're importing, or whether you want to skip duplicate records in the
   import. Click Update.

5. View Zoho's summary of the import. Here, Zoho tells you how many records were added, updated, and/or skipped. There's a History link you can click to see the history of imports. Click Go To ListView to see the data you've imported.

 The import process is the same whether you're adding employees, designations, job openings, or other kinds of data.

Customizing Tabs

Figure 14.3 shows People's standard tabs. You're not stuck with this arrangement of tabs, though. You can hide some tabs, add others, and move displayed tabs around. To do this, click Settings and then click the left menu's Tab Customization button. This opens the page shown in Figure 14.4.

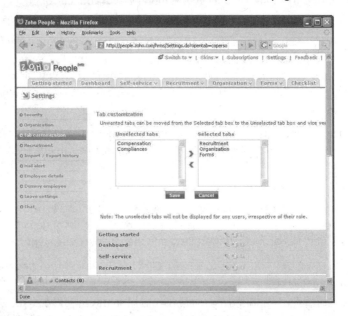

Figure 14.4
Hide or rearrange tabs here.

The Tab Customization page has two boxes: Unselected Tabs on the left and Selected Tabs on the right. To show currently hidden tabs, choose the tab or tabs you want in the Unselected Tabs box and click the right-pointing arrow to shift them over to the Selected Tabs box. To hide currently displayed tabs, reverse the process: Choose tabs from the Selected Tabs box and click the left-pointing arrow to move them over to the Unselected Tabs box. Click Save to apply your changes.

 Tabs listed in the Unselected Tabs box are unavailable to everyone using your Zoho People account, no matter what their role.

The following tabs can't be hidden:

- Getting Started
- Dashboard
- Self-Service
- Checklist

As upcoming sections explain, these tabs are essential to learning and using People, so you probably wouldn't want to hide them anyway.

 Tip If you want, you can remove the Getting Started tab. Open the tab and, in the extreme bottom right, click the Remove Tab Getting Started link, and then click OK to confirm. The Getting Started tab is a central location for common tasks and an in-application Help page, so think twice before you remove it from People. Once it's gone, you can't get it back.

Rearranging Tabs

You can move tabs around so that they're displayed in a way that makes sense to you. You move tabs using the list of tabs that appears below the Unselected Tabs and Selected Tabs boxes. In this list, tabs appear in black text on a light blue background. (That's in People's standard blue theme; if you've chosen a different skin, the background will reflect the color scheme you chose.) Some of the tabs are expanded to show their forms; click the far-right, upward-pointing arrow to collapse the section and make the tab easier to move.

To move a tab, place your cursor on any tab in the list so that the cursor becomes a four-way arrow. When the cursor changes, click and then drag your selected tab into its new position. Let up on the mouse button to drop it there. In the list, the tab at the top is the leftmost tab across the top of the screen. So to move a tab to the right, drag it downward in the list; to move a tab to the left, drag it upward. After you've dragged and dropped a tab to a new location, Zoho shows a dialog box confirming the move. Click OK to close the box.

 Info To change People's color scheme, click Skins at the top of any page. From the menu that appears, choose the color scheme you want. Current options are blue (the standard), green, orange, and black.

Setting Up Security

People has different roles—Admin, Director, Manager, Recruiter, and Team Member—and each of those roles can have different degrees of access to records in People. When you're getting started with People, you'll probably want to tweak the roles and their associated permissions: the kinds of access each role has to People's forms and fields. For example, by default, team members have permission to view and edit all fields on their own Employee form—which might not always be a good idea. For example, team member Erica Employee could sign in, change her role to Admin, and then upload a picture of her cat to replace the company logo (or more seriously, give herself a big raise or delete her rivals from People).

Understanding Roles

You want to make sure users can view and edit only the data they should have access to. And you do that by setting permissions for each role. Click Settings and then click Security in the left menu. The Security page, shown in Figure 14.5, opens, showing these built-in roles:

- **Admin**—As the creator of your organization's Zoho People account, that's you—although you can assign this role to others to share administrative duties. The Admin role has access to all forms, fields, and tabs in People, as well as organization-level settings (such as security and the company profile).

- **Manager**—Managers get full access to the data for the people they manage. Managers cannot tweak organizational settings or work with data for other managers' staff.

- **Team Member**—These are the rank-and-file employees. Their permissions are more limited than managers'. For example, they have no access to Exit Details forms, whereas managers can view Exit Details records related to the people who report to them.

The three roles just listed are the standard roles in People—and the minimum the most organizations need. You can't delete these roles.

Your new People account has a couple other suggestions for roles: Director and Recruiter. You can keep these roles or delete them—whatever makes sense for your organization. You can also create new roles to reflect your organization's structure; see the upcoming section "Managing Employees" for the details.

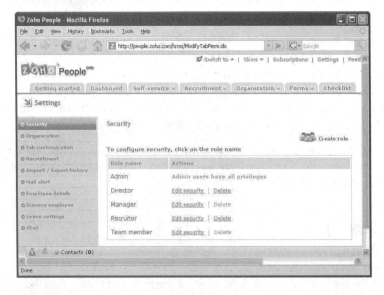

Figure 14.5
People comes with a number of built-in roles.

Setting Role Permissions

To fine-tune the permissions given to various roles, click Edit Security for any role on the Security page to open the Form Permission tab shown in Figure 14.6. (You can edit the permissions for any role on this tab.)

The Permission tabs let you edit these kinds of permissions for each role:

- **Form Permission**—Adjust a role's permission to create, view, edit, or delete data in a particular form. Set permissions to apply to everyone's data, the person's own data, or subordinates' data.

- **Field Permission**—Set permissions to a form on a field-by-field basis. For each field, a checked box means that people in this role have access to the field. Check or uncheck boxes to allow or restrict access. For fields that users can access, choose Only View or View & Edit.

- **Action Permission**—This tab has a list of boxes you can check (to allow the action) or uncheck (to prohibit the action) for performing the following actions on specific forms:

  - Import
  - Export
  - Mail Alert
  - Form Customization
  - Embed Form

- **Global Permission**—This tab gives across-the-board permissions for these sections to appear, along with relevant data, on the role's Dashboard:

  - View Pending Request
  - Announcement
  - Birthday Buddy
  - New Joinee List
  - Department Data
  - Recruitment

Whichever tab you're on, choose the role for which you're setting permissions from the drop-down list at the top of the tab. For permissions relating to specific forms (Form Permission, Field Permission, and Action Permission tabs), choose the form you want as well. Alternatively, you can use the Previous Form and Next Form arrows to go through all the forms one at a time.

Creating a New Role

You might want to create a new role, such as Team Leader, that reflects your organization's hierarchy. You create a new role by cloning an existing role, which means that you copy an existing role as the basis for the new role. Once the new role is created, you can fine-tune its permissions (see the previous section) to reflect what's appropriate for users in that role.

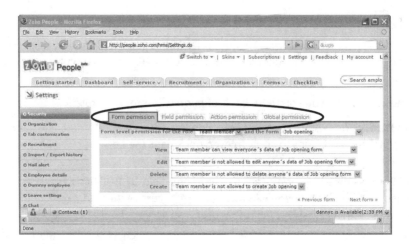

Figure 14.6
Choose a kind of permission (circled) at the top of the page; then set specific permissions for a role.

You create a new role on the Security page (Settings, Security). Above and to the right of the list of current roles, click the Create Role link. The New Role dialog box opens. Give the new role a name and, from the Existing Role drop-down, choose the role you want to clone. Click Create Role.

Zoho adds the new role to the list on the Security page (and to the Role drop-down list on the Add Employee form). Click the role's Edit Security link to set its specific permissions.

Adding Employees

Before your organization starts using People, you'll want to add some employees. There are three ways to do this:

- **Quick Create**—On the Getting Started tab, click the Quickly Add Employee link. This opens the Quick Create dialog box, which captures four basic pieces of information about the employee: first name, last name, employee ID, and email ID. Click Save.

- **On the Organization tab**—Put your cursor on the Organization tab, and a menu appears. From this menu choose Employee, Add. This opens the Add Employee form shown in Figure 14.7. The only required fields are those that are also in the Quick Create box. Fill out those fields (and any others you want to provide data for) and click Save (or Save & New to add another employee).

 If you're adding an employee and you find that the department or designation you need isn't on the list for those fields, click the green plus sign next to the drop-down list. A dialog box opens that lets you create a new department (or designation or whatever the field contains) and add it to the list.

- **By importing spreadsheet data**—Need to transfer a few dozen—or a few hundred—employees from a spreadsheet to People? Do it by importing the employee data listed in your spreadsheet. Choose Organization, Employee, Import Data. Then follow the steps in this chapter's "Importing a List of Departments" section.

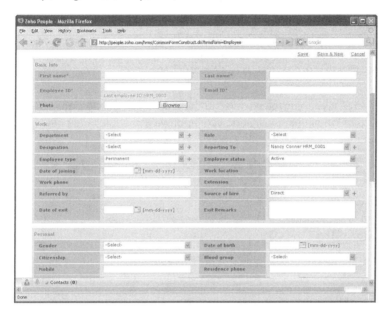

Figure 14.7
Select Organization, Employee, Add to open this form.

 Tip 4U If you think the Add Employee form suffers from TMI (too much information), edit the form to hide the fields you don't need. The section "Customizing a Form" tells you how.

The Zoho People Dashboard

People's home page, for admins and employees alike, is the Dashboard. This tab keeps you up to date on what's happening in your organization and gives you a heads-up on events and approvals you need to attend to.

The Dashboard, shown in Figure 14.8, contains these sections:

- **Waiting for Your Approval**—If you have the authority to approve or reject certain kinds of requests, such as job openings or travel requests, your pending requests are listed here.
- **Announcements**—Company-wide announcements appear in this box. Admins can send messages, as well. Just click the Add link in the upper-right part of the box to open a dialog box where you can give your announcement a title and type its text.

- **Birthday Buddies**—When one of your coworkers has a birthday, you see a reminder here.

- **New Joinees**—This section lists the name, department, and hire date of employees who've joined the company within the last 30 days.

- **My Department**—This section provides an at-a-glance list of everyone who works with you in your department, including phone extension and email address.

 Tip 4U Need to find an employee fast? Use the upper-right Search box that appears on every page of People. Click the downward-pointing arrow on the left side of the search box to choose a field to search by, such as Last Name or Department.

- **Recruitment**—If you're involved in recruitment activities, this section shows tasks related to hiring, such as job openings awaiting your approval, scheduled interviews, and resumes to be evaluated.

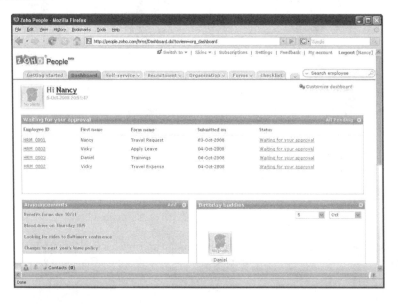

Figure 14.8
The Zoho People Dashboard shows up-to-date information and to-do's.

You can rearrange the Dashboard as you like. Put your cursor on the title bar of any section; when the cursor becomes a four-way arrow, click-and-drag the section into its new position and then let go of the mouse button to drop it there.

To hide a section so that it doesn't show on your Dashboard, click its upper-right X and then click OK. Hiding a section doesn't remove that section from the Dashboard for good. If you want to display a hidden section, click the Dashboard's upper-right Customize Dashboard link. This opens the Customize – Dashboard dialog box, which lists all six Dashboard sections, each with a check box. When a box is checked, that section is displayed; when it's unchecked, the section is hidden. Check or uncheck the boxes as you want and then click Save.

Creating and Customizing Forms

People comes with a number of prebuilt forms you can use to add data to the application: new employees, job openings, upcoming holidays, travel expenses, performance appraisals, and over a dozen others. (To see all the forms in People, click Settings and then choose Tab Customization; the list of active tabs shows the forms on each). You may find that these standard forms suit your organization's needs perfectly. More likely, though, you'll probably find that some forms work great, others need tweaking, and still others you don't need at all. Or you may need a form that People doesn't offer. This section explains how to create a new, custom form and how to edit existing forms to customize them for your business.

Creating a Form from Scratch

If you subscribe to one of People's pricing plans, you can also create your own forms. (Users of the free Basic Edition cannot create custom forms.) The number of custom forms you can create depends on your subscription plan (refer back to Table 14.1). It's easy to create a new form; on the Tab Customization page, find the tab to which you want to add your new form and click its Add Form icon (a couple of sheets of paper with a plus sign).

On the page that opens, the left side of the screen shows different field types, such as text, number, picklist (multiple choice), lookup, and so on. To add a field, simply click- and-drag the field type onto your form and then drop it where you want it to appear.

When you drop the field, an Adding dialog box, like the one shown in Figure 14.9, opens. The contents of this box depend on the kind of field you're adding; Figure 14.9 shows a text field as an example. For each field you add, whatever the type, you can give the field a name, specify whether the field is required when users fill out the form, indicate whether the field can be audited, and add a description to pop up as a tooltip. When you've filled out the Adding dialog box, click Done to add the field.

 To learn about field types, see Chapter 5, "Zoho Reports: Online Databases and Reports."

Well-organized forms group related fields into sections. To create a section, click the upper-left Add Section link. This opens the New Section dialog box, where you name the section, add an optional description, and position the section in your form (making it the first or the last section). Click Create Section to add the new section so you can start filling it up with fields.

 If you use People's Basic Edition, you can't create brand-new custom forms. Instead, find a form you don't use and customize that form to meet your needs. The next section tells you how.

Customizing a Form

You can customize any of the forms in Zoho People, tailoring them to your organization's needs and practices: You can add new fields, edit existing ones, and disable any fields that you don't need. You can change field labels and form names, move a field from one section to another, as well as add or rearrange sections.

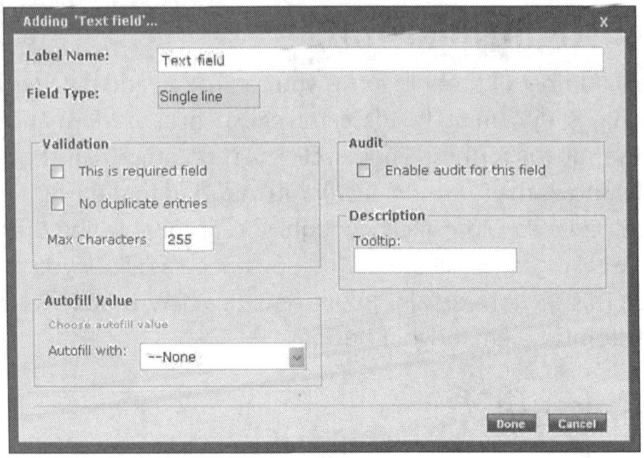

Figure 14.9
Build a custom form, field by field.

If the form you want to customize is already open, click the Customize Form link at the top of the page, or click Form Actions, Customize form. Otherwise, put your cursor on the tab where the form appears, and from the context menu, choose the form you want and click Customize form. So if you wanted to customize the form for adding an employee, you'd choose Organization, Employee, Customize Form. If you wanted to customize the form for submitting travel expenses, you'd select Forms, Travel Expense, Customize Form.

When a form opens in edit mode, you can move any field to a new position—just click, drag, and drop, and Zoho saves the change automatically.

You can also edit any field; hover your cursor over the new field to highlight it. A pencil icon appears at the left side of the field. Move your cursor to the pencil so that a menu appears; from that menu, select Edit This Field to open the Editing Field dialog box. The Editing box is just like the Adding box shown in Figure 14.9, with the current values already filled in. Make the changes you want, such as giving the field a new name, and then click Done to save those changes.

Adding a Field to an Existing Form

If you're a paying subscriber who's already created a custom form or two in People, adding a field works the same way. Select a field type from the left menu and then drag, drop, and name the field.

Basic Edition subscribers won't see the left menu of field types. Instead, your form will look like the one in Figure 14.10. Existing fields are at the top of the page, followed by a section called *Other Fields*. The Other Fields section has boxes representing different field types. Place your cursor over the field type you want so that it becomes a four-way arrow; then click-and-drag the field type into position on the form and drop it there.

Info 4U For Basic Edition users, the number of fields you can add to a form you're customizing is limited by the number of fields and field types that appear in the Other Fields section.

After you have the field in place, put your cursor on the field to highlight it. Move the cursor onto the pencil icon (on the left) and then select Edit This Field. The Editing box opens, where you can name the new field and tweak its properties.

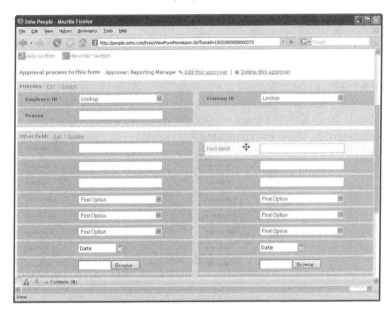

Figure 14.10
Click, drag, and drop fields to add them to a form.

 After you've customized a form, it's a good idea to check the form's security settings to make sure permissions are set the way you want them, at both form and field levels. See the earlier section "Setting Role Permissions."

Enabling or Disabling a Field

When you add fields to a form, those new fields are disabled by default—which means they won't appear when a user fills out the form. To enable a field, put your cursor on the field to highlight it and move it to the pencil icon on the left. When your cursor reaches the pencil, a menu appears; select Disable/Enable. If the field is currently disabled, this option takes it live. If the field is currently enabled, the option hides the field.

 When you're editing a form, you can tell whether a field is enabled or disabled by looking at the field's name. The names of enabled fields are in a bold black font; the names of disabled fields are gray.

Renaming a Section

To give a form's section a new name, find the section you're renaming and click the Edit link to its right. (You can see this link in Figure 14.10.) This puts the section's name in a text box; click inside the box, make your changes, and then click Save. That's all there is to it.

Moving Sections

Just as you can move around the fields on a form, you can also rearrange its sections. To do that, click the Reorder Section link at the top of the editable form. This opens the dialog box shown in Figure 14.11. Select the section you want to move (you can select only one section at a time) and then use the up or down arrow to move it to its new location. When you're done, click Save Order, and Zoho rearranges the form's sections.

Figure 14.11
Use this box to move a section up or down in a form.

Disabling or Enabling a Section

Disabled sections don't appear in the form that users see for adding or viewing data. When you disable a section, you hide the section, its fields, and all its data.

You disable (or reenable) a section in a form's edit mode. When you're customizing a form, each section name has two links to its right: Edit (previous section) and Disable (or Enable if the section is currently hidden). To disable the section, click Disable, and Zoho immediately hides that section. To reenable a hidden section, click its Enable link.

Renaming a Form

If you find that the name of a form in People doesn't match up with the terminology of your organization or industry, it's easy to rename the form. For example, it might be clearer to your users to have a Job Title form than a Designation form.

To change a form's name, click Settings and then choose Tab Customization from the left menu. The page that opens lists People's tabs; each tab lists its associated forms. In that list, find the form whose name you want to change and click the pencil icon to its right. The name of the form changes to a text box; use the box to type the form's new name. Click Save (the icon that looks like a computer disk) to complete the name change.

If you change a form's name, don't forget to customize the form and rename relevant sections and fields as well.

Moving a Form

You can move a form to a different location in the list of forms for its tab—you can even move it to a whole new tab. (This can be helpful if you've run out of custom forms at your subscription level: You can customize a disabled form and use it on a different tab.)

To move a form, click Settings and then click Tab Customization. Hover your cursor on the tab you want to move, making it become a four-way arrow. Then click, drag, and drop the form onto its new tab. A dialog box appears, telling you your update was successful. Click OK to close the dialog box.

Disabling or Enabling a Form

Zoho People comes with a lot of standard forms, and when you create an account, all those forms are enabled. But you may find that there are some forms you don't really need—and you don't want users trying to view or add data to those forms. You can hide any forms your organization doesn't need by disabling them.

You disable a form from the Tab Customization page (Settings, Tab Customization). This page lists all the tabs in People, and for each tab, this page lists its form. In the list, a green flag to the right of a form's name means the form is currently enabled. Click Enabled (next to that green flag) to hide the form. The flag changes to red, and the link changes to Disabled. To bring the form out of hiding, click Disabled—the flag turns green, and the form appears on its tab.

Setting Up an Approval Process

Some forms, such as requests for time off or travel, need approval from a supervisor or manager before a new record can be processed. On some of Zoho's standard forms, the approval process is already built in. (These forms display the message *On submit, a request will be sent to the approver to approve this form* at the top when someone adds a new record.) But you can require approval for any form.

To do this, open the form in edit mode. (Point your cursor to the tab and then the form's name; then click Customize Form.) Above the form's name, click the Add Approver link. Just below the link, the page expands (as shown in Figure 14.12) to offer these options:

- Any Admin
- Reporting Manager of the Employee
- Allow the Employee to Choose Any Employee as Approver

Enable the radio button of the approver you want. (In most cases, you'll probably choose the employee's manager.) When you make your choice, Zoho immediately updates the form to require approval from the person you chose.

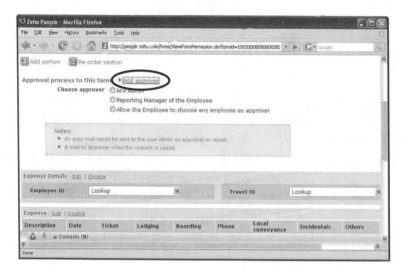

Figure 14.12
Click Add Approver (circled) and then select who's responsible for approving records submitted through this form.

When someone submits a record that requires approval, the approver receives an email notifying him or her that the record awaits approval. The approval request also appears on the approver's Dashboard.

When you see a request for approval on your Dashboard, click the link that says Waiting for Your Approval to open the record and view its details. At the top of the record is a box labeled Waiting for Approval. Check over the details of the request and then enable one of these radio buttons:

- **Approve**—This accepts the request and adds the record to People.
- **Reject**—This blocks the request. When you choose this radio button, a text box appears so you can add a reason (optional) for rejecting the request.

After you've chosen Approve or Reject, click OK. Zoho puts a note on the record saying it has been accepted or rejected and sends the requester an email with your decision.

After you've added an approver to a form, that form's Add Approver link is replaced by two new links:

- **Edit This Approver**—Click this link to display the approver options, shown in Figure 14.12. Enable a different radio button to change the approver.
- **Delete This Approver**—Click this link to stop requiring approval for this form.

Working with Checklists

Often, a new record comes with its own to-do list. For example, think of everything that you and your staff need to do when your organization hires a new employee: schedule an orientation session, assign a phone extension and email address, add that email address to the company newsletter, order business cards—you need a system to make sure everything gets done.

In People, that system is called a *checklist*, and it lays out the tasks that need to be done to support, for example, the addition of a new employee or the announcement of a training session or class. You can create a checklist from scratch, or you can edit an existing checklist. You work with checklists on the Checklist tab, and this section shows you how.

Creating a New Checklist

To create a new checklist, start by clicking the Checklist tab. Then, click Configure Checklist, Create Checklist. This opens the Create Checklist dialog box, shown in Figure 14.13, where you make these choices (all required):

- Give the checklist a name.
- Choose the form that links to the checklist.
- Tell Zoho when the checklist goes into action: when a record is created, edited, approved, or rejected.

For example, imagine you're creating a checklist of tasks that need to be done once a manager has approved the scheduling of a training seminar. You'd call the checklist something like *Training course is approved*, you'd associate it with People's Trainings form, and you'd select On Approve from the Start checklist drop-down. Then, you'd click Create & Add Checklist Item.

Figure 14.13
To create a checklist, give the checklist a name and link it to a form.

Zoho opens the page for your new checklist. Click the Add New Task link to open the Add Checklist Item box shown in Figure 14.14. In this box, add the checklist's first task. For the Training Course Is Approved checklist, for example, this first item might be *Advertise course to managers*. The Add Checklist Item box collects the following information:

- **Item Label**—This is the step that appears on the checklist, so make it descriptive and concise.
- **Description**—It can be helpful to explain briefly what the step involves, and this is the place to add that explanation.
- **Days Limit**—How long does the assigned person have to do the task? Choose the number of days until the due date from this drop-down.

■ **Owner(s)**—Who's responsible for the task? You can choose a specific person, a department (team), role, or form field (such as the person listed as Owner in the form associated with this checklist).

When you've filled out the box, click Add Checklist Item. Zoho adds the item and returns you to the checklist's configuration page. As you add items to the checklist, the Configure Checklist page looks like the one shown in Figure 14.15.

Figure 14.14
Use this box to add individual tasks to a checklist.

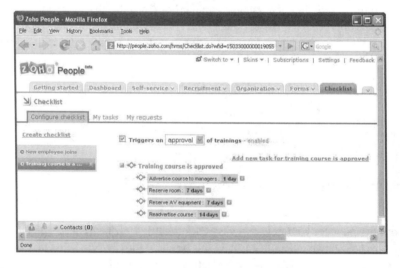

Figure 14.15
As you add tasks to a checklist, they appear on the Configure Checklist page.

Viewing Tasks

To see what checklist tasks you need to be attending to, click the Checklist tab and then click My Tasks. The My Tasks page, shown in Figure 14.16, displays a list of all pending checklist tasks assigned to you. Here's what you can do with items on the list:

- **View history**—Click the far-left View History icon in the History column to see the task's checklist, including which tasks have been completed.

- **Read a description of the task**—Hover your cursor over a task's name to see a tooltip with the task's description (if any).

- **See the form related to the checklist**—Click a link in the For column to see the filled-in form that generated this task.

- **Check off a task as done**—When you've completed a task, check the Status column's check box to remove that task from your list. On the checklist, Zoho marks the task with its completion date.

- **Add a comment**—To add a note to a task, click the Comments column's Add/View comments icon. A box appears that lets you type in a comment or read existing comments.

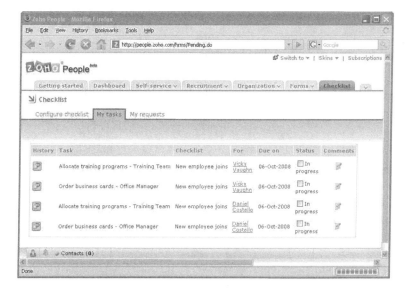

Figure 14.16
View your tasks and check them off the list when done.

Managing Employees

Earlier sections of this chapter tell how to add employees, create and assign roles, and set permissions for those roles. There are a few other things you can do to manage employees within People, as this section explains.

Zoho Chat and Zoho People

In Zoho People accounts, the standard is to have Zoho Chat enabled. Chat (discussed in Chapter 8, "Instant Communication with Zoho Chat") is Zoho's instant messaging program, and it can be a helpful feature when someone has a quick question related to filling out a form or approving a request.

Chatting from People

To launch a chat, click the Contacts link in the lower-left part of the screen and then find the person you want to chat with. (A green dot next to a person's name or ID means that person is available for chatting.) Click the person's ID to open a small window for chatting; type in your message at the bottom of the chat window and then press Enter. A similar chat window opens on the other person's screen, and you can chat back and forth.

Disabling Chat

As an admin, it's up to you whether you want Chat enabled in People. If you find people are chatting about last night's reality show and not doing their work, you can disable chatting in People.

Click Settings and then click Chat. The Chat page has two radio buttons: Disabled and Enabled. Turn on the Disabled radio button to remove chatting from People.

Later, if you decide you want to allow chatting in People after all, come back to the Chat page and turn on the Enabled radio button.

The Self-Service Tab

Admins have the ability to manage People at the application level and to create, view, edit, and delete data in all its forms. Depending on the permissions you've set, other roles such as Manager and Team Member have more limited ability to work with People. Most of what employees do with People happens on the Self-Service tab, shown in Figure 14.17.

Using the left menu, employees select from these Self-Service tab options:

- **My Profile**—On this page, employees can view and edit their personal information (according to the permissions you've set for their role).
- **Company Details**—Here, employees can view the company information that you or another admin entered in People's settings.
- **Organization**—On this page, employees can view lists of departments, designations (job titles), and employees.
- **Forms**—This page lists the forms to which the employee's role has access, whether to add a record, view all data, or view his or her own data. Typically, information that appears on this page relates to company policy and holidays, leave, training, and travel.
- **All**—This page shows all the forms and data to which the employee's role has access.

If employee Daniel wants to request a day off for personal time, for example, he clicks the Self-Service tab and then selects Forms from the left menu. On the page that opens, he goes to the Apply Leave section and clicks Add. This opens the form to apply for time off. After Daniel fills out and has submitted the form, he gets a message from Zoho that his request is now waiting for approval. The request appears in the View My Data list of the Apply Leave section.

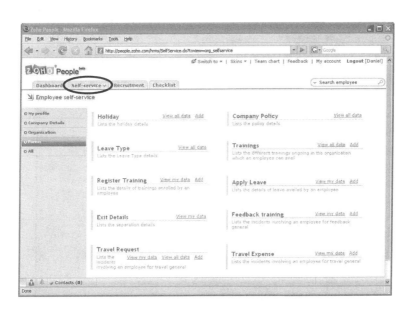

Figure 14.17
Employees use the Self-Service tab to view, edit, and add data.

Managing Recruitment

Zoho People streamlines your hiring process with its easy-to-follow, automated workflow:

- You can create job openings. After job openings have been approved, you can post them to the website.
- As resumes come in, you can add them to your resume database. You can collect resumes directly through an embedded form in your website.
- You can search resumes and send those that look promising to a hiring manager.
- You can schedule interviews.
- You can make an offer with just one click and then track the offer's status online.
- When a candidate accepts your offer, you can switch that person from applicant to employee with a single click.

Figure 14.18 shows the Recruitment tab, the central location for all your hiring activity.

Creating and Posting Job Openings

Adding a job opening is like adding any other kind of record in People. A recruiter who wants to start the hiring process clicks the Recruitment tab and then clicks Add New Job Opening (in the Getting Started section) to open the Job Details form. This collects details such as the job posting's title, the hiring manager, department, target hire date, skill set and experience required, and so on. When the recruiter clicks Save, Zoho notifies the hiring manager that a posting is waiting for approval.

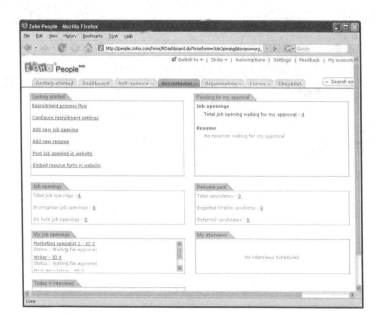

Figure 14.18
The Recruitment tab centralizes your hiring activities.

 Before recruiters start creating new job openings, customize the form so it fits your industry and organization. See the section "Customizing a Form," earlier in this chapter, to find out how.

The hiring manager sees how many jobs await approval in the Recruitment tab's Pending for My Approval section. (Pending job openings also appear in the Waiting for Your Approval section of the hiring manager's Dashboard.) When the hiring manager clicks the number representing pending job openings, Zoho opens a list of those openings for the hiring manager to review and then approve or reject. After approval, the job opening becomes In Progress; the number of in-progress job openings appears in the Recruitment tab's Job Openings section.

Next, the recruiter (or the hiring manager) can post the approved job opening on the company website. On the Recruitment tab, look in the Getting Started section and click Post Job Opening in Website to open the Post Created JobOpenings in Website box shown in Figure 14.19. This box collects information about what should be shown in the website post: job openings, field contents from the job-opening form, display font and colors. A preview shows what the posting will look like on the web page.

When the selections have been made, click Generate Code. Based on the settings, Zoho creates some HTML code that will display the postings on the company website. Copy the code and then paste it into an HTML document and upload the document to the site. Now, visitors to the site can browse, click, and read job openings there.

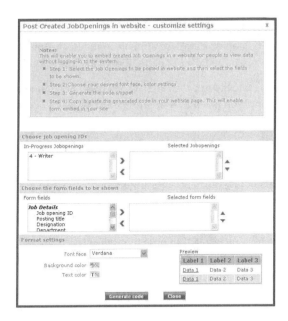

Figure 14.19
Select the job openings, details, and formatting to display on the website.

Managing Resumes

As resumes come in, recruiters can add them to People's resume pool. On the Recruitment tab's Getting Started section, click Add New Resume to open the Add Resume form. This form collects information about the applicant and the resume's contents, such as name, contact information, work experience, education level, and so on. The resume can be attached to the form to make it available to hiring managers and interviewers with one-click access.

 Make sure that Add Resume collects the essential information you need. Before you take People live in your organization, review and customize the Add Resume form. See the "Customizing a Form" section to get the details on tweaking a form to fit your organization's needs.

Collecting Resumes Through Your Organization's Website

If you advertise job openings on your company website, you'll want interested job-hunters to be able to apply for those job from the website as well. Adding the Add Resume form to your website also saves your recruitment staff a lot of time; candidates fill out the form and attach their resumes themselves—and the resumes go straight into your resume pool.

To embed the Add Resume form in your website, go to the Recruitment tab's Getting Started section and click Embed Resume Form in Website. A box opens, displaying the HTML code you need to put the form on a web page. Copy the code and paste it into an HTML document. Upload that document to your site, and you're ready to start collecting resumes from site visitors.

Finding Resumes and Matching Them to Job Openings

The number of resumes in People's database appears in the Recruitment tab's Resume pool section. Click the number to open the Resume page, shown in Figure 14.20.

At the top of the Resumes page, you can search for a particular resume or set of resumes: Select a field to search and a condition (such as *Is* or *Starts with*), type in your search terms, and then click the Search button.

Tip 4U To search in more than one field of the Add Resume form, click the Add More link.

A list of resumes appears below the Search Resume section. View an attached resume by clicking its View Resume link (on the right). This downloads the resume to your computer and opens it in an appropriate program (such as Microsoft Word for DOC files).

To associate a resume with a particular job opening, select the resume you want by checking its box. (You can select more than one.) Click Move Resume To and then select a job opening from the list. Zoho grays out the candidate's check box on the Resume page's list and moves it to the hiring manager's Pending for My Approval box. From there, the hiring manager clicks the number of pending resumes to see a page that shows the job opening and lists the applicants whose resumes look like a good match for that job.

Info 4U A resume can be associated with only one job opening at a time.

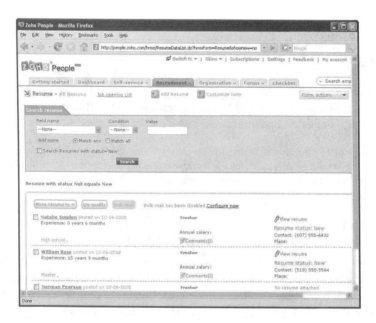

Figure 14.20
Manage resumes on the Resume page.

Evaluating Candidates

The hiring manager looks at candidates for a job opening on the Job Opening page, shown in Figure 14.21. The job opening appears at the top of the page; candidates whose resumes have been associated with that opening are listed at the bottom of the page.

Figure 14.21
Open positions appear on the Job Opening page.

In the list of candidates, the hiring manager can click a candidate's name to view his or her Add Resume form or click the View Resume link to download and read an attached resume. If you're the hiring manager, when you've decided whether you want to schedule an interview, click Evaluate. In the Evaluate dialog box that opens, select Call for Interview or Do Not Call for Interview and then click Ok.

 To send the also-rans a "thanks but no thanks" email en masse, check the boxes of those whom you don't plan to interview and click Bulk Mail. This opens a box where you can compose your email (and, if you want, save it as a template) and send the email to multiple recipients. An Admin must enable bulk mail: Click Settings, Mail Alert, Enabled.

Setting Up an Interview

Clicking Call for Interview puts the candidate on the Shortlist. When you make that call, click Schedule Interview – Level 1 below the candidate's name to open the dialog box shown in Figure 14.22. This box allows you to choose an interviewer, as well as a date and time for the interview. The Schedule Interview box also has fields where you can specify the type of interview (such as "in person" or "by phone"), assign a venue, choose a comment sheet to attach to the interview, and add notes for the interview. Click Schedule & Finish to complete interview setup or Schedule & Notify to send a confirmation email to the candidate.

People comment sheets come in two flavors: General and Personality. They're designed to capture the interviewer's impressions of a candidate. To customize comment sheets, click Settings, Recruitment. Then find the sheet you want at the bottom of the page. Click Edit and then customize as you would any other form.

After you've scheduled an interview, it appears in the interviewer's My Interviews section of the Recruitment tab and on the Interview tab of the relevant Job Opening page. Any relevant notes appear there as well.

To schedule multiple interviews, click the Schedule Interview link below the candidate's name and repeat the process.

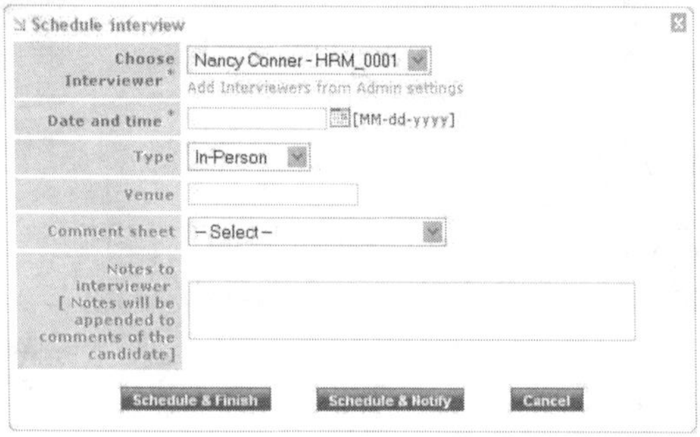

Figure 14.22
Use this form to schedule an interview.

After the Interview

When you've completed the interview, find the candidate on the Interview tab and click Make Your Decision. The page expands to look like the one in Figure 14.23. If a comment sheet was attached to the interview, click the Fill Interview Comment link to open a dialog box containing the comment sheet form. If there were multiple interviewers, you can see their comment sheets and recommendations as well. Choose Selected or Rejected and then click Save.

Zoho records your recommendation. To see what others recommended, click Consensus on Interview to open a dialog box of the same name. In this box, you can choose from these actions: To Be Offered, On Hold, Rejected, and Rejected–Hirable. Make your selection and click OK. The consensus is added to that candidate's profile in the list of candidates for the job.

Making an Offer and Adding a Candidate as an Employee

When you've decided to offer a position to a candidate, click Offer to open the Make Offer dialog box, shown in Figure 14.24. This box has two steps:

- **Step 1 – Make Offer**—Here you select an expected start date, the offered salary or wages, and how the offer will be communicated (by phone, by email, and so on). You can also add comments, if you want.

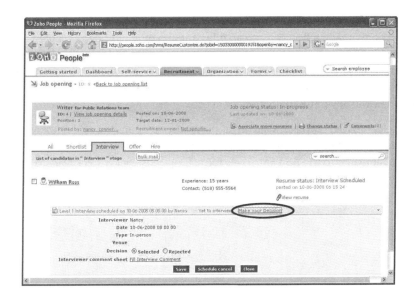

Figure 14.23
Click Make Your Decision to recommend whether to hire the candidate.

■ **Step 2 – Offer Status**—Use this section to track the status of your organization's offer. Choose Accepted, Declined, or Withdrawn from the Offer Status box, confirm the start date, adjust the salary (if necessary), and add any relevant notes.

Be sure to click Save after each step.

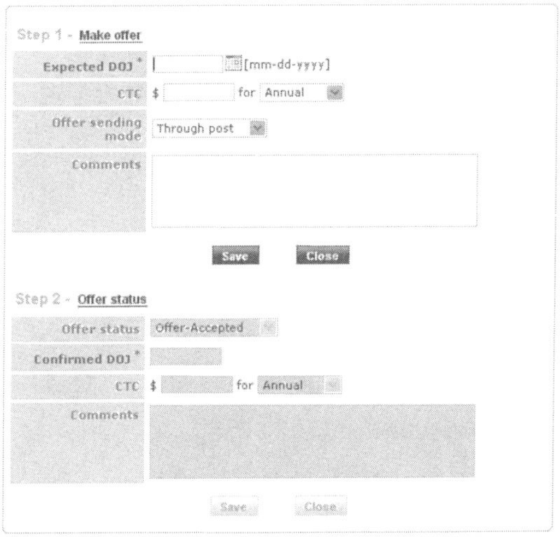

Figure 14.24
Make and track a job offer here.

After a successful search—you've identified and advertised a job opening, selected and interviewed candidates, made a decision and an offer, and the offer has been accepted—all that's left to do now is add the successful candidate as an employee. To do that, find the candidate on the Offer tab and, beneath his or her name, click Hire. This opens the dialog box shown in Figure 14.25. In the Candidate Status field, choose Joined or (in the worst-case scenario) No-Show and then add any notes HR the Comments box.

When you select Joined and click Make as Employee, Zoho opens the Add Employee form (refer to Figure 14.7), with information from the candidate's Add Resume form already filled in. If you need to add more info to the Add Employee form, fill in those fields. Click Save to add the employee and generate the New Employee Joins checklist. Congratulations on your new hire!

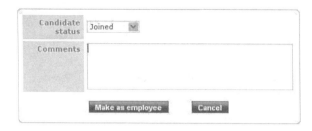

Figure 14.25
Convert an accepted candidate to an employee using this box.

Index

Symbols

% Completed option (Projects task assignments), 339

= (equals sign) in formulas (Sheet), 123

2D/3D views, switching between in dashboard charts (CRM), 330

A

Access URL dialog box (Reports), 167

accessing shared documents (Writer), 41

accounts (email), setting up in Mail, 210-212

accounts (Google), signing into Zoho through, 5-6

accounts (Yahoo!), signing into Zoho through, 5-6

accounts (Zoho), creating, 4-5

Accounts module (CRM), 318

Action Permission tab (People), 367

Actions button (Meeting Presenter toolbar), 260

ActiveX viewer for meetings (Meeting), 264

Actual Size button (Meeting Participant toolbar), 265

Add Chart dialog box (Sheet), 118
moving, 119

Add Checklist Item dialog box (People), 377

Add Column option (Reports column editing), 154

Add Comment button (Writer Formatting toolbar), 24

Add Comment dialog box (Writer), 47

Add Component dialog box (CRM), 311

Add Custom Message option (Notebook Share Object dialog box), 74

Add Filter page (Mail), 209

Add Form option (Creator New Form page), 184

Add Formula Column option (Reports column editing), 154

Add Group dialog box (Reports), 165

Add New Customer page (Invoice), 296

Add New Invoice page (Invoice), 303

Add Project page (Projects), 336

Add Resume form (People), embedding in websites, 383

Add RSS dialog box (Notebook), 62

Add Show dialog box (Notebook), 62

Add URL dialog box (Notebook), 62

Add Video dialog box (Notebook), 61

Add Web Page dialog box (Notebook), 57

adding. See also inserting
attachments to messages (Mail), 202
client users to projects (Projects), 338
components (CRM), 311
contacts (Chat), 223
to Contacts list (Mail), 217-218
content to applications (Creator), 179
customers (Invoice), 295-297
departments (People), 363
employees (People), 368-369

fields
in CRM, 326
to forms (People), 372-373
forms to applications (Creator), 171-173
labels to charts (Sheet), 119-121
links to projects (Projects), 352-353
notes to meetings (Projects), 343
photos to profiles (Mail), 217
range of cells (Sheet), 125
sections to forms (People), 371
tasks
to checklists (People), 377-378
to task lists (Projects), 341
users
in CRM, 312-313
to projects (Projects), 337-338

Adding dialog box (People), 371

Address (Billing) option (Invoice Add New Customer page), 297

Address (Shipping) option (Invoice Add New Customer page), 297

Address Book (Mail), 200

Address Information section (CRM Create User page), 313

addresses (Mail), blocking/allowing, 206-207

addressing messages (Mail), 199

admin permissions (CRM profiles), 317

Admin role (People), 366

Administrator profile (CRM), 315

Agenda option (Meeting Create Meeting tab), 255

Alignment button (Sheet), 113

alignment buttons (Writer Formatting toolbar), 22